Deltora Quest

デルトラクエスト

Volume 1

Story by Emily Rodda

Manga by Makoto Niwano

Translated by Mayumi Kobayashi

Adapted by Michael Braff

Lettered by North Market Street Graphics

KC
KODANSHA COMICS

Deltora Quest volume 1 is a work of fiction. Names, characters, places, and incidents are the products of the author's imagination or are used fictitiously. Any resemblance to actual events, locales, or persons, living or dead, is entirely coincidental.

A Kodansha Comics Trade Paperback Original

Deltora Quest volume 1 copyright © 2005 Emily Rodda and Makoto Niwano
English translation copyright © 2011 Emily Rodda and Makoto Niwano

All rights reserved.

Published in the United States by Kodansha Comics, an imprint of Kodansha USA Publishing, LLC, New York.

Publication rights for this English edition arranged through Kodansha Ltd, Tokyo.

First published in Japan in 2005 by Kodansha Ltd., Tokyo

ISBN 978-1-935-42928-9

Printed in the United States of America

www.kodanshacomics.com

9 8 7 6 5 4 3 2 1

Translator: Mayumi Kobayashi
Adapter: Michael Braff
Lettering: North Market Street Graphics

Deltora Quest
デルトラクエスト

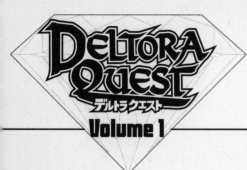

Volume 1

CONTENTS

HONORIFICS EXPLAINED

Throughout the Kodansha Comics books, you will find Japanese honorifics left intact in the translations. For those not familiar with how the Japanese use honorifics and, more important, how they differ from American honorifics, we present this brief overview.

Politeness has always been a critical facet of Japanese culture. Ever since the feudal era, when Japan was a highly stratified society, use of honorifics—which can be defined as polite speech that indicates relationship or status—has played an essential role in the Japanese language. When addressing someone in Japanese, an honorific usually takes the form of a suffix attached to one's name (example: "Asuna-san"), is used as a title at the end of one's name, or appears in place of the name itself (example: "Negi-sensei," or simply "Sensei!").

Honorifics can be expressions of respect or endearment. In the context of manga and anime, honorifics give insight into the nature of the relationship between characters. Many English translations leave out these important honorifics and therefore distort the feel of the original Japanese. Because Japanese honorifics contain nuances that English honorifics lack, it is our policy at Kodansha not to translate them. Here, instead, is a guide to some of the honorifics you may encounter in Kodansha Comics.

-san: This is the most common honorific and is equivalent to Mr., Miss, Ms., or Mrs. It is the all-purpose honorific and can be used in any situation where politeness is required.

-sama: This is one level higher than "-san" and is used to confer great respect.

-dono: This comes from the word "tono," which means "lord." It is an even higher level than "-sama" and confers utmost respect.

-kun: This suffix is used at the end of boys' names to express familiarity or endearment. It is also sometimes used by men among friends, or when addressing someone younger or of a lower station.

-chan: This is used to express endearment, mostly toward girls. It is also used for little boys, pets, and even among lovers. It gives a sense of childish cuteness.

Bozu: This is an informal way to refer to a boy, similar to the English terms "kid" and "squirt."

Sempai/
Senpai: This title suggests that the addressee is one's senior in a group or organization. It is most often used in a school setting, where underclassmen refer to their upperclassmen as "sempai." It can also be used in the workplace, such as when a newer employee addresses an employee who has seniority in the company.

Kohai: This is the opposite of "sempai" and is used toward underclassmen in school or newcomers in the workplace. It connotes that the addressee is of a lower station.

Sensei: Literally meaning "one who has come before," this title is used for teachers, doctors, or masters of any profession or art.

-[blank]:   This is usually forgotten in these lists, but it is perhaps the most significant difference between Japanese and English. The lack of honorific means that the speaker has permission to address the person in a very intimate way. Usually, only family, spouses, or very close friends have this kind of permission. Known as *yobisute*, it can be gratifying when someone who has earned the intimacy starts to call one by one's name without an honorific. But when that intimacy hasn't been earned, it can be very insulting.

Deltora Quest

デルトラクエスト

1

The Secret Belt

Story by: Emily Rodda
Manga by: Makoto Niwano

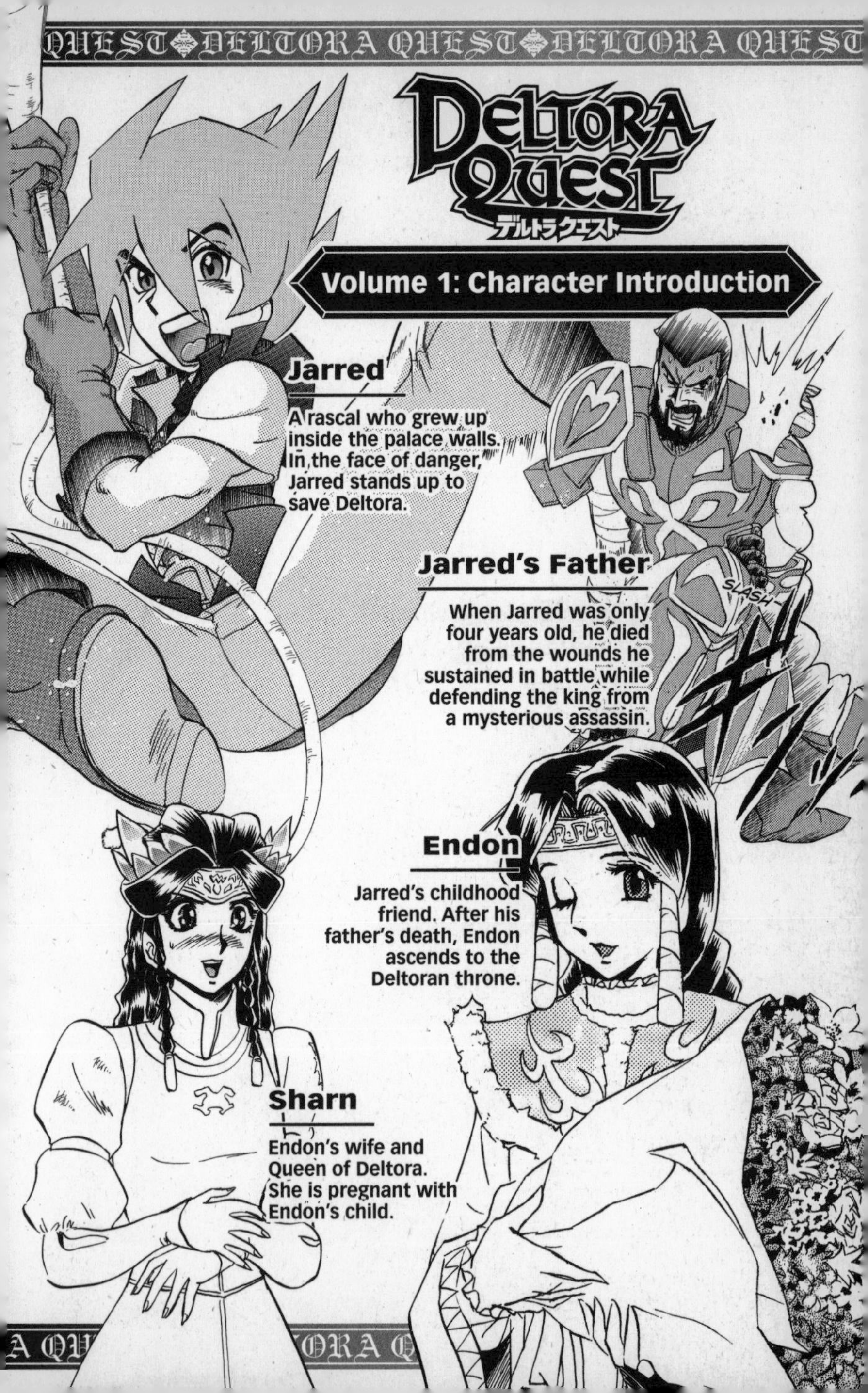
QUEST DELTORA QUEST DELTORA QUEST
DELTORA QUEST
デルトラクエスト
SLASH

Volume 1: Character Introduction

Jarred

A rascal who grew up inside the palace walls. In the face of danger, Jarred stands up to save Deltora.

Jarred's Father

When Jarred was only four years old, he died from the wounds he sustained in battle while defending the king from a mysterious assassin.

Endon

Jarred's childhood friend. After his father's death, Endon ascends to the Deltoran throne.

Sharn

Endon's wife and Queen of Deltora. She is pregnant with Endon's child.

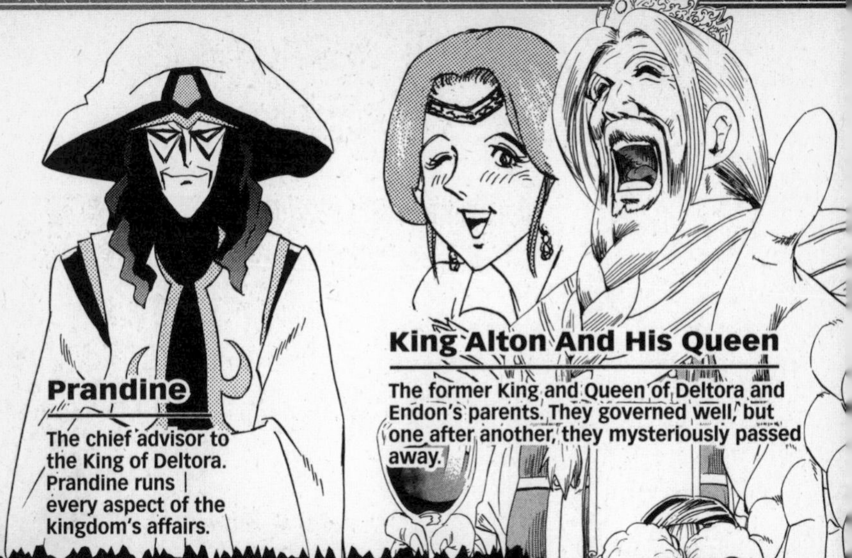

Prandine

The chief advisor to the King of Deltora. Prandine runs every aspect of the kingdom's affairs.

King Alton And His Queen

The former King and Queen of Deltora and Endon's parents. They governed well, but one after another, they mysteriously passed away.

Min

Jarred and Endon's nursemaid. Min loved and raised the two as if they were her own.

What is "The Belt of Deltora?"

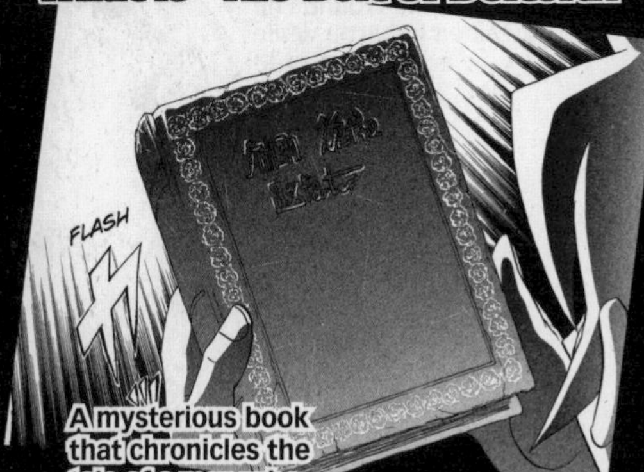
FLASH

A mysterious book that chronicles the tale of a man who defended Deltora against an invading evil enemy, and the great powers the Belt of Deltora bestowed him. The book's author and origin remains a mystery.

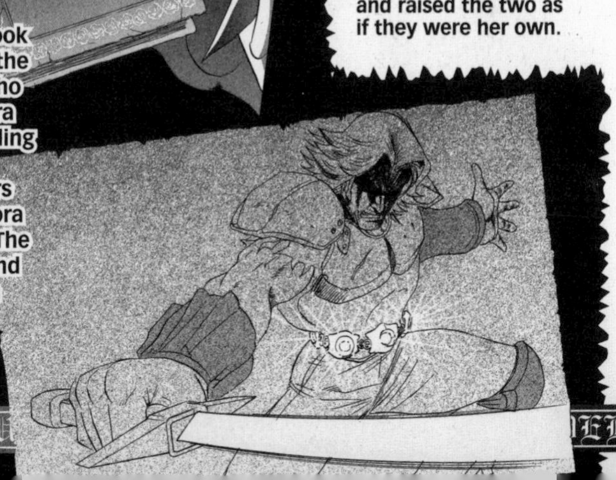

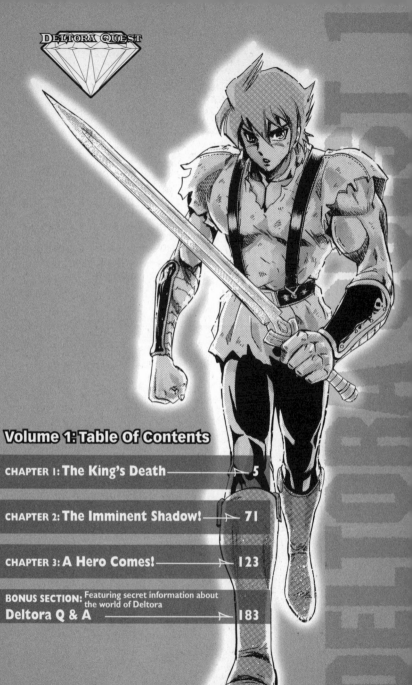

Volume 1: Table Of Contents

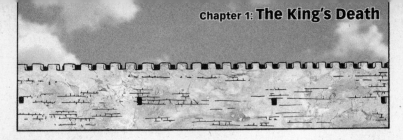

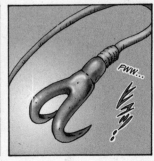

Chapter 1: The King's Death

FWW...
ALL RIGHT ...!
FWW!
FWW!
I'M GOING TO DO IT FOR SURE TODAY!

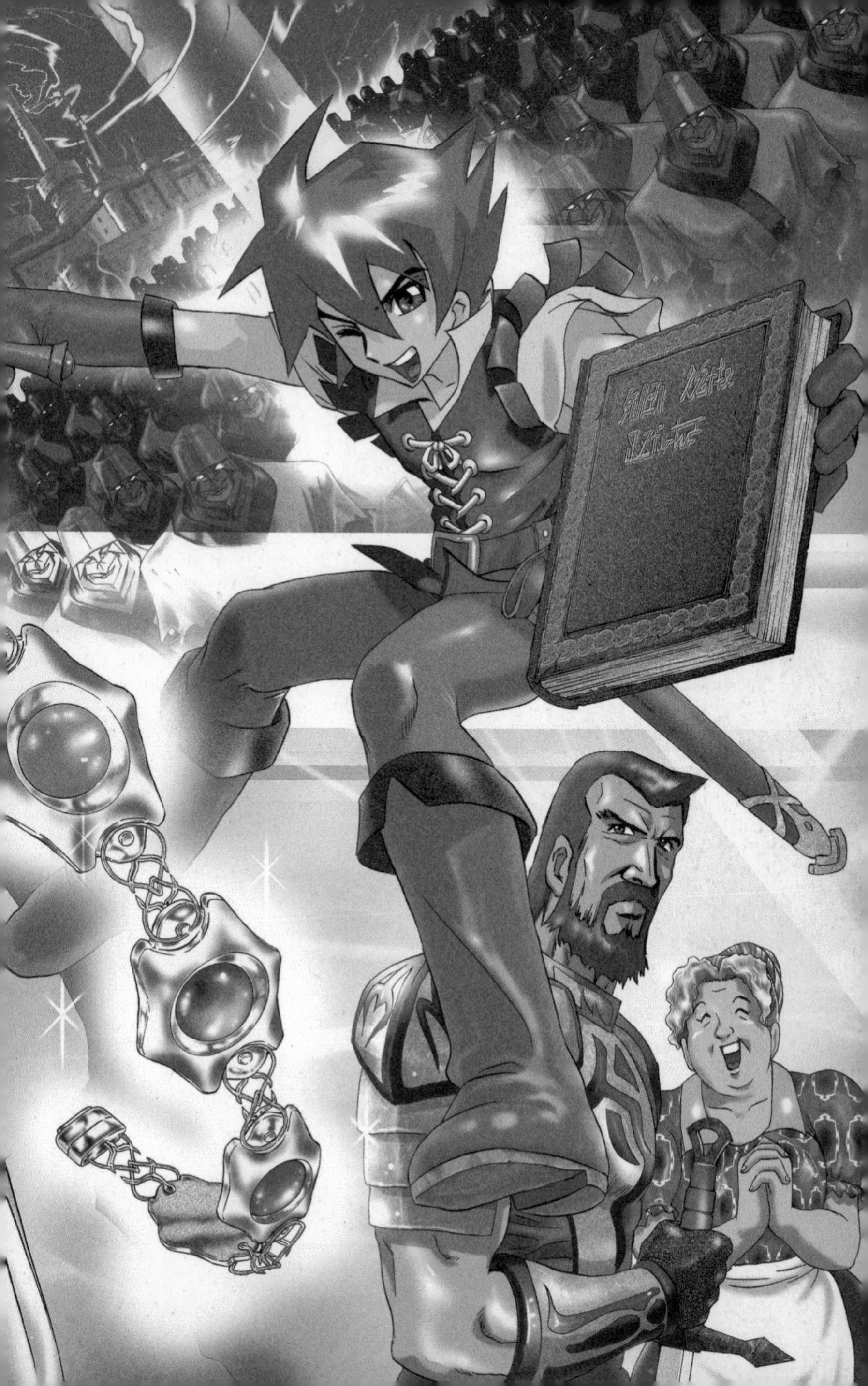

Chapter 1: The King's Death

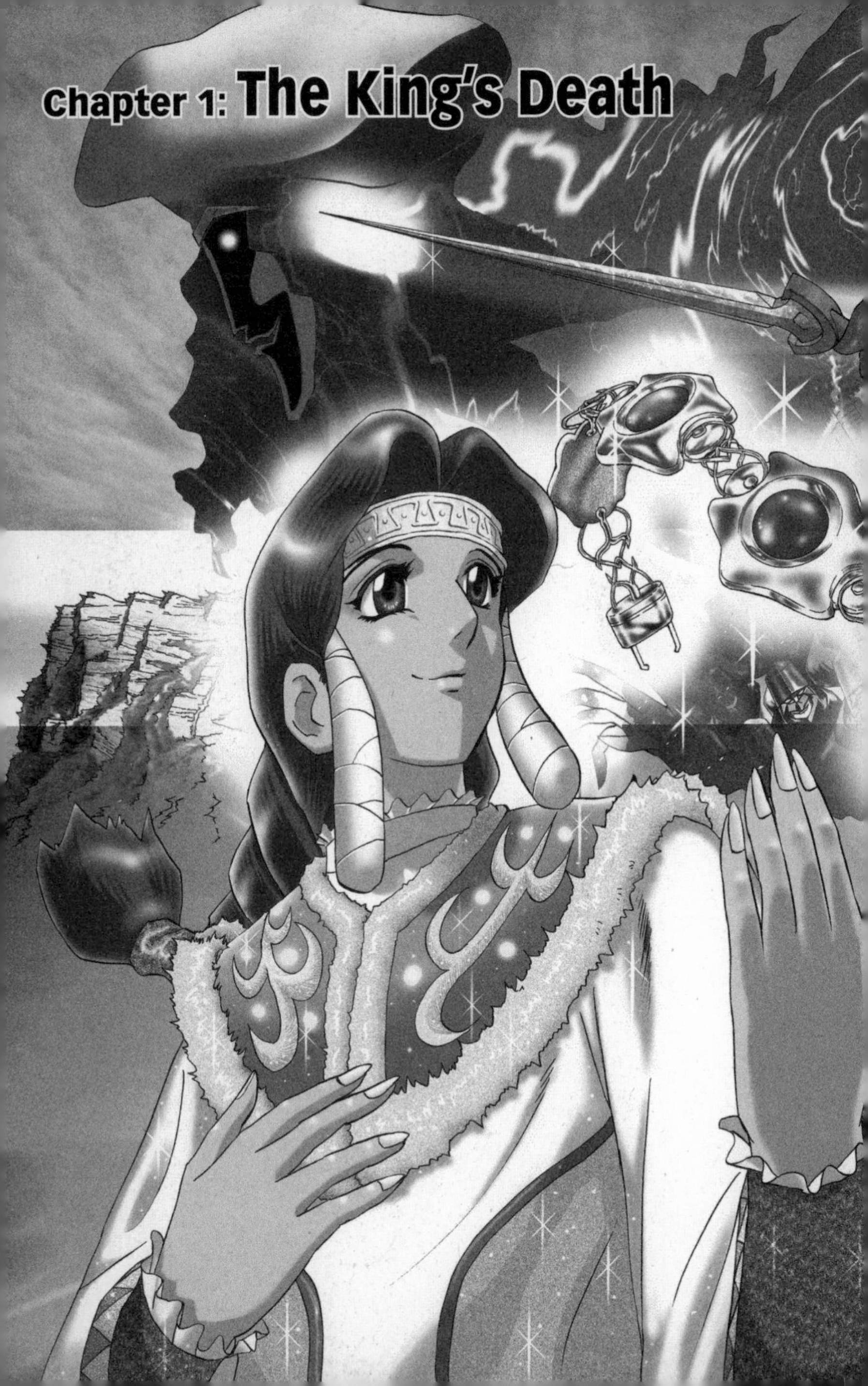

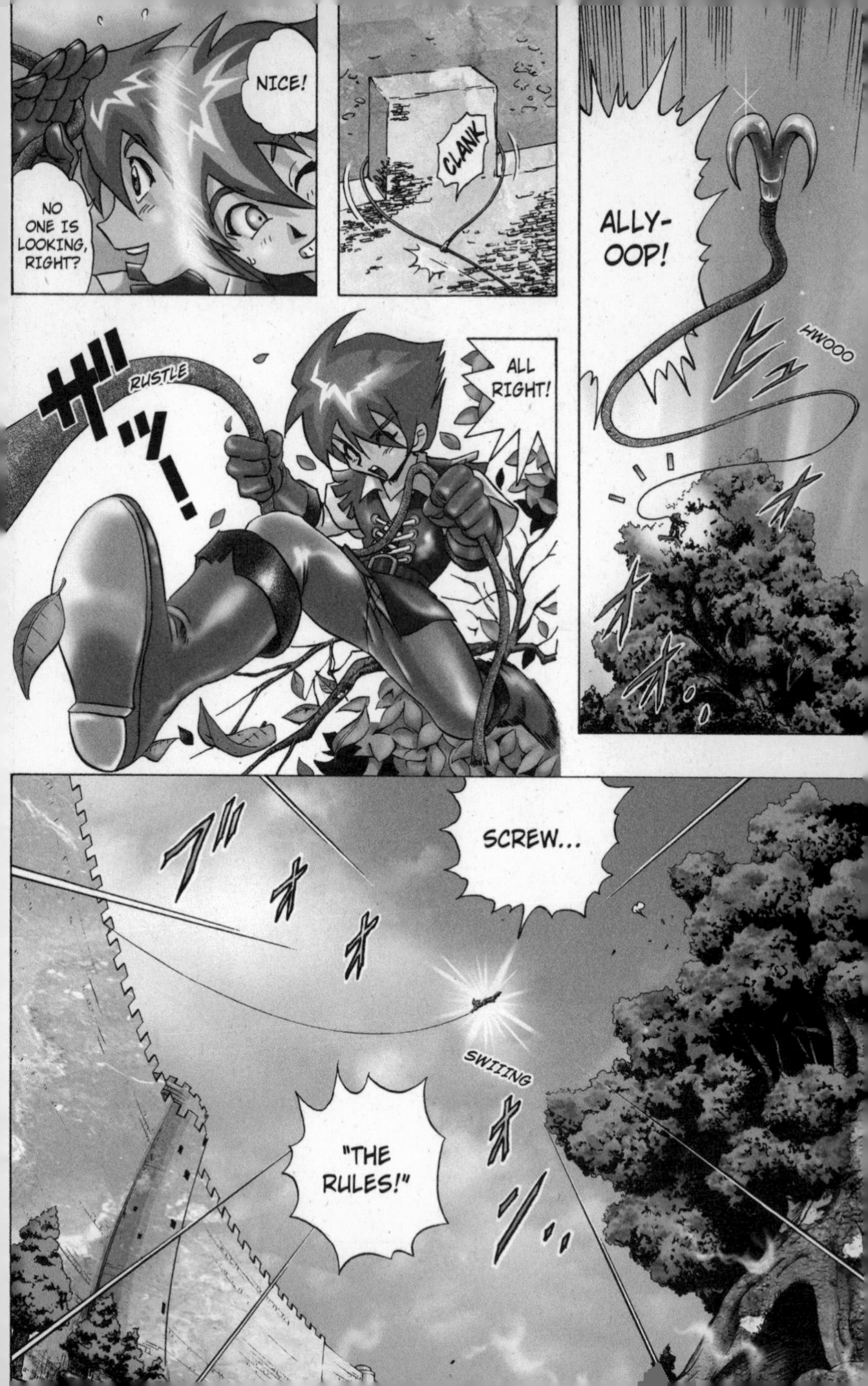
ALLY-OOP!
HWOOO
CLANK
NICE!
NO ONE IS LOOKING, RIGHT?
ALL RIGHT!
RUSTLE
SCREW...
SWIIING
"THE RULES!"

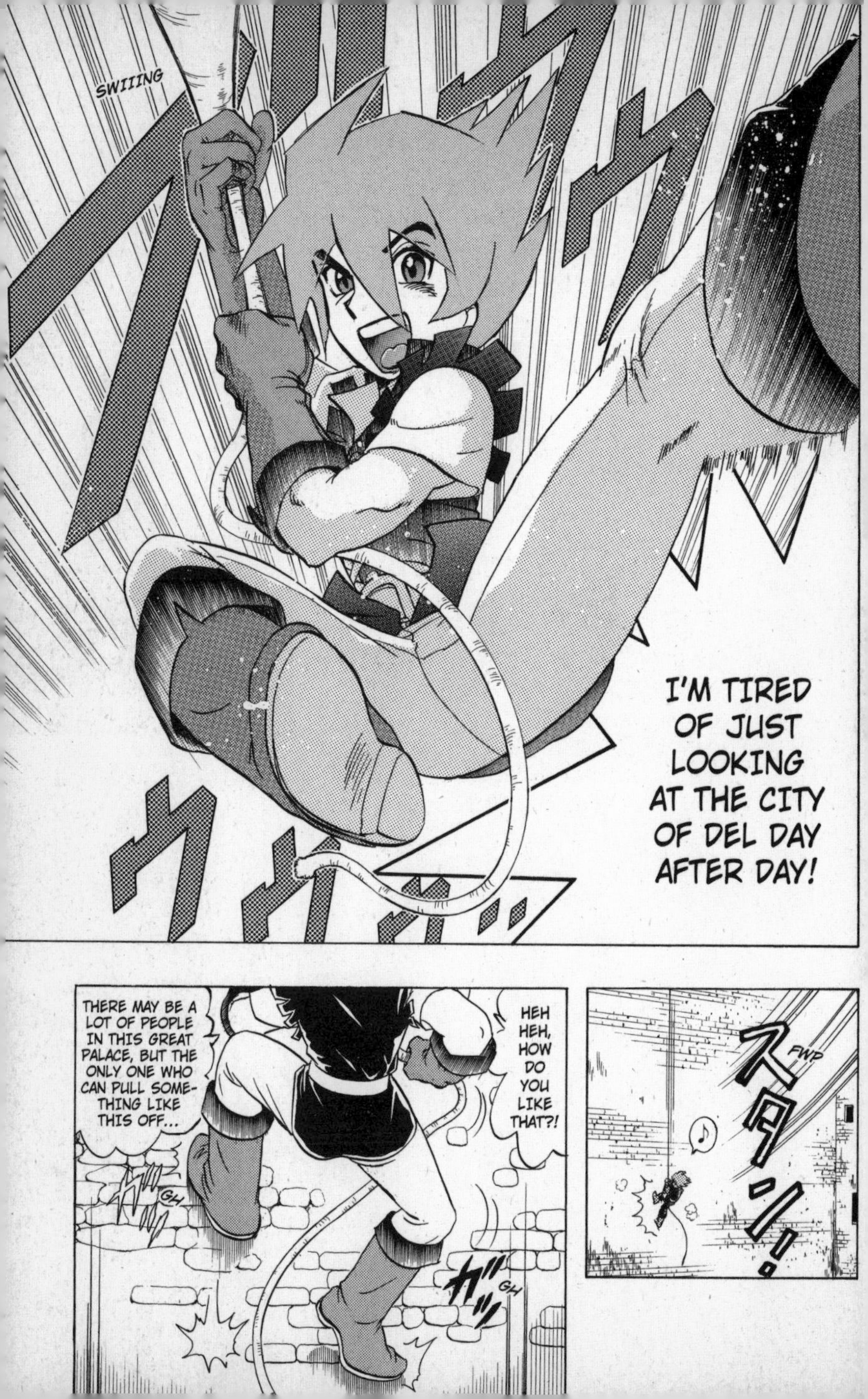
SWIIING
I'M TIRED OF JUST LOOKING AT THE CITY OF DEL DAY AFTER DAY!
FWP
♪
HEH HEH, HOW DO YOU LIKE THAT?!
THERE MAY BE A LOT OF PEOPLE IN THIS GREAT PALACE, BUT THE ONLY ONE WHO CAN PULL SOME-THING LIKE THIS OFF...
GH
GH

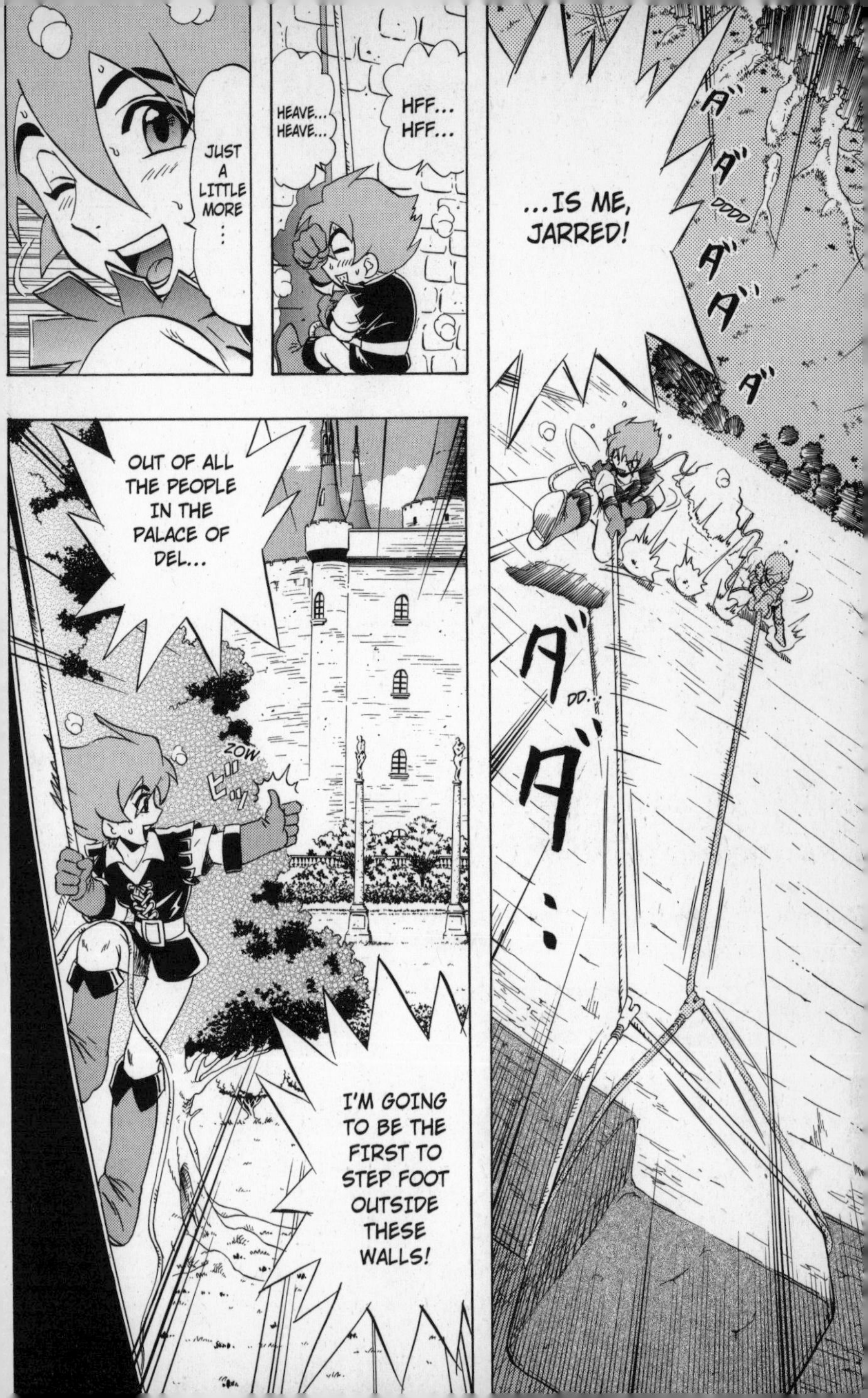

JUST A LITTLE MORE . . .
HEAVE... HEAVE...
HFF... HFF...
OUT OF ALL THE PEOPLE IN THE PALACE OF DEL...
ZOW
I'M GOING TO BE THE FIRST TO STEP FOOT OUTSIDE THESE WALLS!
...IS ME, JARRED!
DDDD
DD...

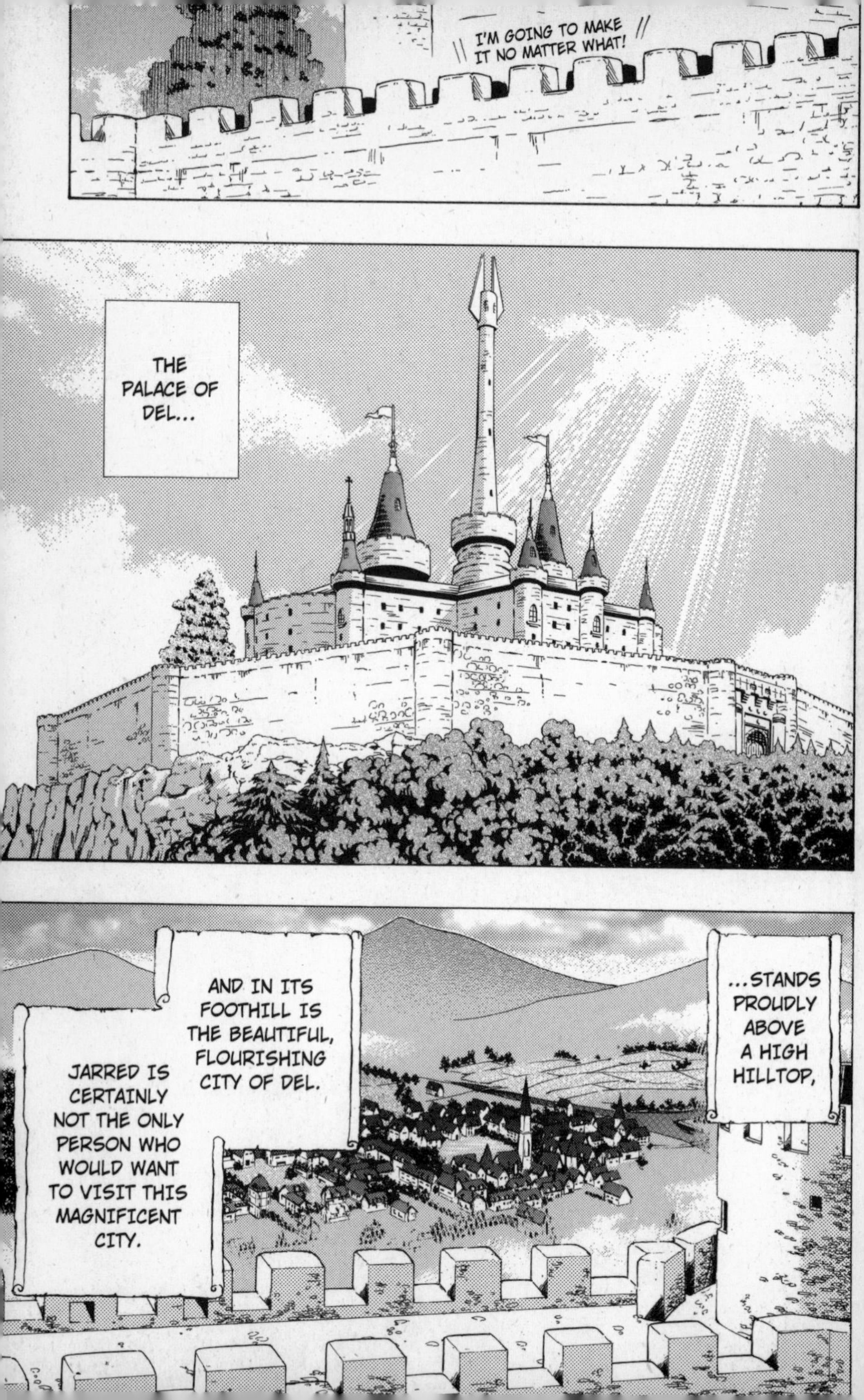
I'M GOING TO MAKE IT NO MATTER WHAT!
THE PALACE OF DEL...
...STANDS PROUDLY ABOVE A HIGH HILLTOP,
AND IN ITS FOOTHILL IS THE BEAUTIFUL, FLOURISHING CITY OF DEL.
JARRED IS CERTAINLY NOT THE ONLY PERSON WHO WOULD WANT TO VISIT THIS MAGNIFICENT CITY.

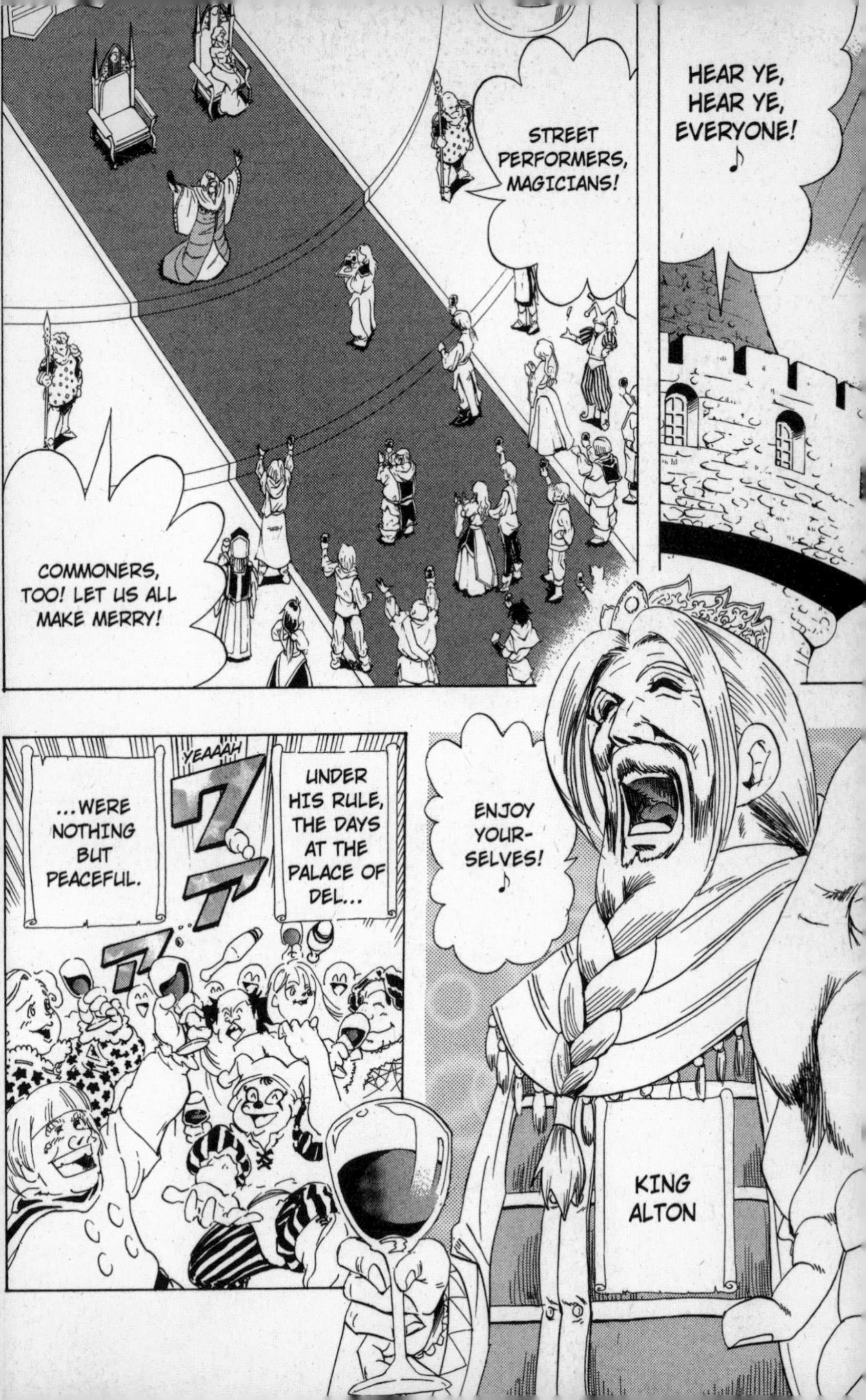
HEAR YE, HEAR YE, EVERYONE! ♪
STREET PERFORMERS, MAGICIANS!
COMMONERS, TOO! LET US ALL MAKE MERRY!
ENJOY YOUR-SELVES! ♪
KING ALTON
UNDER HIS RULE, THE DAYS AT THE PALACE OF DEL...
YEAAAH
...WERE NOTHING BUT PEACEFUL.

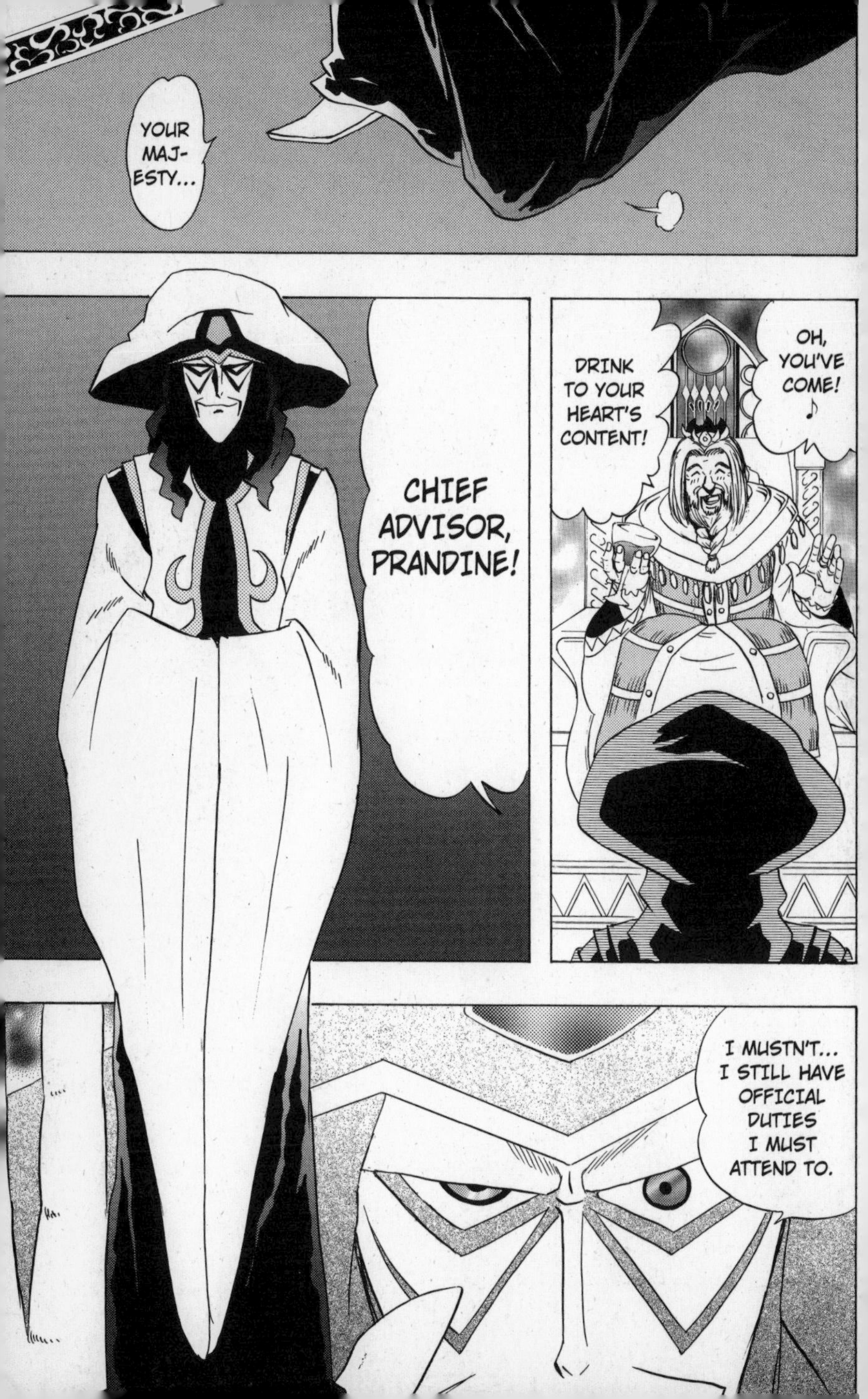
YOUR MAJ-ESTY...
OH, YOU'VE COME! ♪
DRINK TO YOUR HEART'S CONTENT!
CHIEF ADVISOR, PRANDINE!
I MUSTN'T... I STILL HAVE OFFICIAL DUTIES I MUST ATTEND TO.

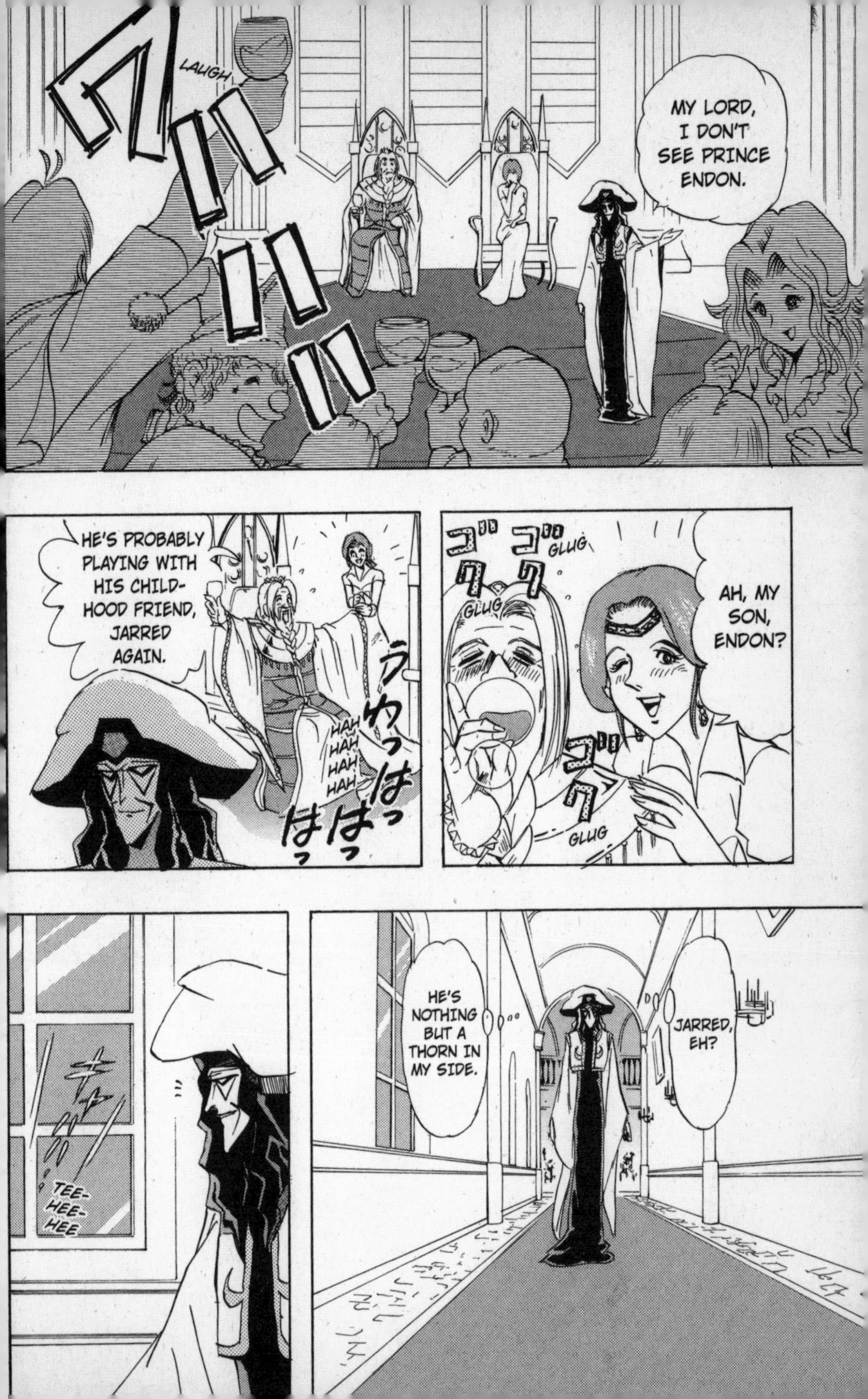
LAUGH
MY LORD, I DON'T SEE PRINCE ENDON.
GLUG
GLUG
AH, MY SON, ENDON?
GLUG
HE'S PROBABLY PLAYING WITH HIS CHILD-HOOD FRIEND, JARRED AGAIN.
HAH HAH HAH HAH
JARRED, EH?
HE'S NOTHING BUT A THORN IN MY SIDE.
TEE-HEE-HEE

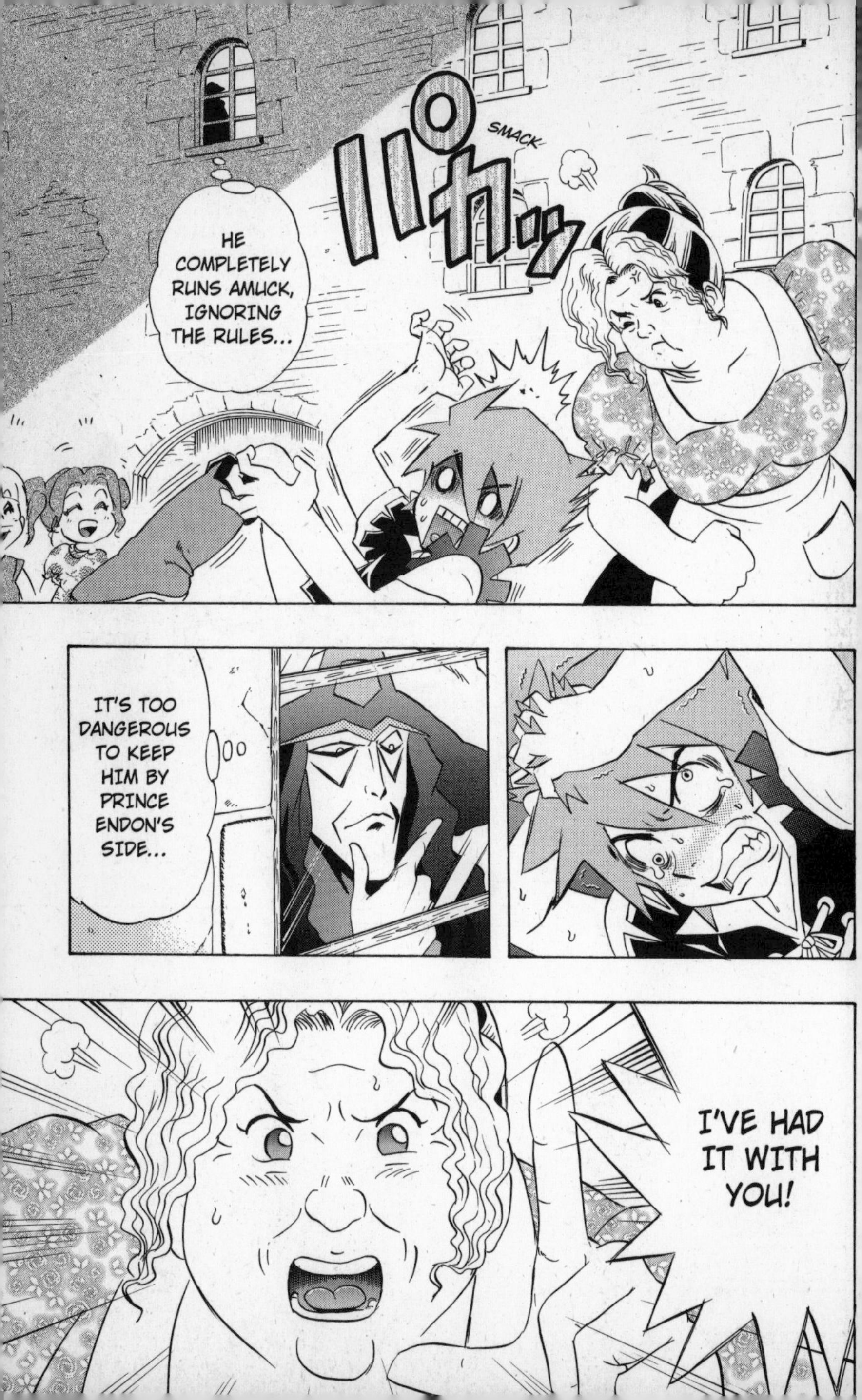
パカッ
SMACK
HE COMPLETELY RUNS AMUCK, IGNORING THE RULES...
IT'S TOO DANGEROUS TO KEEP HIM BY PRINCE ENDON'S SIDE...
I'VE HAD IT WITH YOU!

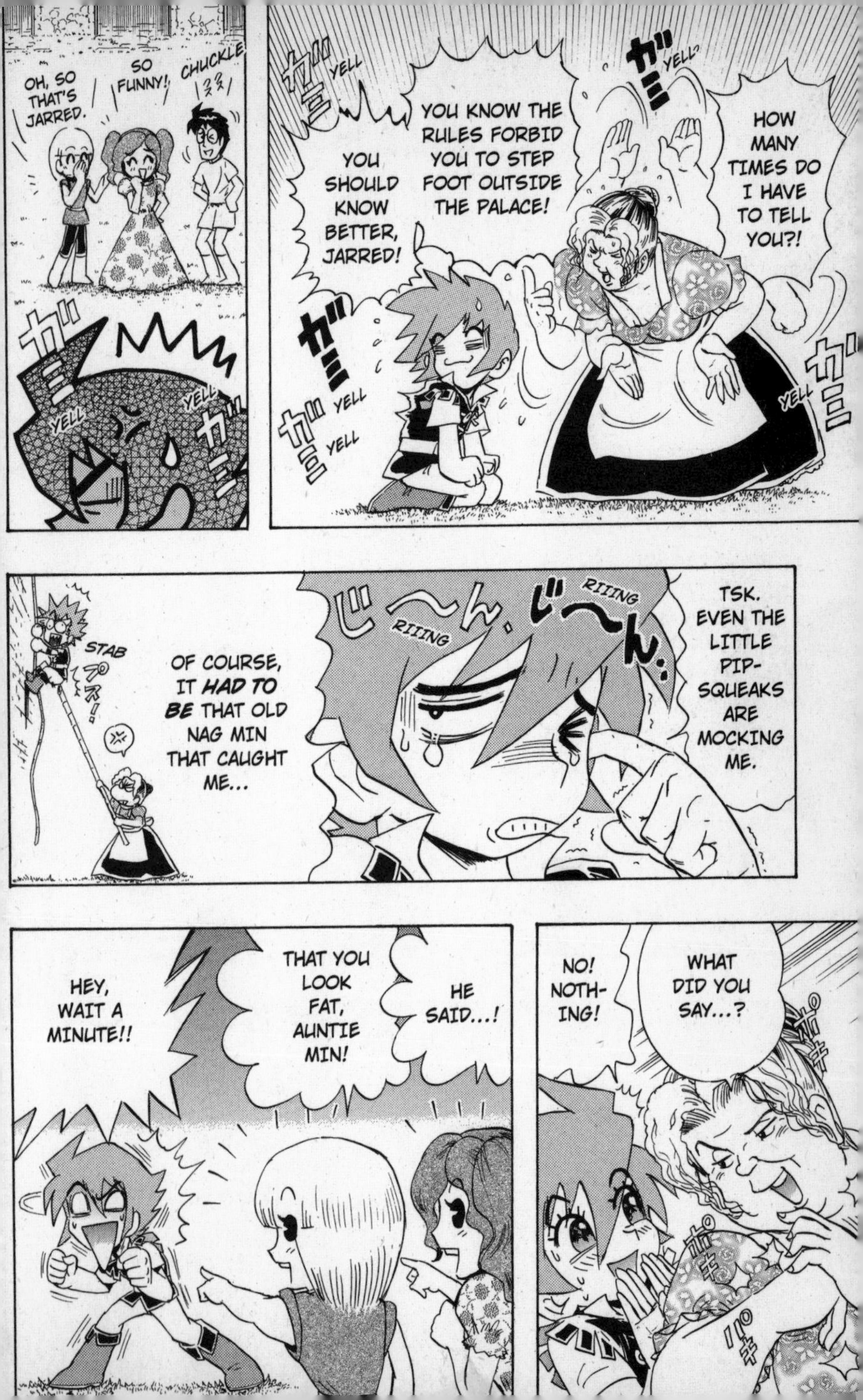
ガミ YELL
ガミ YELL
HOW MANY TIMES DO I HAVE TO TELL YOU?!
YOU KNOW THE RULES FORBID YOU TO STEP FOOT OUTSIDE THE PALACE!
YOU SHOULD KNOW BETTER, JARRED!
ガミ YELL
ガミ YELL
ガミ YELL
CHUCKLE
SO FUNNY!
OH, SO THAT'S JARRED.
ガミ YELL
ガミ YELL
TSK. EVEN THE LITTLE PIP-SQUEAKS ARE MOCKING ME.
じ〜ん RIIING
じ〜ん RIIING
OF COURSE, IT *HAD TO BE* THAT OLD NAG MIN THAT CAUGHT ME...
STAB
WHAT DID YOU SAY...?
NO! NOTHING!
HE SAID...!
THAT YOU LOOK FAT, AUNTIE MIN!
HEY, WAIT A MINUTE!!

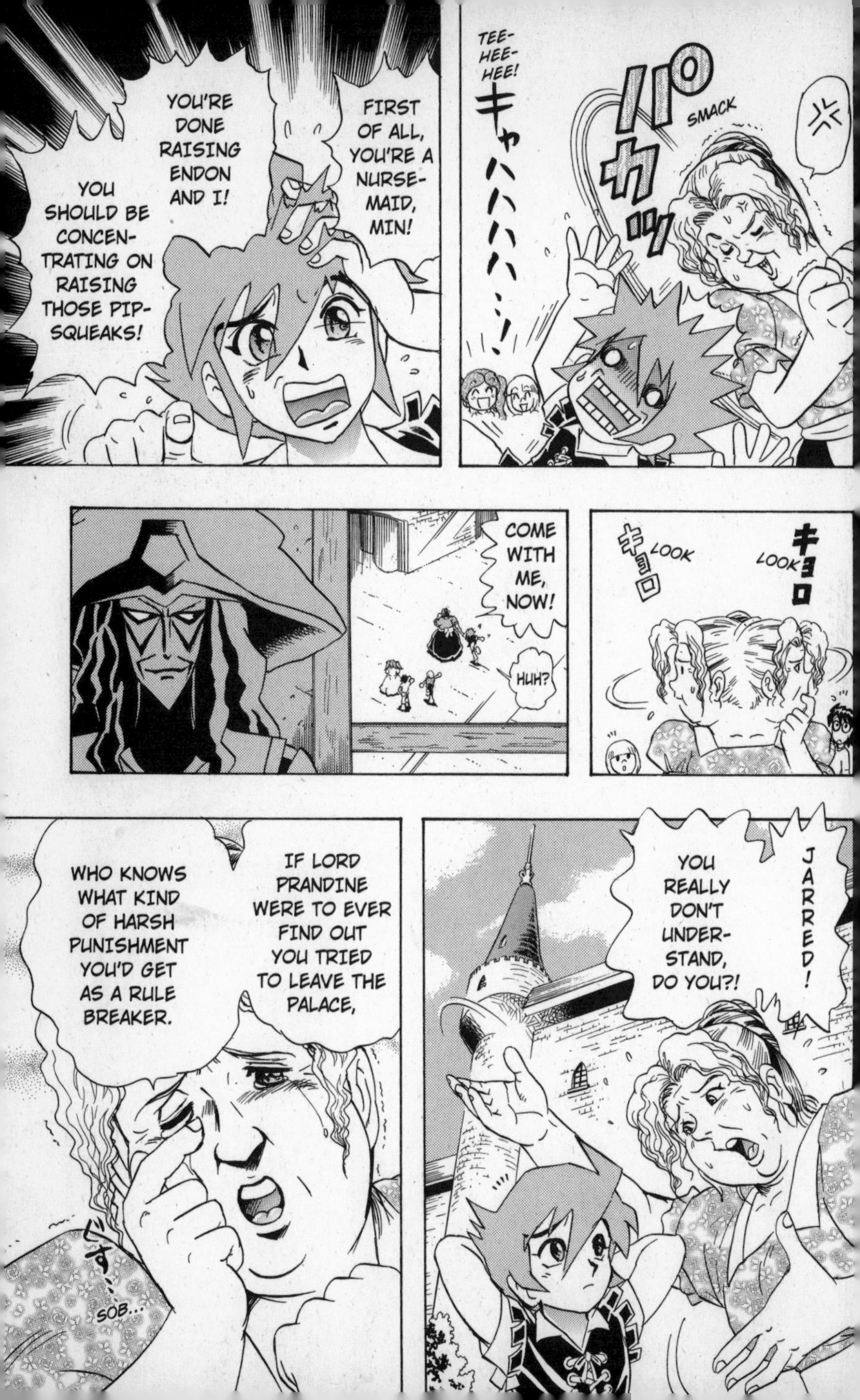
TEE-HEE-HEE!
キャハハハハ…!
パカッ
SMACK
FIRST OF ALL, YOU'RE A NURSE-MAID, MIN!
YOU'RE DONE RAISING ENDON AND I!
YOU SHOULD BE CONCEN-TRATING ON RAISING THOSE PIP-SQUEAKS!
キョロ
LOOK
キョロ
LOOK
COME WITH ME, NOW!
HUH?
JARRED!
YOU REALLY DON'T UNDER-STAND, DO YOU?!
IF LORD PRANDINE WERE TO EVER FIND OUT YOU TRIED TO LEAVE THE PALACE,
WHO KNOWS WHAT KIND OF HARSH PUNISHMENT YOU'D GET AS A RULE BREAKER.
ぐす…
SOB...

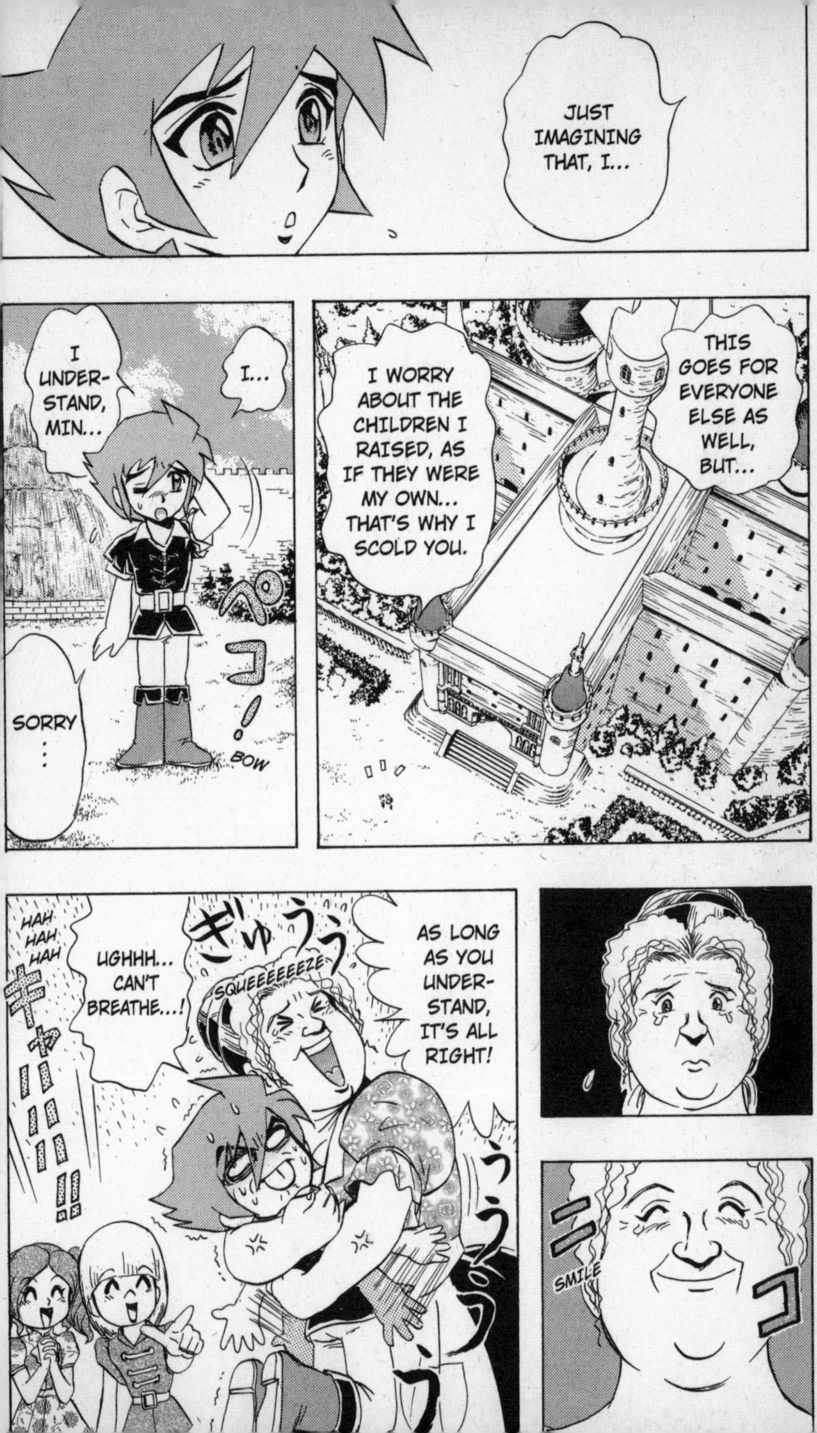
JUST IMAGINING THAT, I...
THIS GOES FOR EVERYONE ELSE AS WELL, BUT...
I WORRY ABOUT THE CHILDREN I RAISED, AS IF THEY WERE MY OWN... THAT'S WHY I SCOLD YOU.
I...
I UNDER-STAND, MIN...
BOW
SORRY...
SMILE
AS LONG AS YOU UNDER-STAND, IT'S ALL RIGHT!
SQUEEEEEEEZE
UGHHH... CAN'T BREATHE...!
HAH HAH HAH

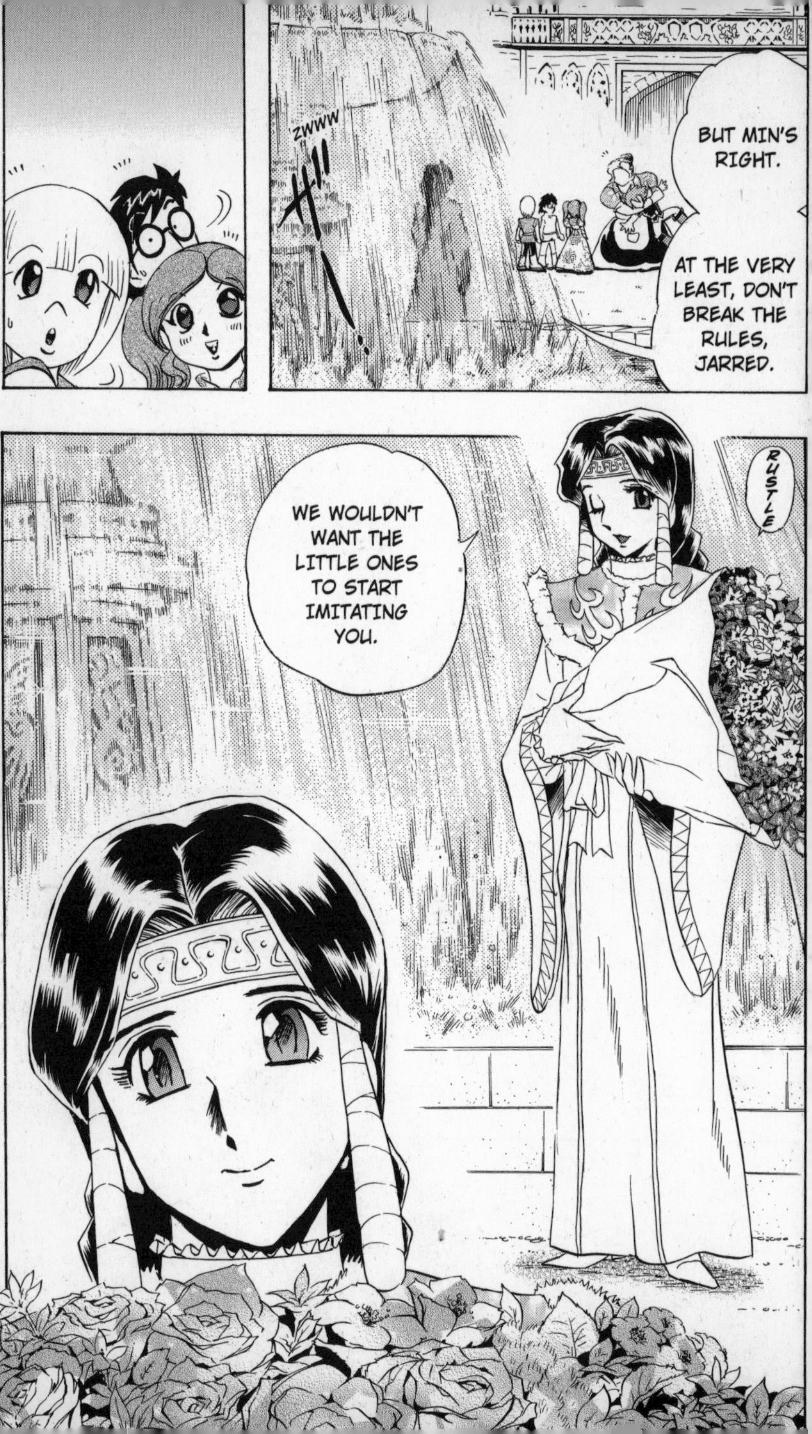
BUT MIN'S RIGHT.
AT THE VERY LEAST, DON'T BREAK THE RULES, JARRED.
ZWWW
RUSTLE
WE WOULDN'T WANT THE LITTLE ONES TO START IMITATING YOU.

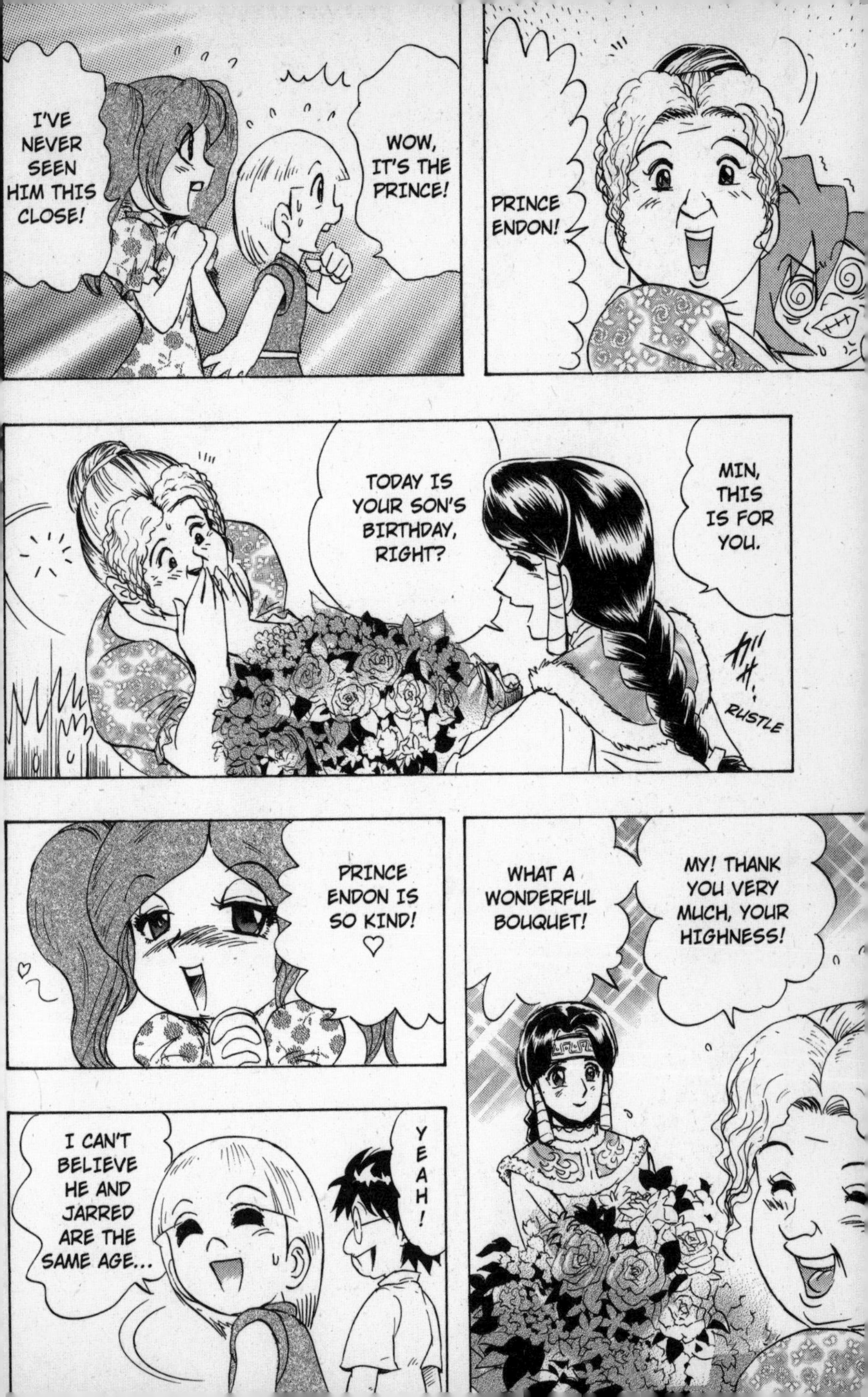
PRINCE ENDON!
WOW, IT'S THE PRINCE!
I'VE NEVER SEEN HIM THIS CLOSE!
MIN, THIS IS FOR YOU.
RUSTLE
TODAY IS YOUR SON'S BIRTHDAY, RIGHT?
MY! THANK YOU VERY MUCH, YOUR HIGHNESS!
WHAT A WONDERFUL BOUQUET!
PRINCE ENDON IS SO KIND! ♡
YEAH!
I CAN'T BELIEVE HE AND JARRED ARE THE SAME AGE...

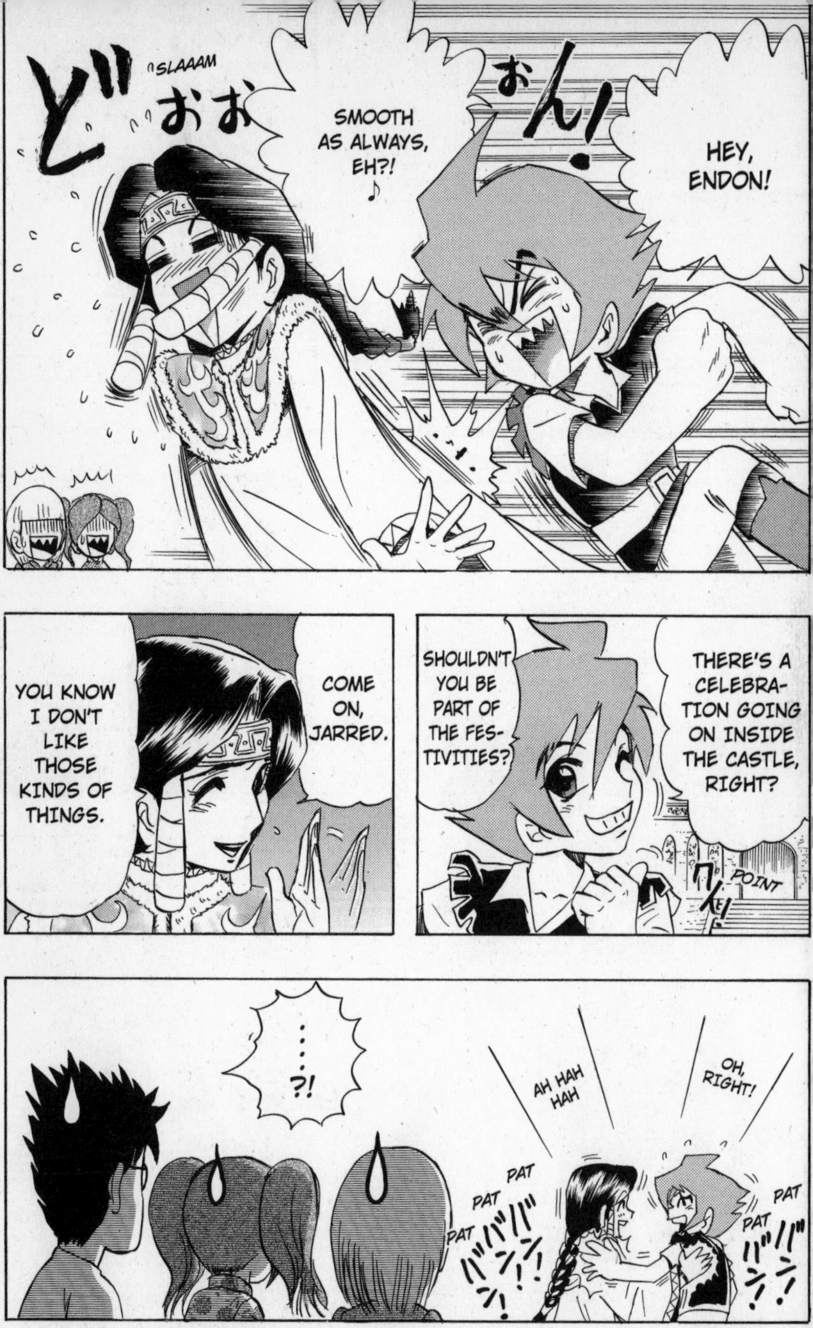
HEY, ENDON!
おん!
SMOOTH AS ALWAYS, EH?! ♪
どおお
SLAAAM
THERE'S A CELEBRATION GOING ON INSIDE THE CASTLE, RIGHT?
SHOULDN'T YOU BE PART OF THE FESTIVITIES?
POINT
COME ON, JARRED.
YOU KNOW I DON'T LIKE THOSE KINDS OF THINGS.
OH, RIGHT!
PAT
PAT
バン!バン!
AH HAH HAH
PAT
PAT
PAT
バン!バン!バン!
....?!

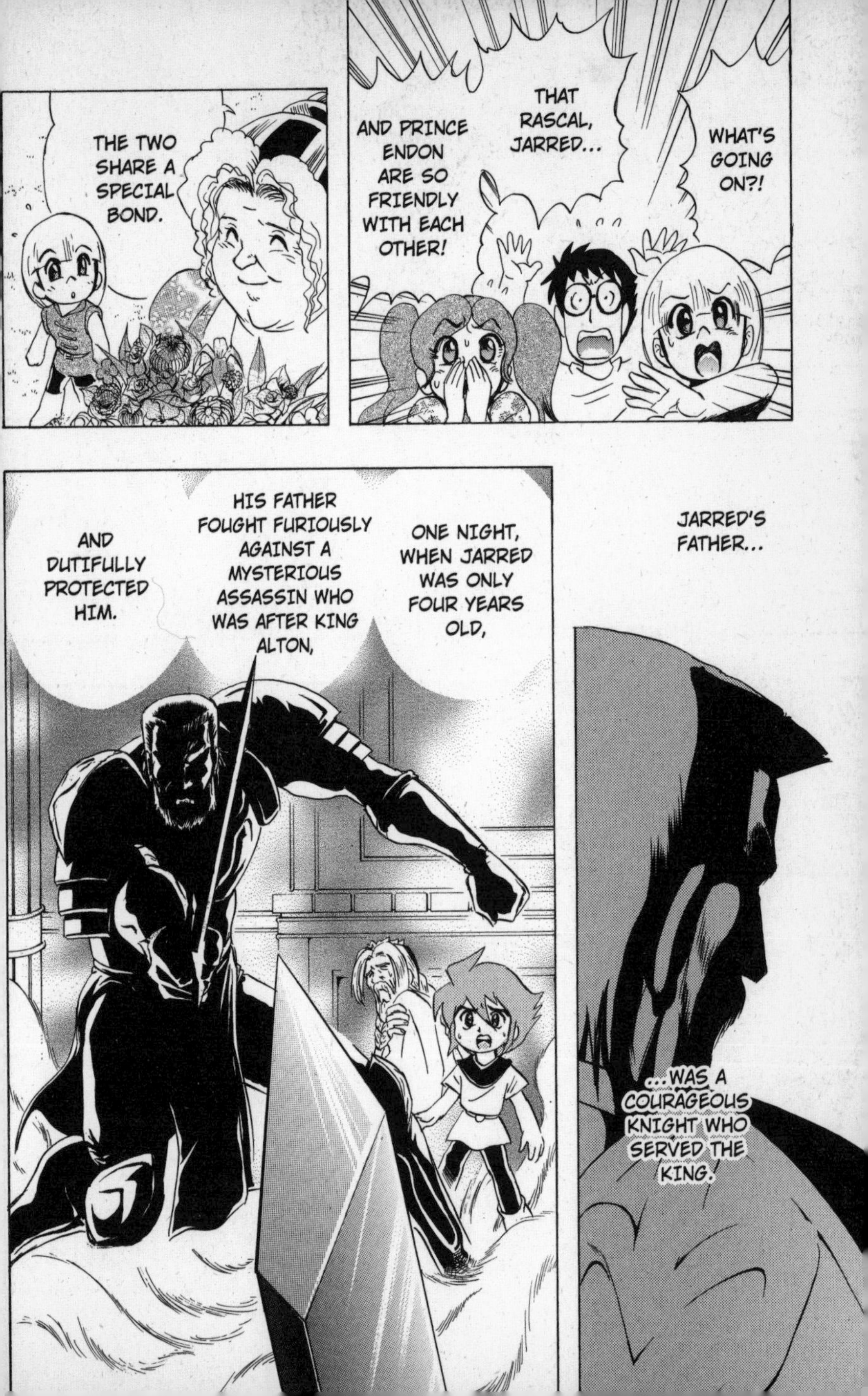
WHAT'S GOING ON?!
THAT RASCAL, JARRED...
AND PRINCE ENDON ARE SO FRIENDLY WITH EACH OTHER!
THE TWO SHARE A SPECIAL BOND.
JARRED'S FATHER...
...WAS A COURAGEOUS KNIGHT WHO SERVED THE KING.
ONE NIGHT, WHEN JARRED WAS ONLY FOUR YEARS OLD,
HIS FATHER FOUGHT FURIOUSLY AGAINST A MYSTERIOUS ASSASSIN WHO WAS AFTER KING ALTON,
AND DUTIFULLY PROTECTED HIM.

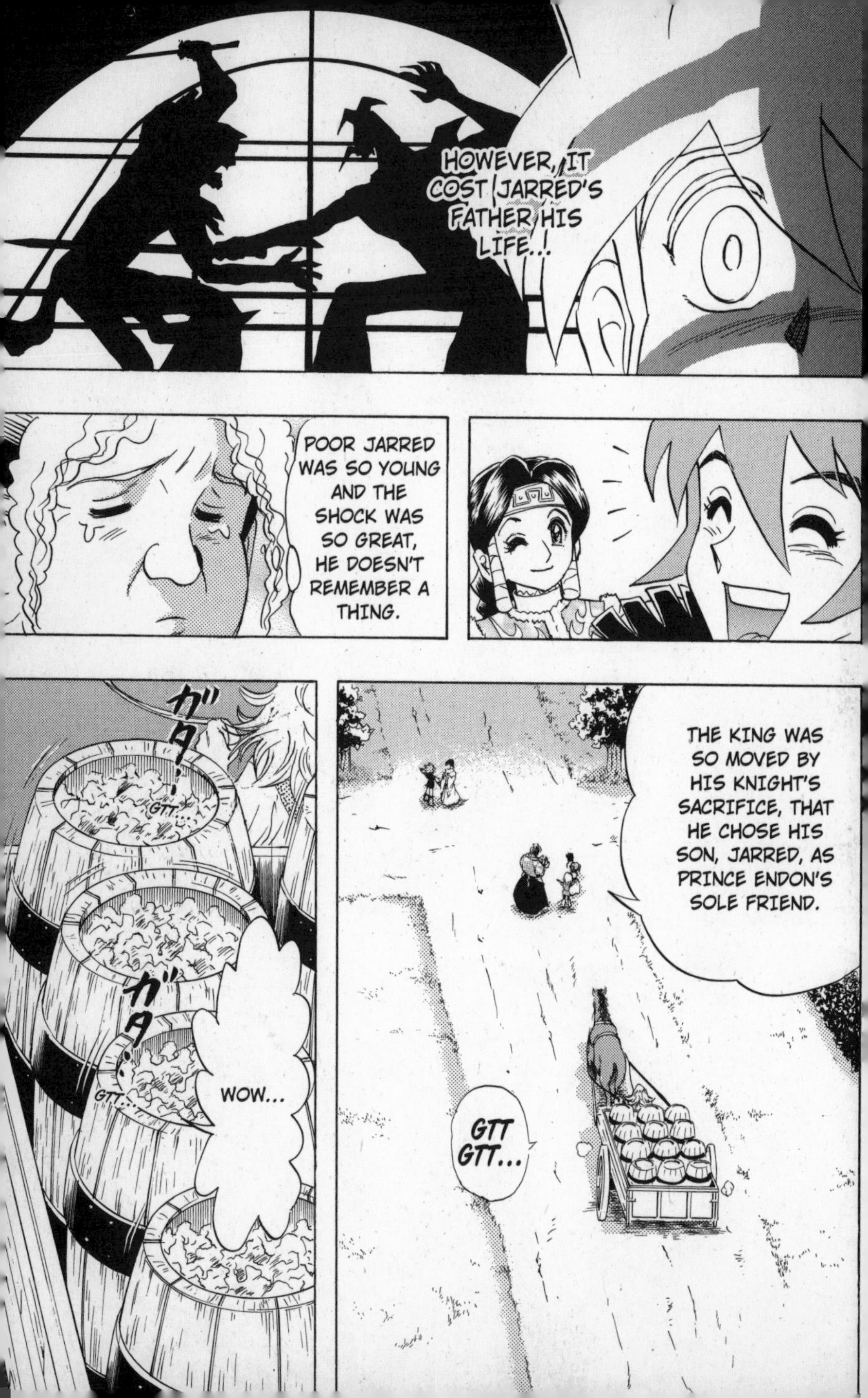
HOWEVER, IT COST JARRED'S FATHER HIS LIFE...!
POOR JARRED WAS SO YOUNG AND THE SHOCK WAS SO GREAT, HE DOESN'T REMEMBER A THING.
THE KING WAS SO MOVED BY HIS KNIGHT'S SACRIFICE, THAT HE CHOSE HIS SON, JARRED, AS PRINCE ENDON'S SOLE FRIEND.
GTT GTT...
ガタ
GTT...
ガタ
GTT...
WOW...

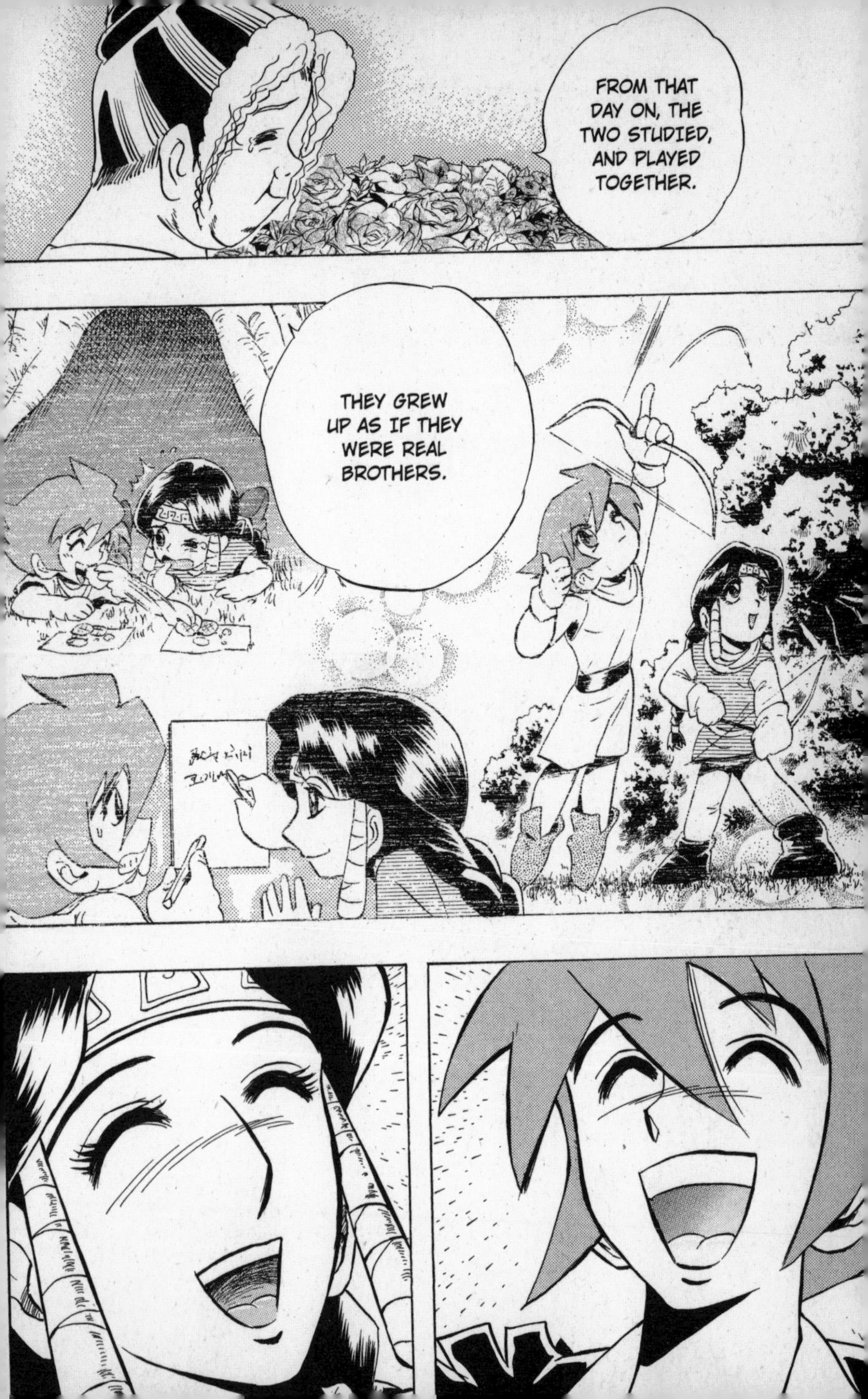
FROM THAT DAY ON, THE TWO STUDIED, AND PLAYED TOGETHER.
THEY GREW UP AS IF THEY WERE REAL BROTHERS.

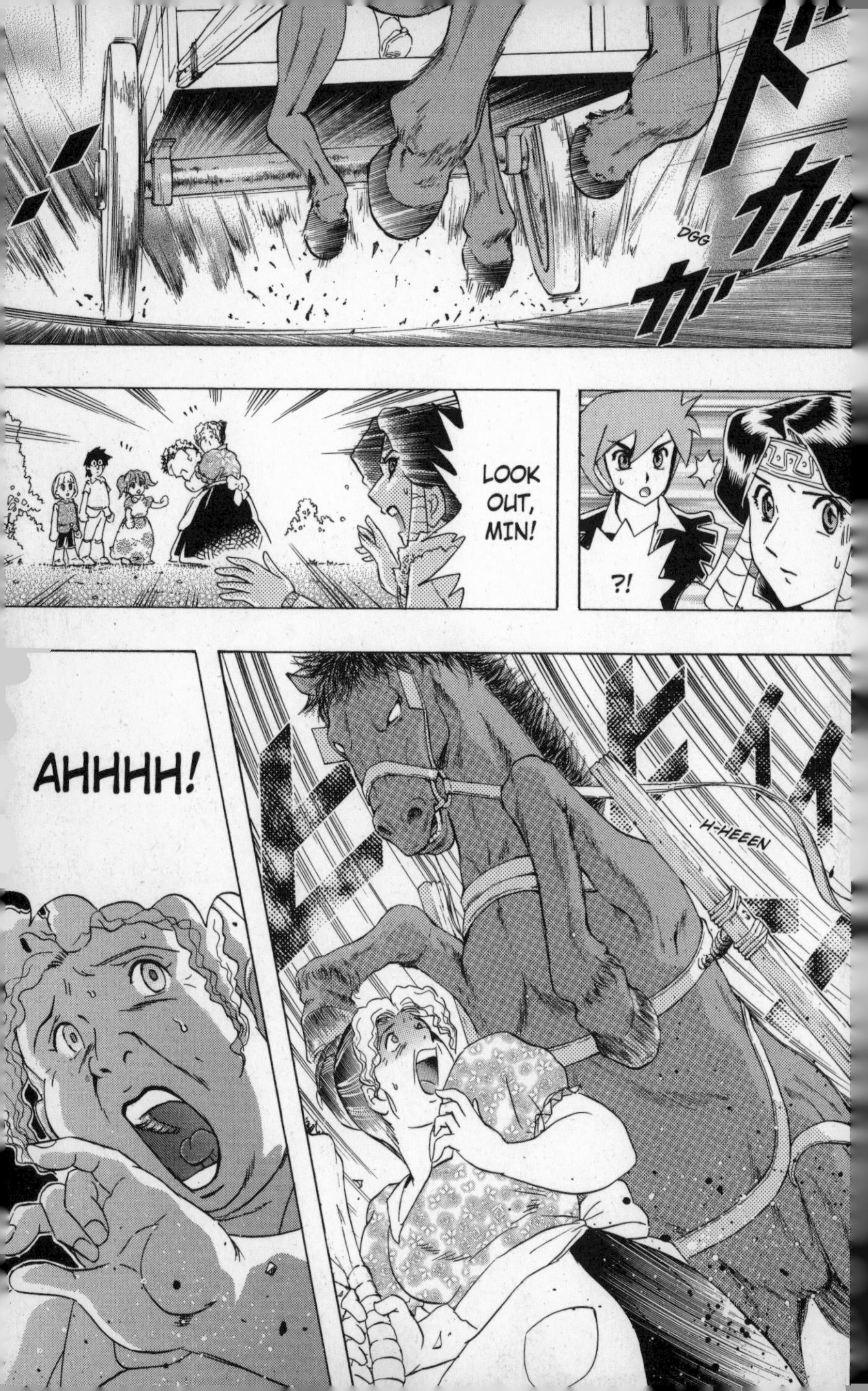
ドカッ
ガッ
DGG
?!
LOOK OUT, MIN!
ヒヒイ—ン
H-HEEEN
AHHHH!

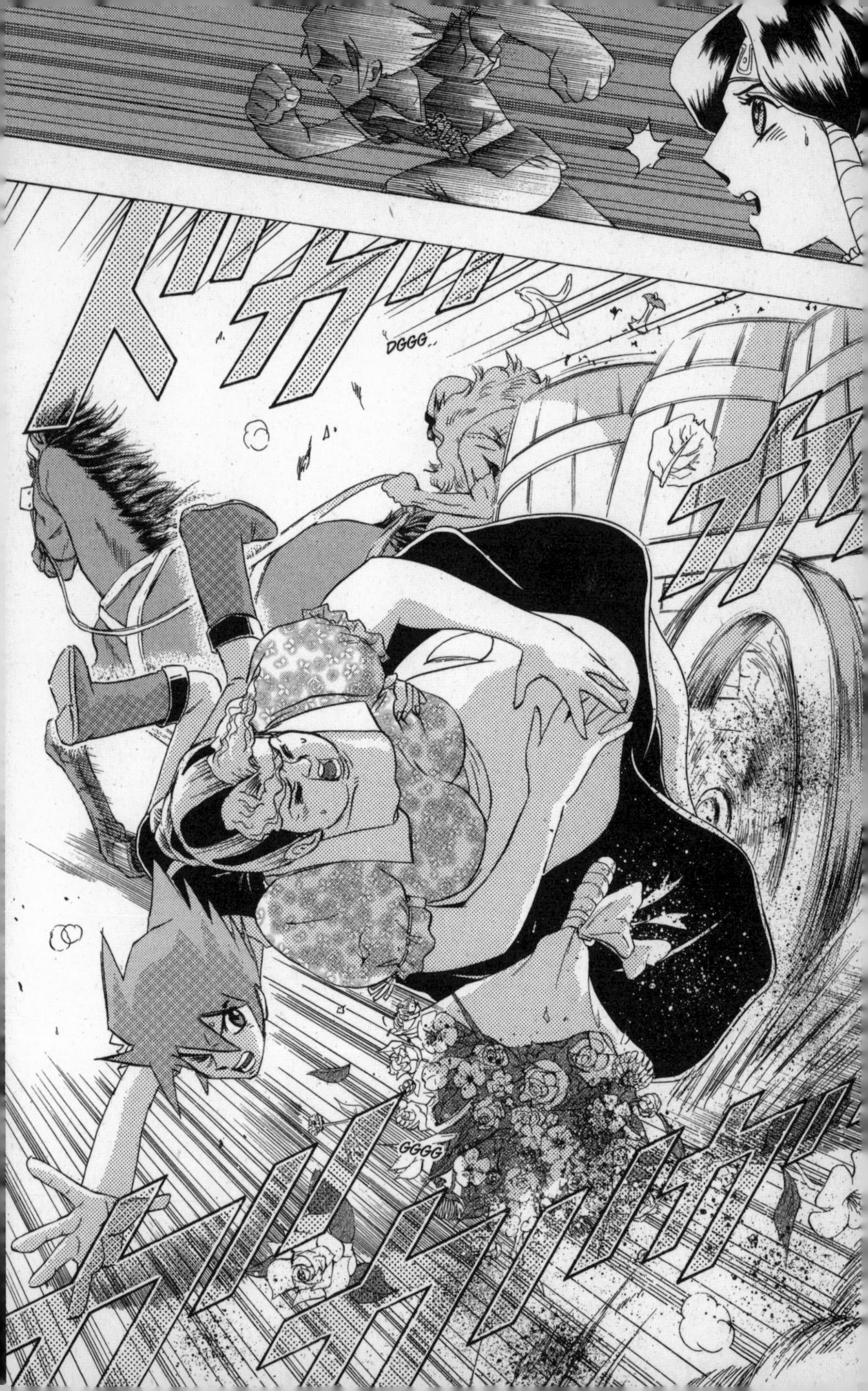
DGGG..
GGGG

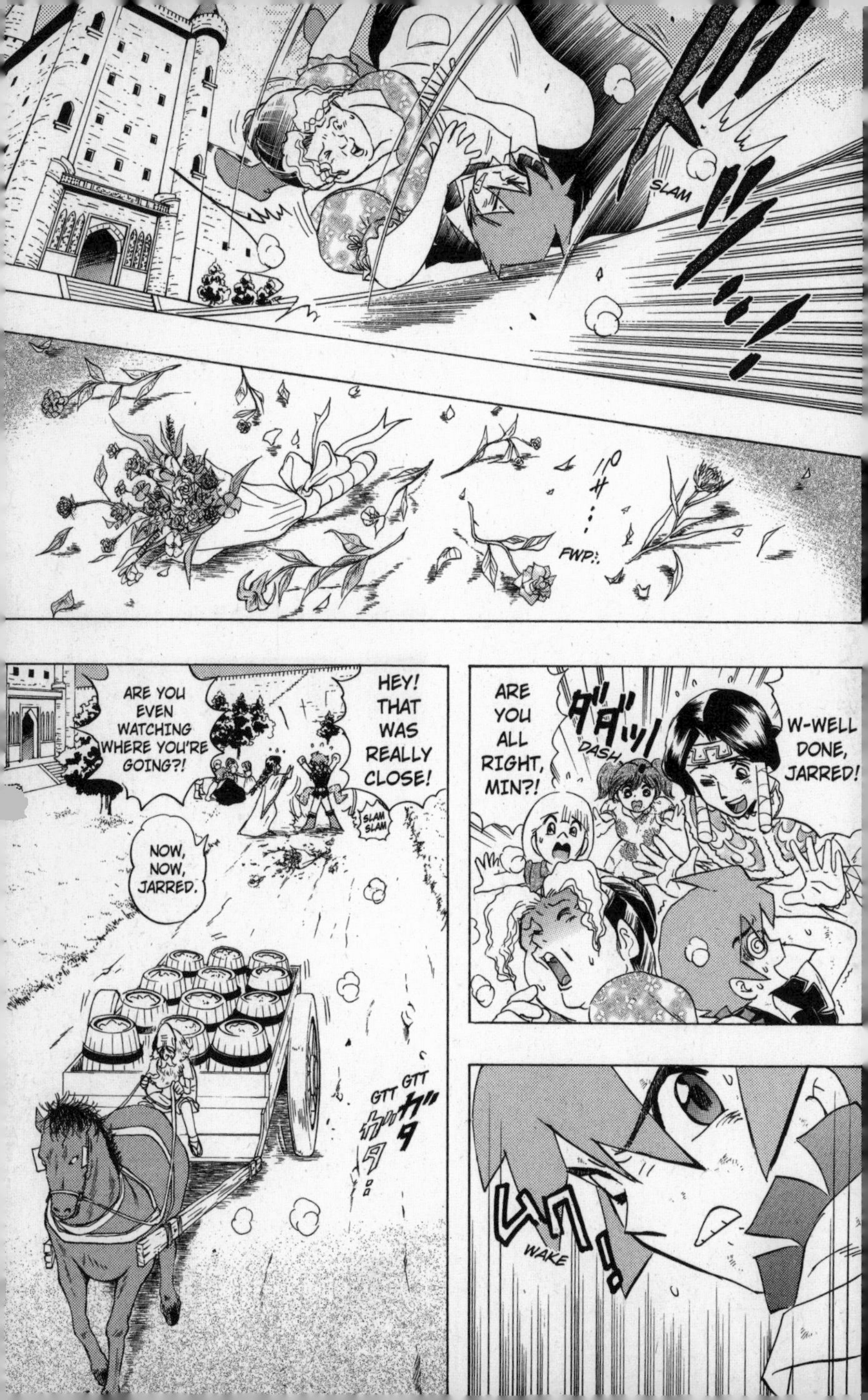
SLAM
FWP:.
W-WELL DONE, JARRED!
DASH
ARE YOU ALL RIGHT, MIN?!
WAKE
HEY! THAT WAS REALLY CLOSE!
SLAM SLAM
ARE YOU EVEN WATCHING WHERE YOU'RE GOING?!
NOW, NOW, JARRED.
GTT GTT

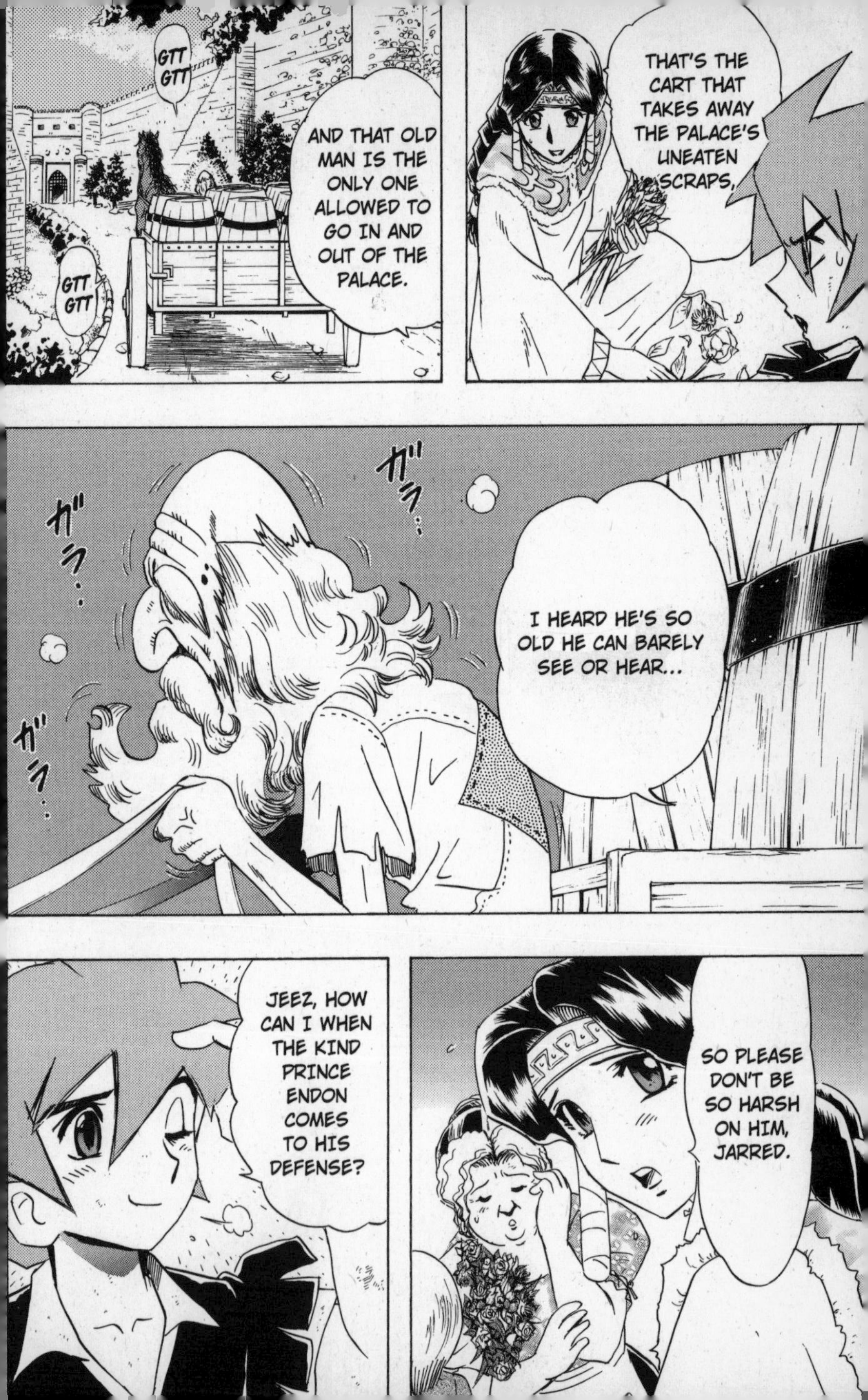
THAT'S THE CART THAT TAKES AWAY THE PALACE'S UNEATEN SCRAPS,
GTT GTT
AND THAT OLD MAN IS THE ONLY ONE ALLOWED TO GO IN AND OUT OF THE PALACE.
GTT GTT
ガラ…
I HEARD HE'S SO OLD HE CAN BARELY SEE OR HEAR...
ガラ…
ガラ…
SO PLEASE DON'T BE SO HARSH ON HIM, JARRED.
JEEZ, HOW CAN I WHEN THE KIND PRINCE ENDON COMES TO HIS DEFENSE?

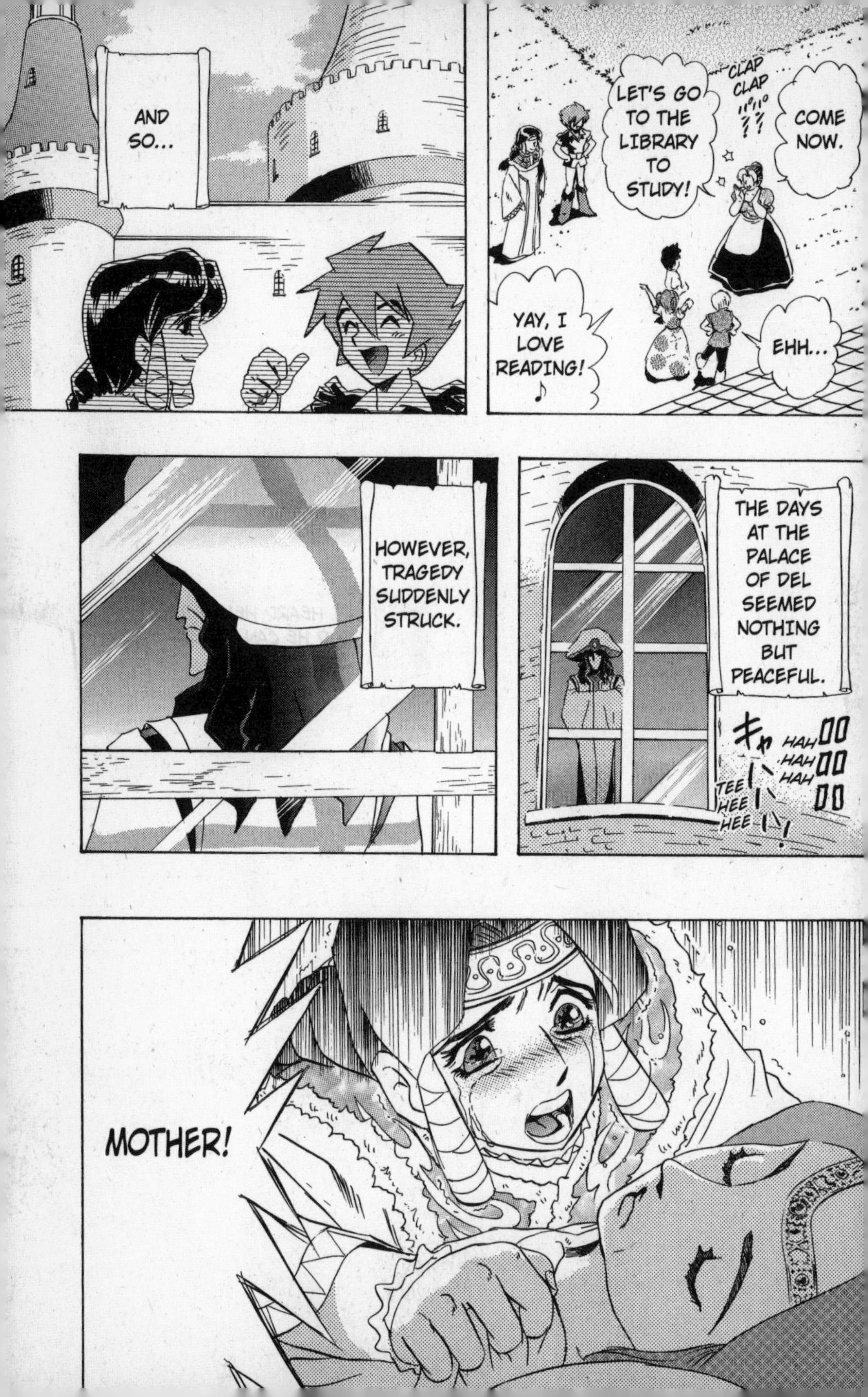
COME NOW.
CLAP CLAP
LET'S GO TO THE LIBRARY TO STUDY!
EHH...
YAY, I LOVE READING! ♪
AND SO...
THE DAYS AT THE PALACE OF DEL SEEMED NOTHING BUT PEACEFUL.
HAH HAH HAH
TEE HEE HEE
HOWEVER, TRAGEDY SUDDENLY STRUCK.
MOTHER!

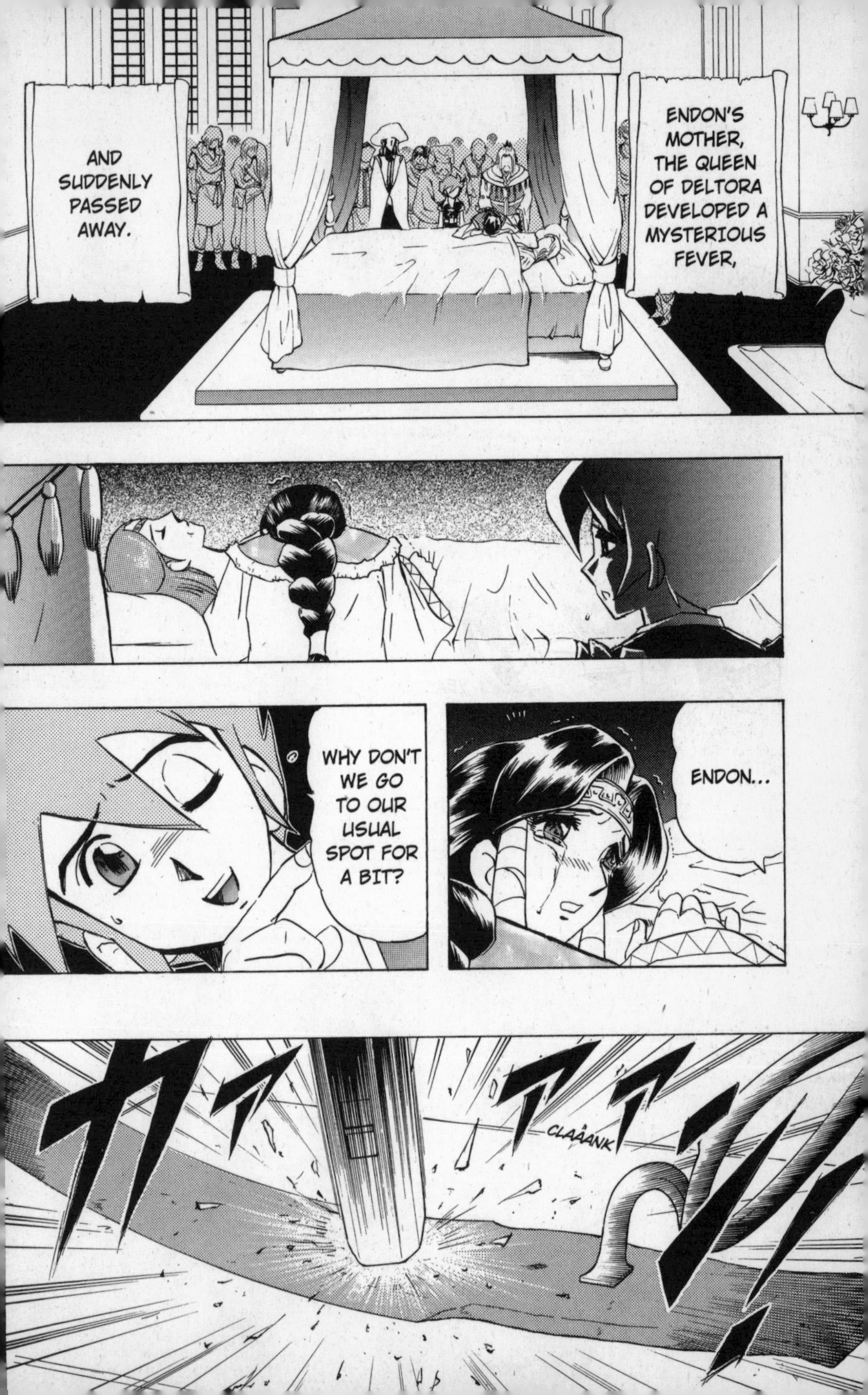
ENDON'S MOTHER, THE QUEEN OF DELTORA DEVELOPED A MYSTERIOUS FEVER,
AND SUDDENLY PASSED AWAY.
ENDON...
WHY DON'T WE GO TO OUR USUAL SPOT FOR A BIT?
CLAÂANK

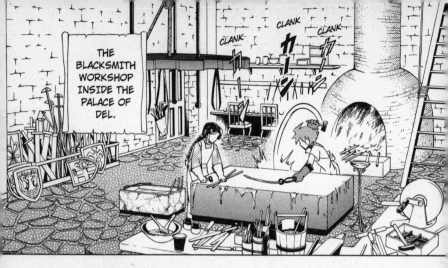

THE BLACKSMITH WORKSHOP INSIDE THE PALACE OF DEL.

CLANK

CLANK

CLANK

......

YEAH, I GUESS...

CLANK

FORGING A SWORD HELPS TAKE YOUR MIND OFF OF THINGS, DOESN'T IT?

WHA-?! JARRED?!

AHHHH!

...

!!

SLAM

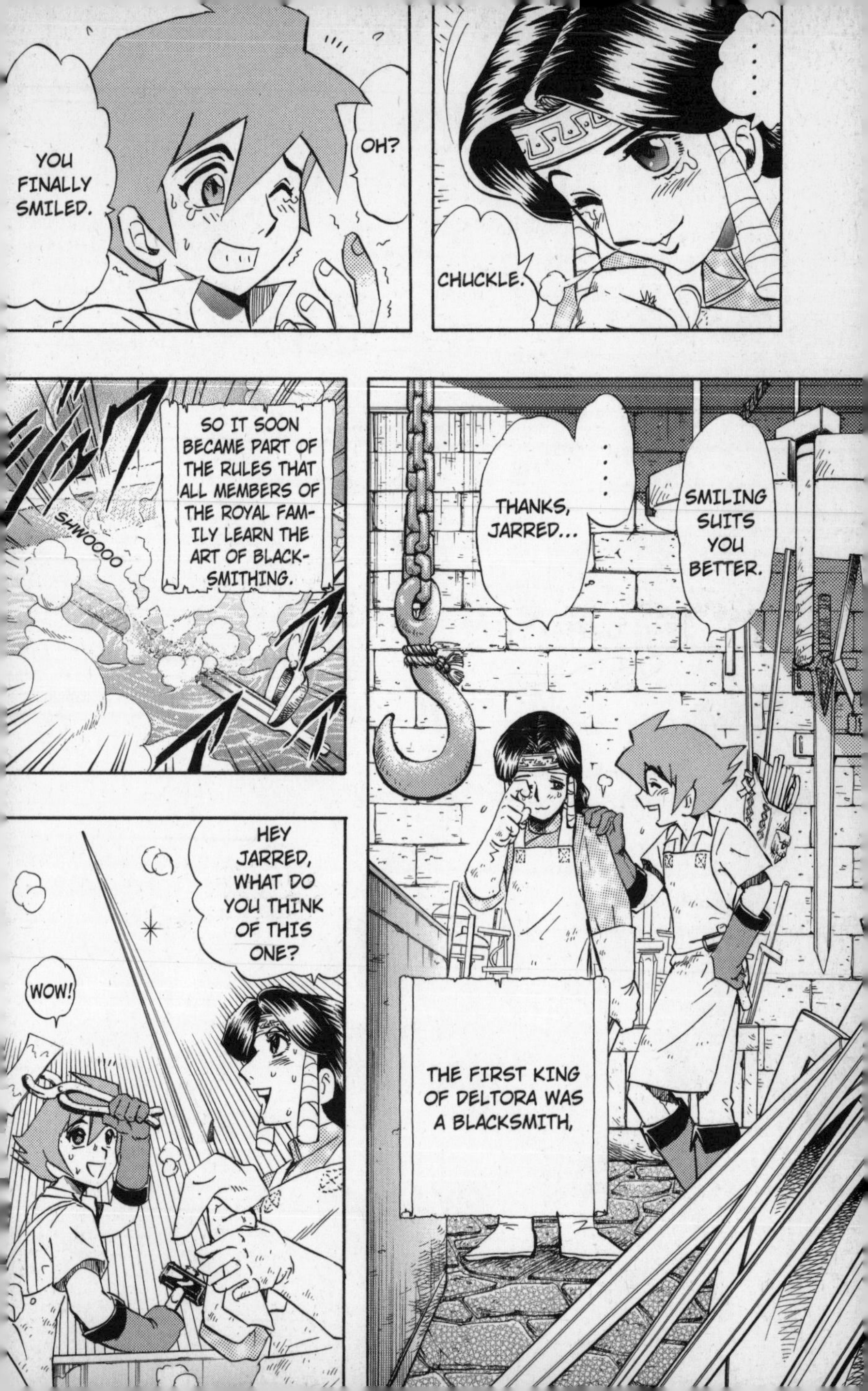

. . . .
CHUCKLE.
OH?
YOU FINALLY SMILED.
SMILING SUITS YOU BETTER.
. . . .
THANKS, JARRED...
THE FIRST KING OF DELTORA WAS A BLACKSMITH,
SO IT SOON BECAME PART OF THE RULES THAT ALL MEMBERS OF THE ROYAL FAMILY LEARN THE ART OF BLACKSMITHING.
SHWOOOO
HEY JARRED, WHAT DO YOU THINK OF THIS ONE?
WOW!

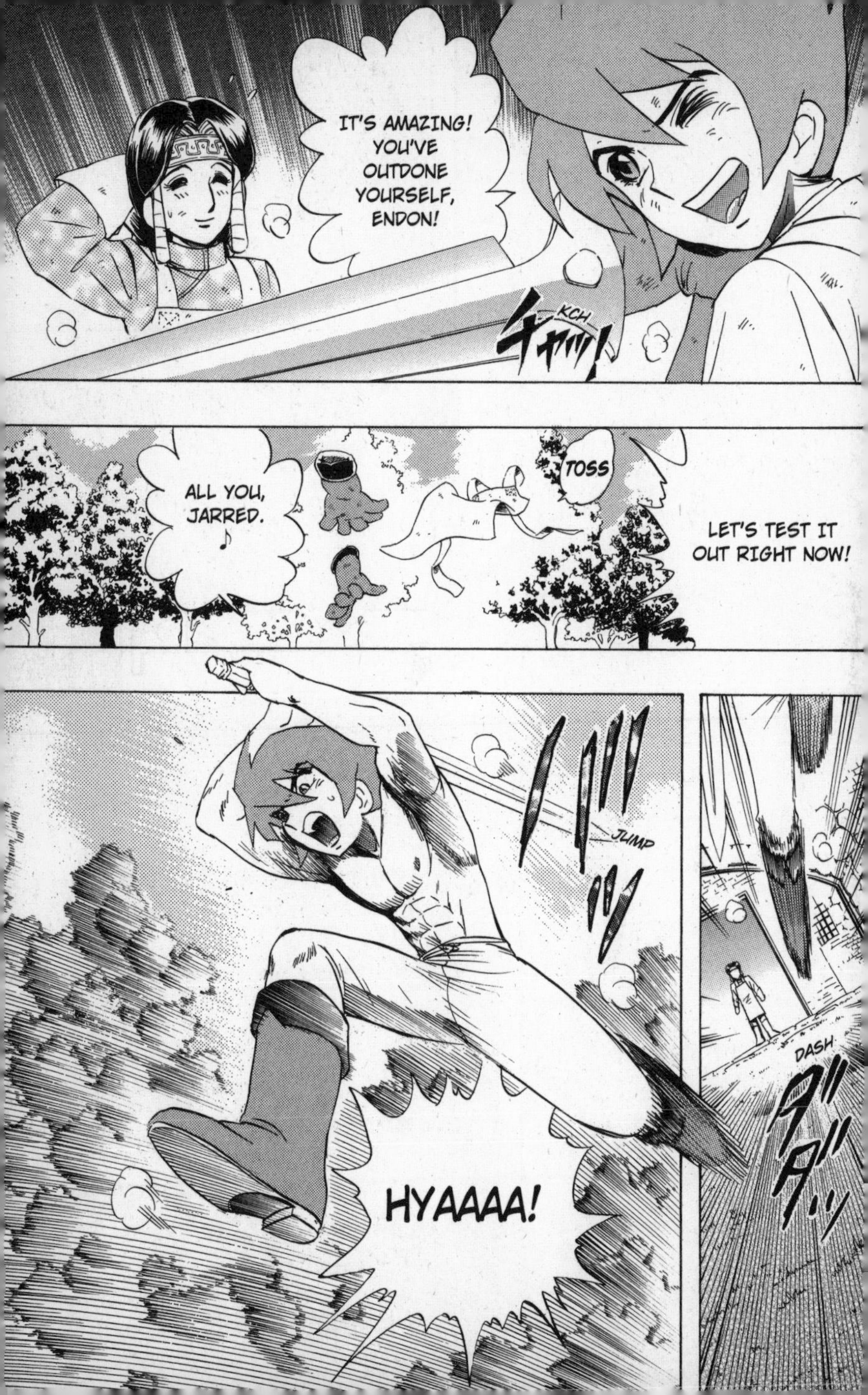
IT'S AMAZING! YOU'VE OUTDONE YOURSELF, ENDON!
KCH
LET'S TEST IT OUT RIGHT NOW!
TOSS
ALL YOU, JARRED. ♪
DASH
JUMP
HYAAAA!

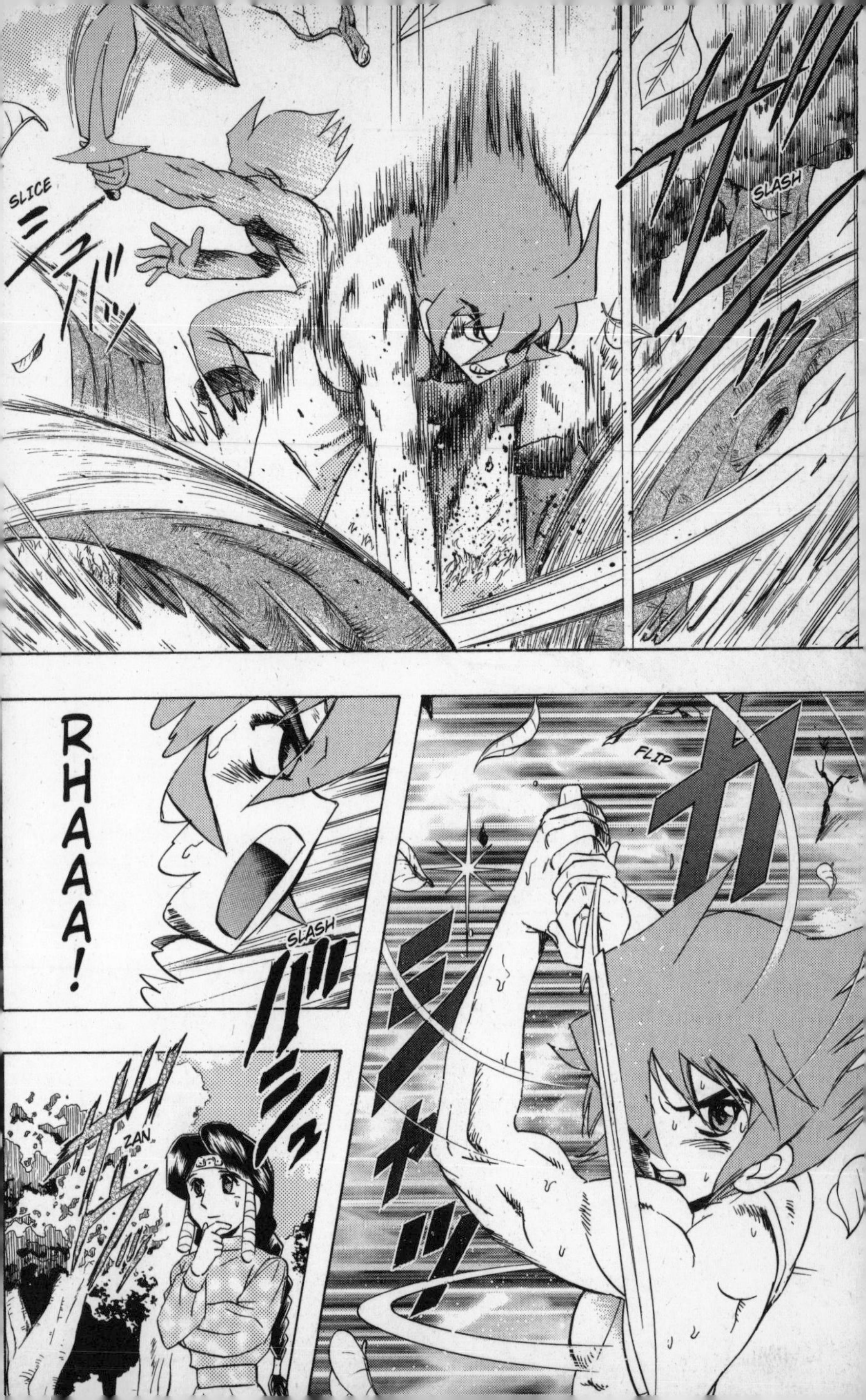
SLASH
SLICE
FLIP
RHAAAA!
SLASH
ZAN

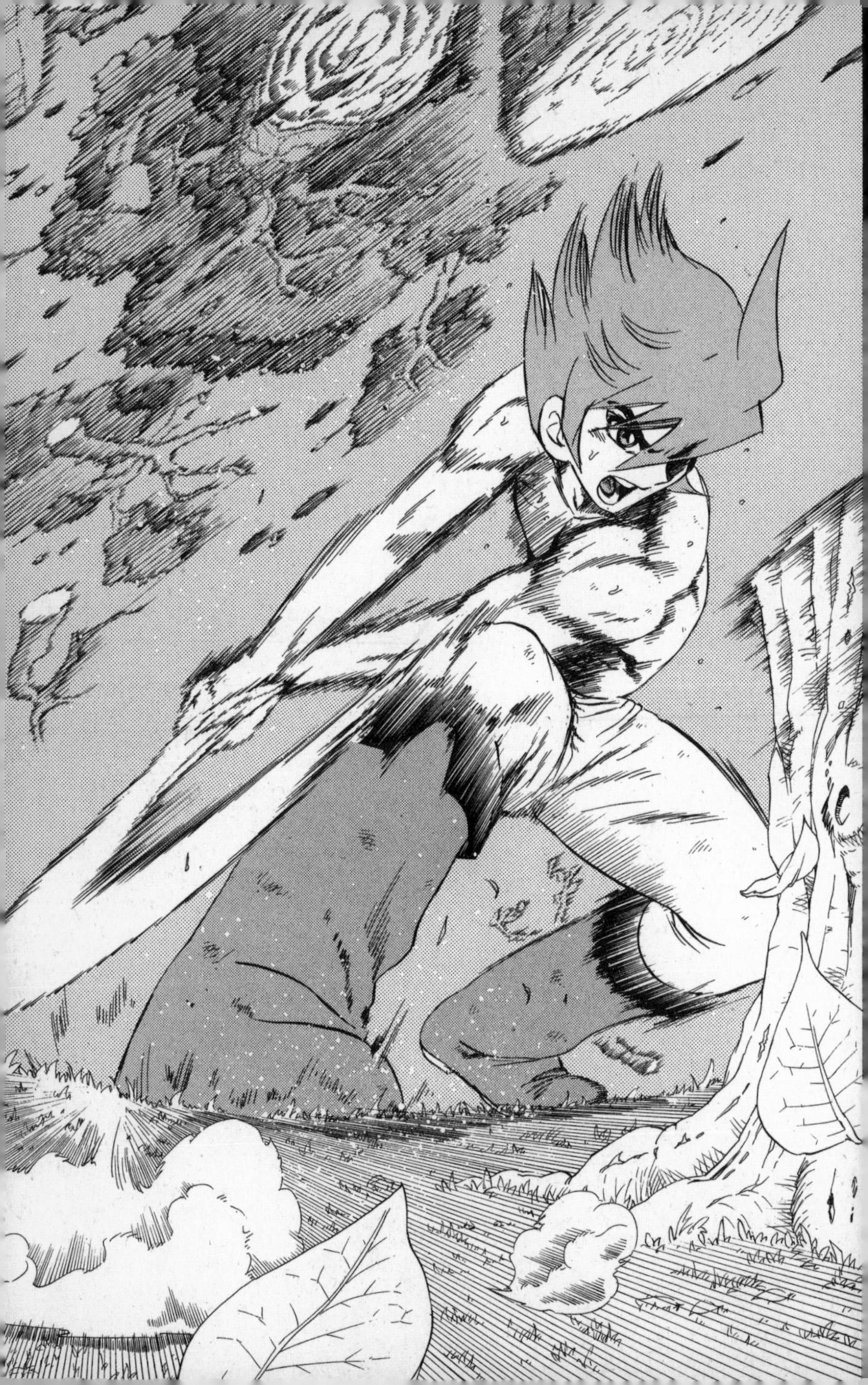

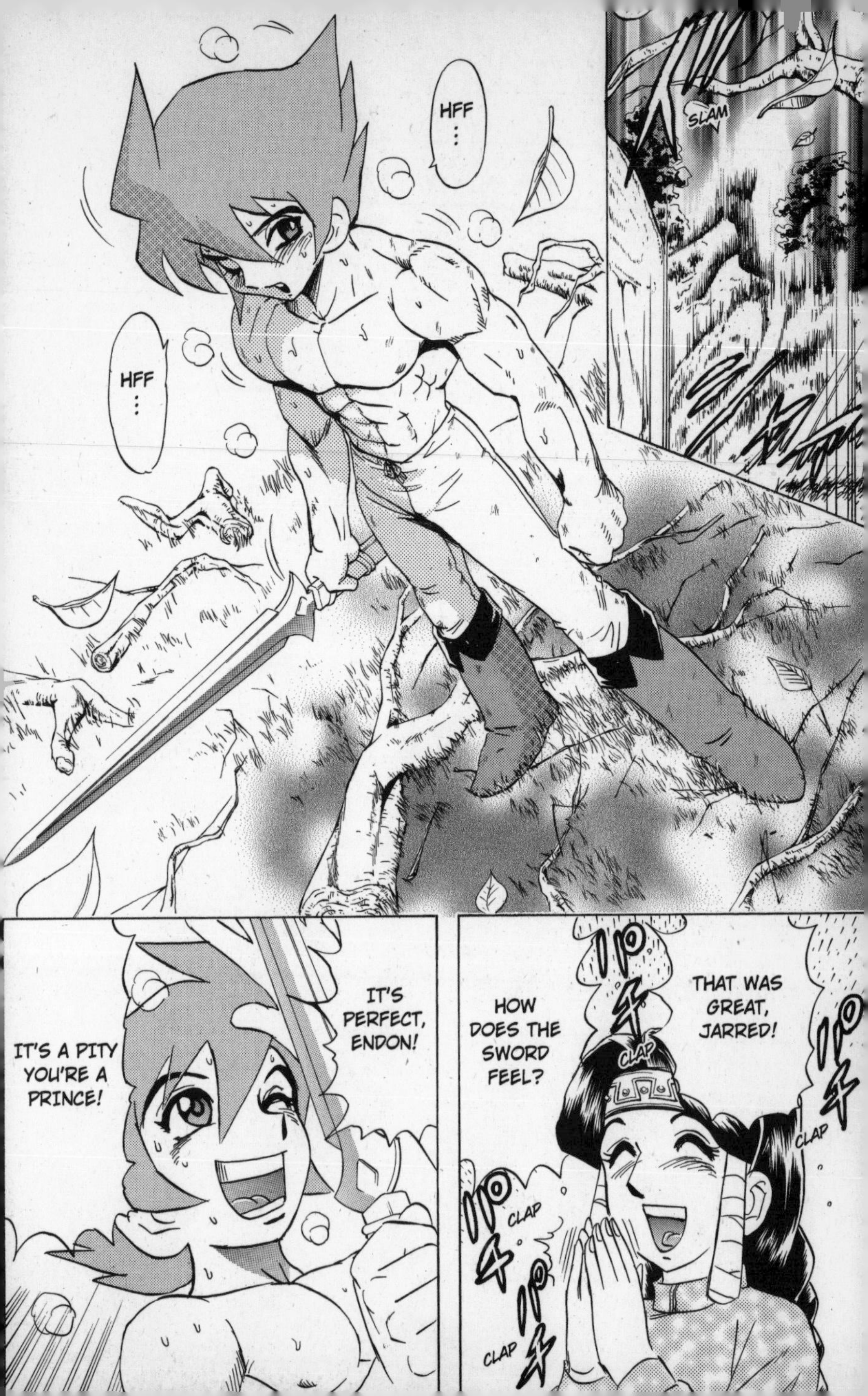
SLAM
HFF...
HFF...
THAT WAS GREAT, JARRED!
HOW DOES THE SWORD FEEL?
CLAP
CLAP
CLAP
CLAP
IT'S PERFECT, ENDON!
IT'S A PITY YOU'RE A PRINCE!

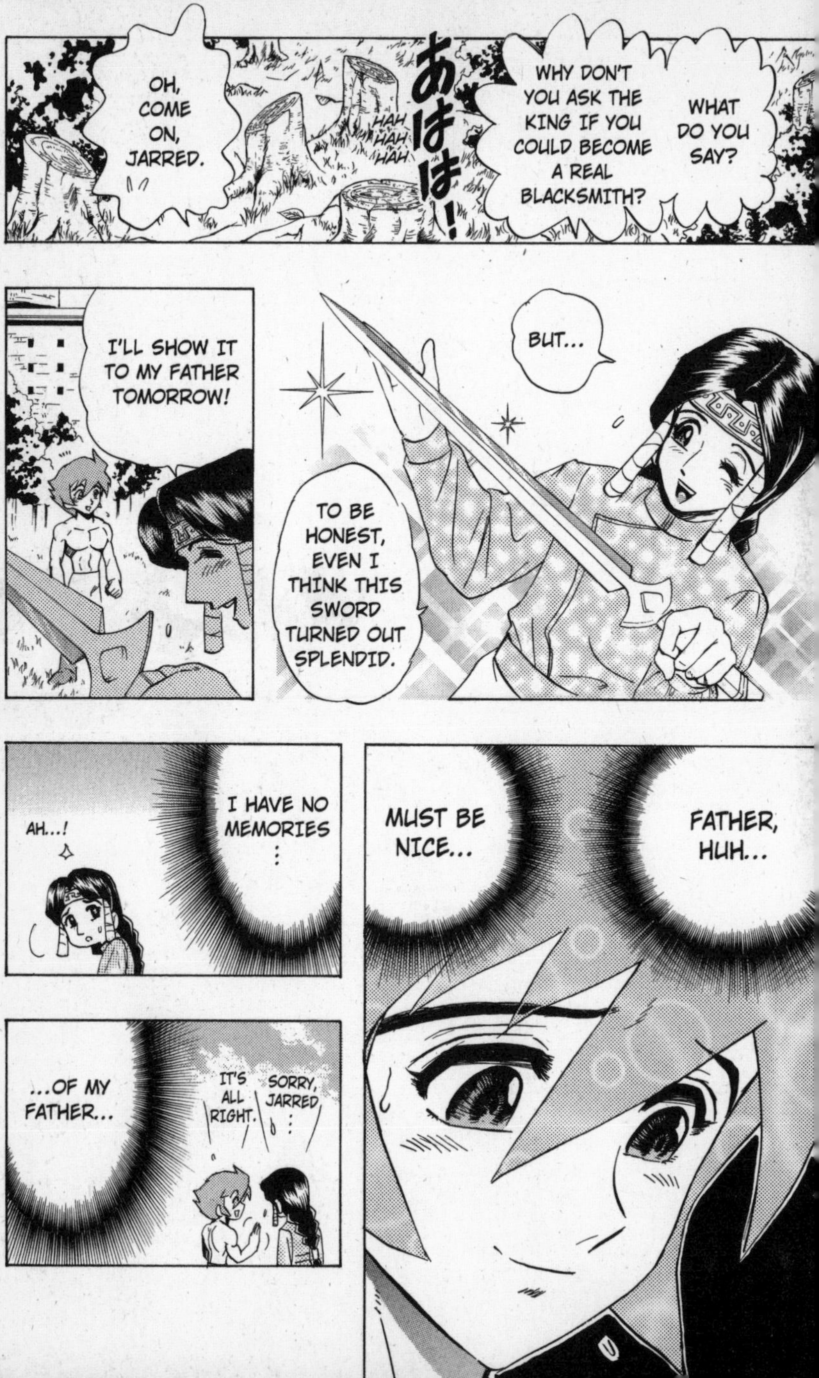
WHAT DO YOU SAY?
WHY DON'T YOU ASK THE KING IF YOU COULD BECOME A REAL BLACKSMITH?
あはは!
HAH HAH HAH
OH, COME ON, JARRED.
BUT...
TO BE HONEST, EVEN I THINK THIS SWORD TURNED OUT SPLENDID.
I'LL SHOW IT TO MY FATHER TOMORROW!
FATHER, HUH...
MUST BE NICE...
I HAVE NO MEMORIES...
AH...!
SORRY, JARRED...
IT'S ALL RIGHT.
...OF MY FATHER...

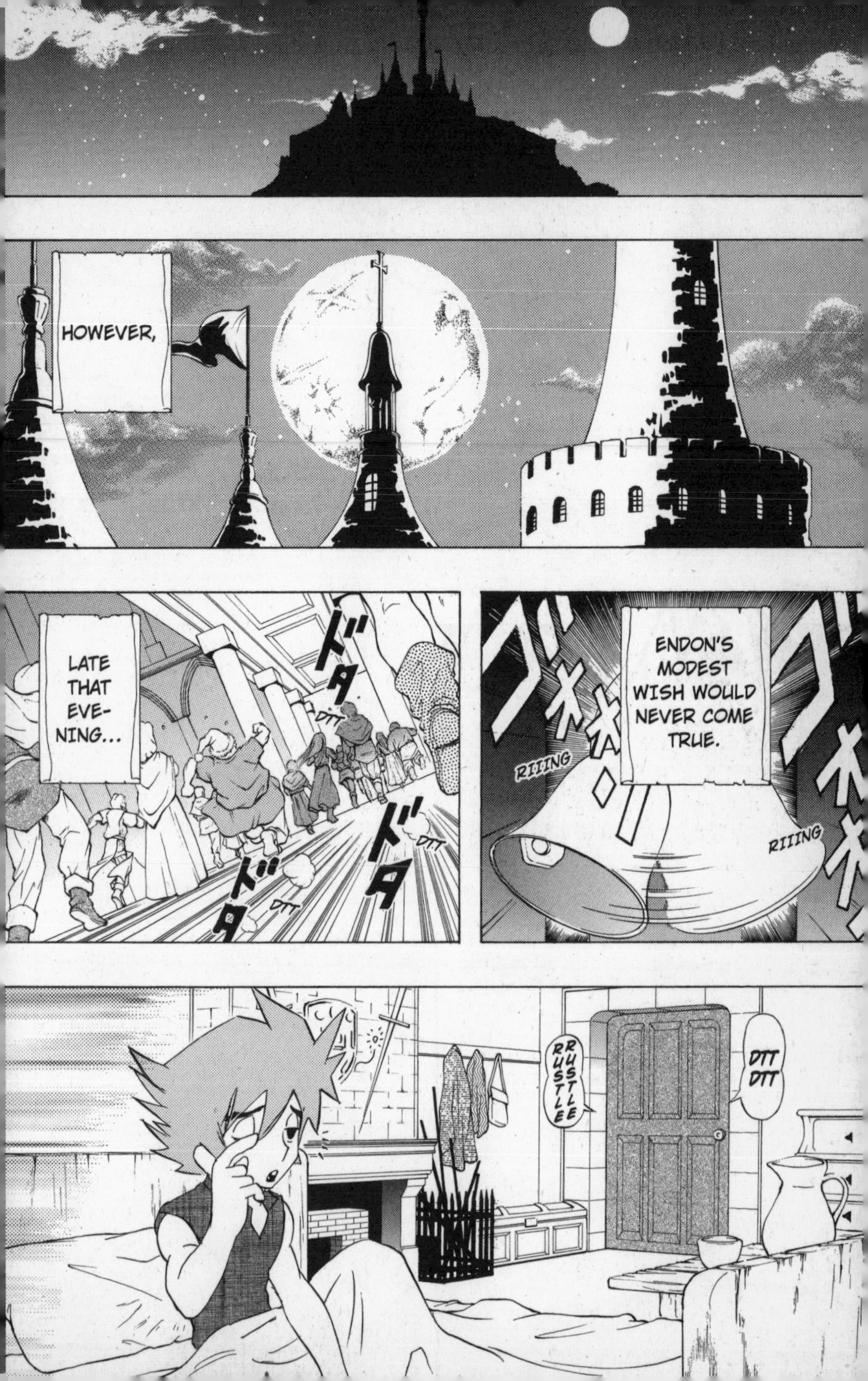
HOWEVER,
ENDON'S MODEST WISH WOULD NEVER COME TRUE.
RIIING
RIIING
LATE THAT EVE-NING...
DTT
DTT
DTT
RUSTLE RUSTLE
DTT DTT

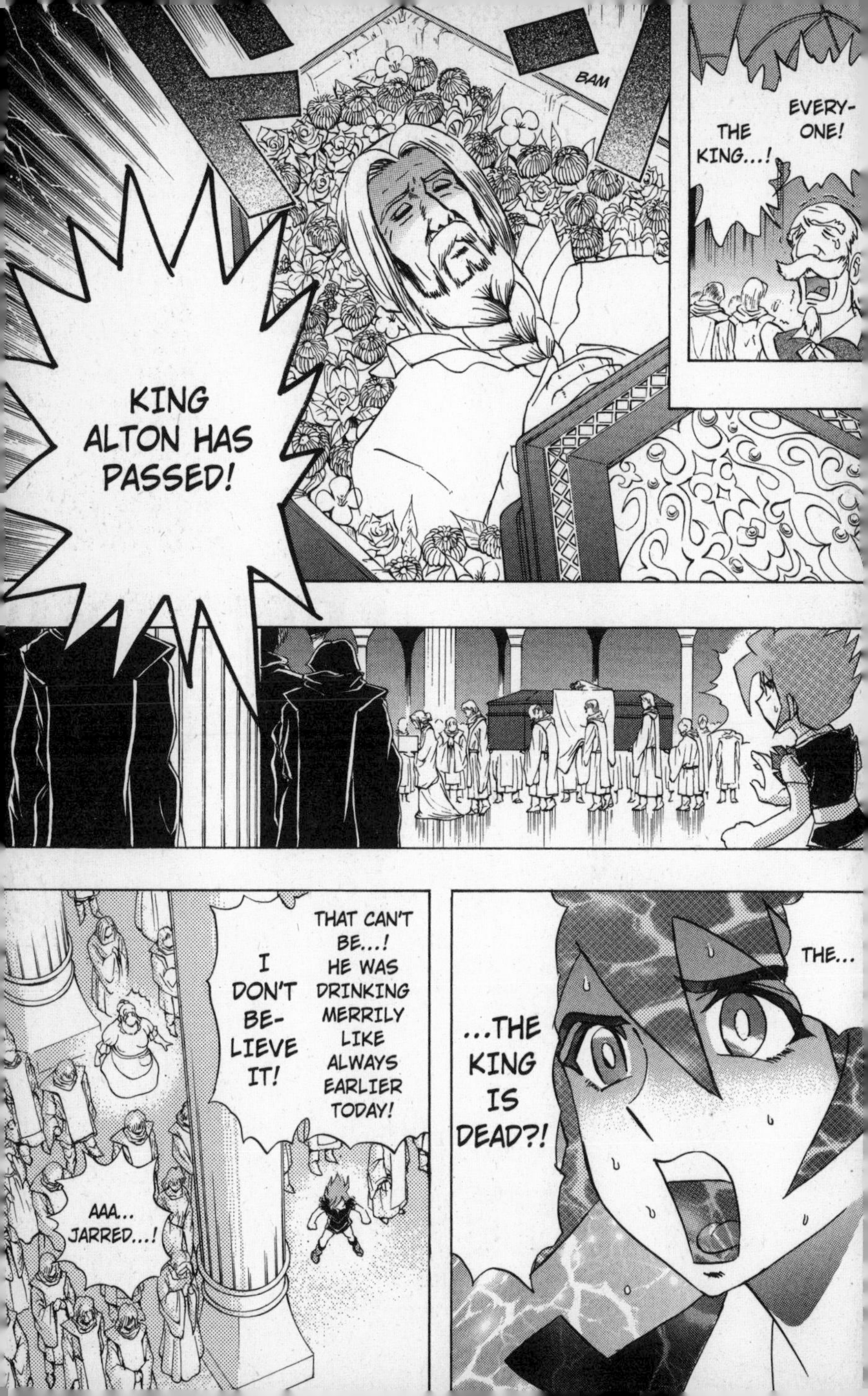
EVERY-ONE!
THE KING...!
BAM
KING ALTON HAS PASSED!
THE...
...THE KING IS DEAD?!
THAT CAN'T BE...! HE WAS DRINKING MERRILY LIKE ALWAYS EARLIER TODAY!
I DON'T BE-LIEVE IT!
AAA... JARRED...!

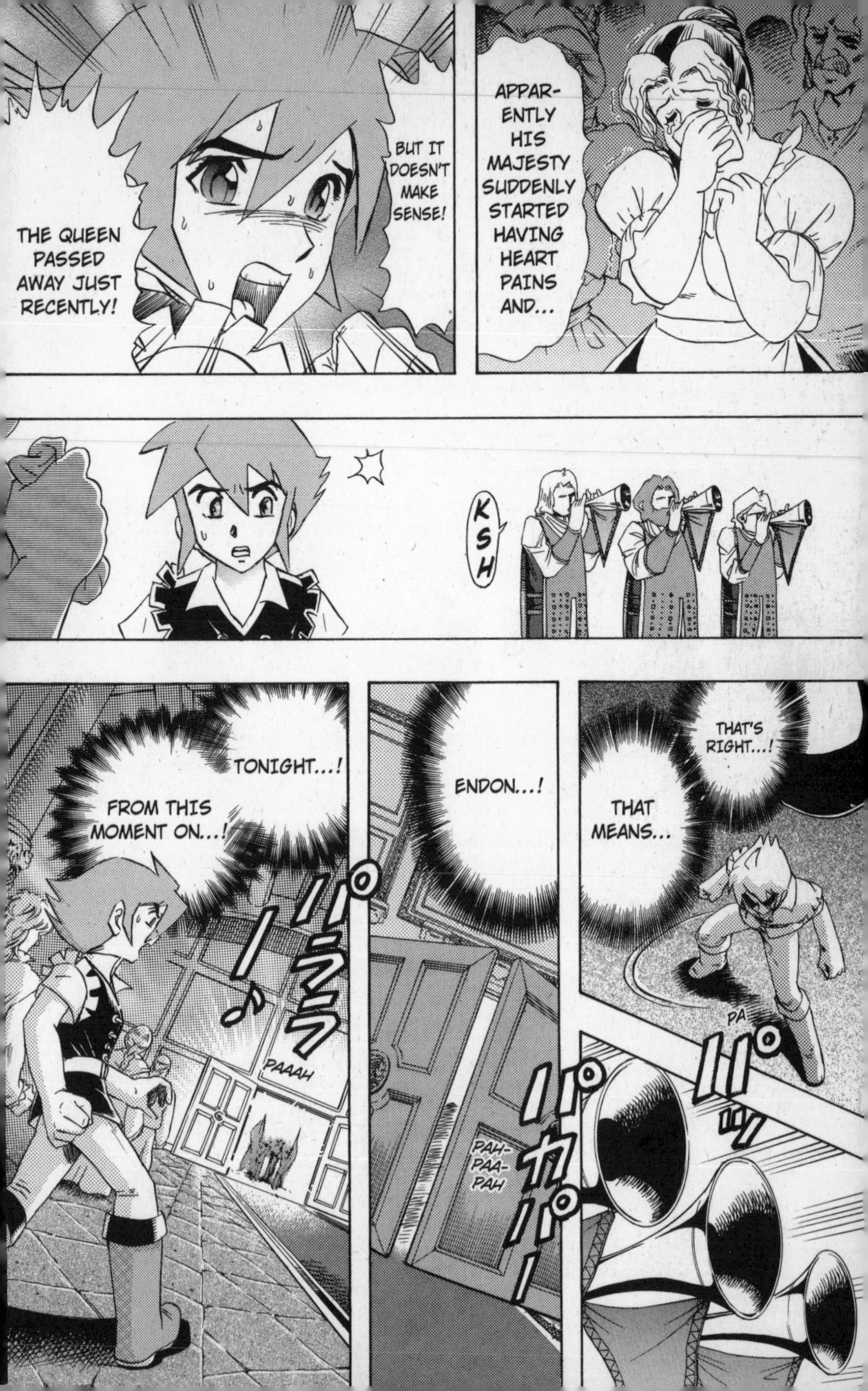
APPARENTLY HIS MAJESTY SUDDENLY STARTED HAVING HEART PAINS AND...
BUT IT DOESN'T MAKE SENSE!
THE QUEEN PASSED AWAY JUST RECENTLY!
KSH
THAT'S RIGHT...!
THAT MEANS...
PA
ENDON...!
PAH-PAA-PAH
TONIGHT...!
FROM THIS MOMENT ON...!
PAAAH

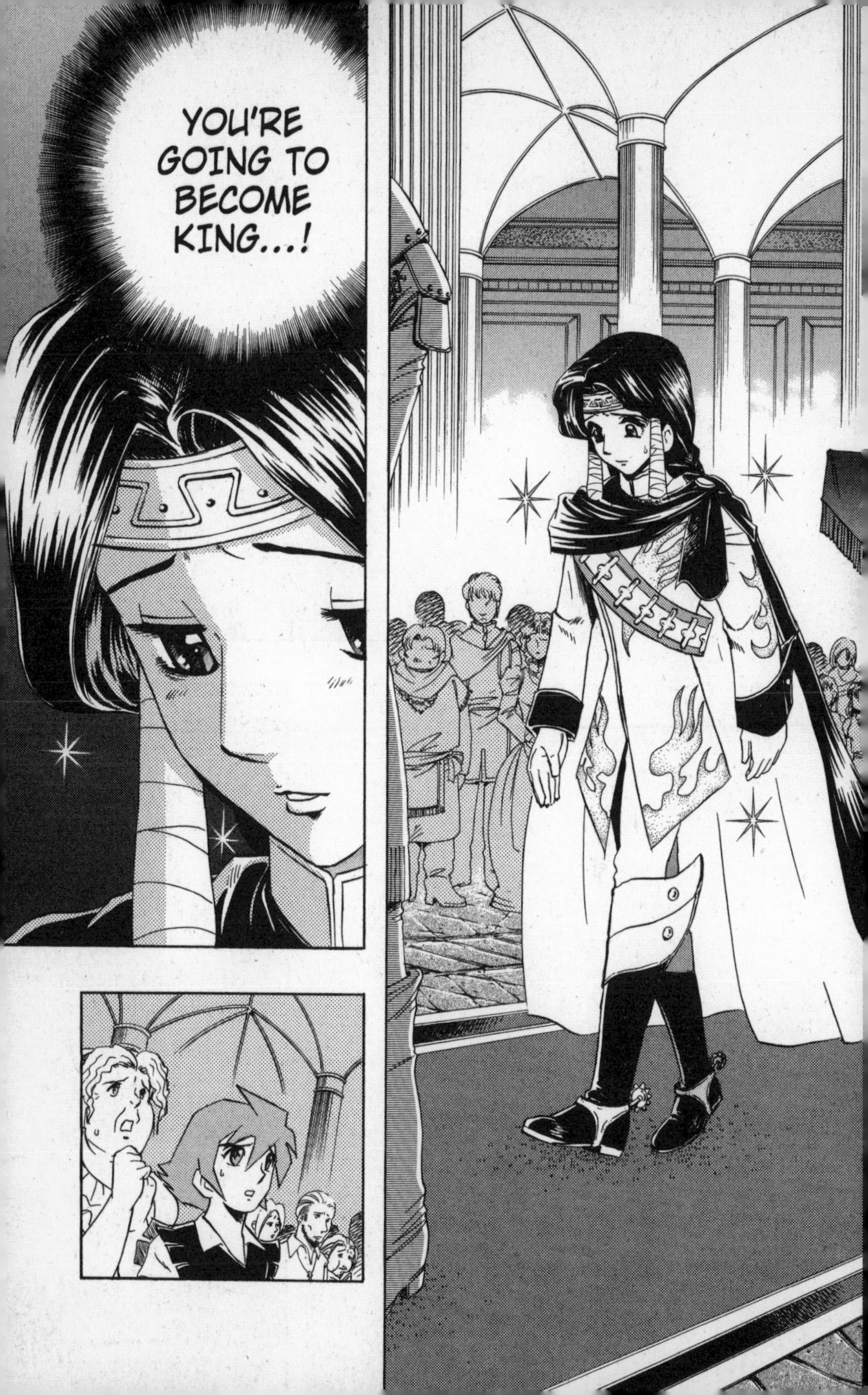
YOU'RE GOING TO BECOME KING...!

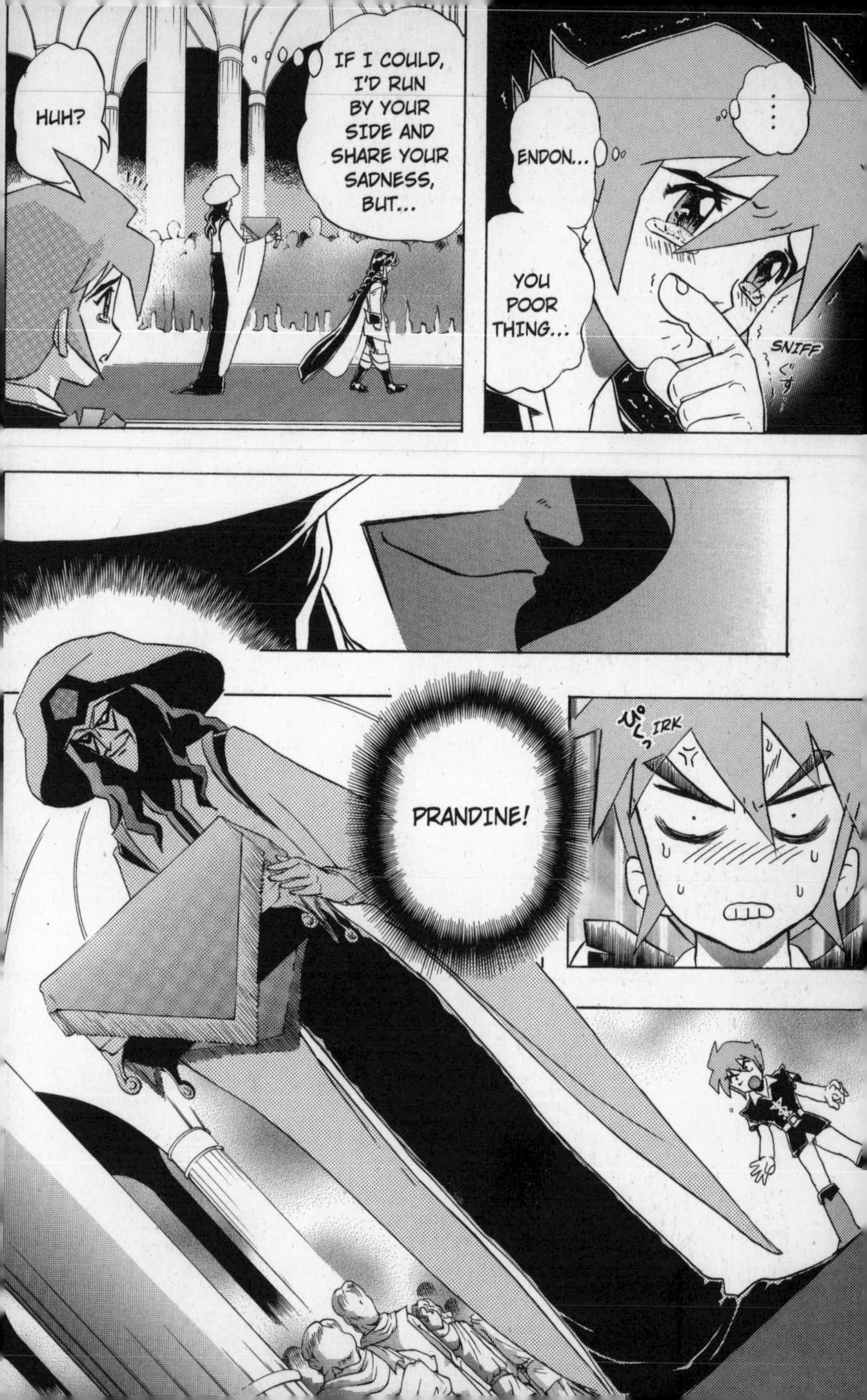
......
ENDON...
YOU POOR THING...
SNIFF
ぐすっ
IF I COULD, I'D RUN BY YOUR SIDE AND SHARE YOUR SADNESS, BUT...
HUH?
ぴくっ
IRK
PRANDINE!

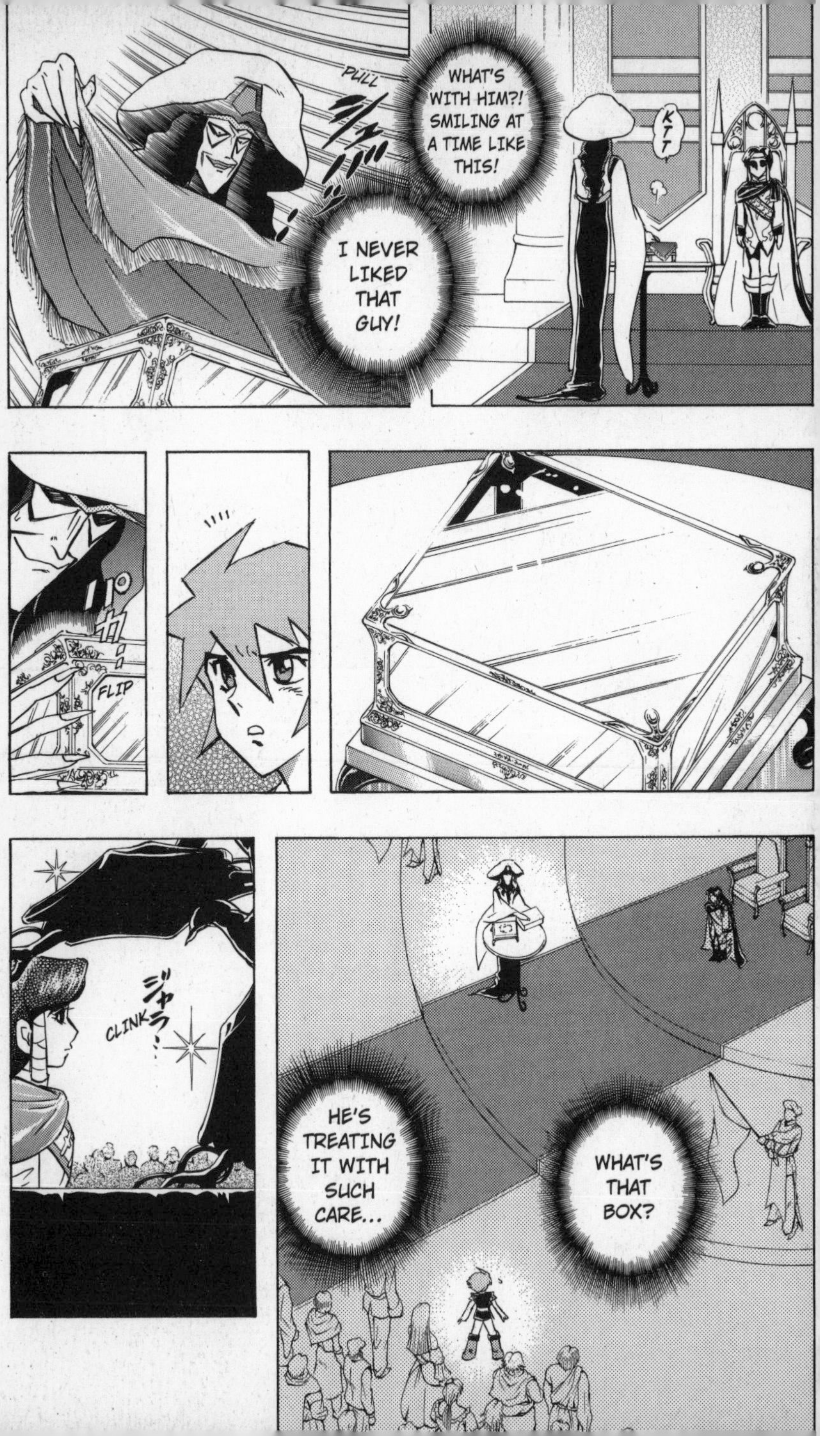
KTT
WHAT'S WITH HIM?! SMILING AT A TIME LIKE THIS!
I NEVER LIKED THAT GUY!
PULL
FLIP
WHAT'S THAT BOX?
HE'S TREATING IT WITH SUCH CARE...
CLINK

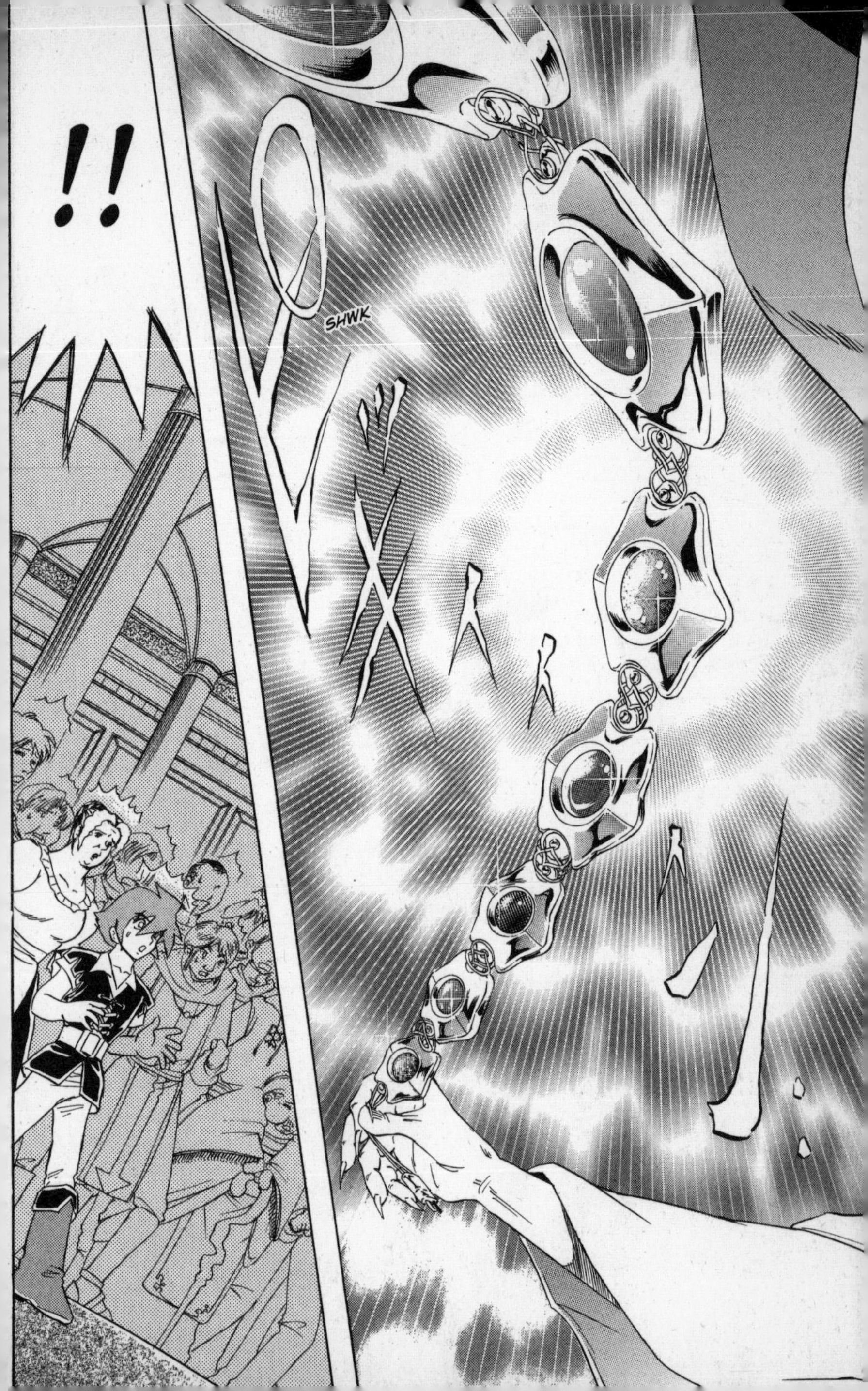
!!
SHWK

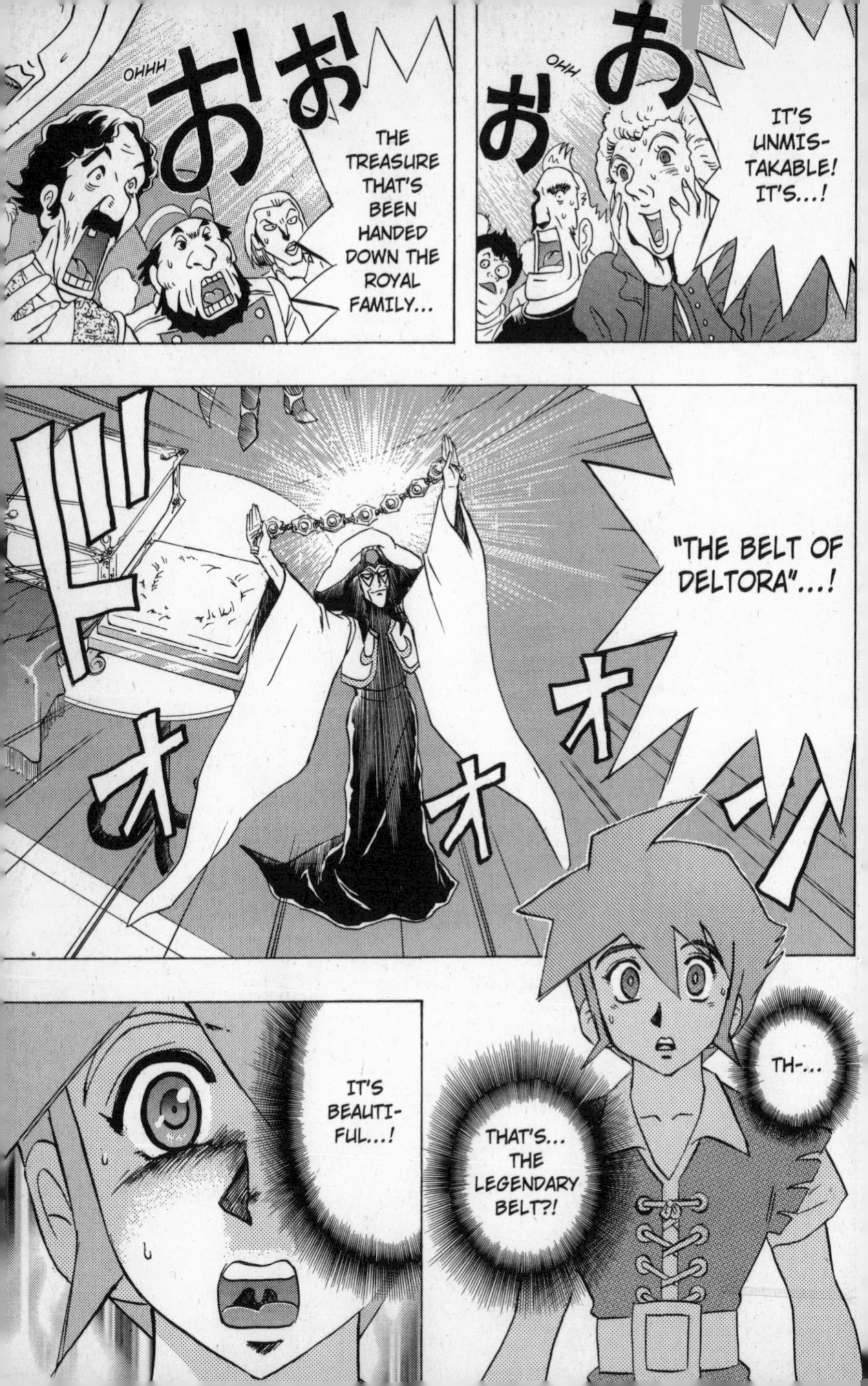
OHH
おぉ
IT'S UNMIS-TAKABLE! IT'S...!
OHHH
おぉ
THE TREASURE THAT'S BEEN HANDED DOWN THE ROYAL FAMILY...
ドオオオーッ
"THE BELT OF DELTORA"...!
TH-...
THAT'S... THE LEGENDARY BELT?!
IT'S BEAUTI-FUL...!

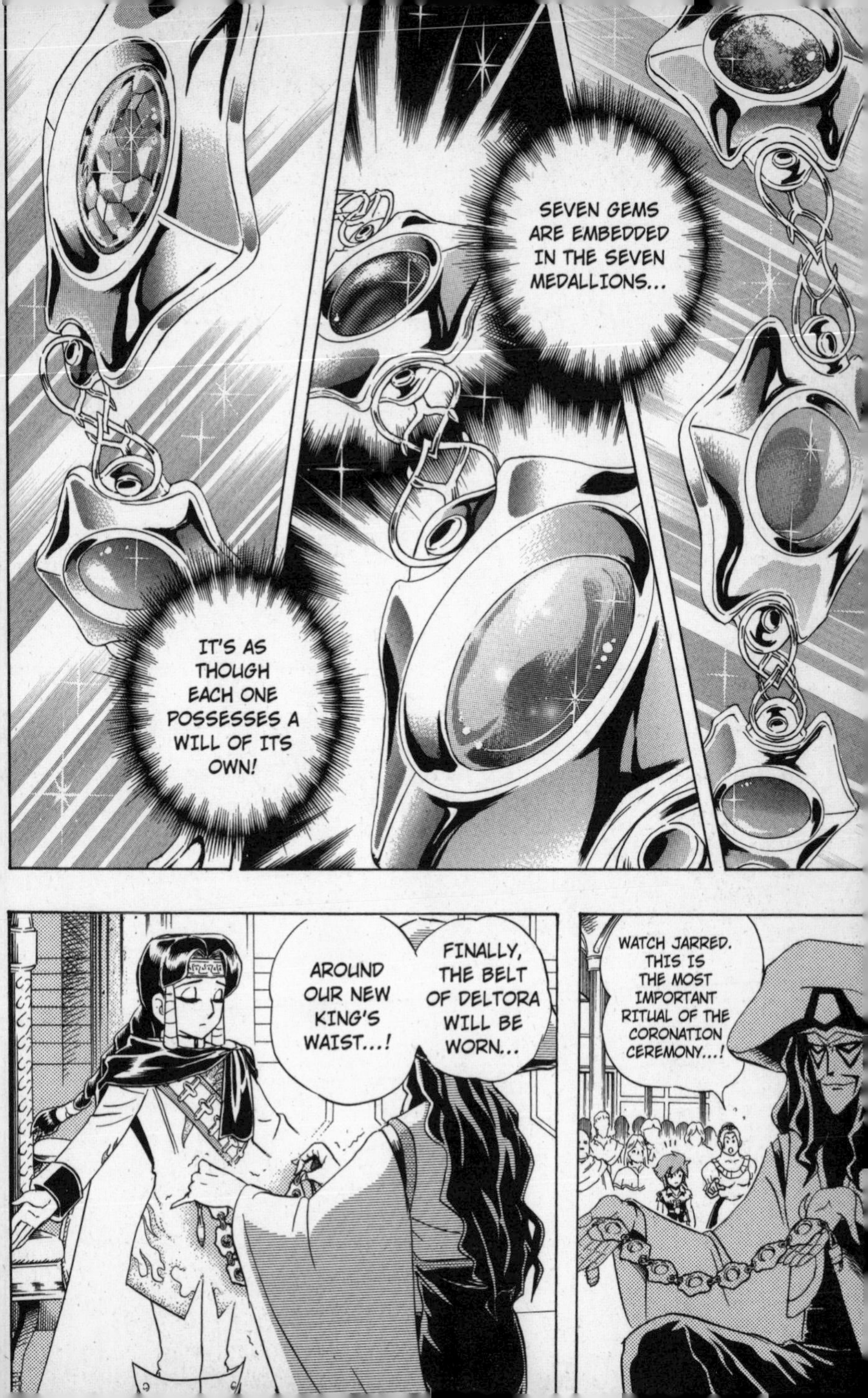
SEVEN GEMS ARE EMBEDDED IN THE SEVEN MEDALLIONS...
IT'S AS THOUGH EACH ONE POSSESSES A WILL OF ITS OWN!
WATCH JARRED. THIS IS THE MOST IMPORTANT RITUAL OF THE CORONATION CEREMONY...!
FINALLY, THE BELT OF DELTORA WILL BE WORN...
AROUND OUR NEW KING'S WAIST...!

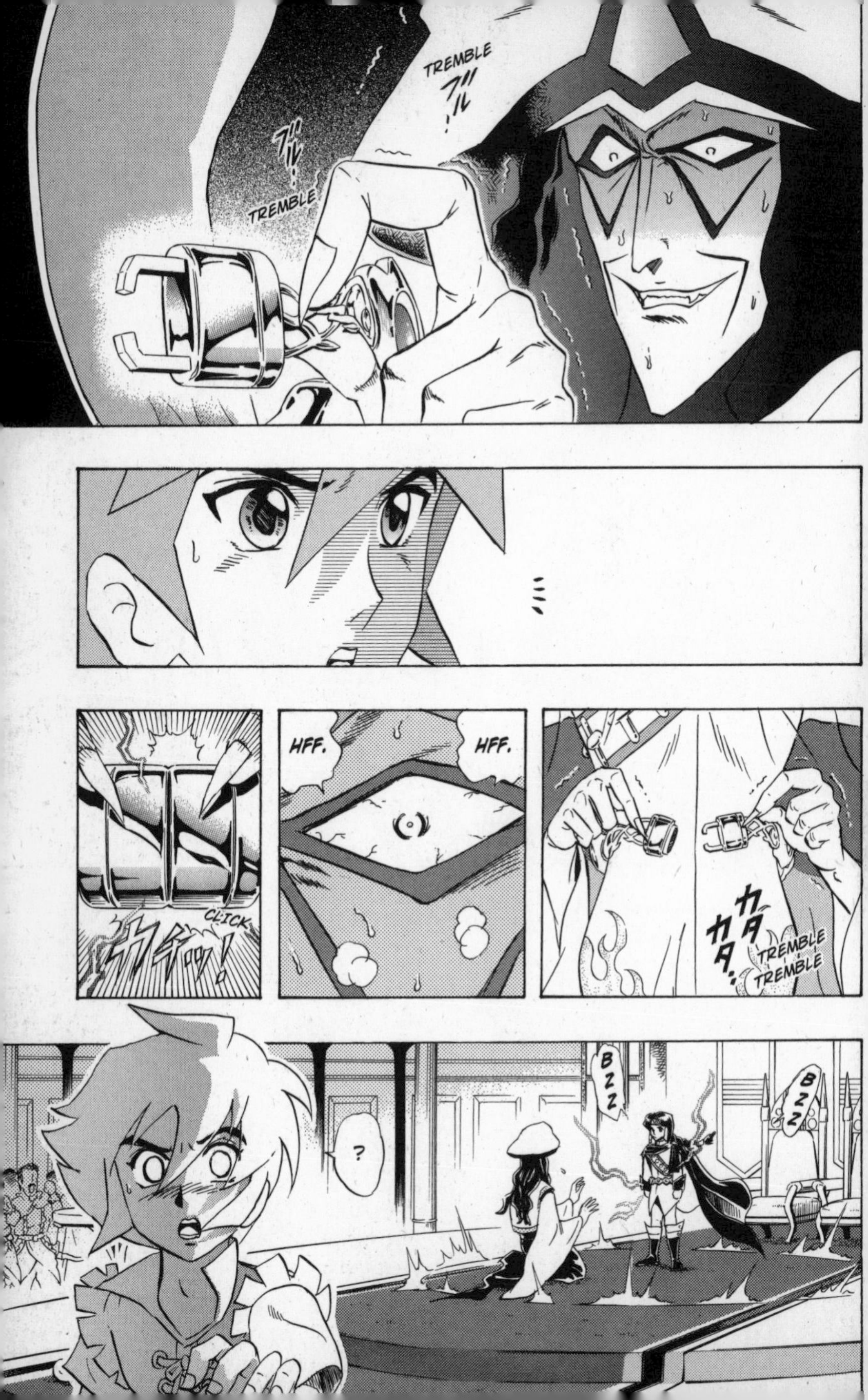
TREMBLE
ブル
ブル
TREMBLE
HFF.
HFF.
CLICK
TREMBLE
TREMBLE
BZZ
BZZ
?

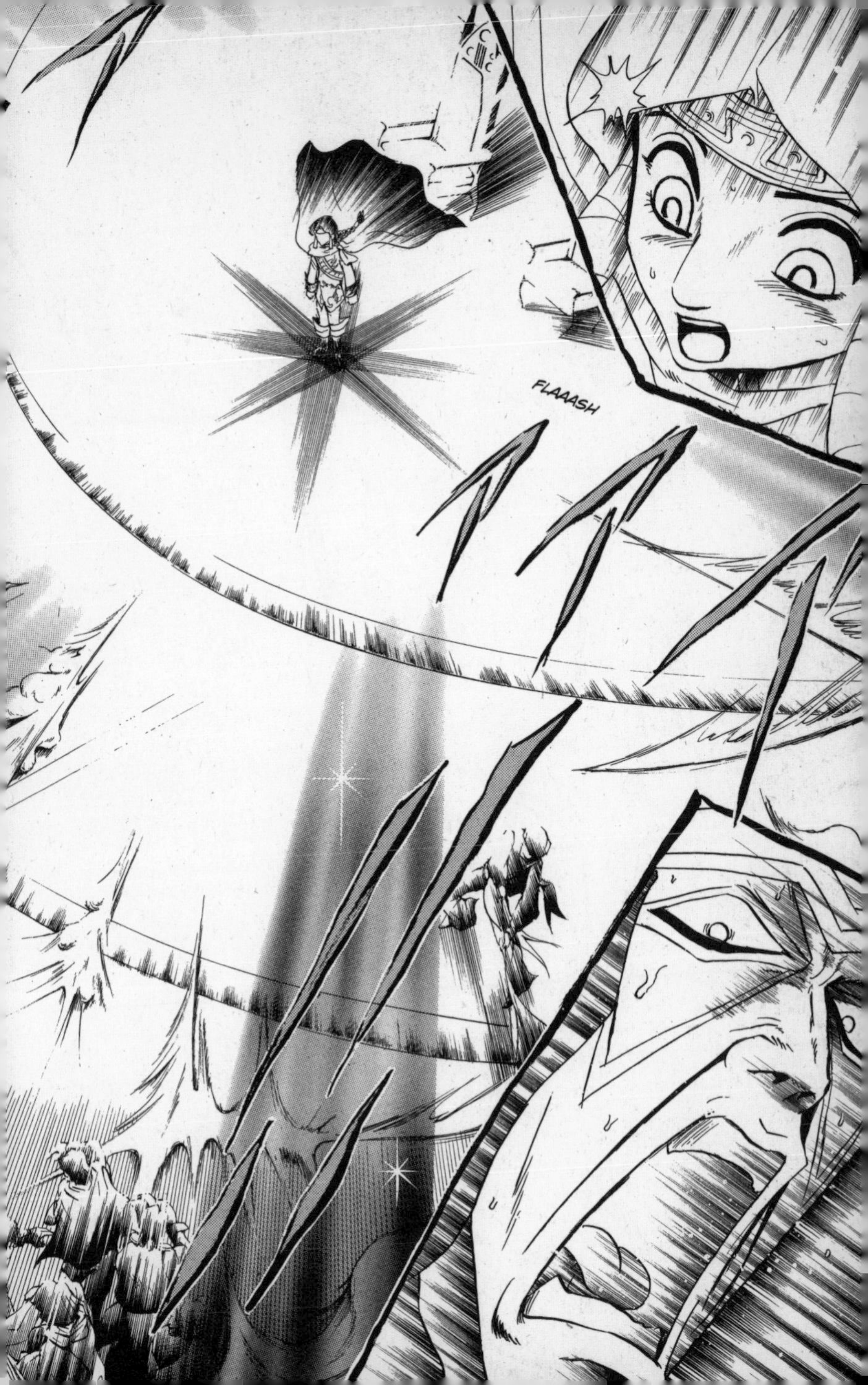
FLAAASH

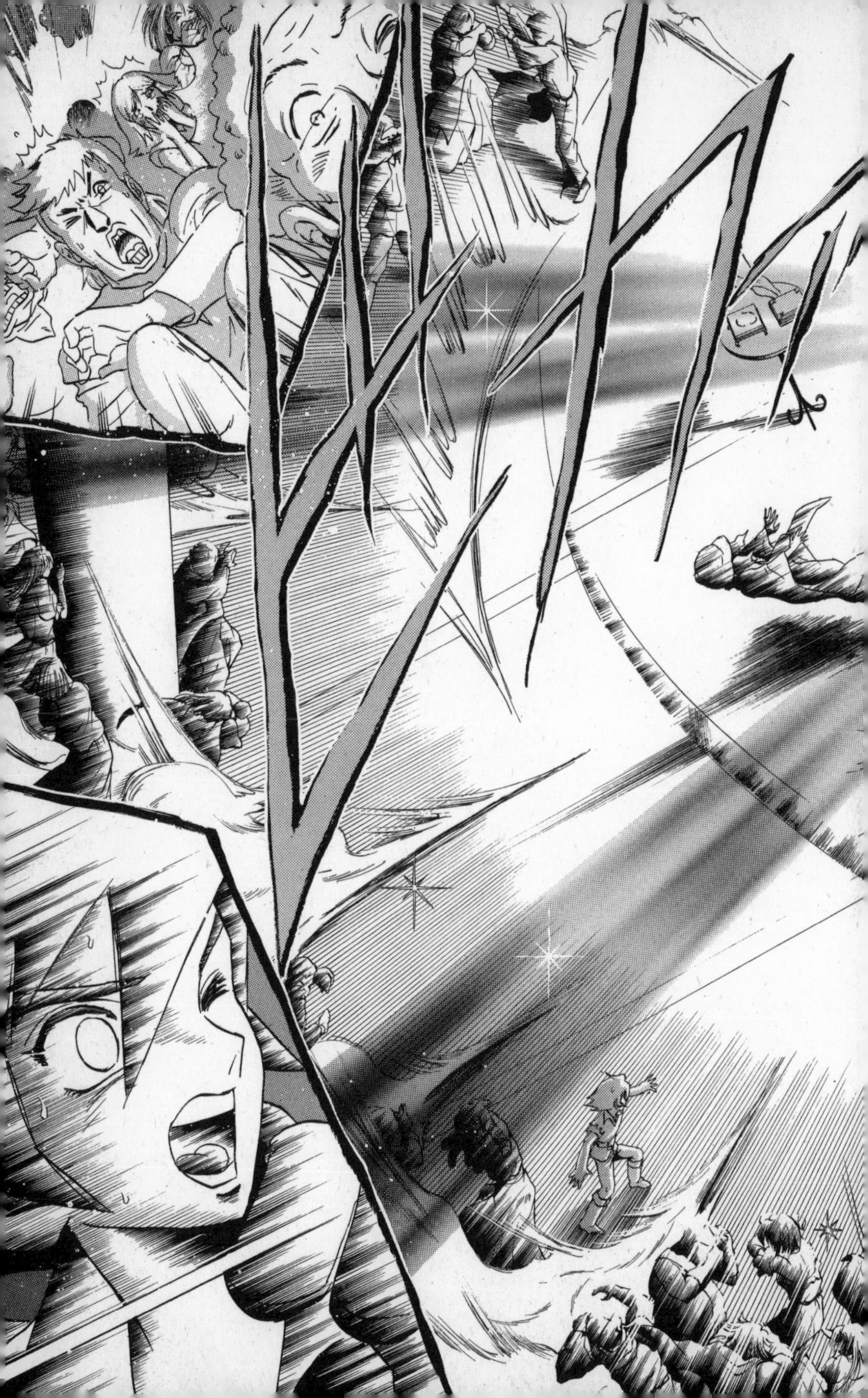

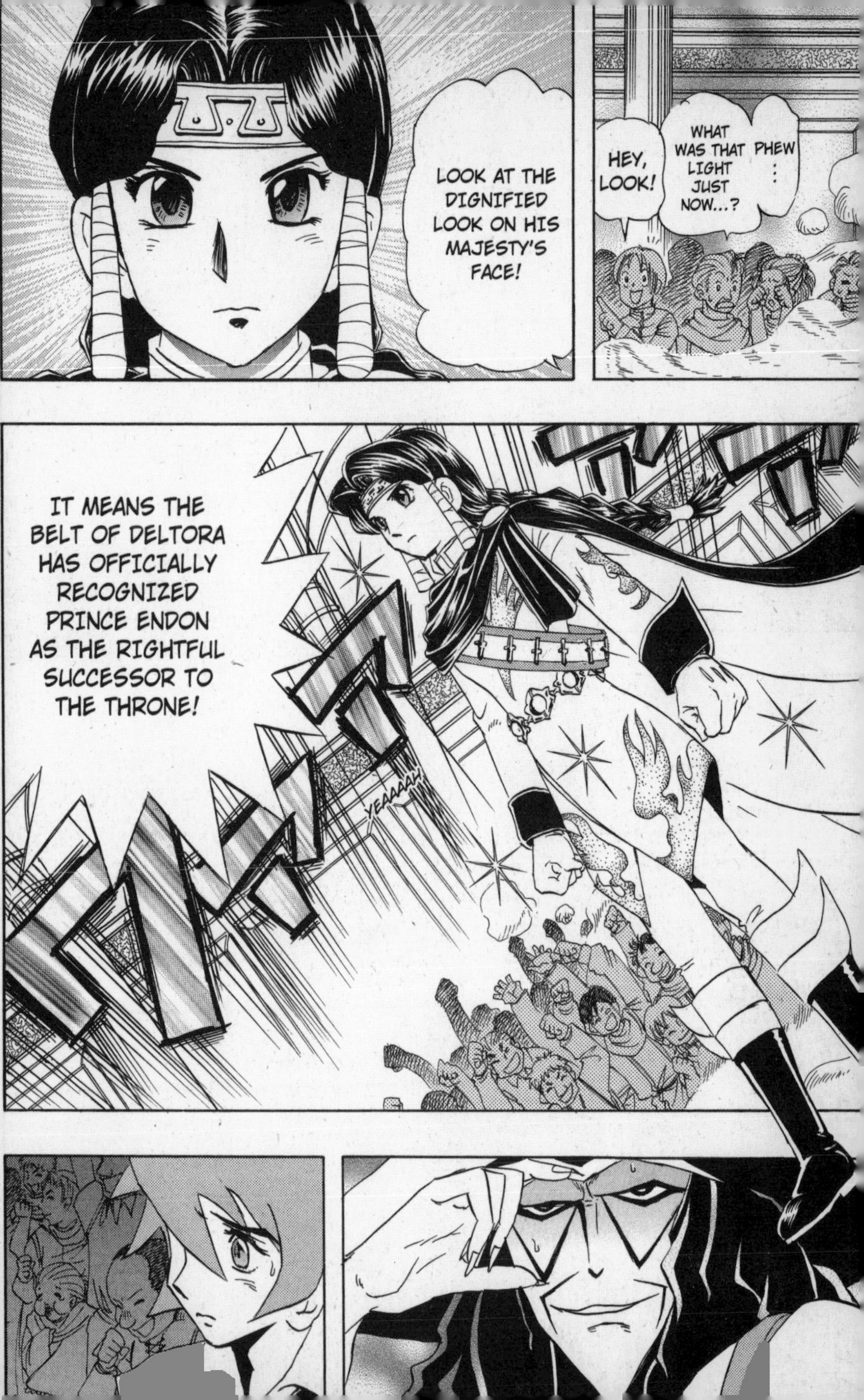
PHEW...
WHAT WAS THAT LIGHT JUST NOW...?
HEY, LOOK!
LOOK AT THE DIGNIFIED LOOK ON HIS MAJESTY'S FACE!
IT MEANS THE BELT OF DELTORA HAS OFFICIALLY RECOGNIZED PRINCE ENDON AS THE RIGHTFUL SUCCESSOR TO THE THRONE!
YEAAAAH

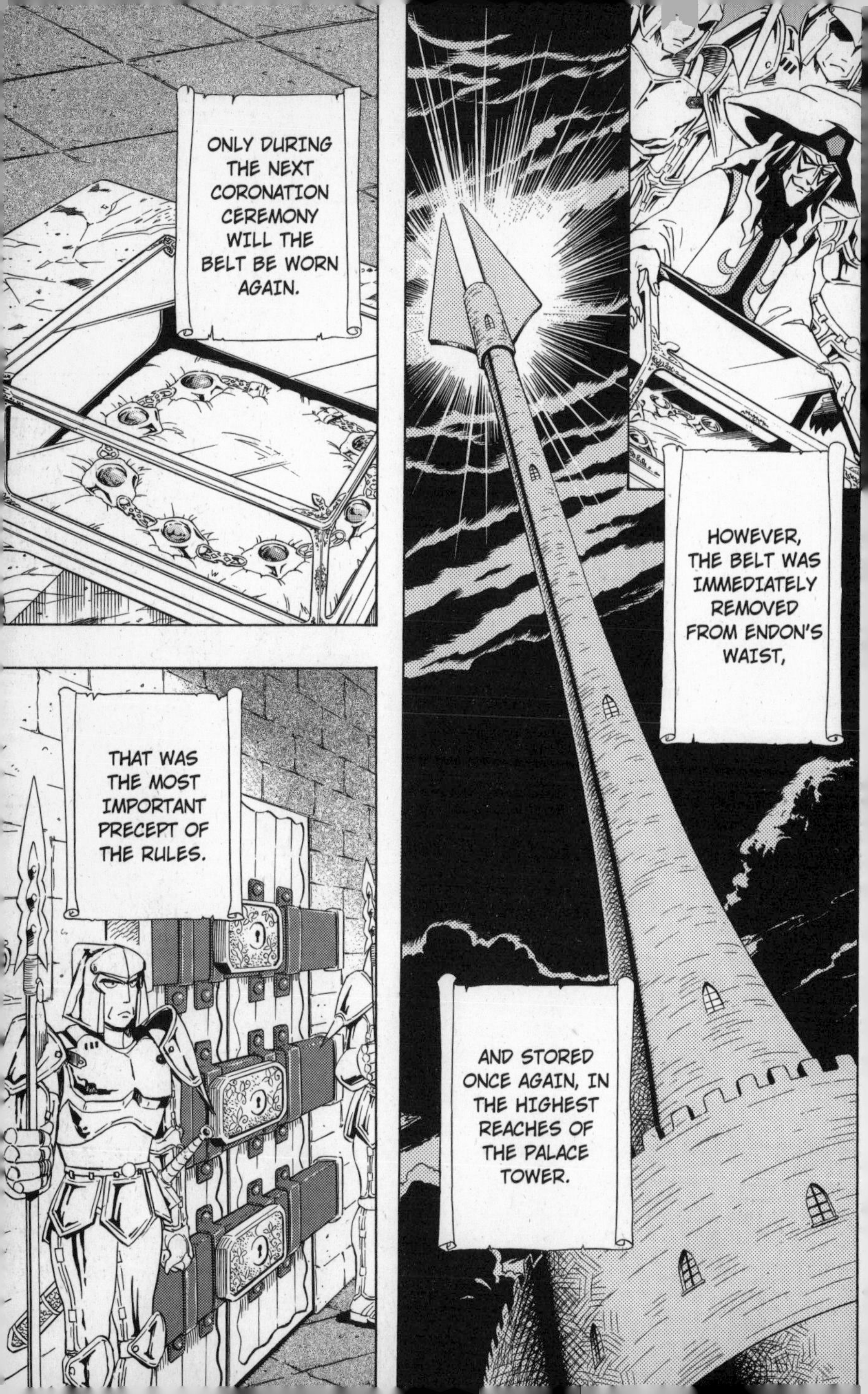
HOWEVER, THE BELT WAS IMMEDIATELY REMOVED FROM ENDON'S WAIST,
AND STORED ONCE AGAIN, IN THE HIGHEST REACHES OF THE PALACE TOWER.
ONLY DURING THE NEXT CORONATION CEREMONY WILL THE BELT BE WORN AGAIN.
THAT WAS THE MOST IMPORTANT PRECEPT OF THE RULES.

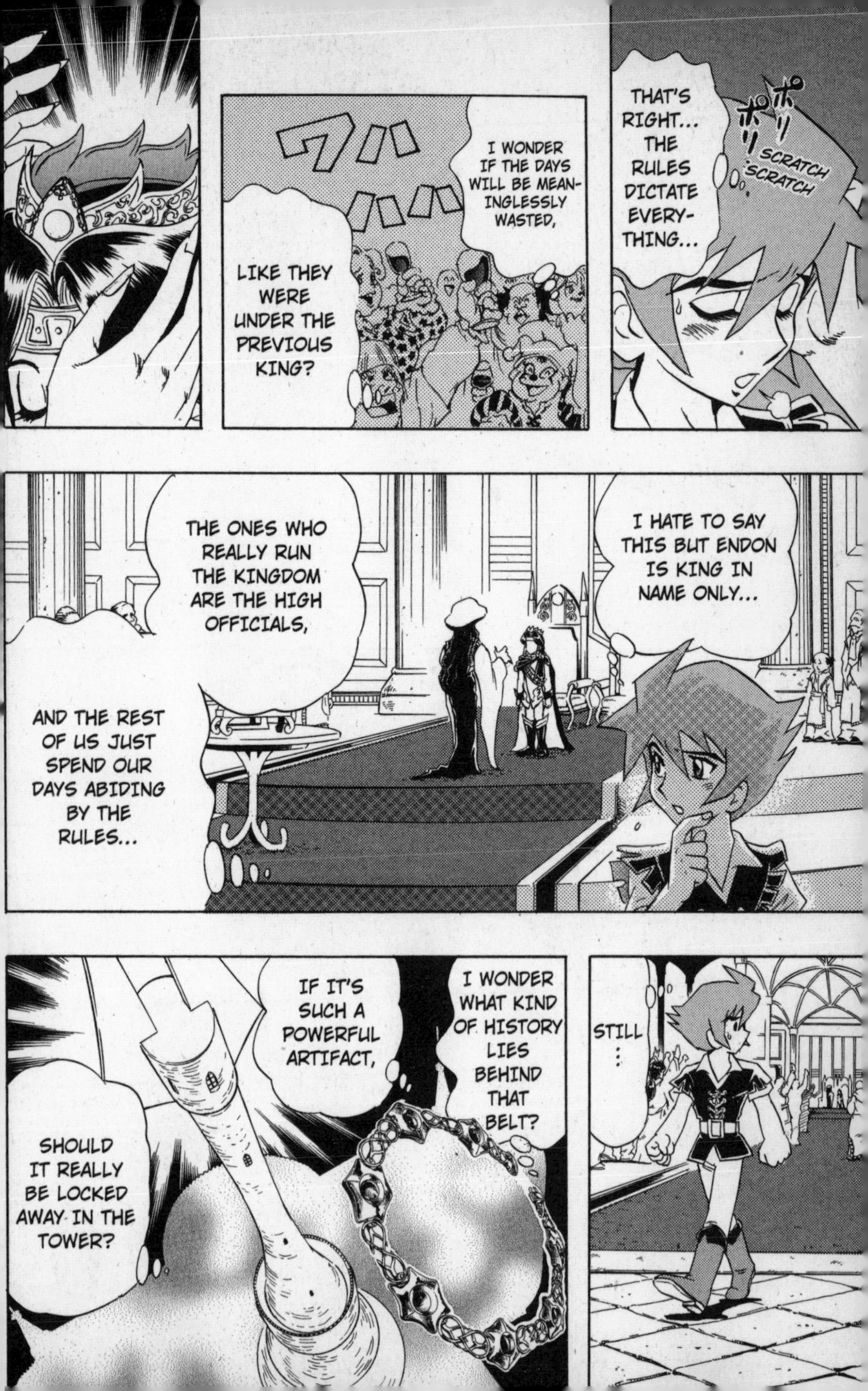
THAT'S RIGHT... THE RULES DICTATE EVERY-THING...
ポリポリ
SCRATCH SCRATCH
I WONDER IF THE DAYS WILL BE MEAN-INGLESSLY WASTED,
LIKE THEY WERE UNDER THE PREVIOUS KING?
ワハハハ
I HATE TO SAY THIS BUT ENDON IS KING IN NAME ONLY...
THE ONES WHO REALLY RUN THE KINGDOM ARE THE HIGH OFFICIALS,
AND THE REST OF US JUST SPEND OUR DAYS ABIDING BY THE RULES...
STILL...
I WONDER WHAT KIND OF HISTORY LIES BEHIND THAT BELT?
IF IT'S SUCH A POWERFUL ARTIFACT,
SHOULD IT REALLY BE LOCKED AWAY IN THE TOWER?

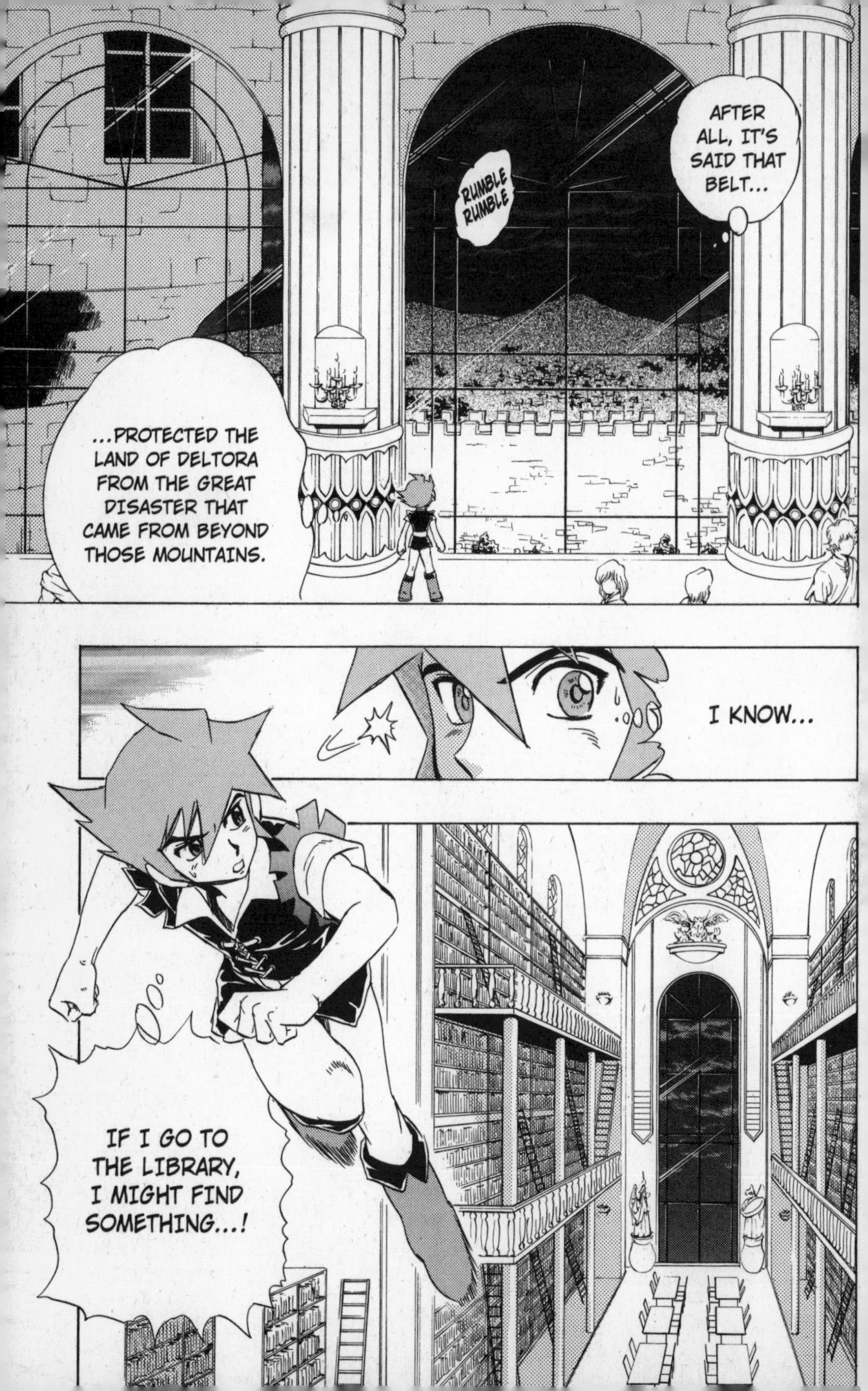
AFTER ALL, IT'S SAID THAT BELT...
RUMBLE RUMBLE
...PROTECTED THE LAND OF DELTORA FROM THE GREAT DISASTER THAT CAME FROM BEYOND THOSE MOUNTAINS.
I KNOW...
IF I GO TO THE LIBRARY, I MIGHT FIND SOMETHING...!

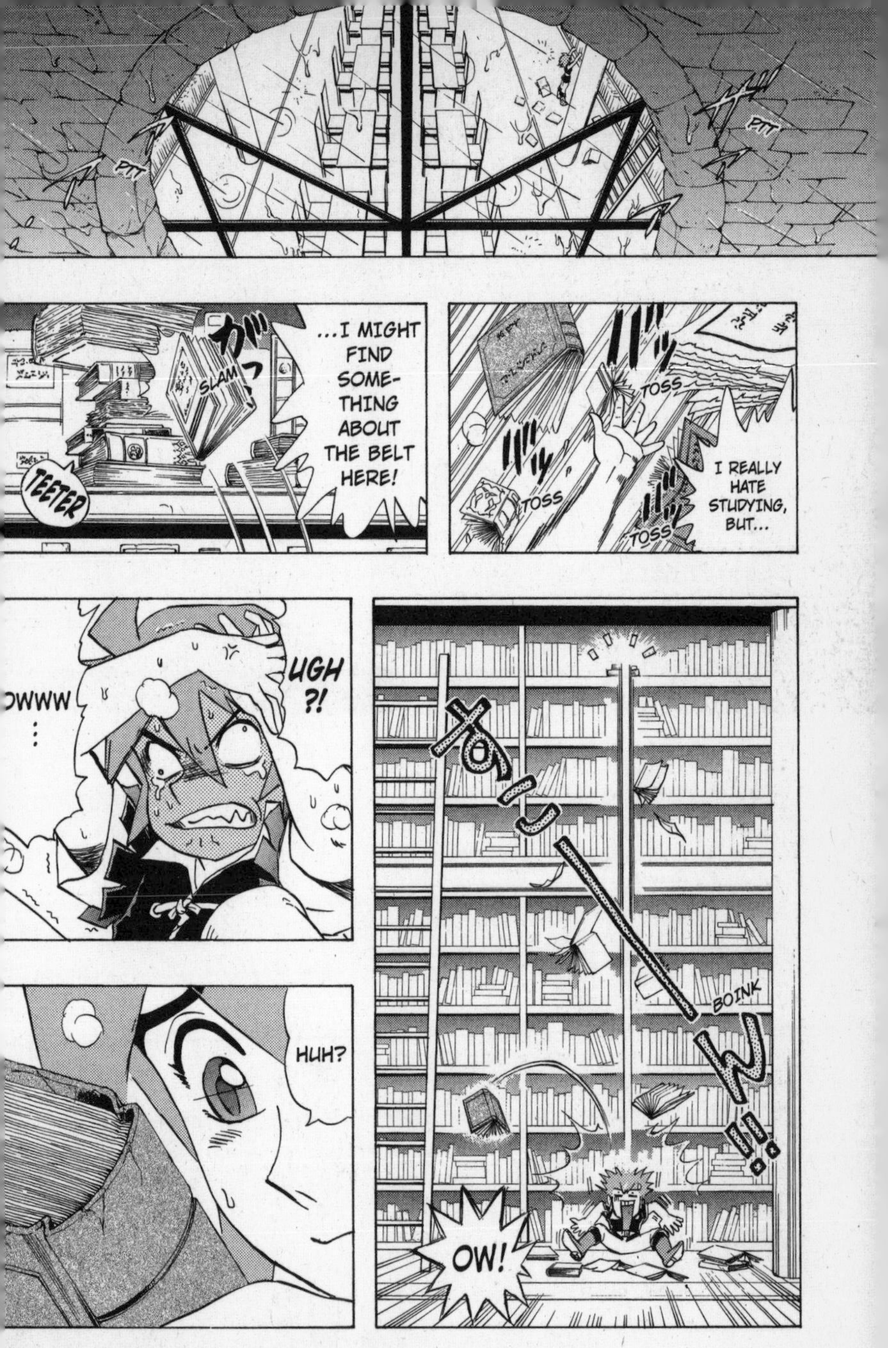
PITT
PITT
I REALLY HATE STUDYING, BUT...
TOSS
TOSS
TOSS
...I MIGHT FIND SOMETHING ABOUT THE BELT HERE!
SLAM
TEETER
BOINK
OW!
UGH ?!
OWWW...
HUH?

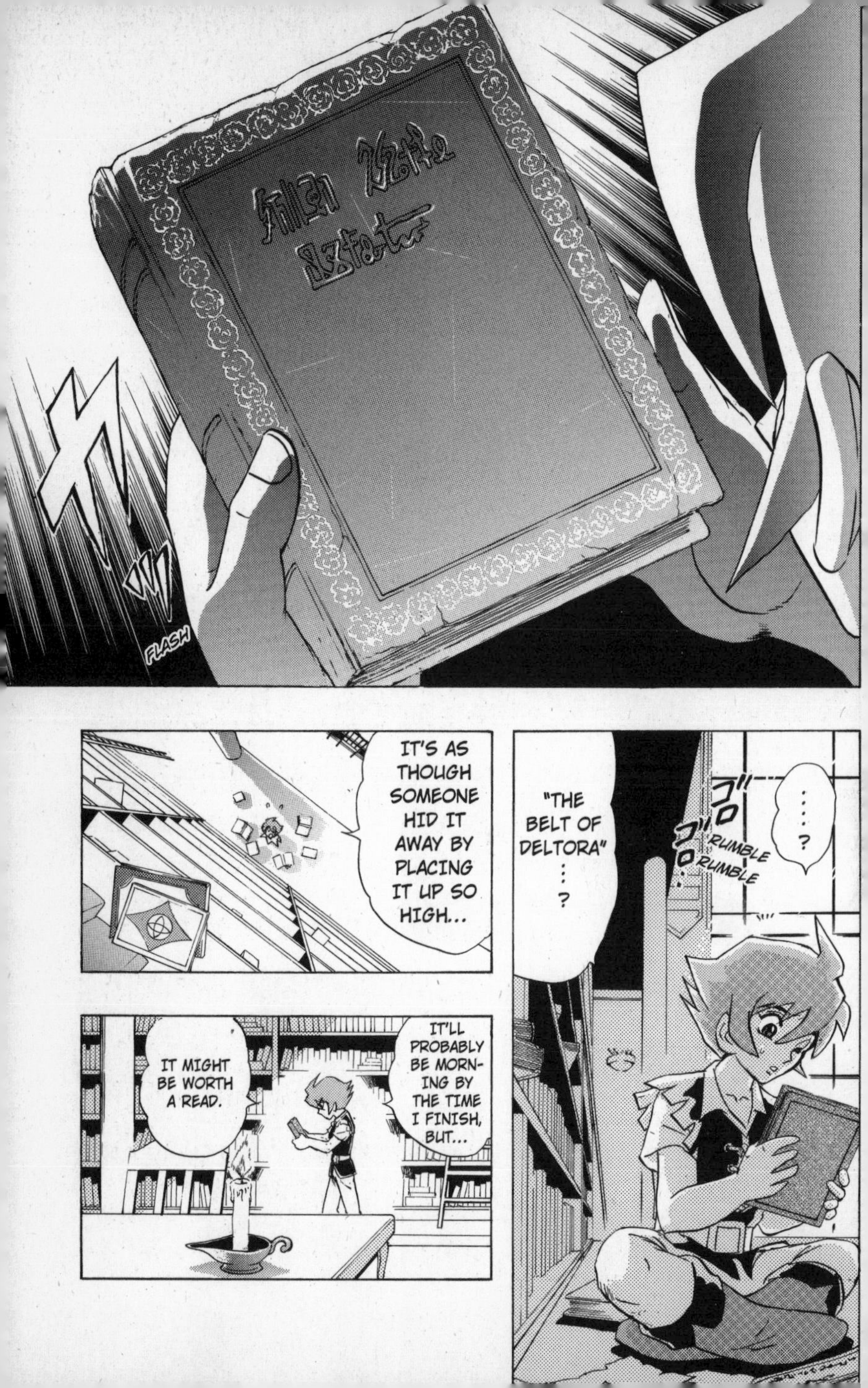
FLASH
....?
RUMBLE RUMBLE
"THE BELT OF DELTORA"...?
IT'S AS THOUGH SOMEONE HID IT AWAY BY PLACING IT UP SO HIGH...
IT'LL PROBABLY BE MORN-ING BY THE TIME I FINISH, BUT...
IT MIGHT BE WORTH A READ.

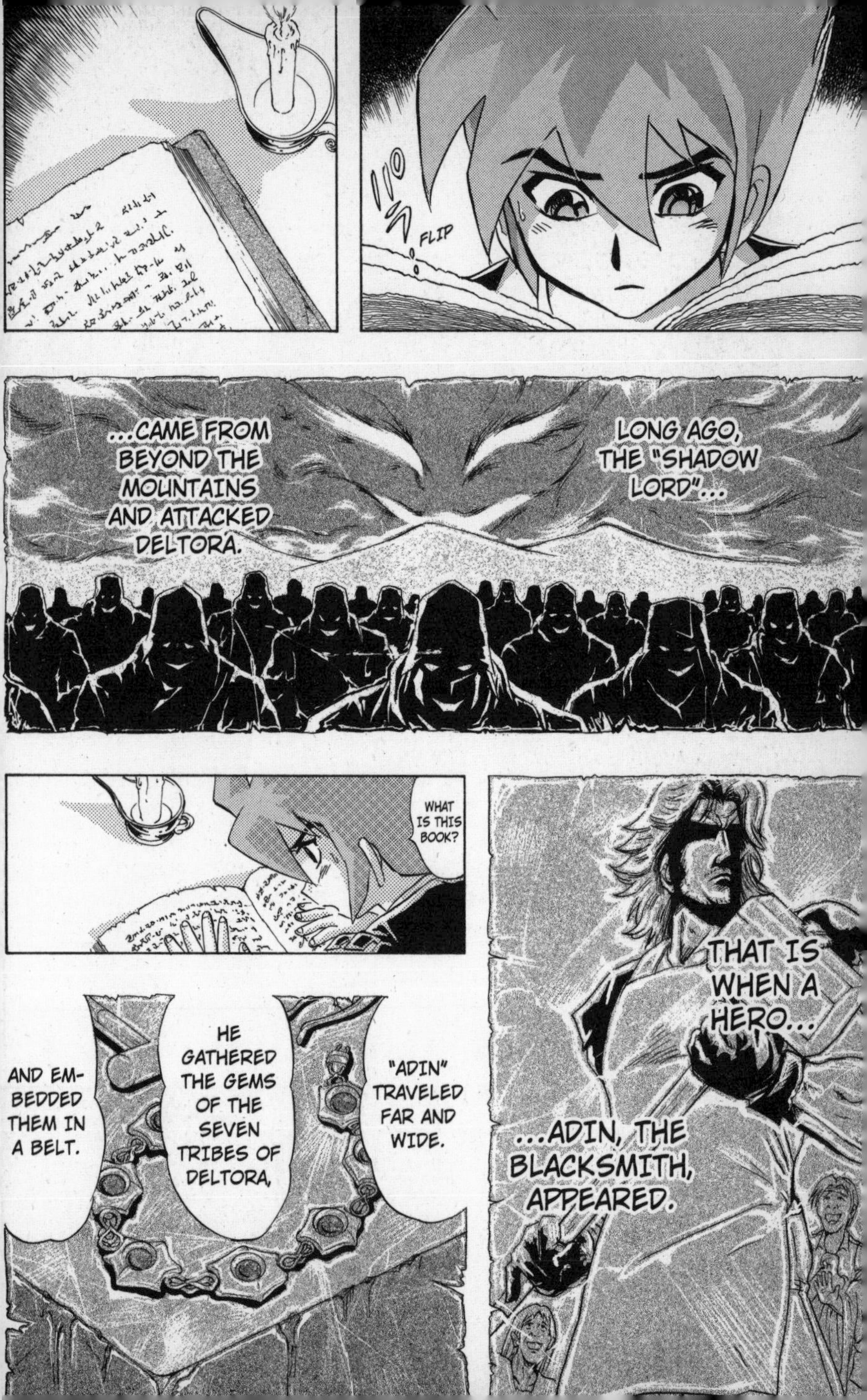
FLIP
LONG AGO, THE "SHADOW LORD"...
...CAME FROM BEYOND THE MOUNTAINS AND ATTACKED DELTORA.
THAT IS WHEN A HERO...
...ADIN, THE BLACKSMITH, APPEARED.
WHAT IS THIS BOOK?
"ADIN" TRAVELED FAR AND WIDE.
HE GATHERED THE GEMS OF THE SEVEN TRIBES OF DELTORA,
AND EM-BEDDED THEM IN A BELT.

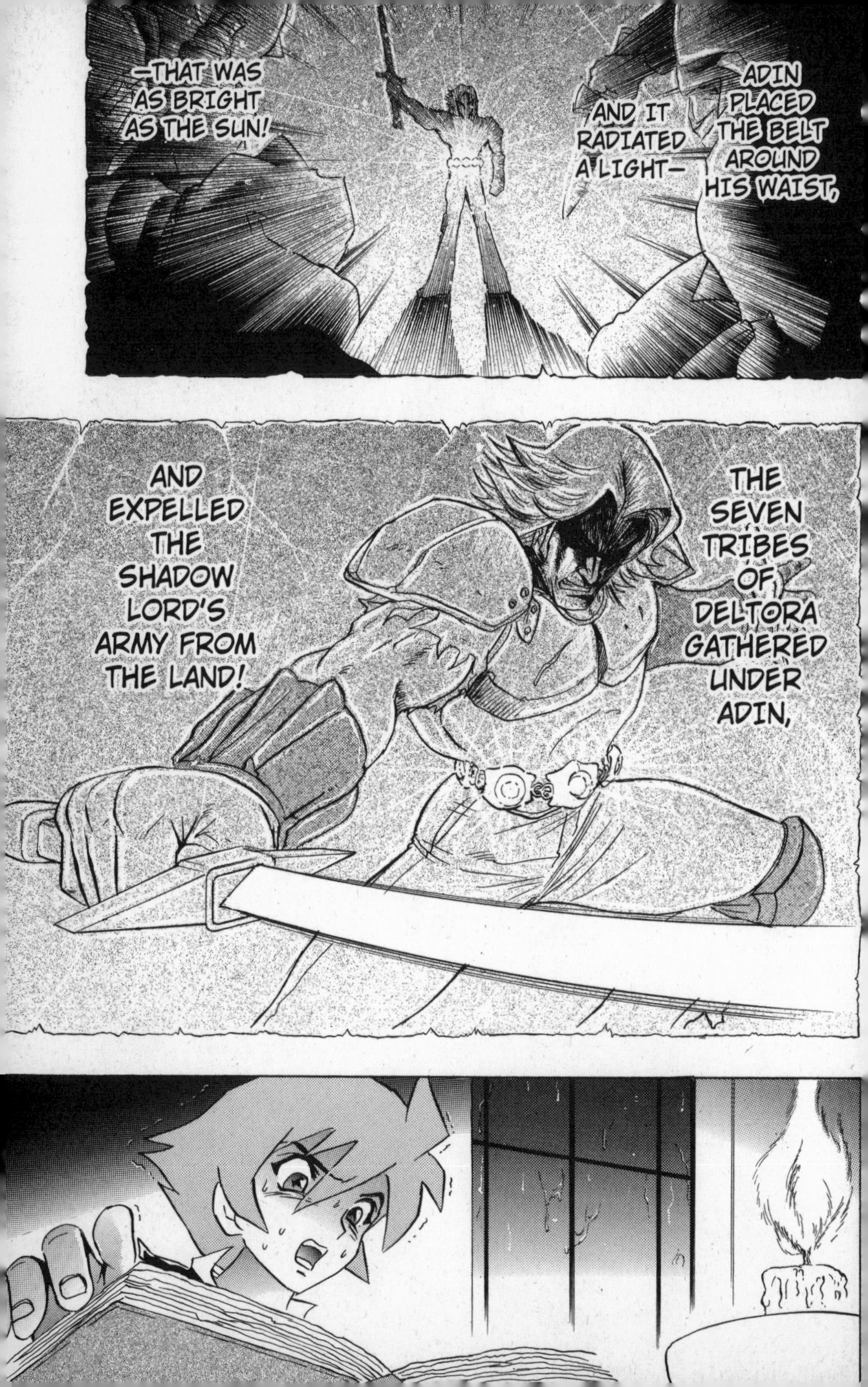
ADIN PLACED THE BELT AROUND HIS WAIST,
AND IT RADIATED A LIGHT—
—THAT WAS AS BRIGHT AS THE SUN!
THE SEVEN TRIBES OF DELTORA GATHERED UNDER ADIN,
AND EXPELLED THE SHADOW LORD'S ARMY FROM THE LAND!

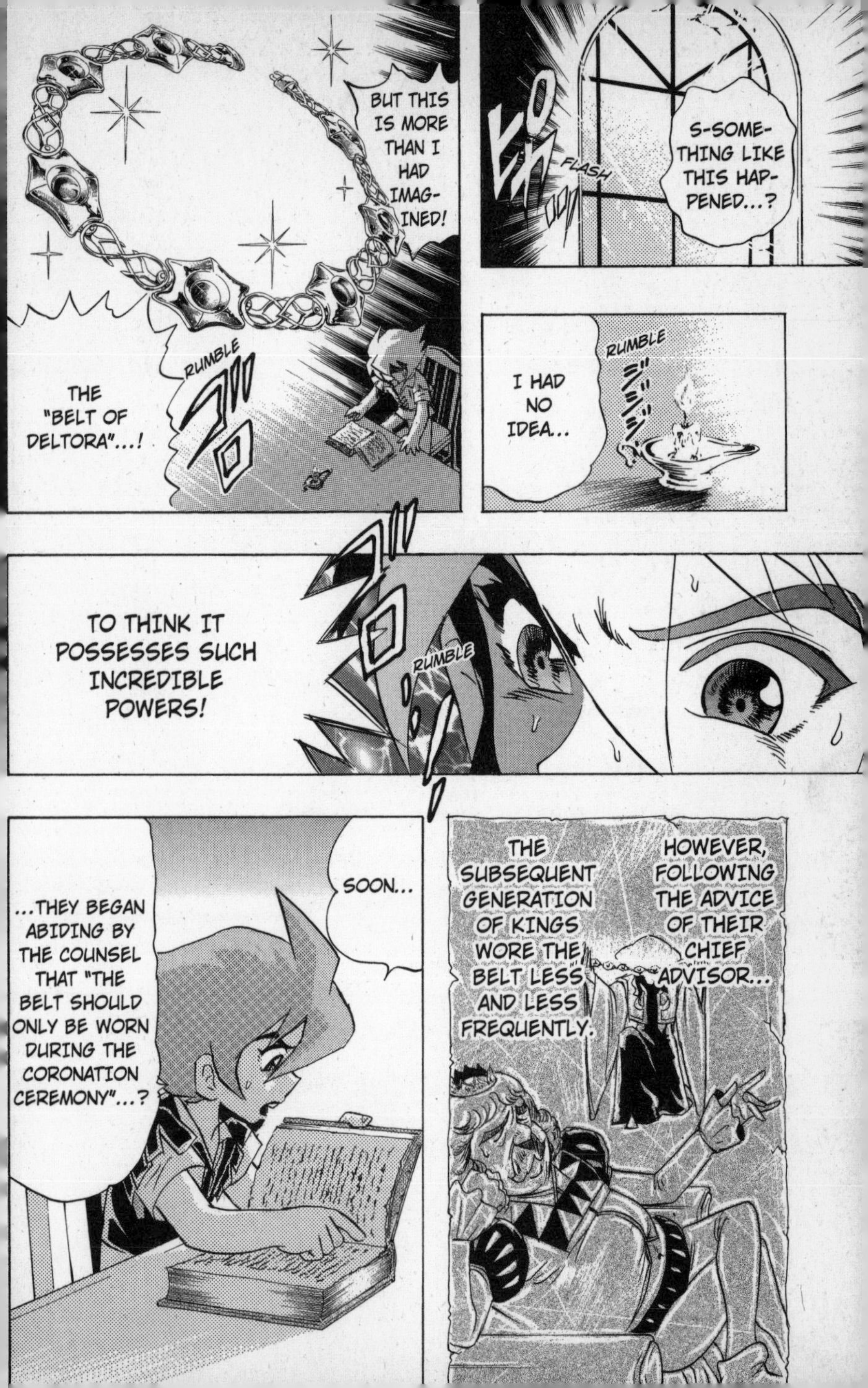
FLASH
S-SOMETHING LIKE THIS HAPPENED...?
RUMBLE
I HAD NO IDEA...
BUT THIS IS MORE THAN I HAD IMAGINED!
RUMBLE
THE "BELT OF DELTORA"...!
RUMBLE
TO THINK IT POSSESSES SUCH INCREDIBLE POWERS!
HOWEVER, FOLLOWING THE ADVICE OF THEIR CHIEF ADVISOR...
THE SUBSEQUENT GENERATION OF KINGS WORE THE BELT LESS AND LESS FREQUENTLY.
SOON...
...THEY BEGAN ABIDING BY THE COUNSEL THAT "THE BELT SHOULD ONLY BE WORN DURING THE CORONATION CEREMONY"...?

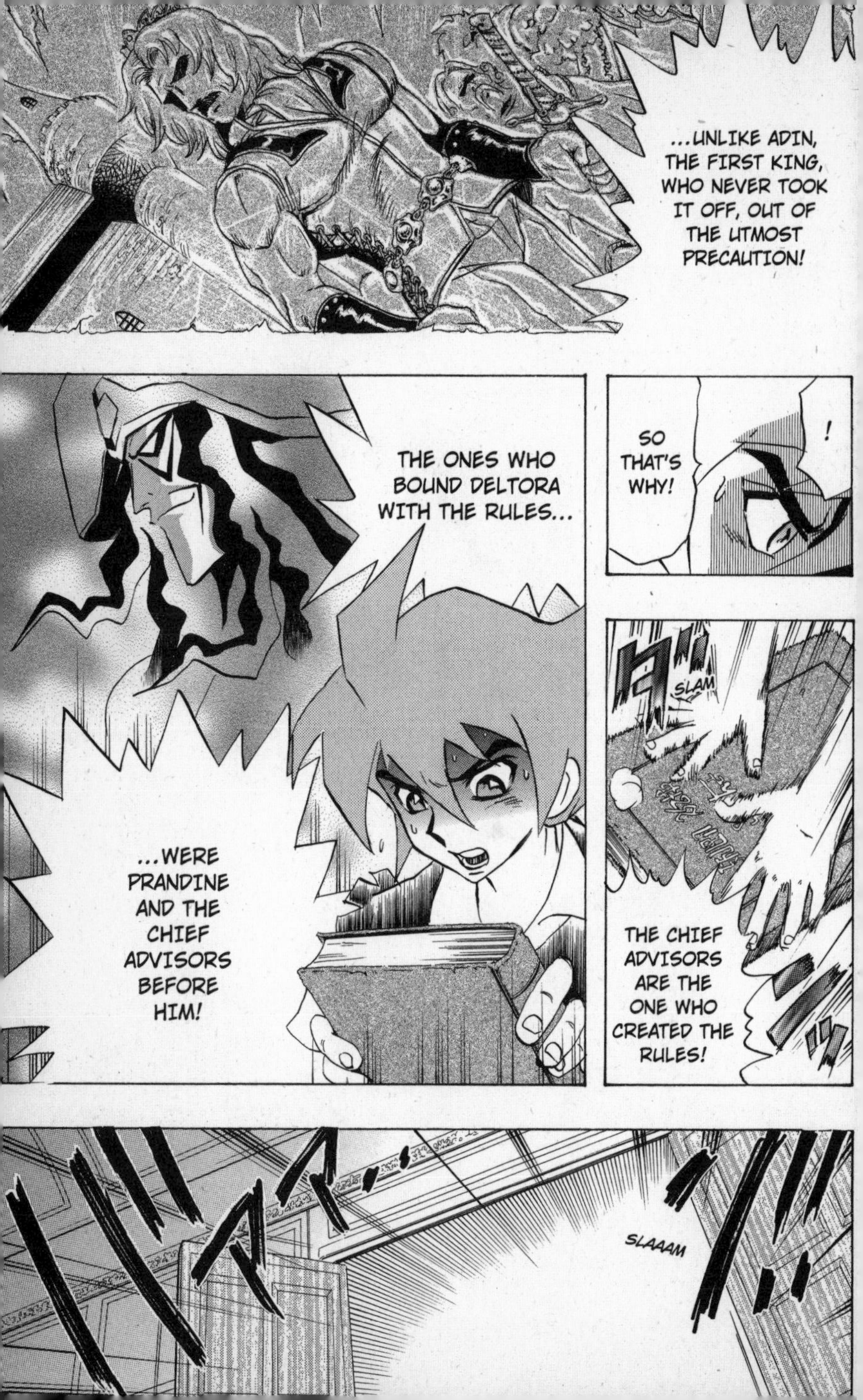
...UNLIKE ADIN, THE FIRST KING, WHO NEVER TOOK IT OFF, OUT OF THE UTMOST PRECAUTION!
SO THAT'S WHY!
!
SLAM
THE CHIEF ADVISORS ARE THE ONE WHO CREATED THE RULES!
THE ONES WHO BOUND DELTORA WITH THE RULES...
...WERE PRANDINE AND THE CHIEF ADVISORS BEFORE HIM!
SLAAAM

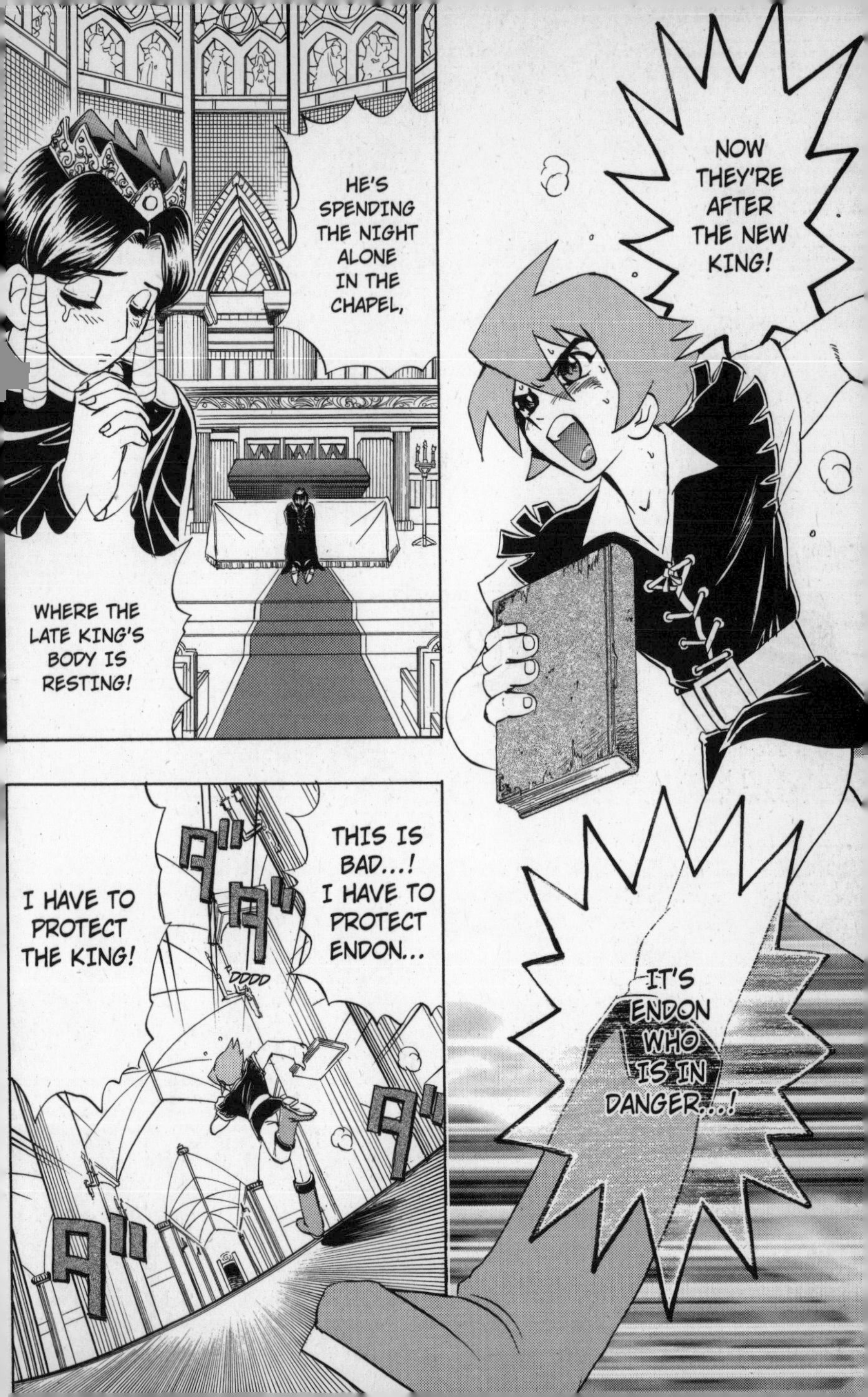
NOW THEY'RE AFTER THE NEW KING!
IT'S ENDON WHO IS IN DANGER...!
HE'S SPENDING THE NIGHT ALONE IN THE CHAPEL,
WHERE THE LATE KING'S BODY IS RESTING!
THIS IS BAD...! I HAVE TO PROTECT ENDON...
I HAVE TO PROTECT THE KING!
DDDD

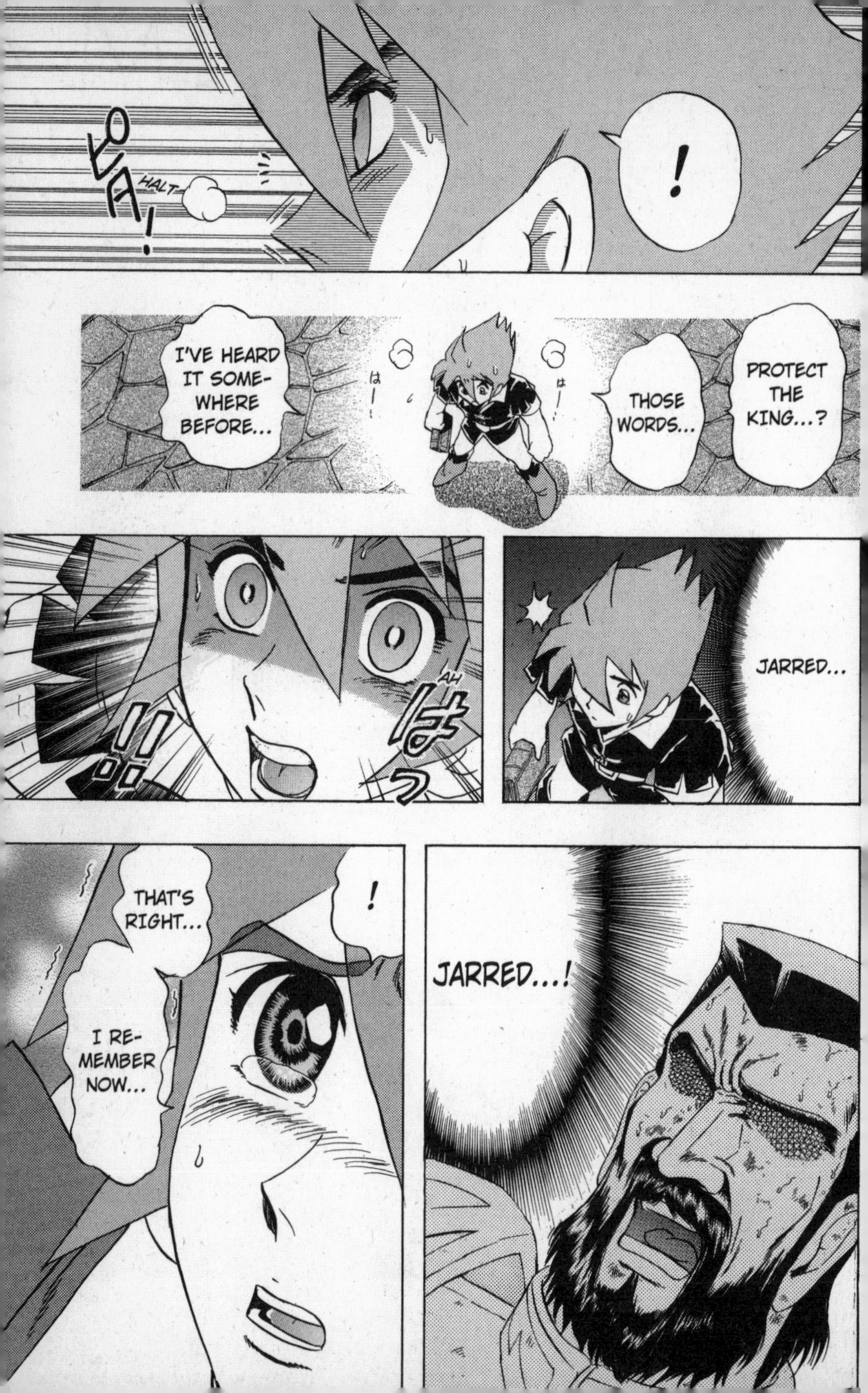
!
ピタ!
HALT
PROTECT THE KING...?
THOSE WORDS...
I'VE HEARD IT SOME-WHERE BEFORE...
JARRED...
はっ
AH
!!
JARRED...!
!
THAT'S RIGHT...
I RE-MEMBER NOW...

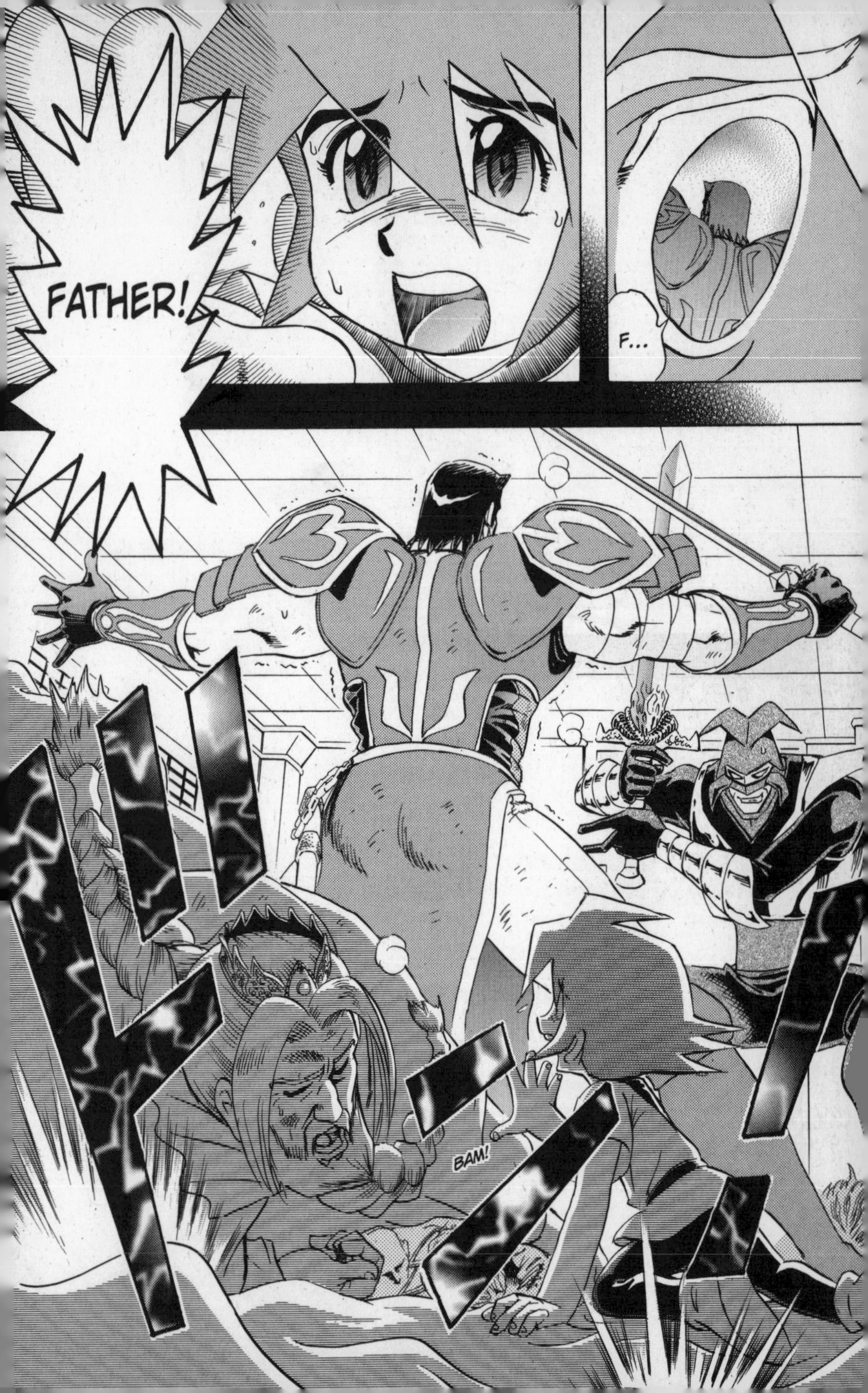
F...
FATHER!
BAM!

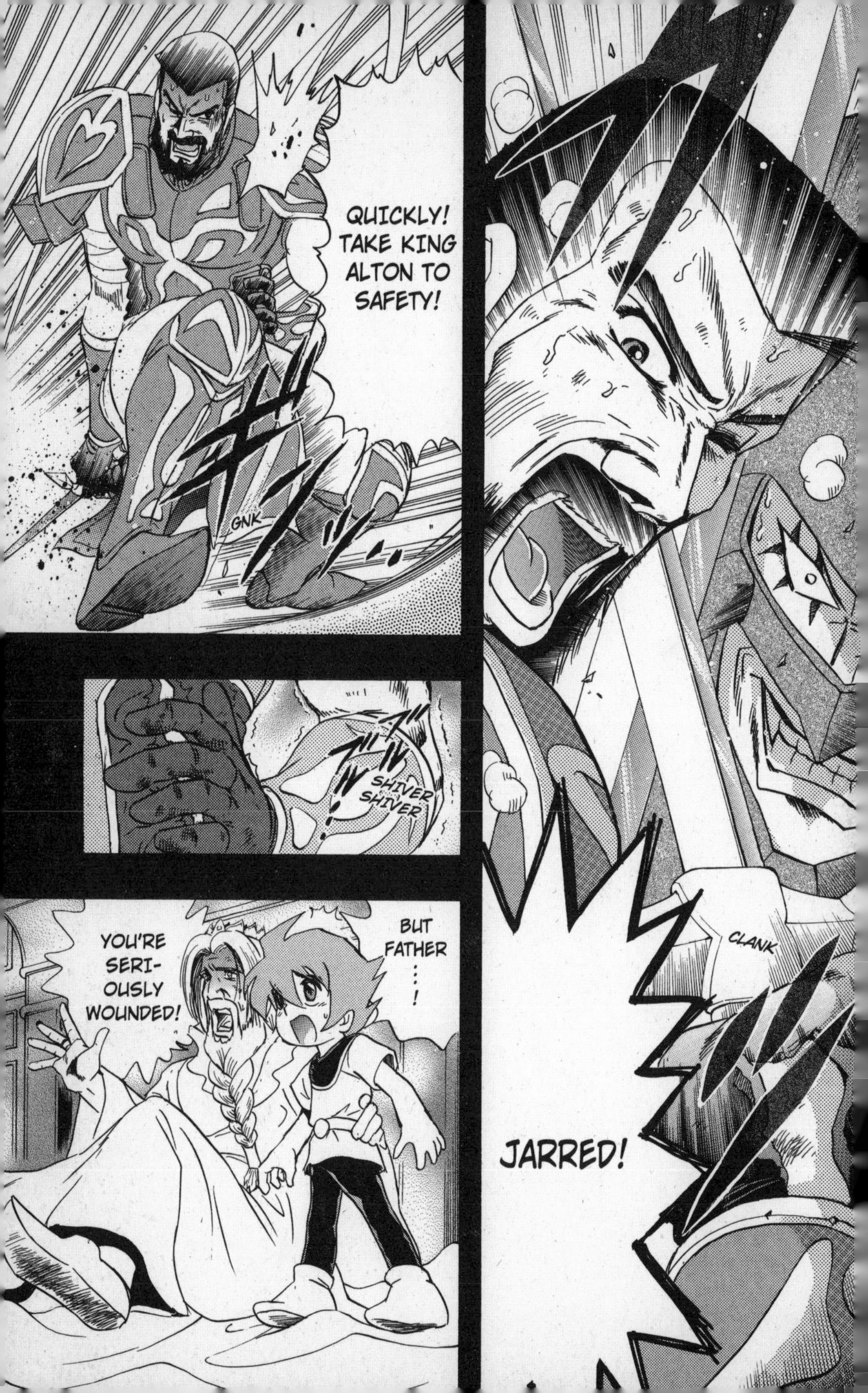
CLANK
JARRED!
QUICKLY! TAKE KING ALTON TO SAFETY!
GNK
SHIVER SHIVER
BUT FATHER ...!
YOU'RE SERI-OUSLY WOUNDED!

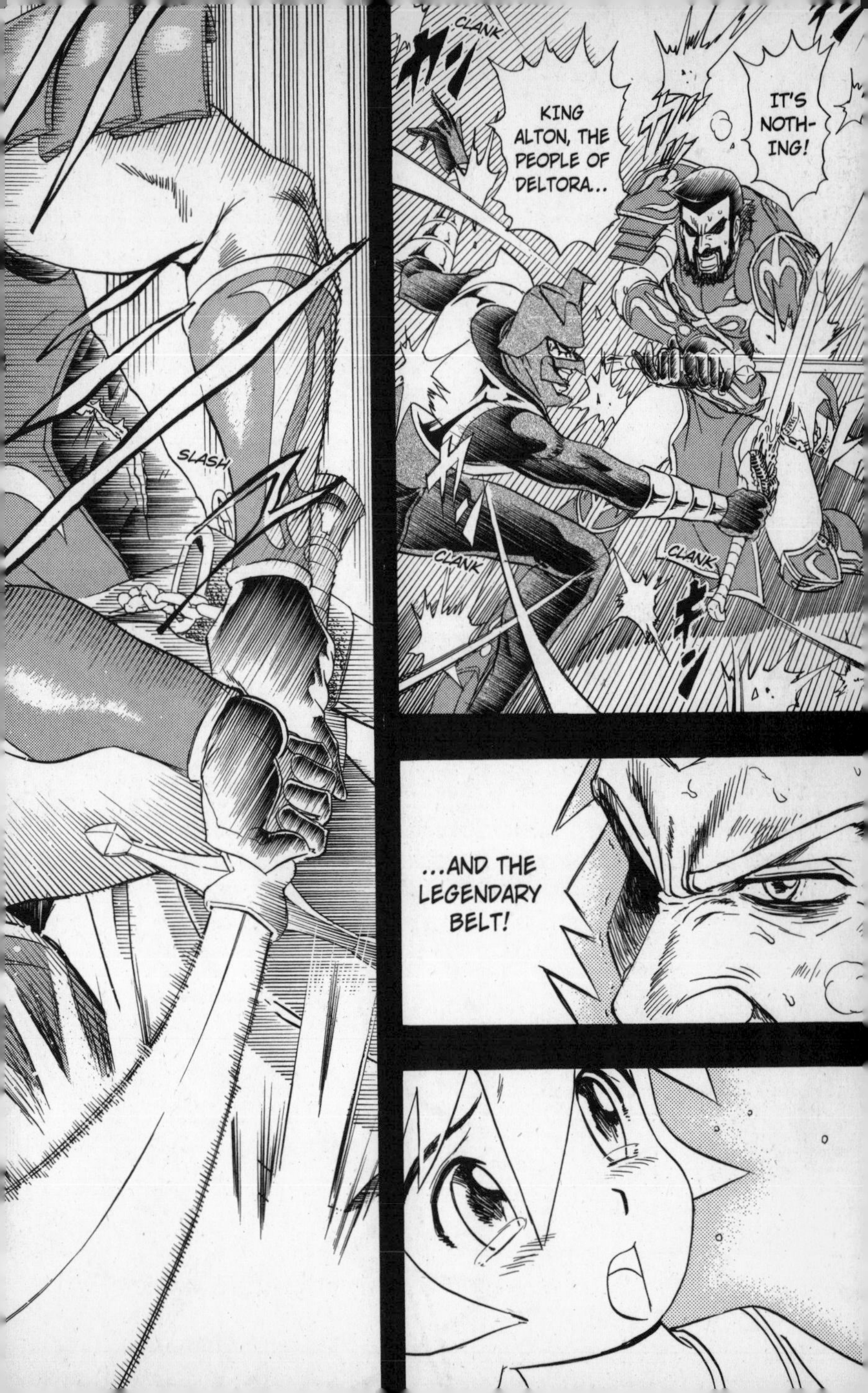
CLANK
IT'S NOTHING!
KING ALTON, THE PEOPLE OF DELTORA...
CLANK
CLANK
...AND THE LEGENDARY BELT!
SLASH

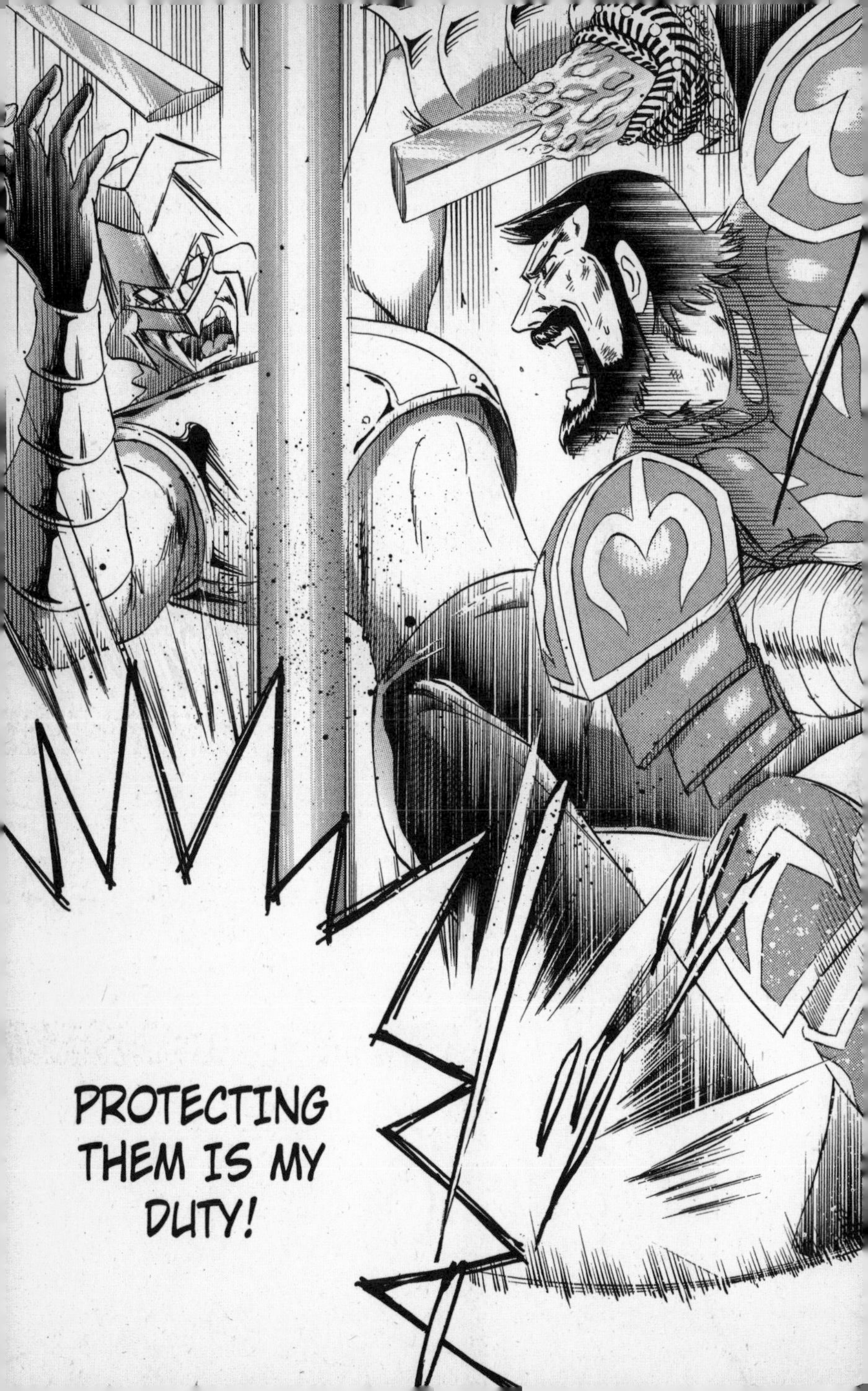
PROTECTING THEM IS MY DUTY!

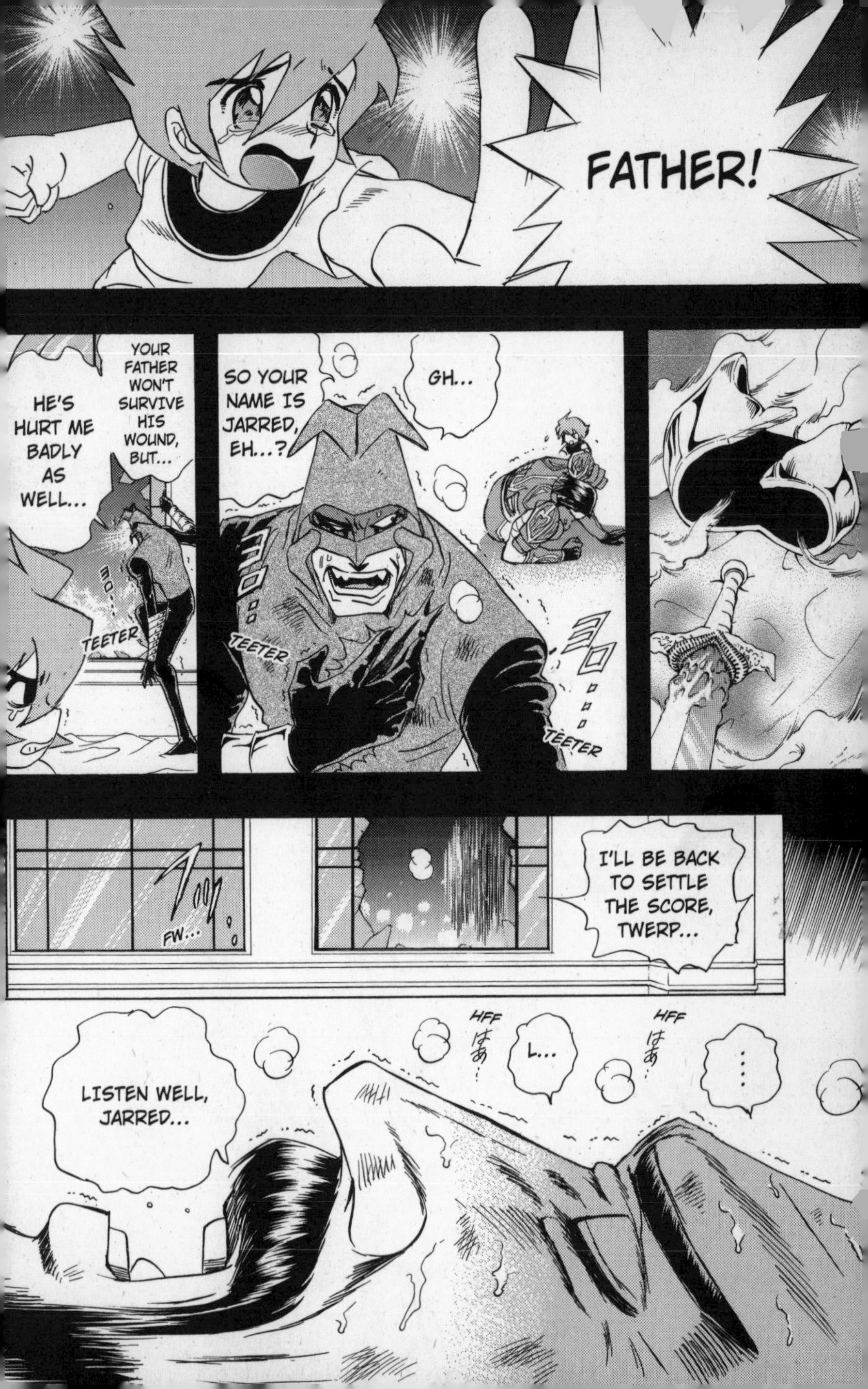
FATHER!
GH...
SO YOUR NAME IS JARRED, EH...?
TEETER
TEETER
YOUR FATHER WON'T SURVIVE HIS WOUND, BUT...
HE'S HURT ME BADLY AS WELL...
TEETER
I'LL BE BACK TO SETTLE THE SCORE, TWERP...
FW...
....
HFF はあ
L...
HFF はあ
LISTEN WELL, JARRED...

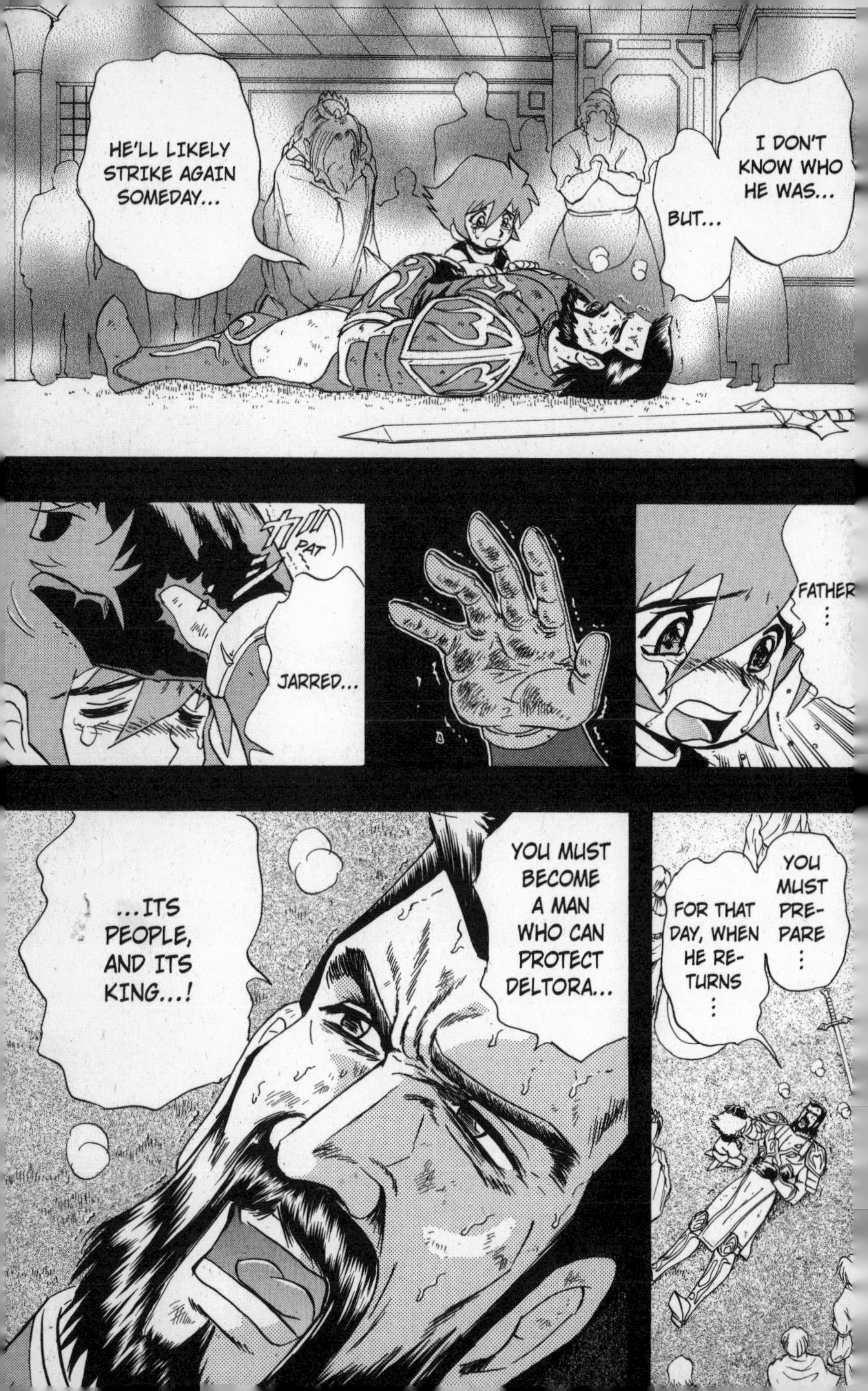
I DON'T KNOW WHO HE WAS...
BUT...
HE'LL LIKELY STRIKE AGAIN SOMEDAY...
FATHER...
PAT
JARRED...
YOU MUST PRE-PARE...
FOR THAT DAY, WHEN HE RE-TURNS...
YOU MUST BECOME A MAN WHO CAN PROTECT DELTORA...
...ITS PEOPLE, AND ITS KING...!

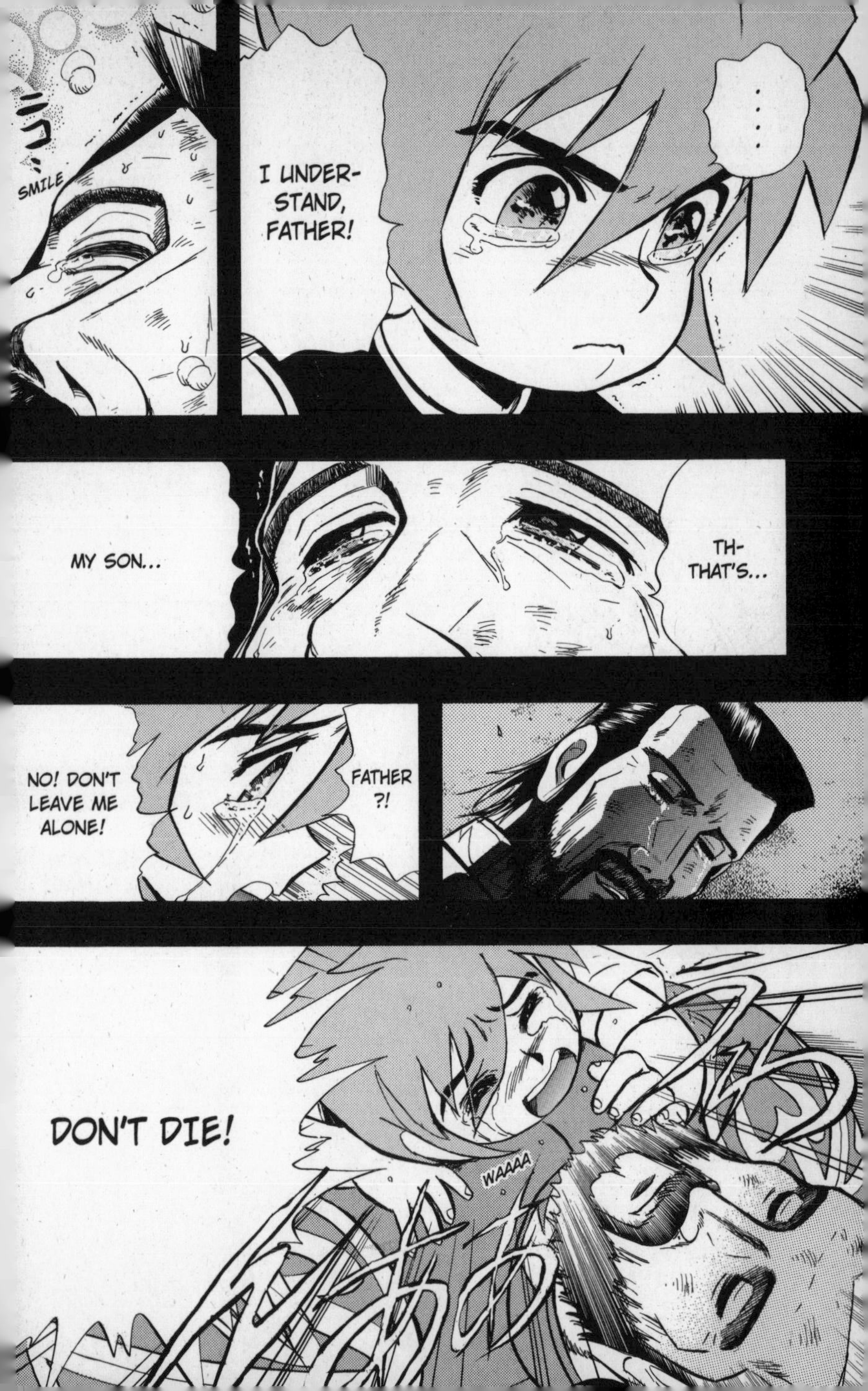
.....
I UNDER-STAND, FATHER!
SMILE
TH- THAT'S...
MY SON...
FATHER ?!
NO! DON'T LEAVE ME ALONE!
WAAAA
DON'T DIE!

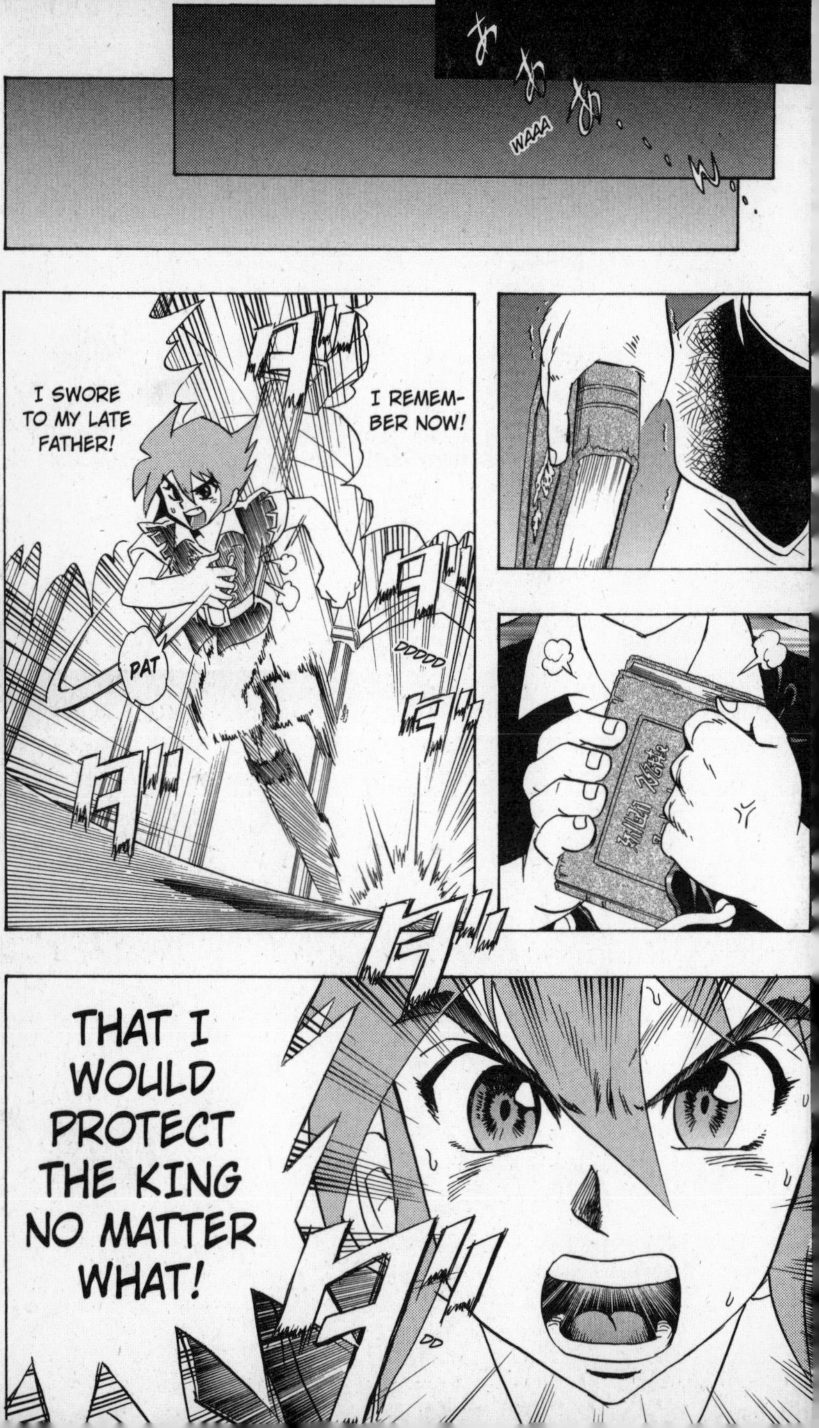
WAAA
I REMEMBER NOW!
I SWORE TO MY LATE FATHER!
PAT
DDDDD
THAT I WOULD PROTECT THE KING NO MATTER WHAT!
DD

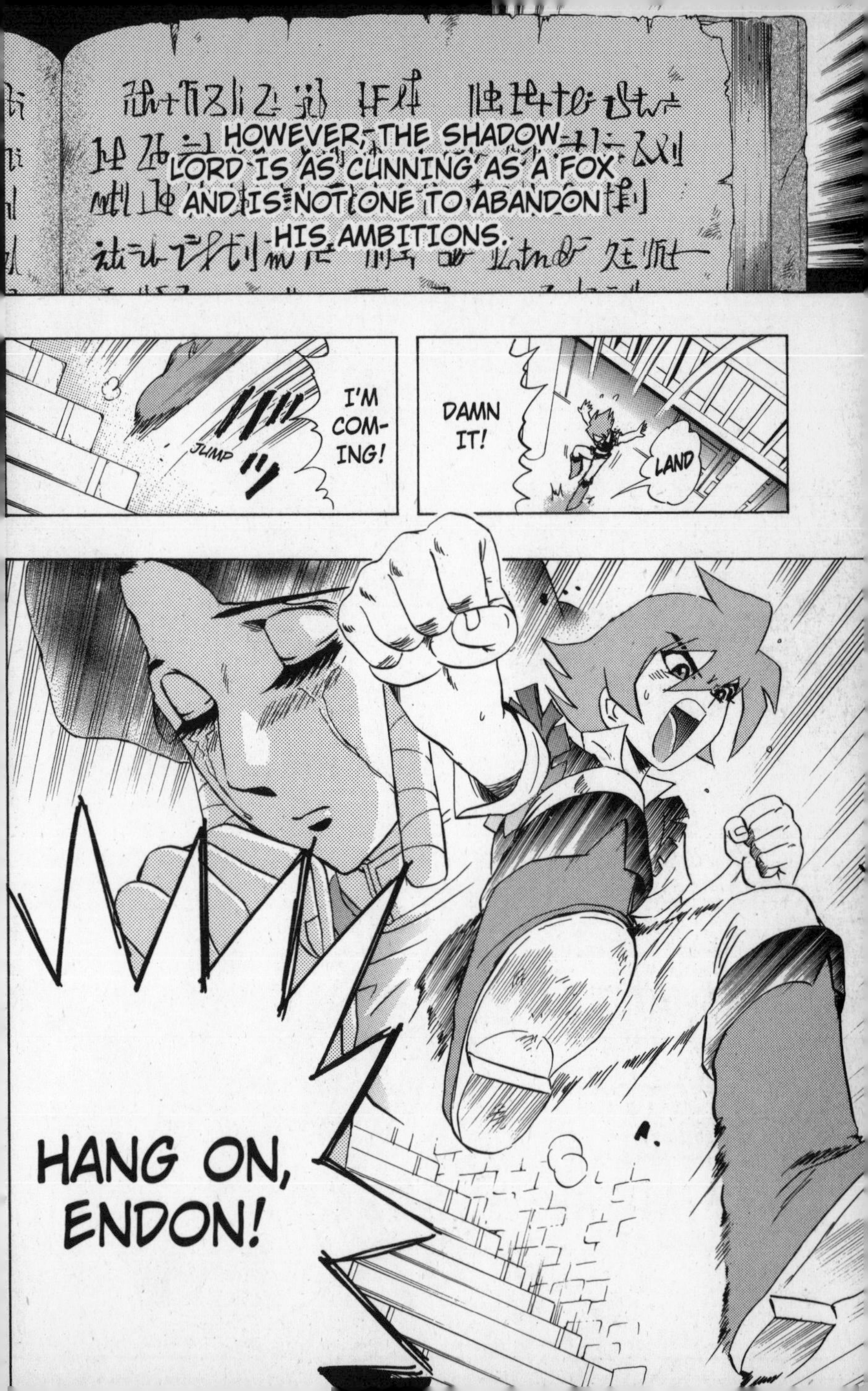
HOWEVER, THE SHADOW LORD IS AS CUNNING AS A FOX AND IS NOT ONE TO ABANDON HIS AMBITIONS.
DAMN IT!
LAND
I'M COM-ING!
JUMP
HANG ON, ENDON!

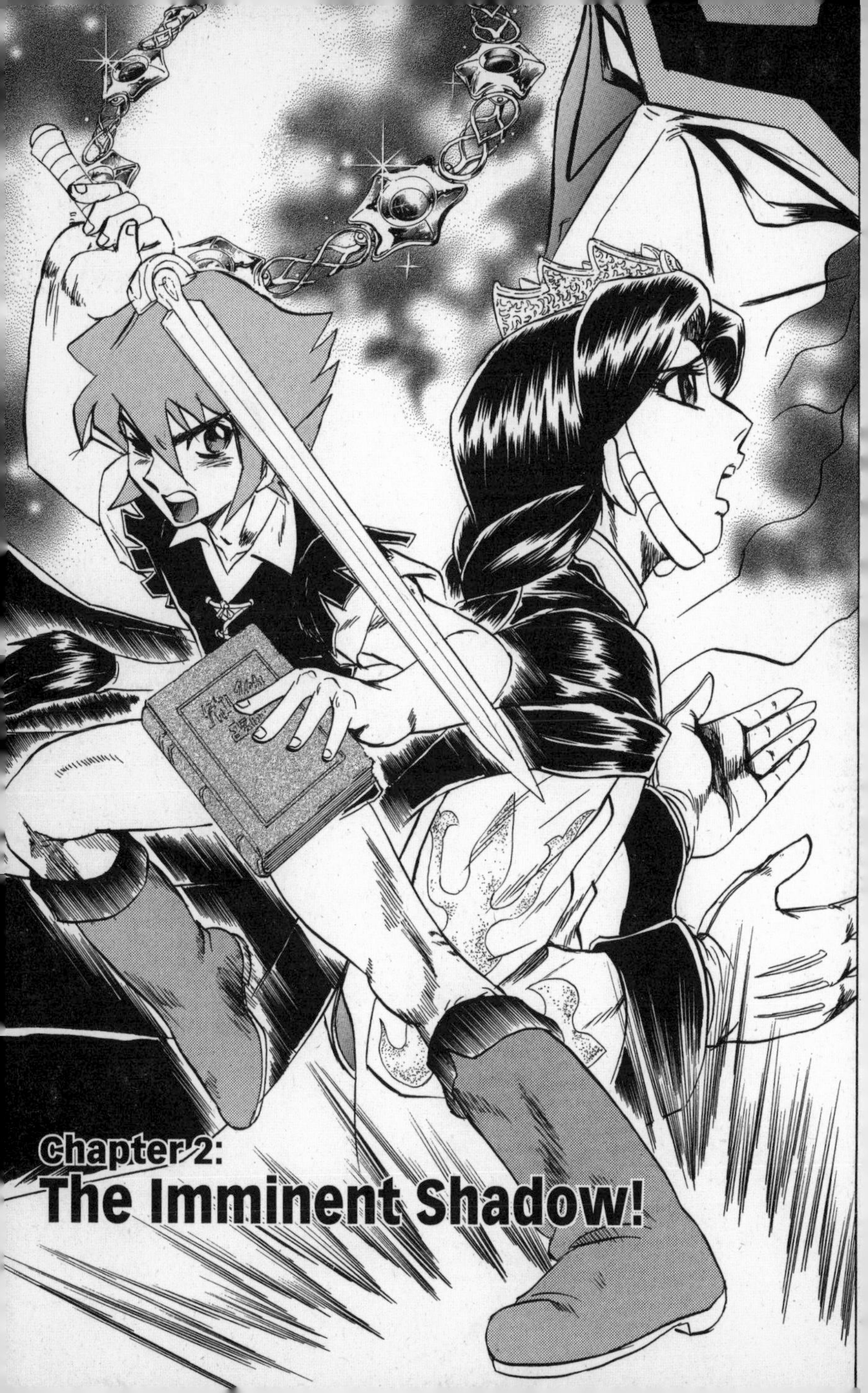
Chapter 2:
The Imminent Shadow!

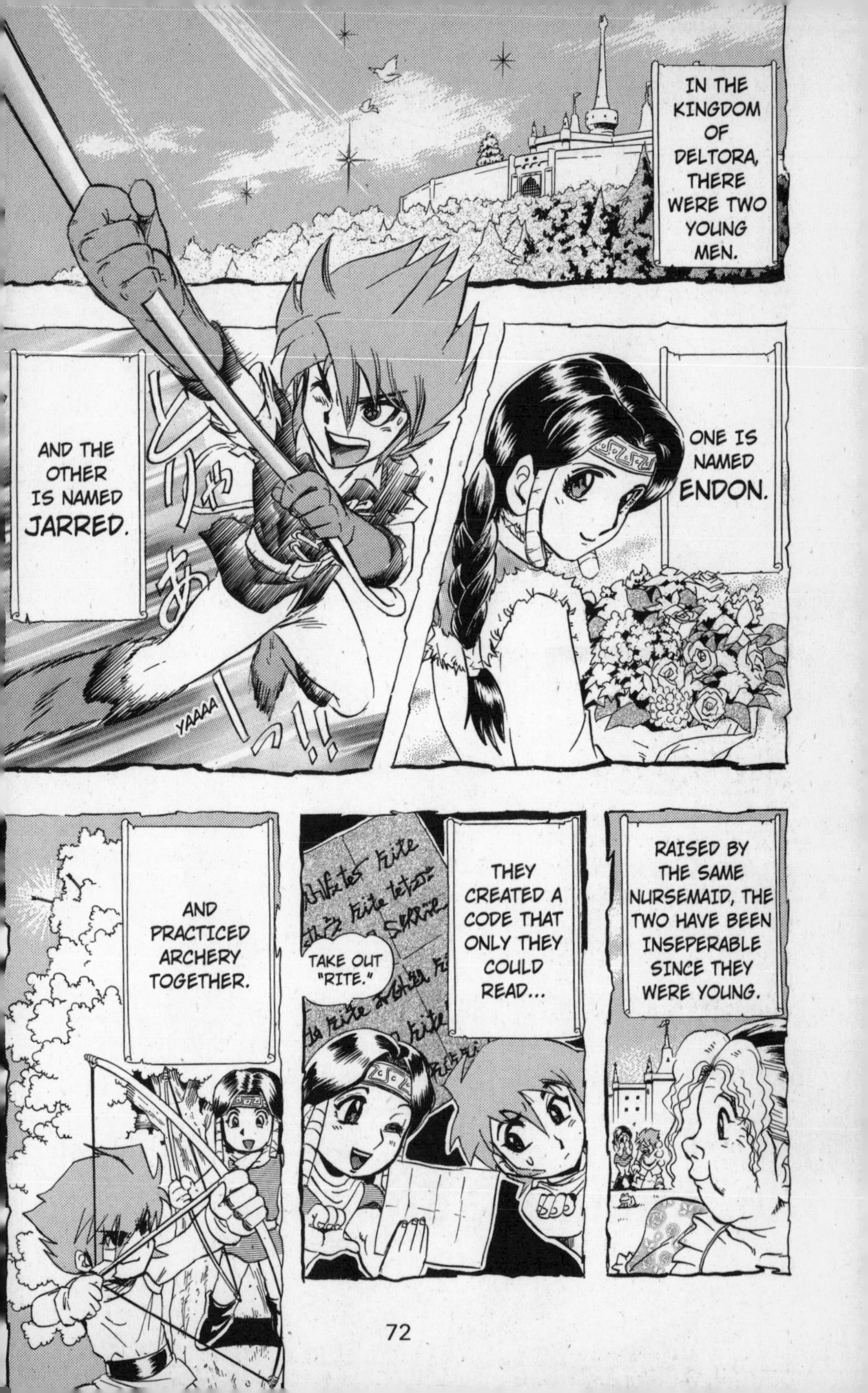
IN THE KINGDOM OF DELTORA, THERE WERE TWO YOUNG MEN.
ONE IS NAMED ENDON.
AND THE OTHER IS NAMED JARRED.
YAAAA
RAISED BY THE SAME NURSEMAID, THE TWO HAVE BEEN INSEPERABLE SINCE THEY WERE YOUNG.
THEY CREATED A CODE THAT ONLY THEY COULD READ...
TAKE OUT "RITE."
AND PRACTICED ARCHERY TOGETHER.

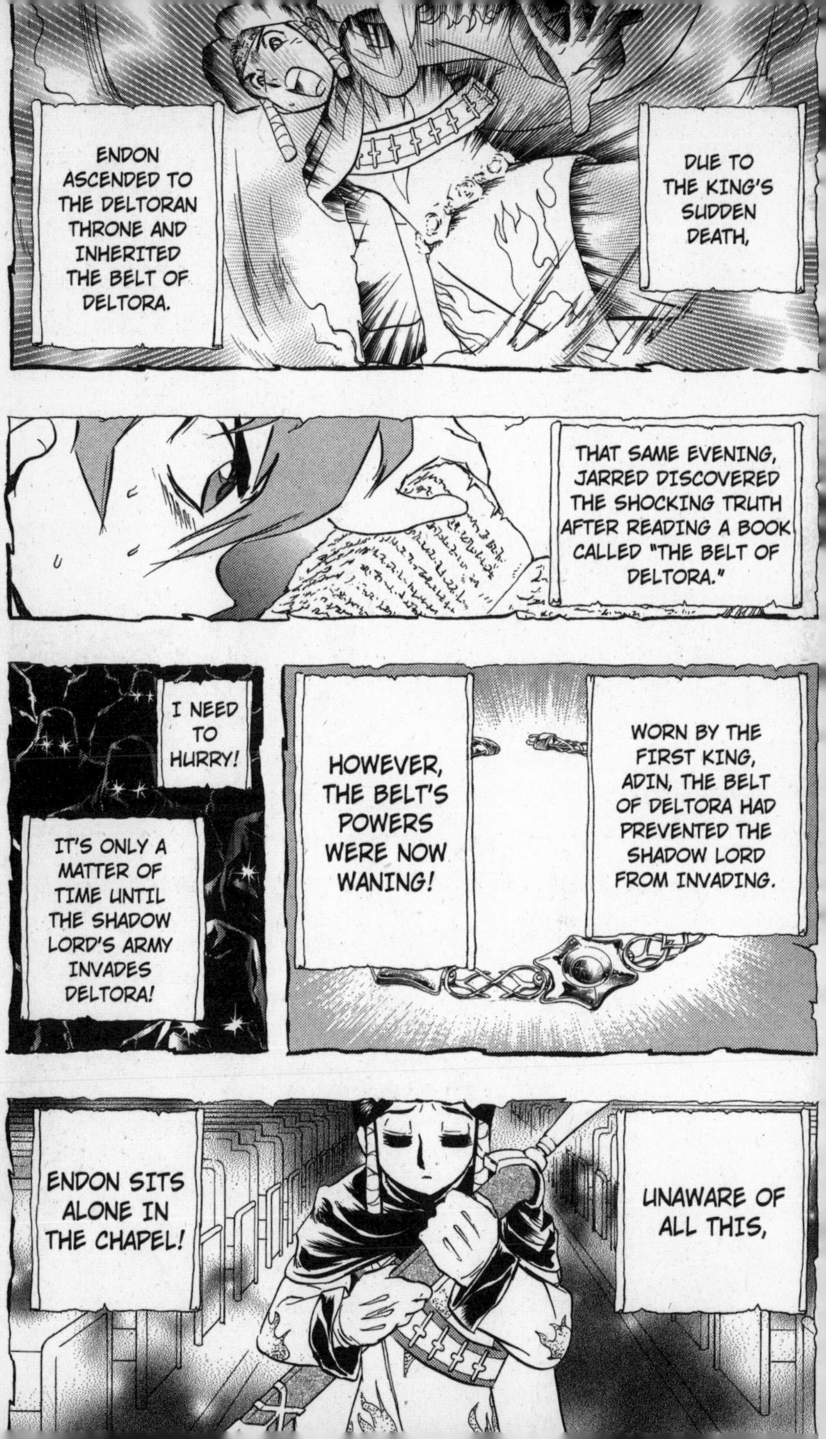
DUE TO THE KING'S SUDDEN DEATH,
ENDON ASCENDED TO THE DELTORAN THRONE AND INHERITED THE BELT OF DELTORA.
THAT SAME EVENING, JARRED DISCOVERED THE SHOCKING TRUTH AFTER READING A BOOK CALLED "THE BELT OF DELTORA."
WORN BY THE FIRST KING, ADIN, THE BELT OF DELTORA HAD PREVENTED THE SHADOW LORD FROM INVADING.
HOWEVER, THE BELT'S POWERS WERE NOW WANING!
I NEED TO HURRY!
IT'S ONLY A MATTER OF TIME UNTIL THE SHADOW LORD'S ARMY INVADES DELTORA!
UNAWARE OF ALL THIS,
ENDON SITS ALONE IN THE CHAPEL!

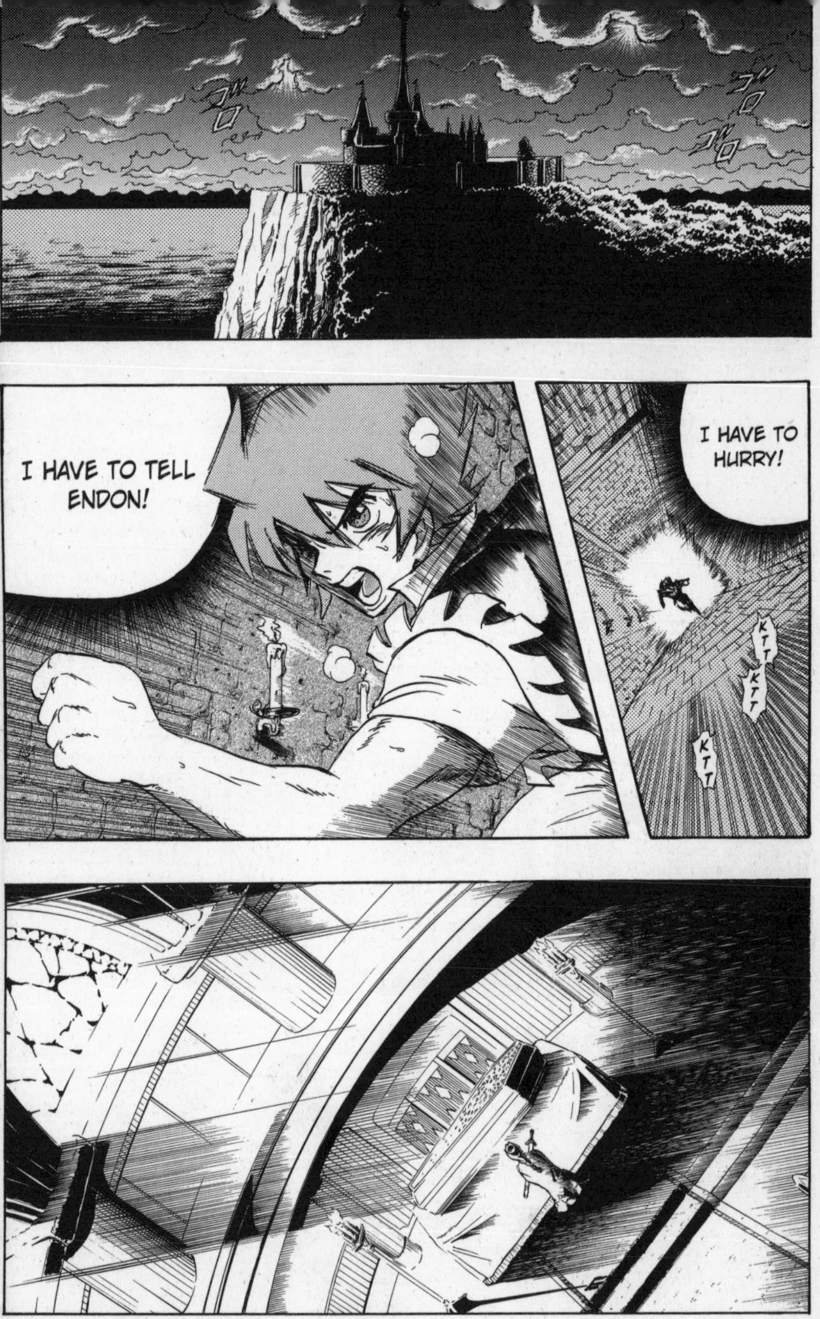
ゴロ
ゴロ
ゴロ
I HAVE TO HURRY!
KTT
KTT
KTT
I HAVE TO TELL ENDON!

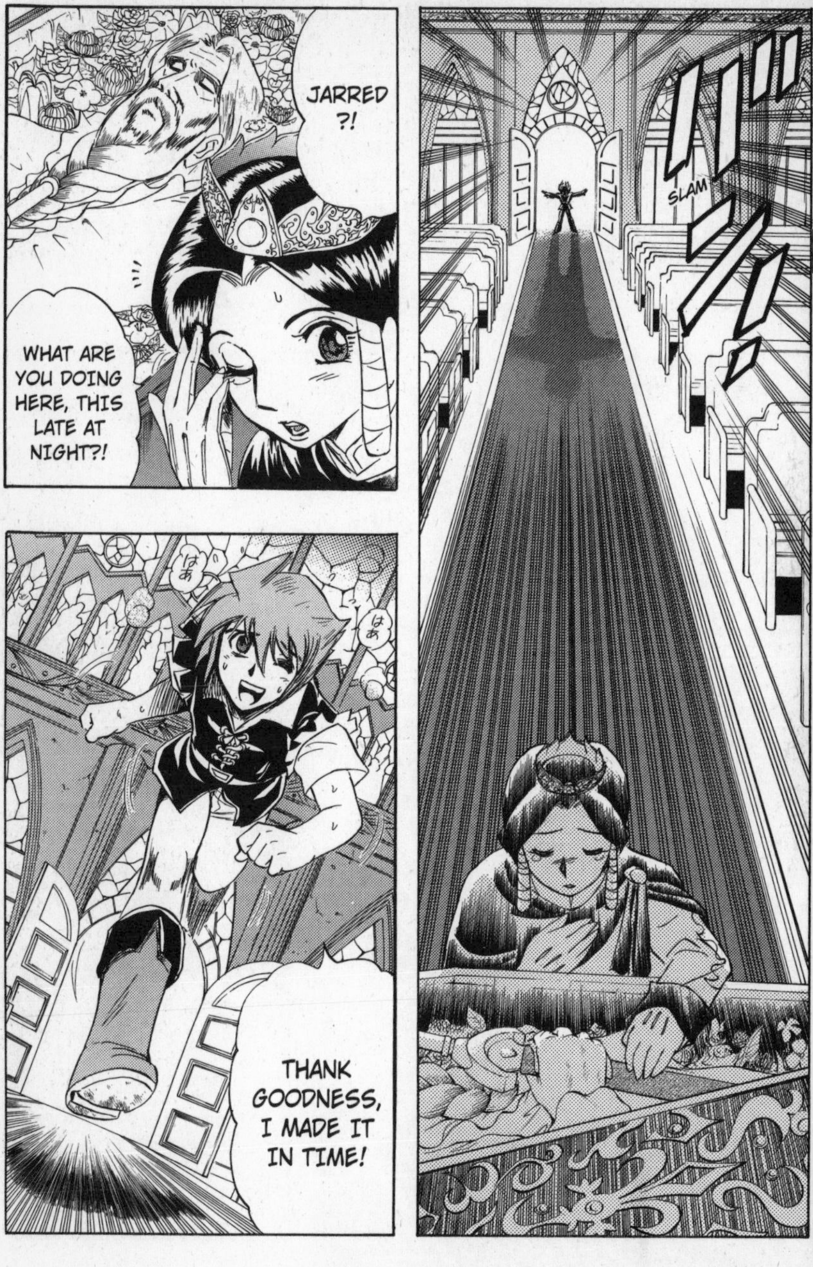
SLAM
JARRED ?!
WHAT ARE YOU DOING HERE, THIS LATE AT NIGHT?!
はあ
はあ
THANK GOODNESS, I MADE IT IN TIME!

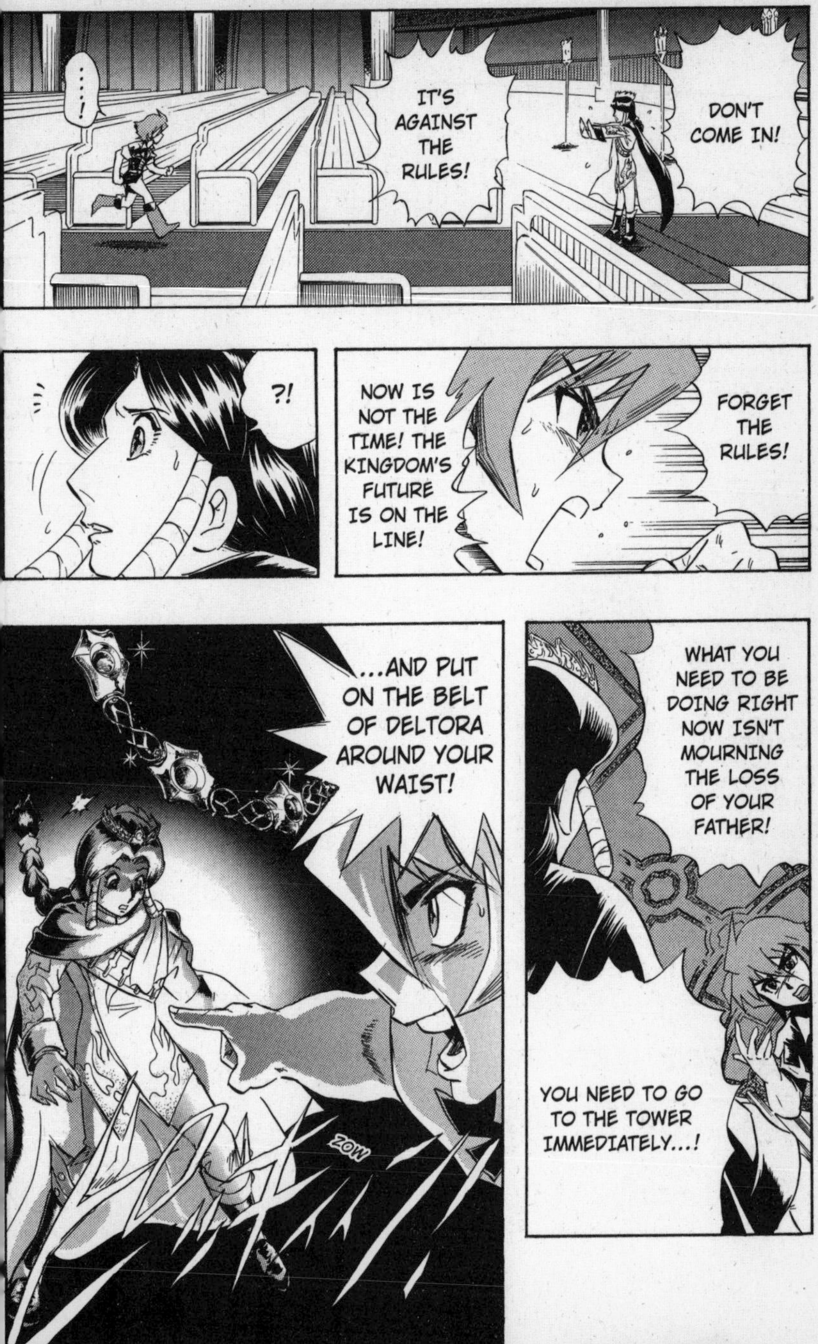
DON'T COME IN!
IT'S AGAINST THE RULES!
....!
FORGET THE RULES!
NOW IS NOT THE TIME! THE KINGDOM'S FUTURE IS ON THE LINE!
?!
WHAT YOU NEED TO BE DOING RIGHT NOW ISN'T MOURNING THE LOSS OF YOUR FATHER!
YOU NEED TO GO TO THE TOWER IMMEDIATELY...!
...AND PUT ON THE BELT OF DELTORA AROUND YOUR WAIST!
ZOW

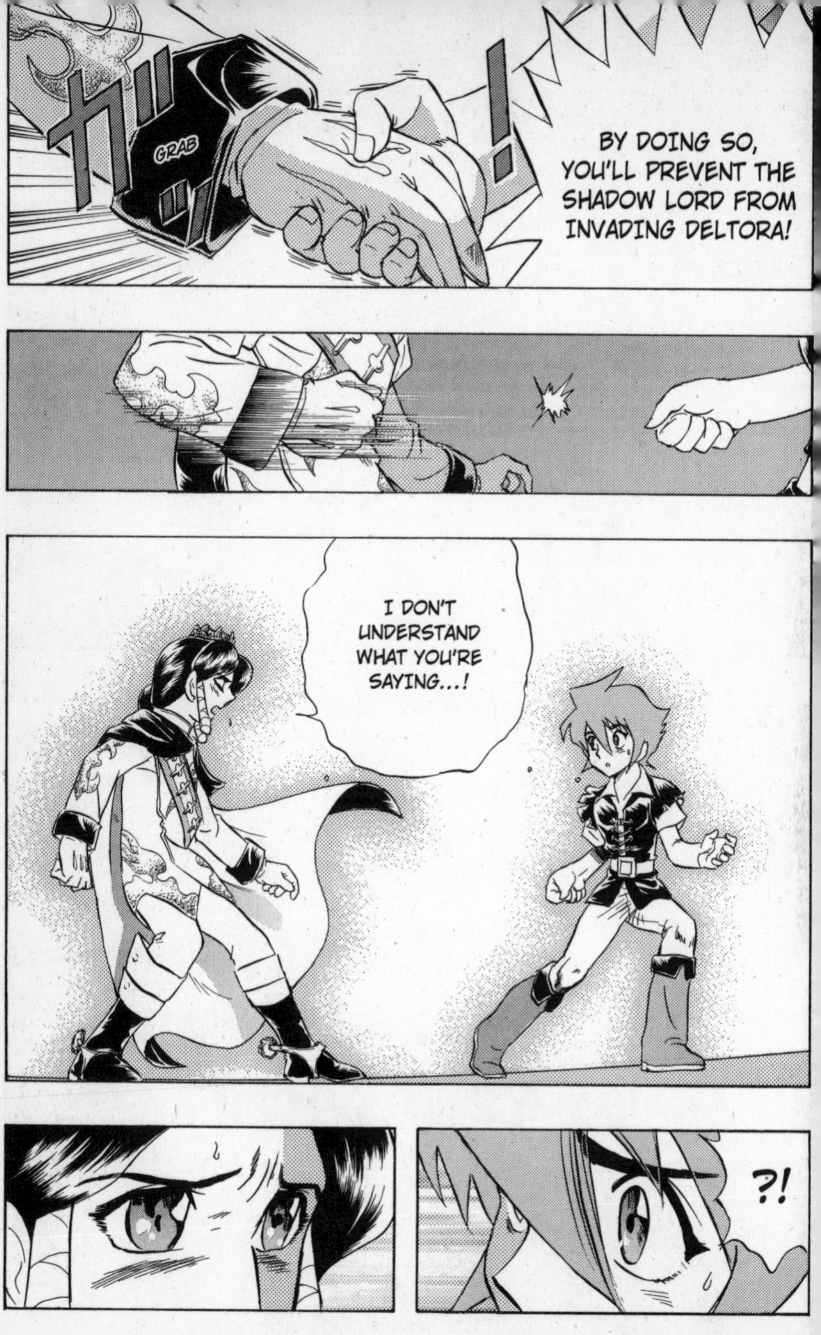
GRAB
BY DOING SO, YOU'LL PREVENT THE SHADOW LORD FROM INVADING DELTORA!
I DON'T UNDERSTAND WHAT YOU'RE SAYING...!
?!

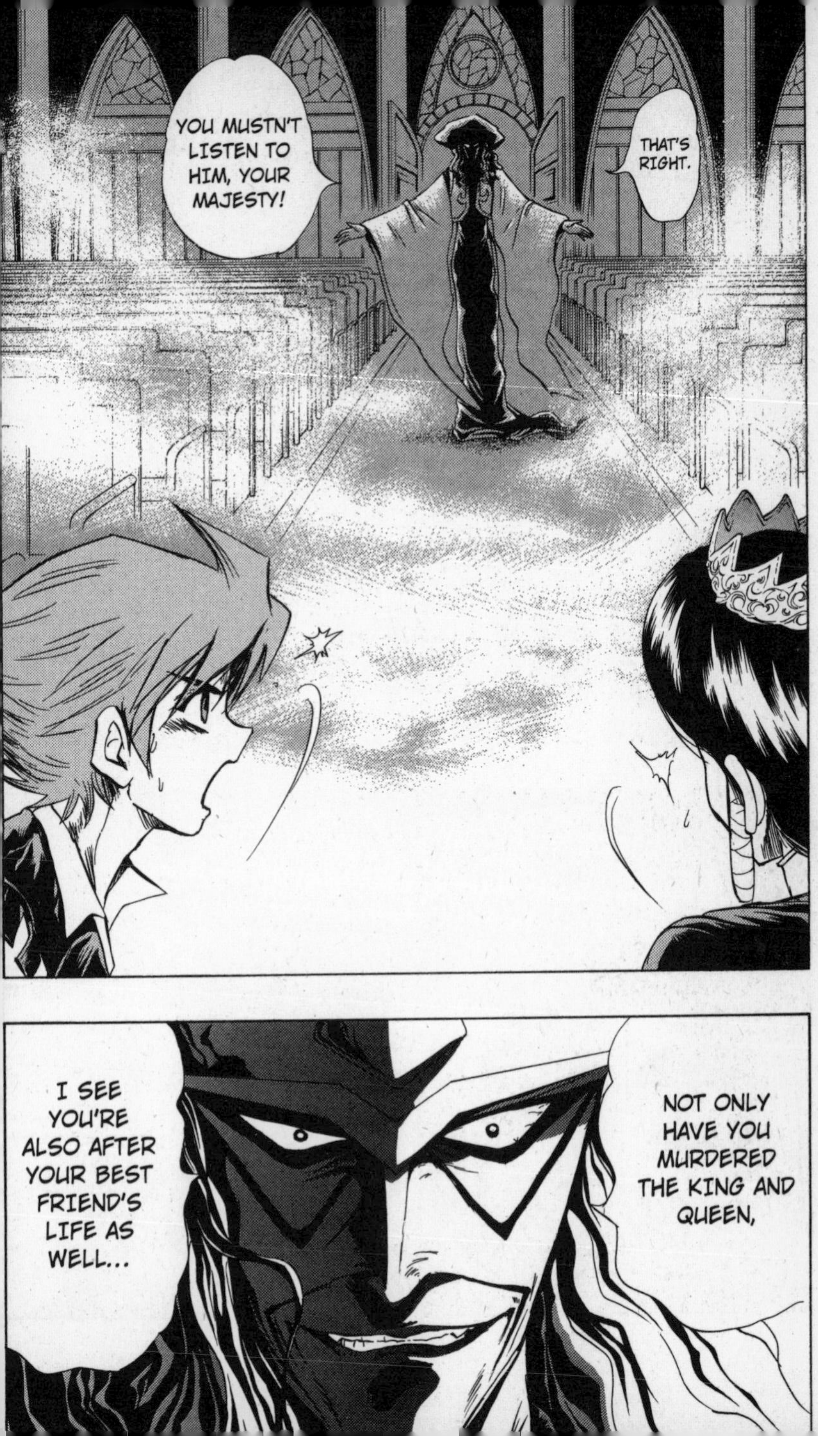
THAT'S RIGHT.
YOU MUSTN'T LISTEN TO HIM, YOUR MAJESTY!
NOT ONLY HAVE YOU MURDERED THE KING AND QUEEN,
I SEE YOU'RE ALSO AFTER YOUR BEST FRIEND'S LIFE AS WELL...

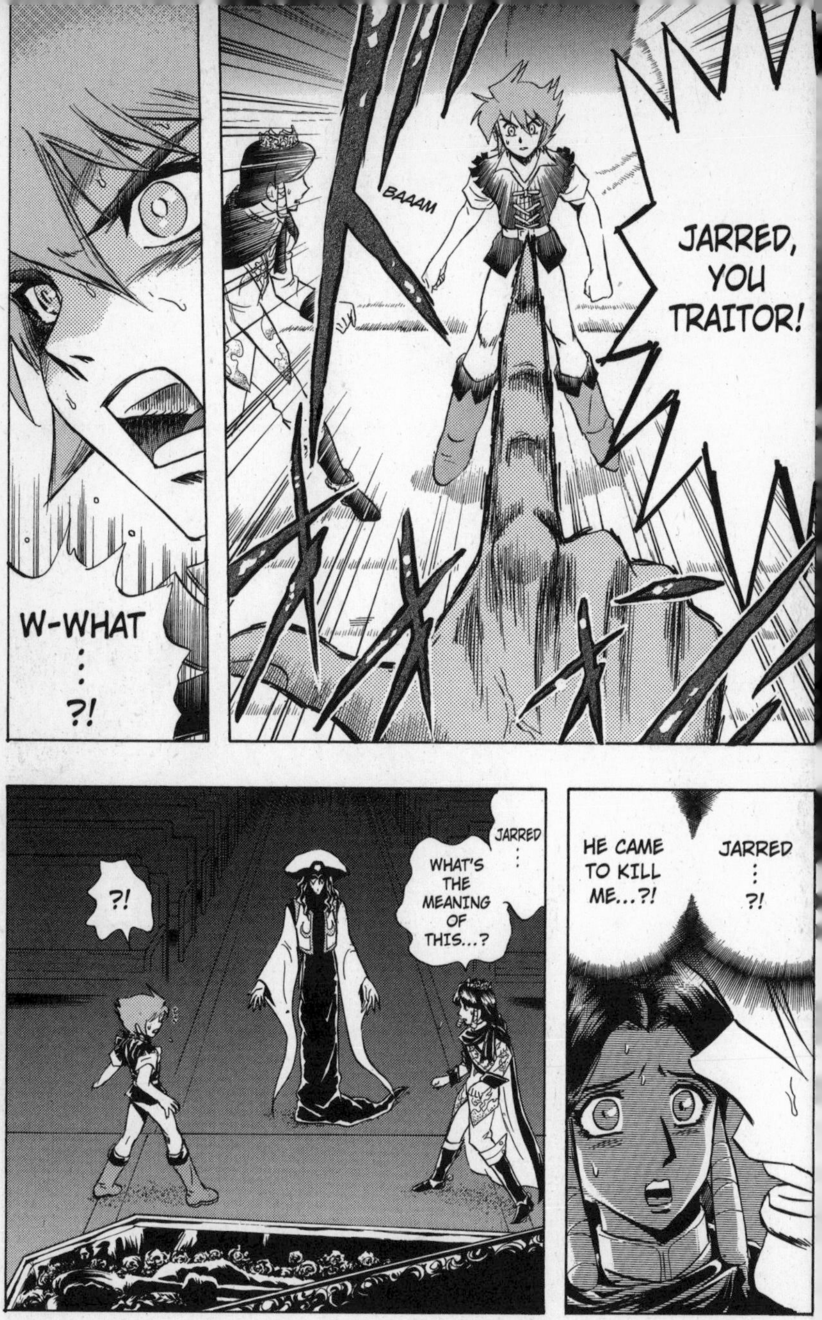
JARRED, YOU TRAITOR!
BAAAM
W-WHAT...?!
JARRED...?!
HE CAME TO KILL ME...?!
JARRED...
WHAT'S THE MEANING OF THIS...?
?!

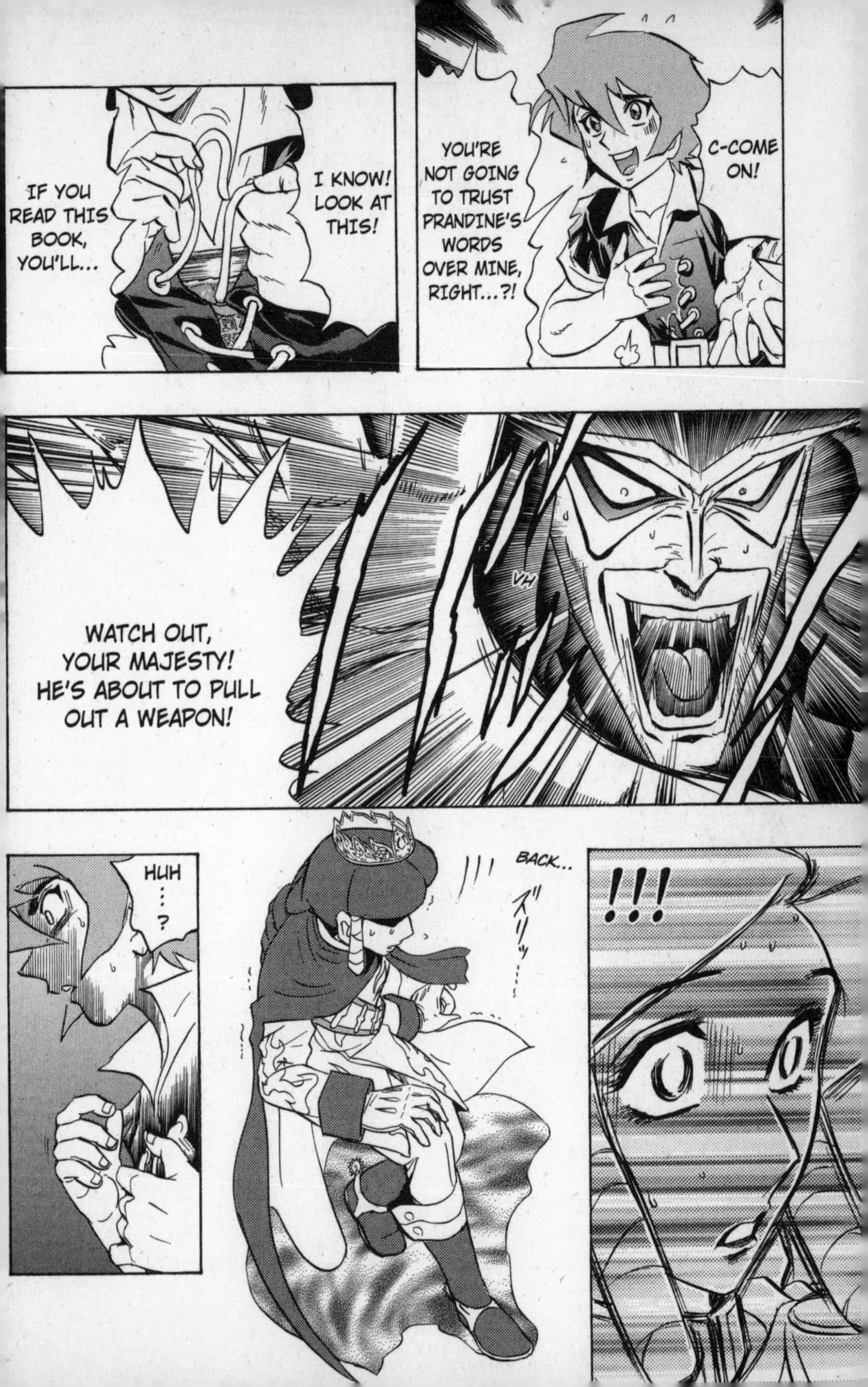
C-COME ON!
YOU'RE NOT GOING TO TRUST PRANDINE'S WORDS OVER MINE, RIGHT...?!
I KNOW! LOOK AT THIS!
IF YOU READ THIS BOOK, YOU'LL...
VH
WATCH OUT, YOUR MAJESTY! HE'S ABOUT TO PULL OUT A WEAPON!
!!!
BACK...
!!!
ズリッ…
HUH...?

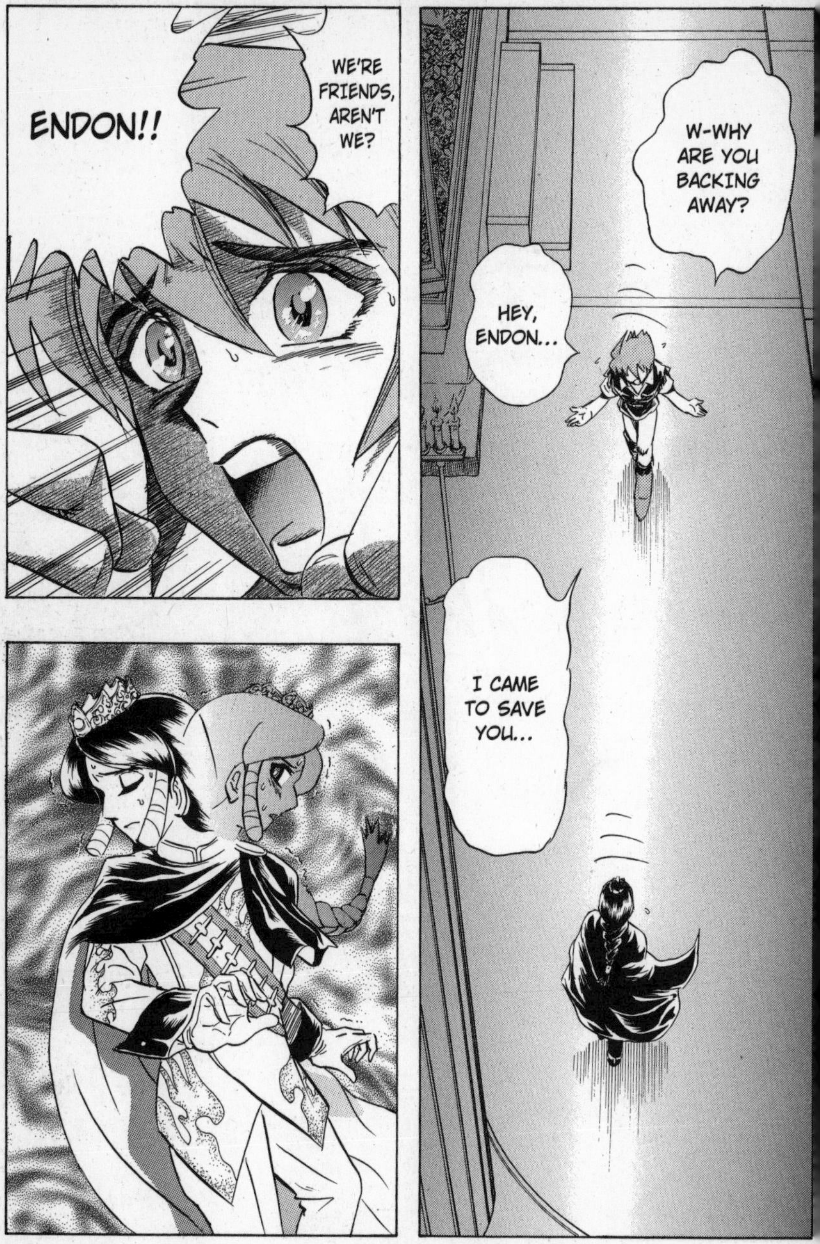
W-WHY ARE YOU BACKING AWAY?
HEY, ENDON...
I CAME TO SAVE YOU...
WE'RE FRIENDS, AREN'T WE?
ENDON!!

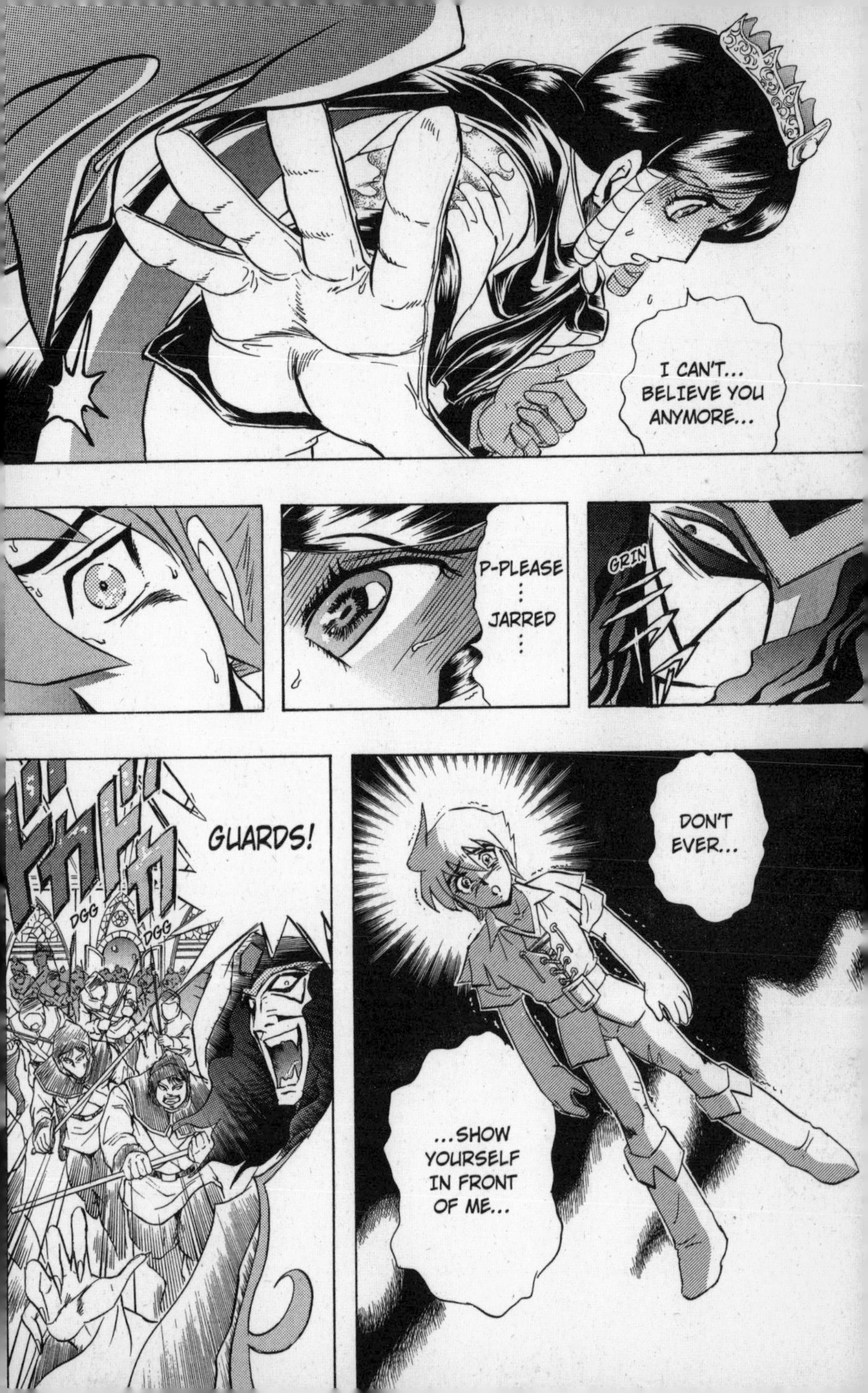
I CAN'T... BELIEVE YOU ANYMORE...
GRIN
P-PLEASE ... JARRED ...
DON'T EVER...
...SHOW YOURSELF IN FRONT OF ME...
GUARDS!
DGG
DGG

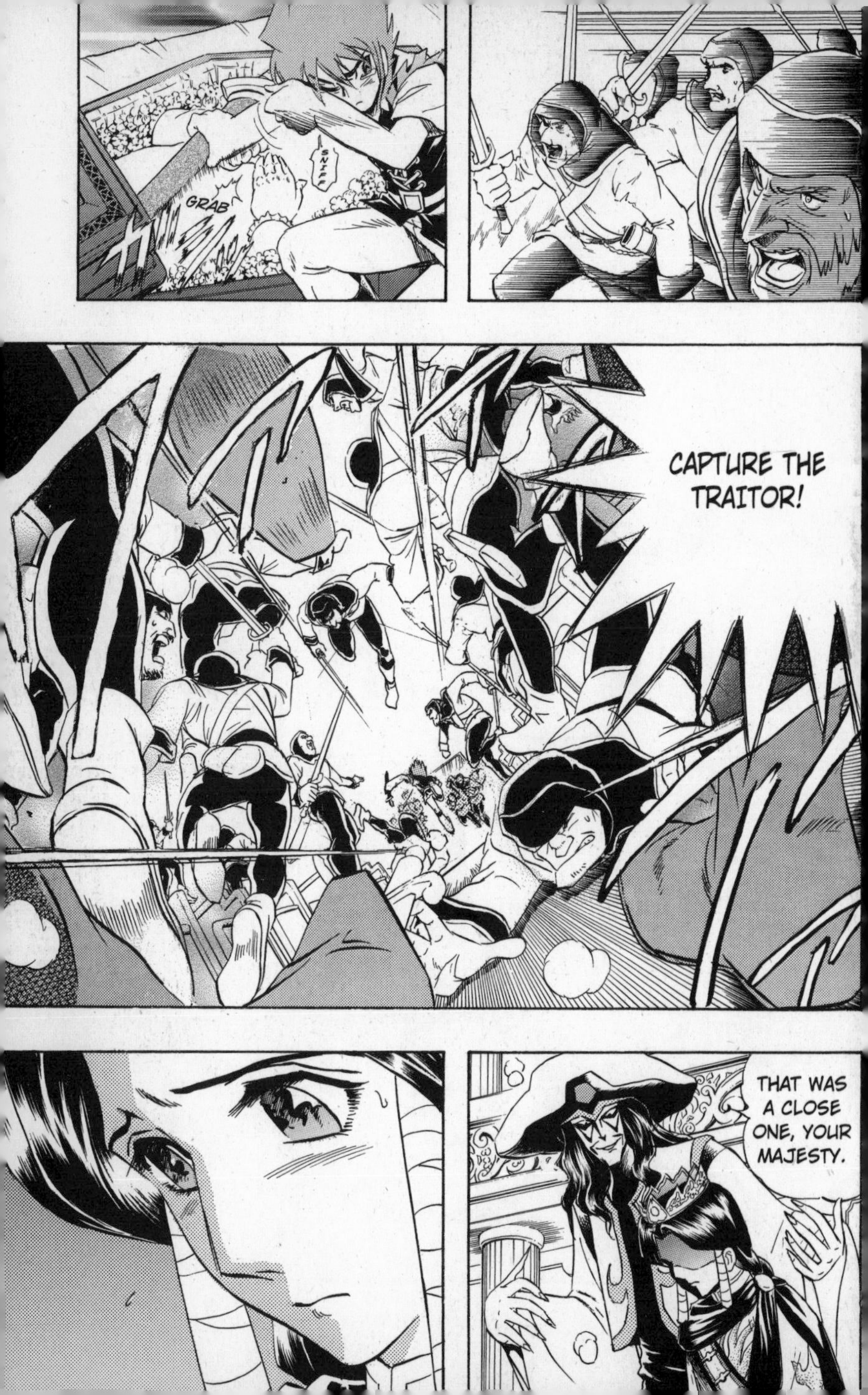
SNIFF
GRAB
CAPTURE THE TRAITOR!
THAT WAS A CLOSE ONE, YOUR MAJESTY.

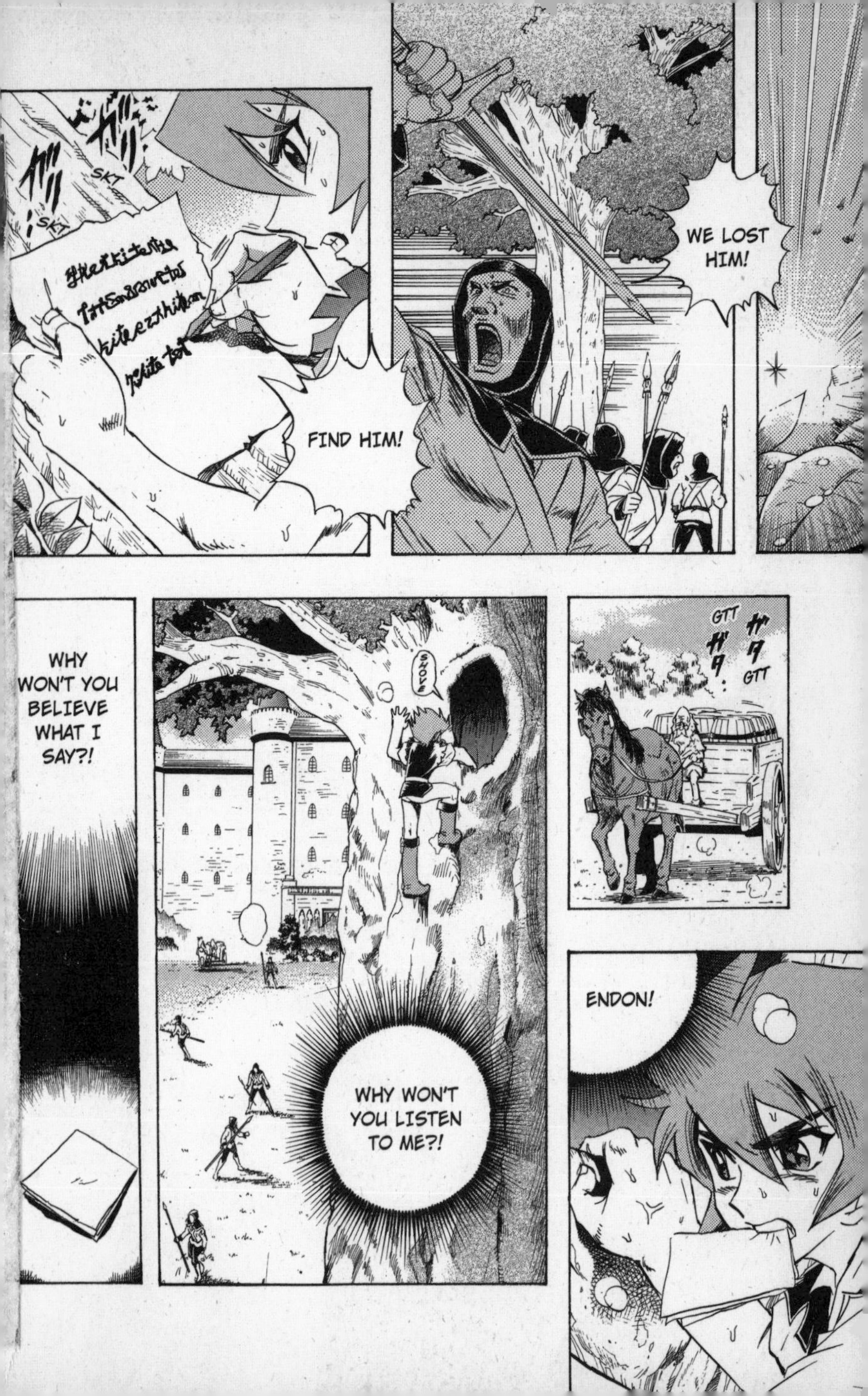

WE LOST HIM!
FIND HIM!
SKT
SKT
GTT
GTT
ENDON!
SHOVE
WHY WON'T YOU LISTEN TO ME?!
WHY WON'T YOU BELIEVE WHAT I SAY?!

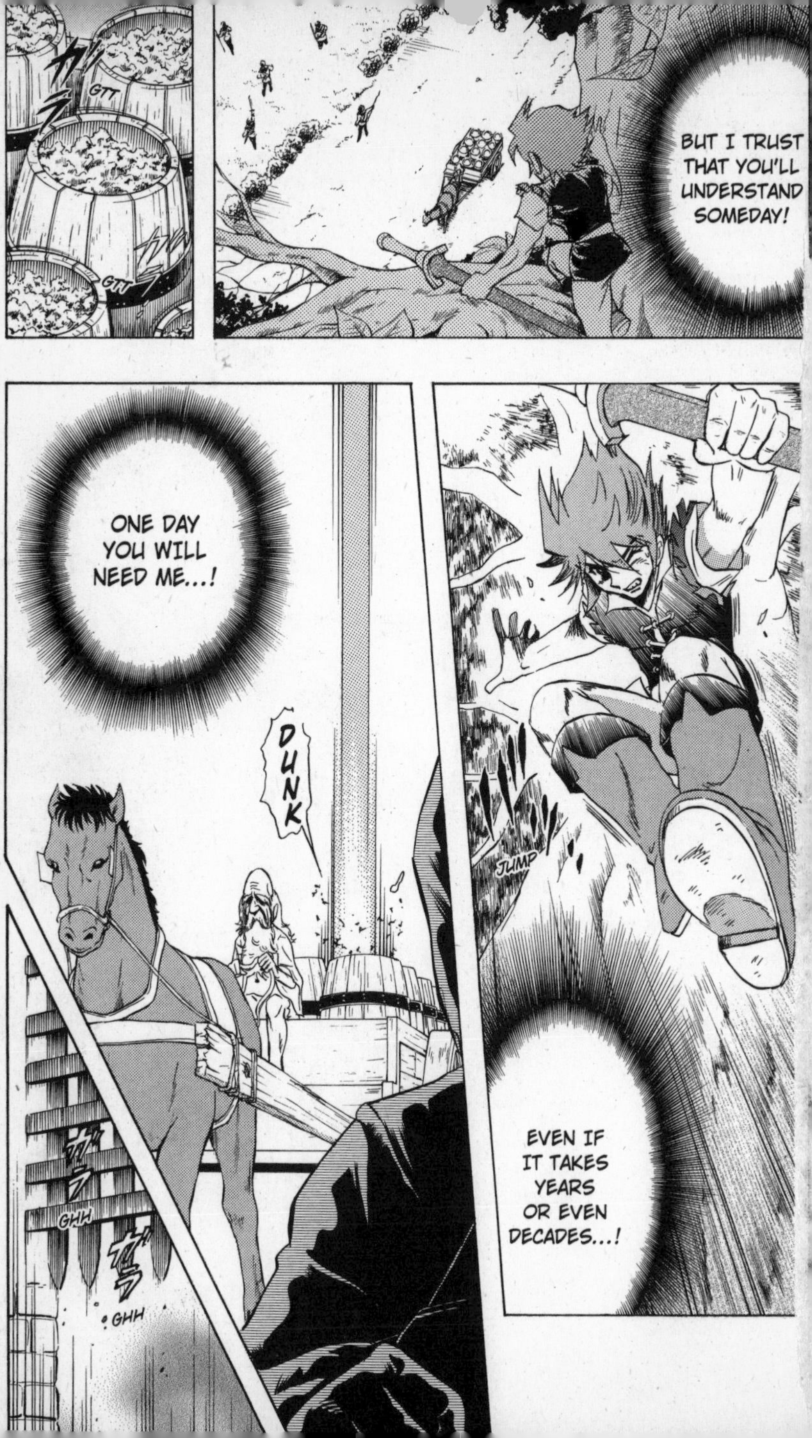
BUT I TRUST THAT YOU'LL UNDERSTAND SOMEDAY!
GTT
GTT
JUMP
EVEN IF IT TAKES YEARS OR EVEN DECADES...!
ONE DAY YOU WILL NEED ME...!
DUNK
GHH
GHH

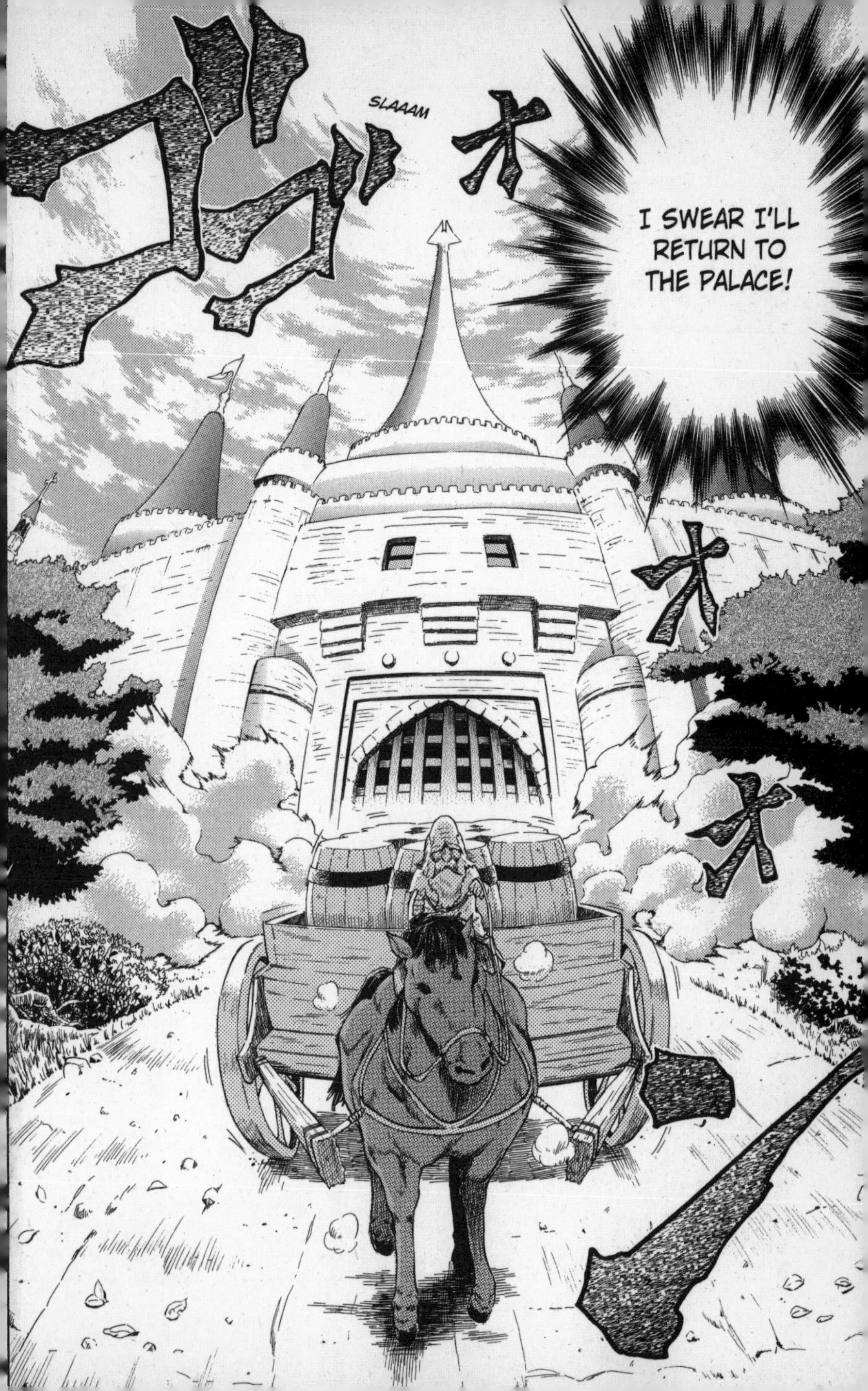
SLAAAM
I SWEAR I'LL RETURN TO THE PALACE!

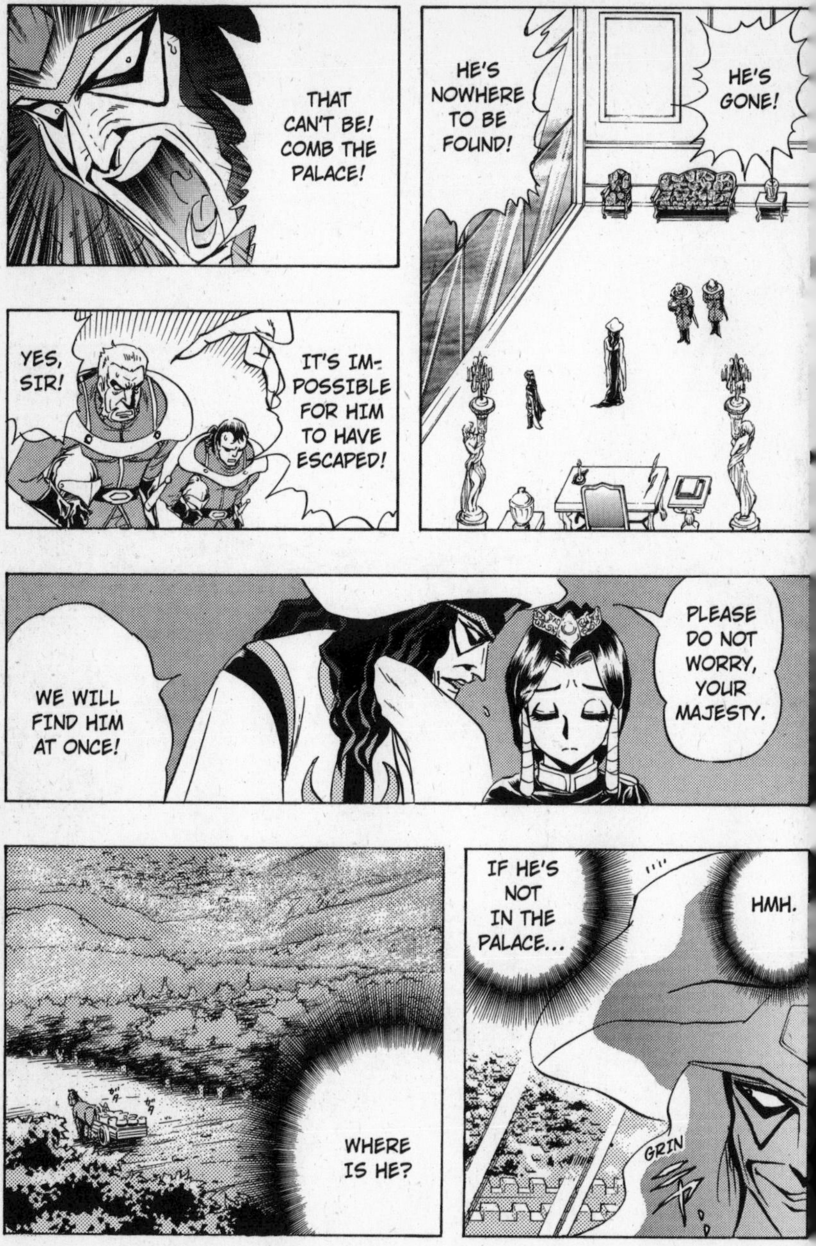
HE'S GONE!
HE'S NOWHERE TO BE FOUND!
THAT CAN'T BE! COMB THE PALACE!
IT'S IM-POSSIBLE FOR HIM TO HAVE ESCAPED!
YES, SIR!
PLEASE DO NOT WORRY, YOUR MAJESTY.
WE WILL FIND HIM AT ONCE!
HMH.
IF HE'S NOT IN THE PALACE...
GRIN
WHERE IS HE?

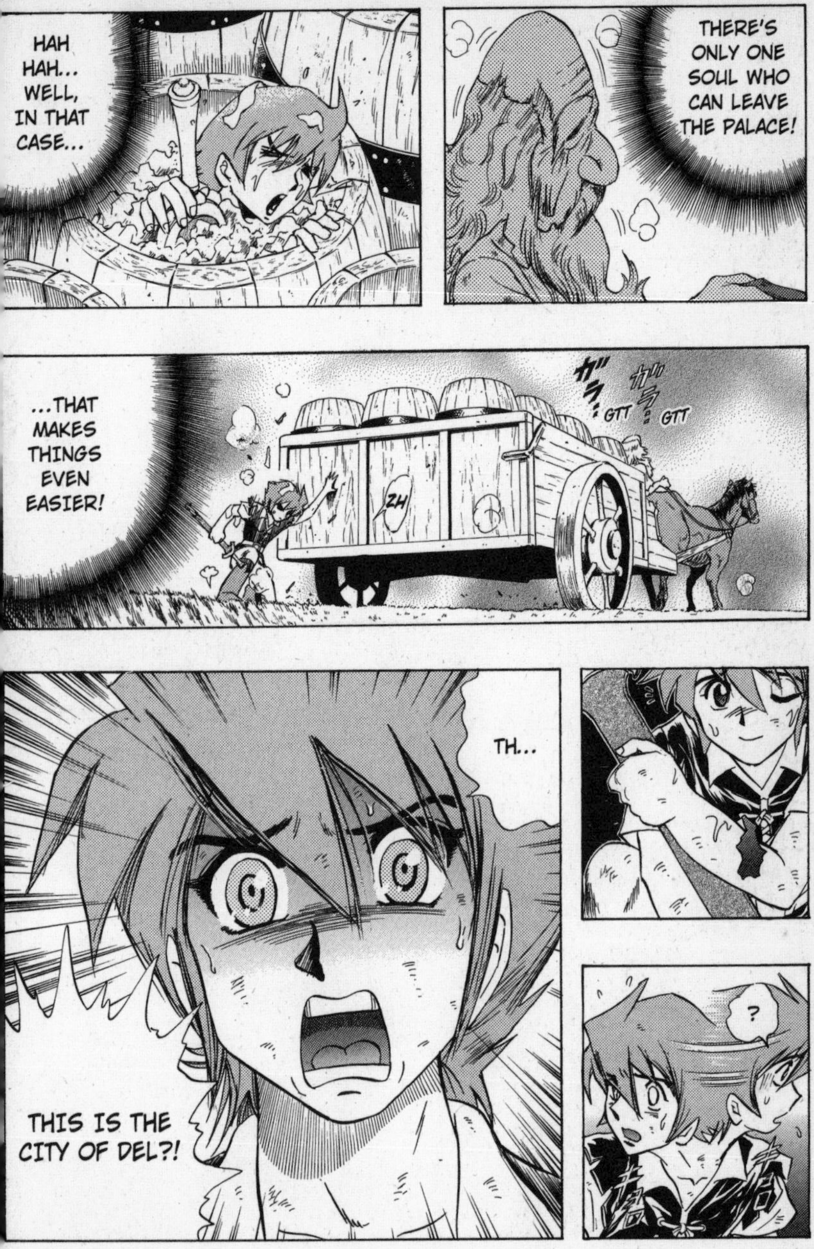
THERE'S ONLY ONE SOUL WHO CAN LEAVE THE PALACE!
HAH HAH... WELL, IN THAT CASE...
ガラ GTT
ガラ GTT
...THAT MAKES THINGS EVEN EASIER!
ZH
?
TH...
THIS IS THE CITY OF DEL?!

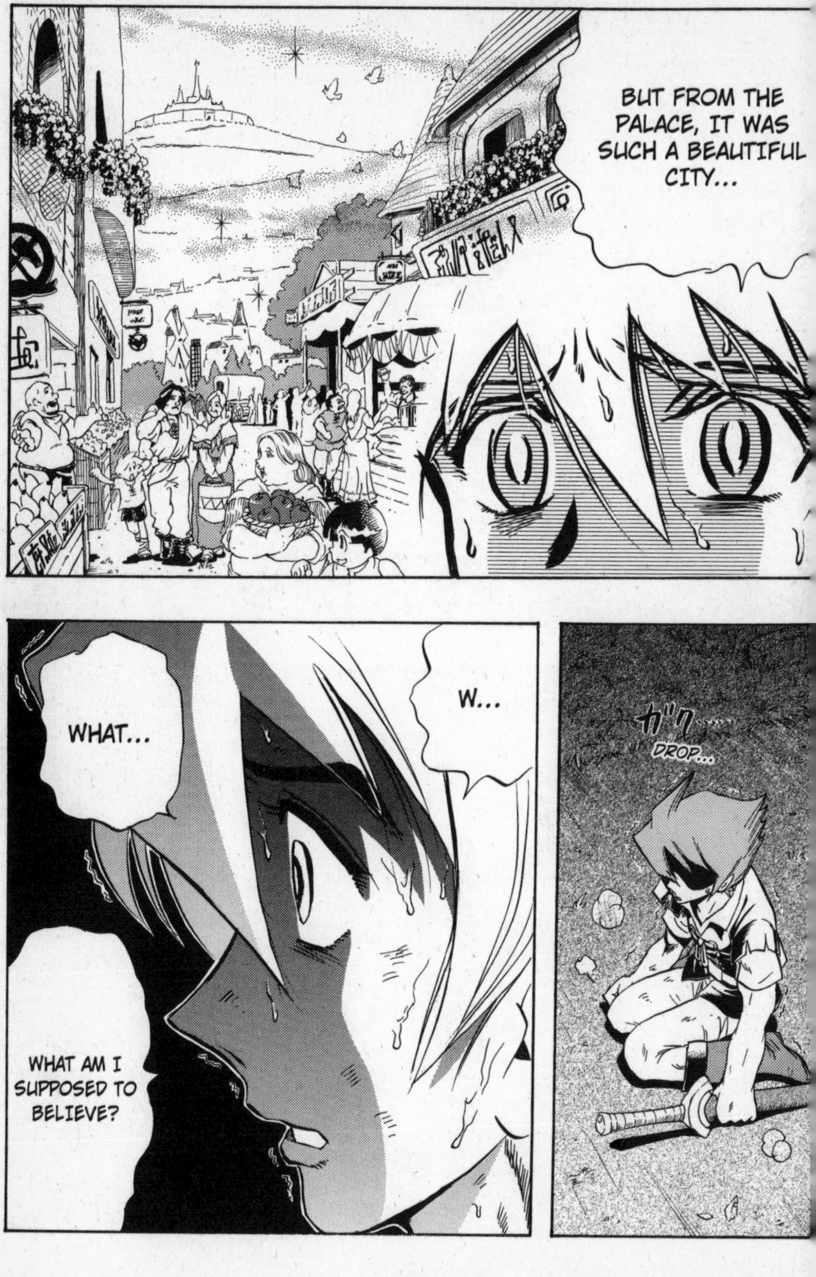
BUT FROM THE PALACE, IT WAS SUCH A BEAUTIFUL CITY...
ガク...
DROP...
W...
WHAT...
WHAT AM I SUPPOSED TO BELIEVE?

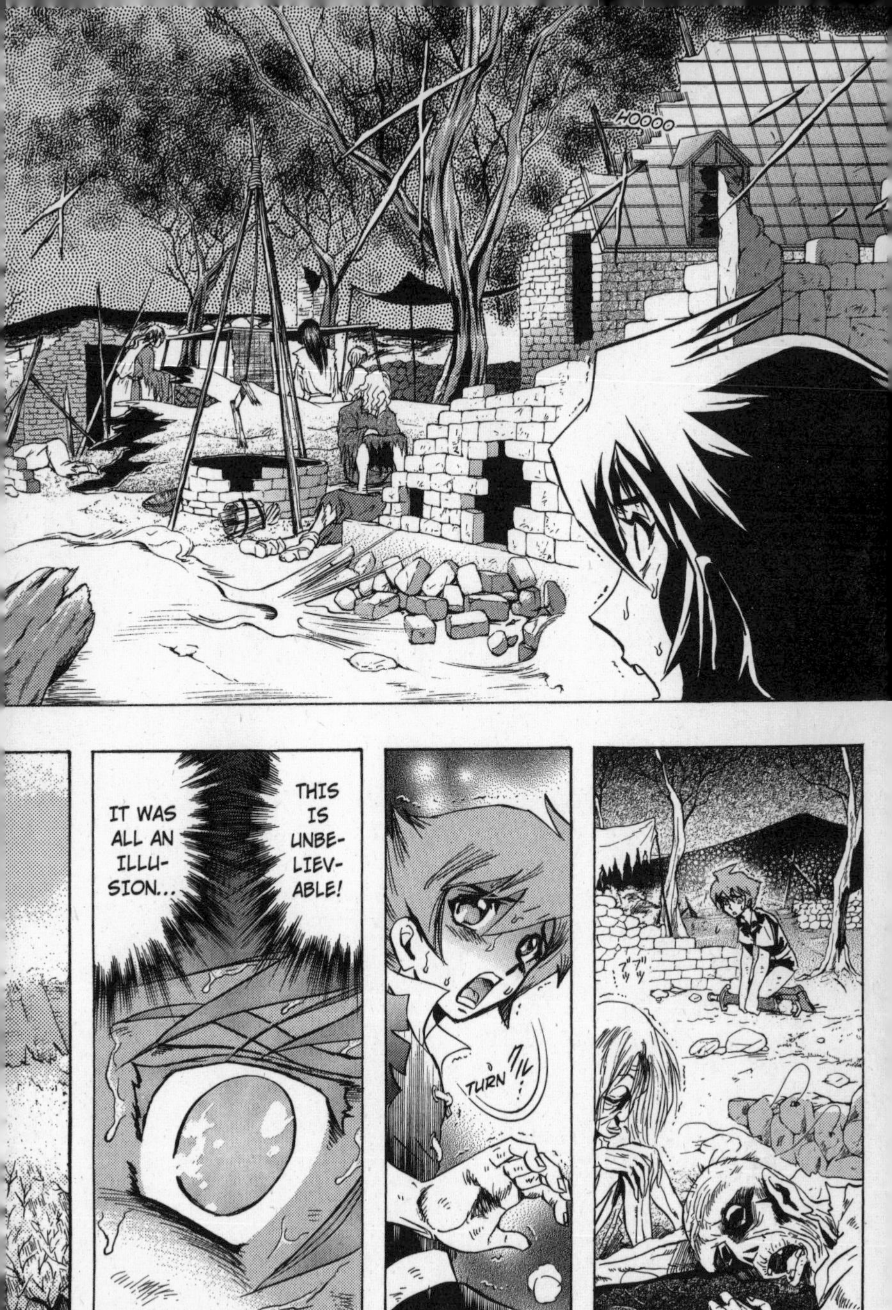
HOOOO
TURN
THIS IS UNBELIEVABLE!
IT WAS ALL AN ILLUSION...

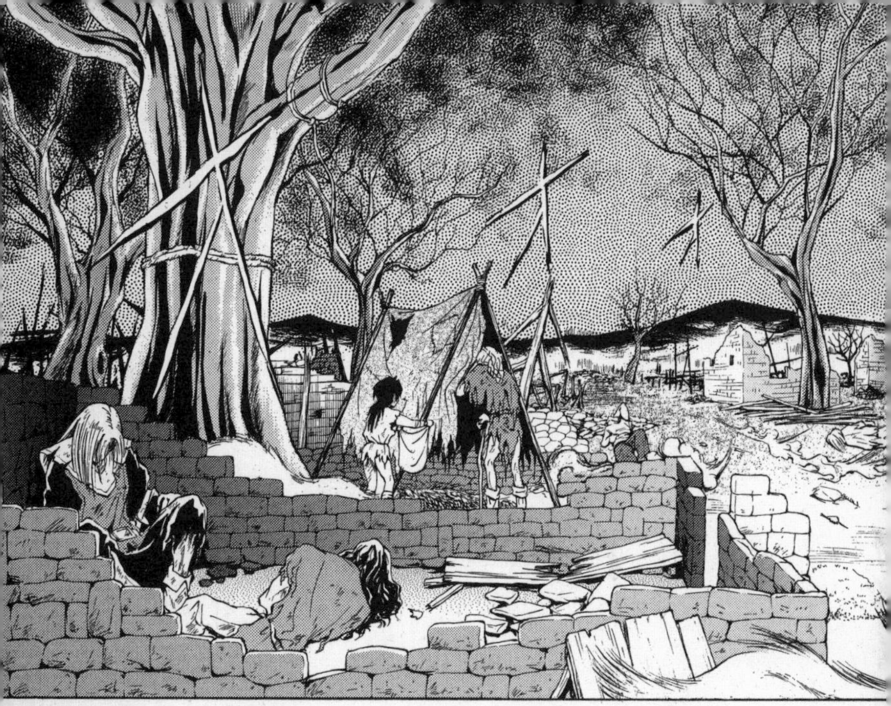

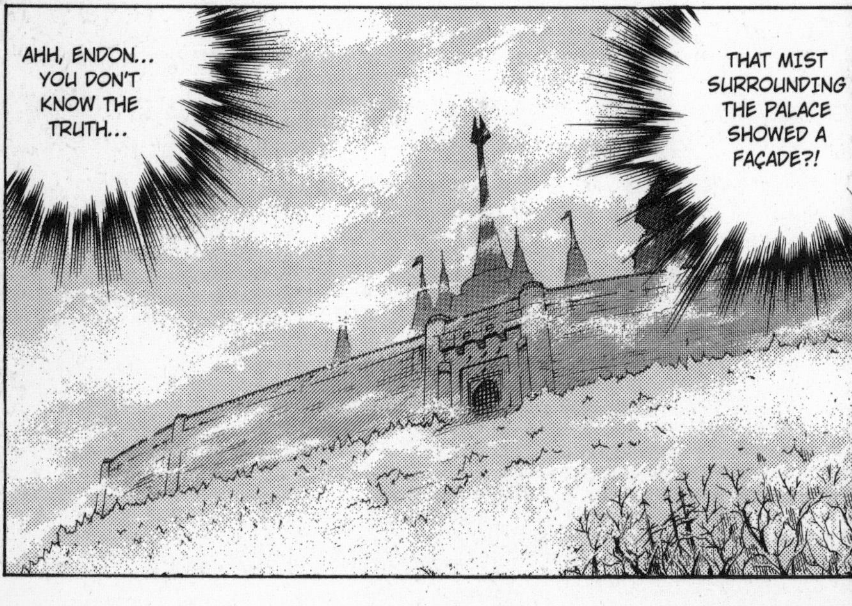
THAT MIST SURROUNDING THE PALACE SHOWED A FAÇADE?!
AHH, ENDON... YOU DON'T KNOW THE TRUTH...

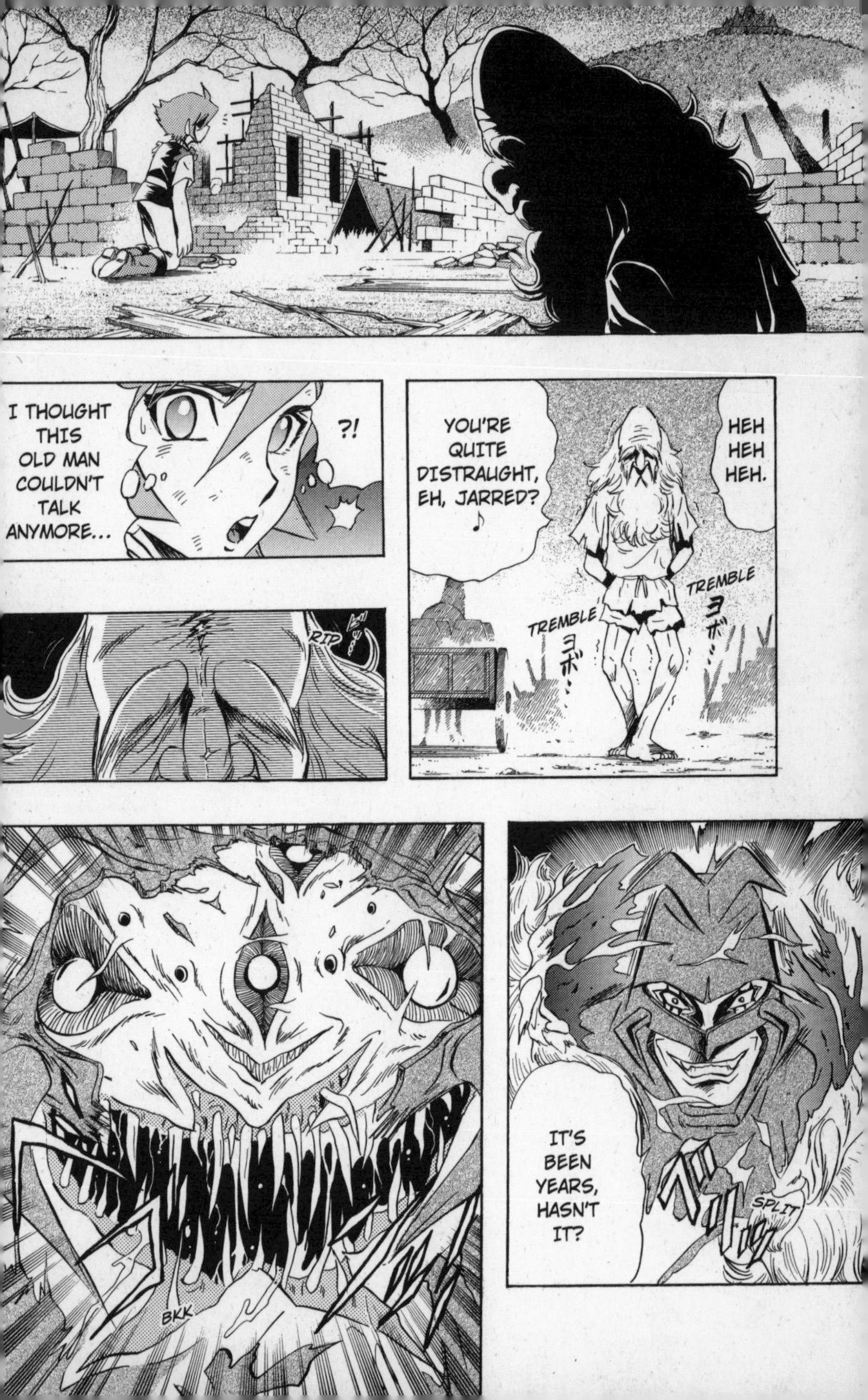
HEH HEH HEH.
YOU'RE QUITE DISTRAUGHT, EH, JARRED? ♪
TREMBLE
ヨボ
TREMBLE
ヨボ
?!
I THOUGHT THIS OLD MAN COULDN'T TALK ANYMORE...
RIP
IT'S BEEN YEARS, HASN'T IT?
SPLIT
BKK

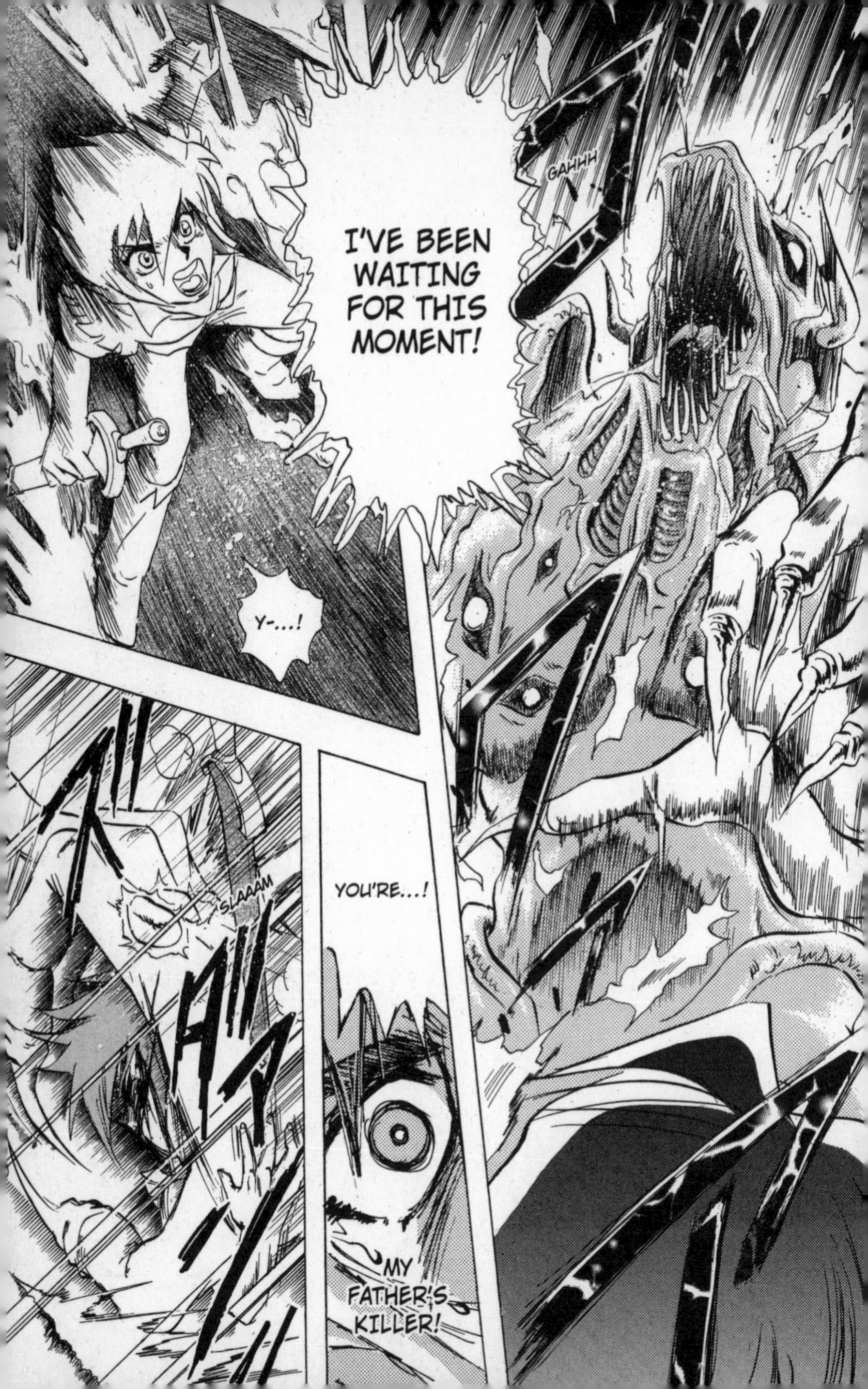
GAHHH
I'VE BEEN WAITING FOR THIS MOMENT!
Y-...!
YOU'RE...!
MY FATHER'S KILLER!
SLAAAM

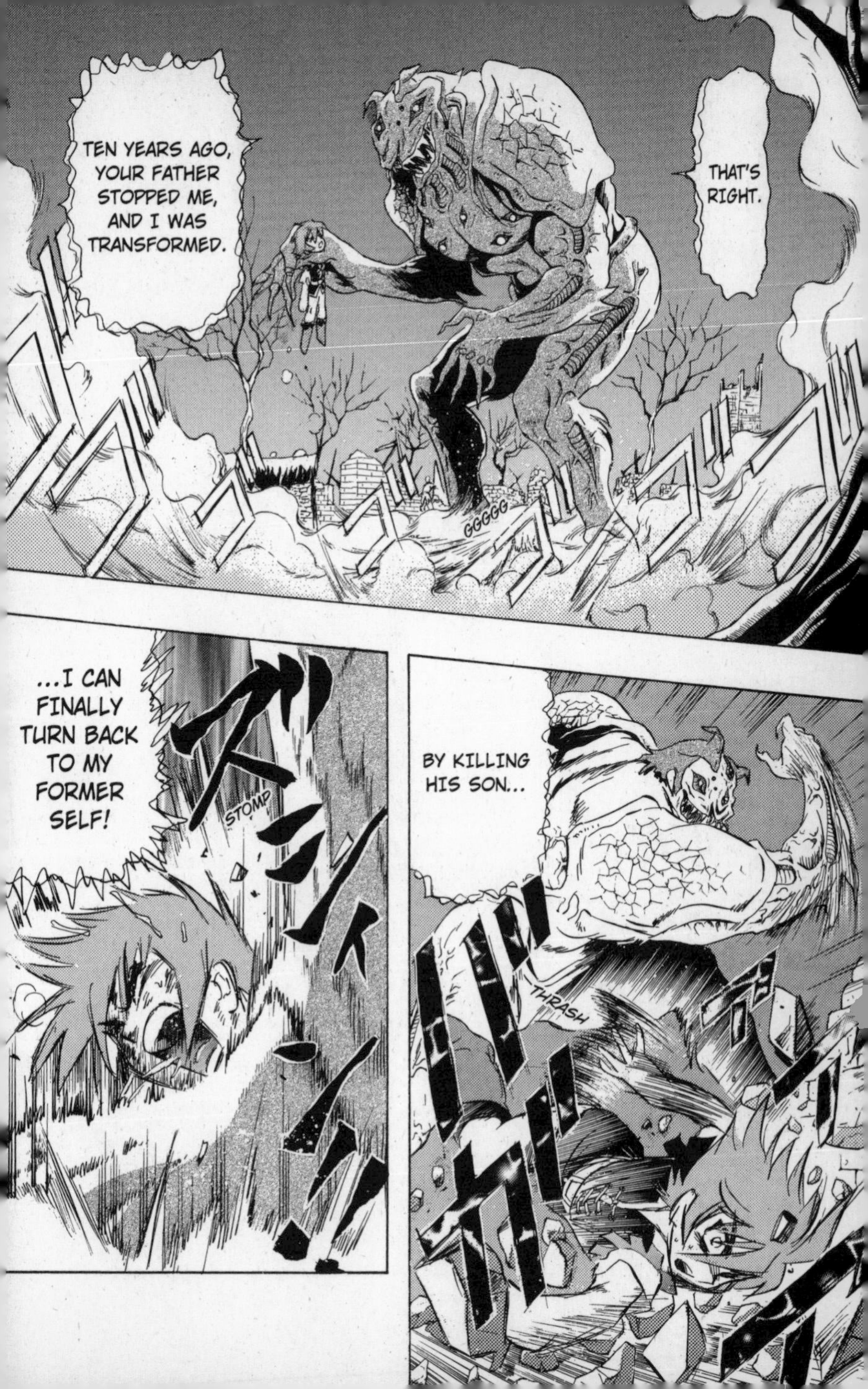
THAT'S RIGHT.
TEN YEARS AGO, YOUR FATHER STOPPED ME, AND I WAS TRANSFORMED.
GGGGG
BY KILLING HIS SON...
THRASH
...I CAN FINALLY TURN BACK TO MY FORMER SELF!
STOMP

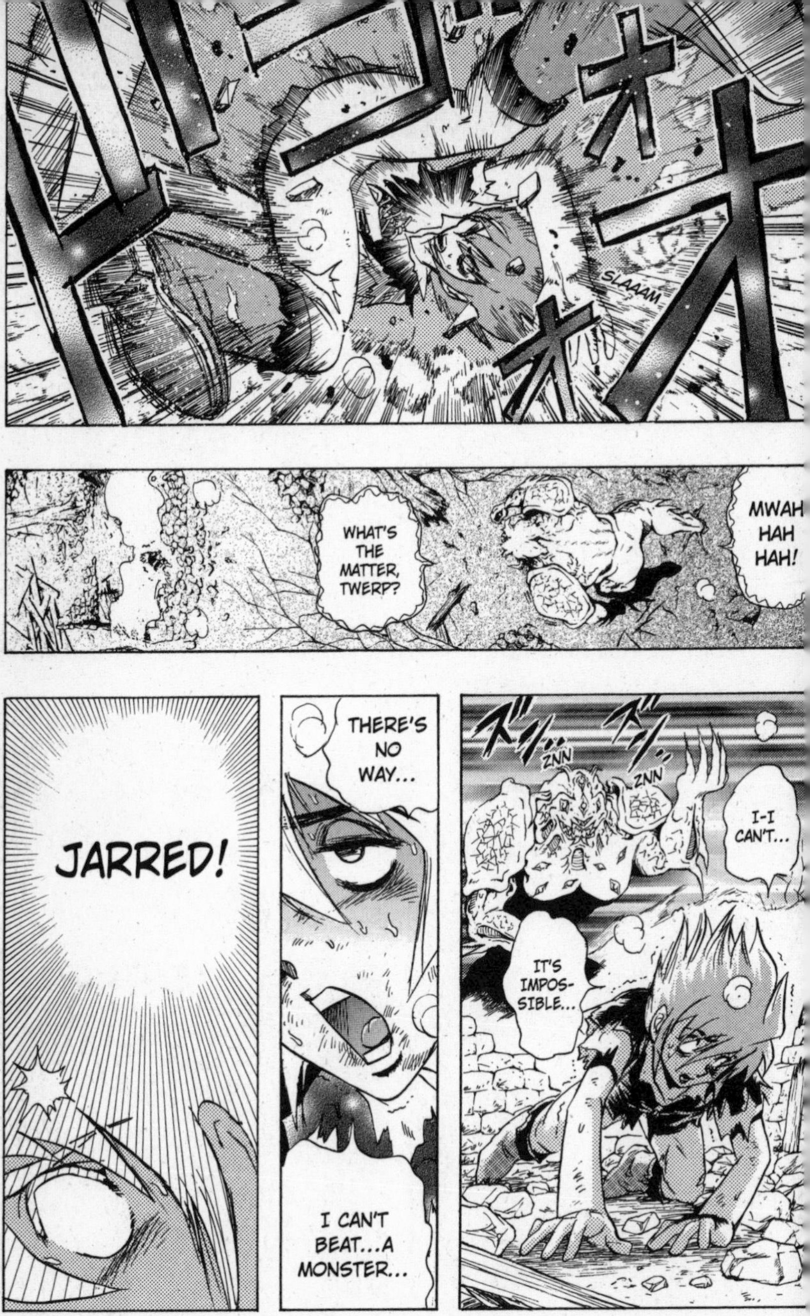
SLAAAM
MWAH HAH HAH!
WHAT'S THE MATTER, TWERP?
ZNN
ZNN
I-I CAN'T...
IT'S IMPOS-SIBLE...
THERE'S NO WAY...
I CAN'T BEAT...A MONSTER...
JARRED!

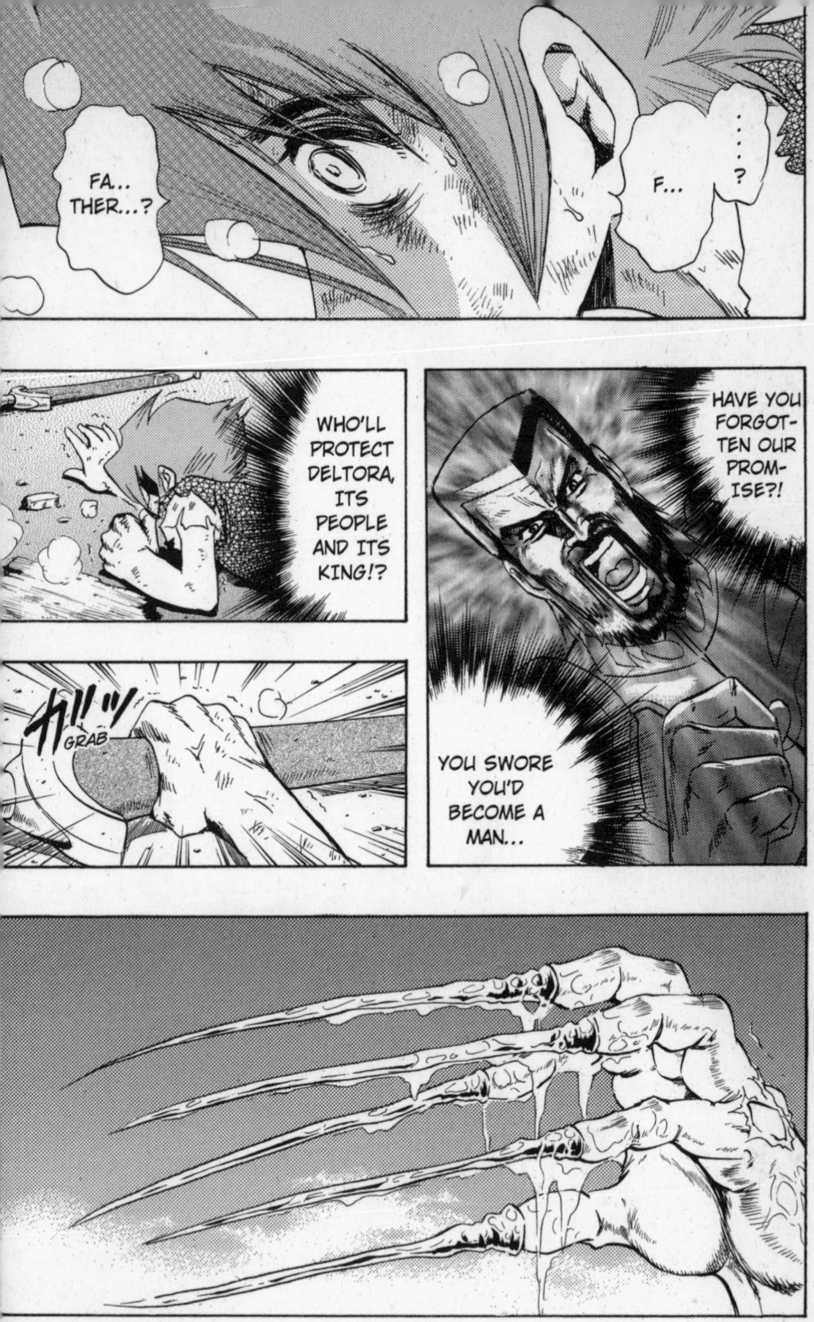
F... ....?
FA... THER...?
HAVE YOU FORGOT-TEN OUR PROM-ISE?!
YOU SWORE YOU'D BECOME A MAN...
WHO'LL PROTECT DELTORA, ITS PEOPLE AND ITS KING!?
カ!!ッ
GRAB

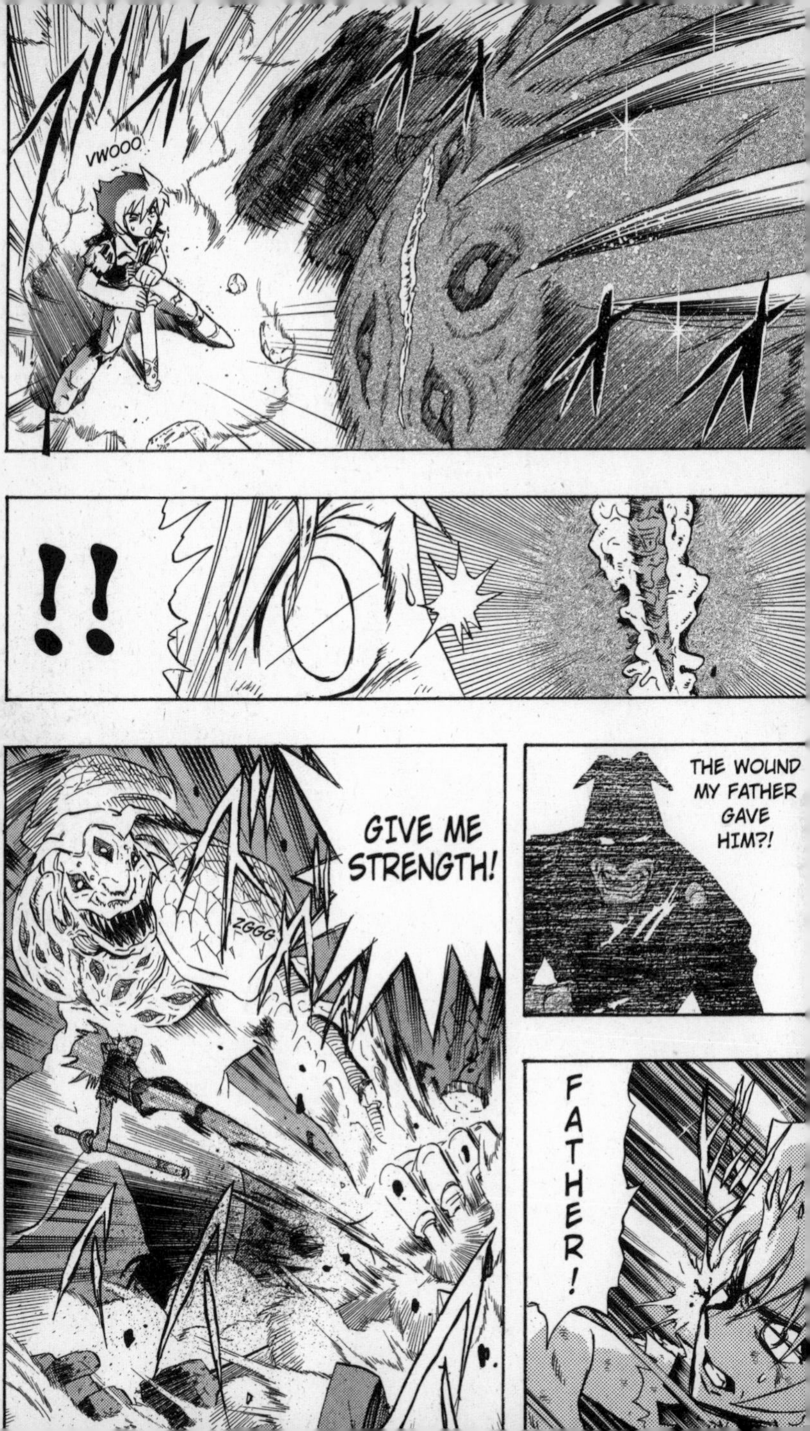
VWOOO
!!
THE WOUND MY FATHER GAVE HIM?!
FATHER!
GIVE ME STRENGTH!
ZGGG

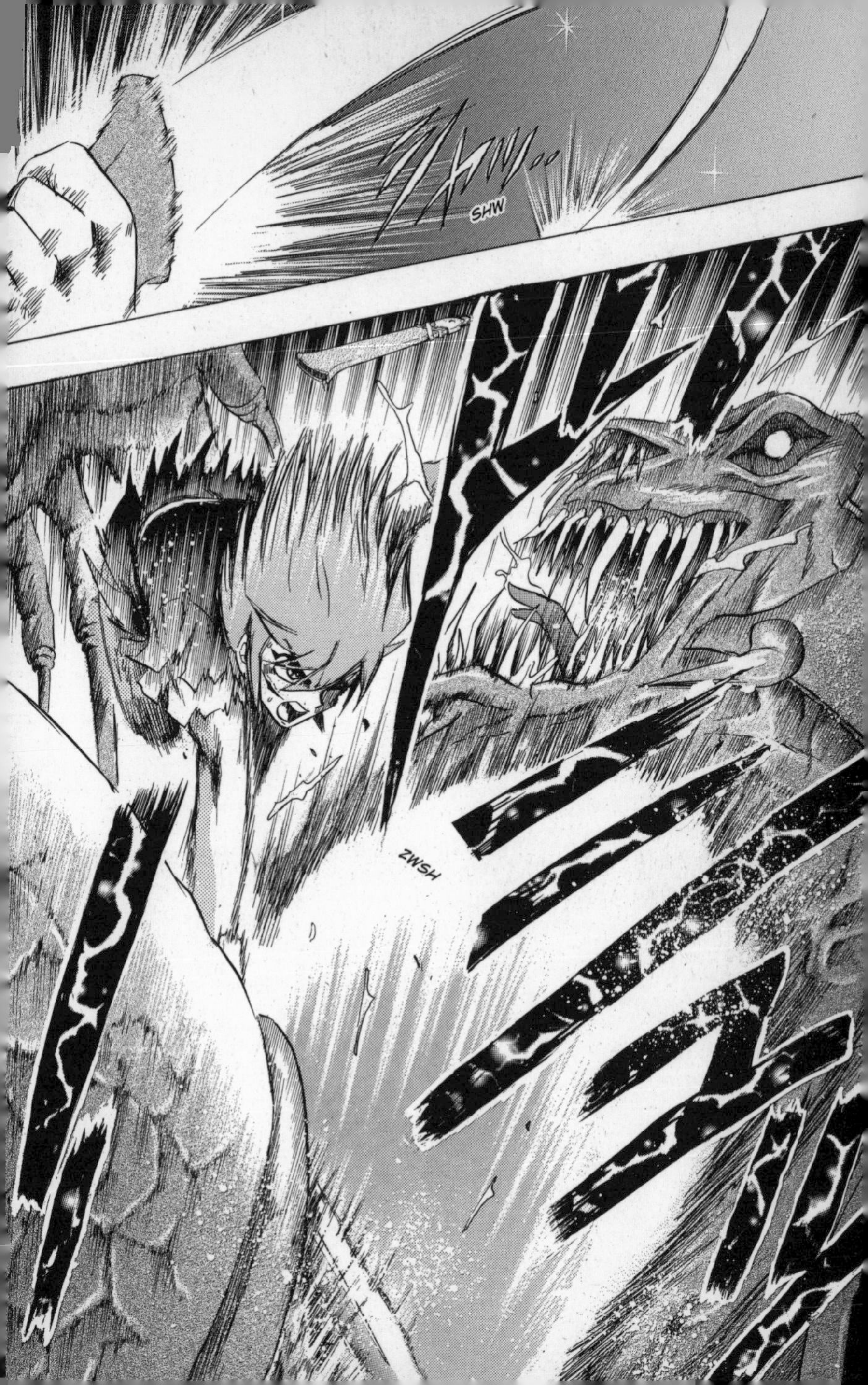
SHW
ZWSH

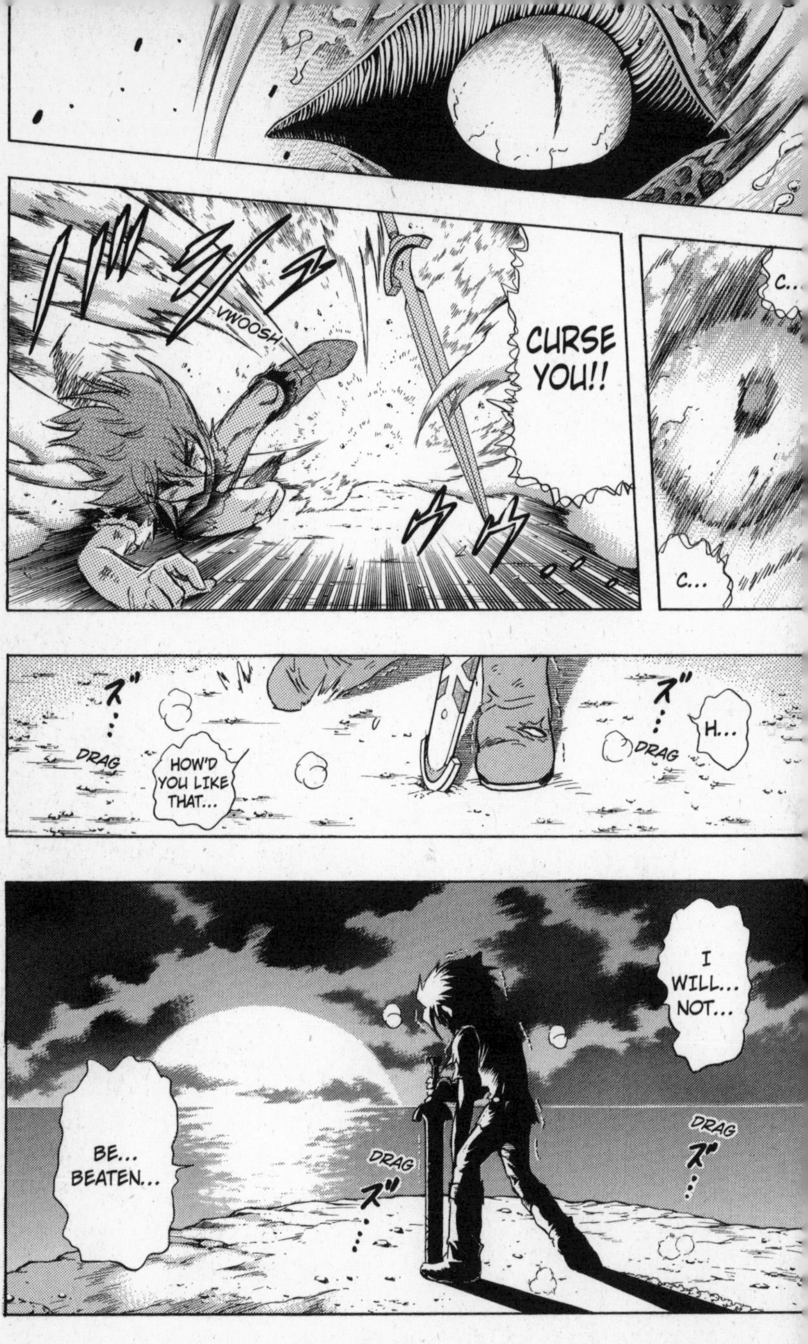
C...
C...
CURSE YOU!!
VWOOSH
H...
DRAG
HOW'D YOU LIKE THAT...
DRAG
I WILL... NOT...
DRAG
DRAG
BE... BEATEN...

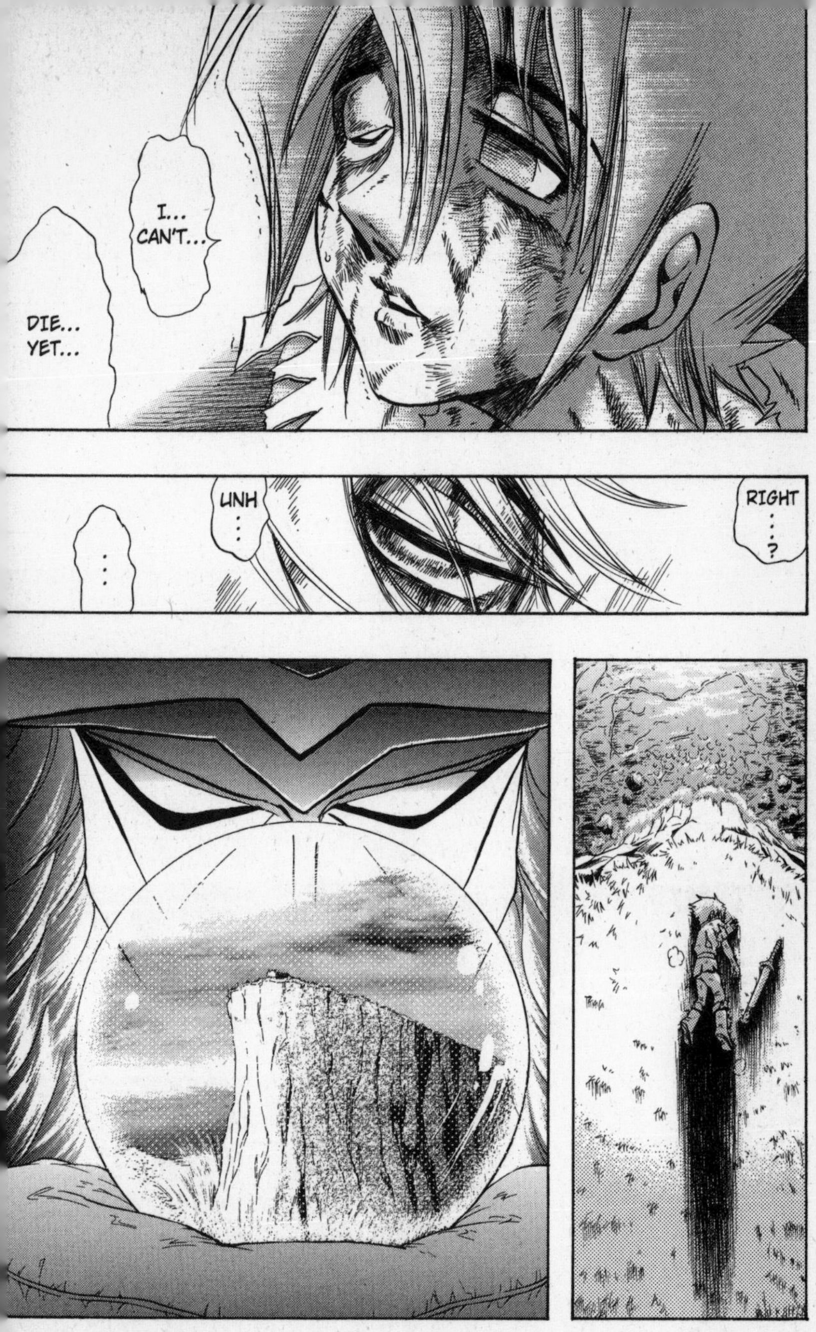
I... CAN'T...
DIE... YET...
RIGHT...?
UNH...
...

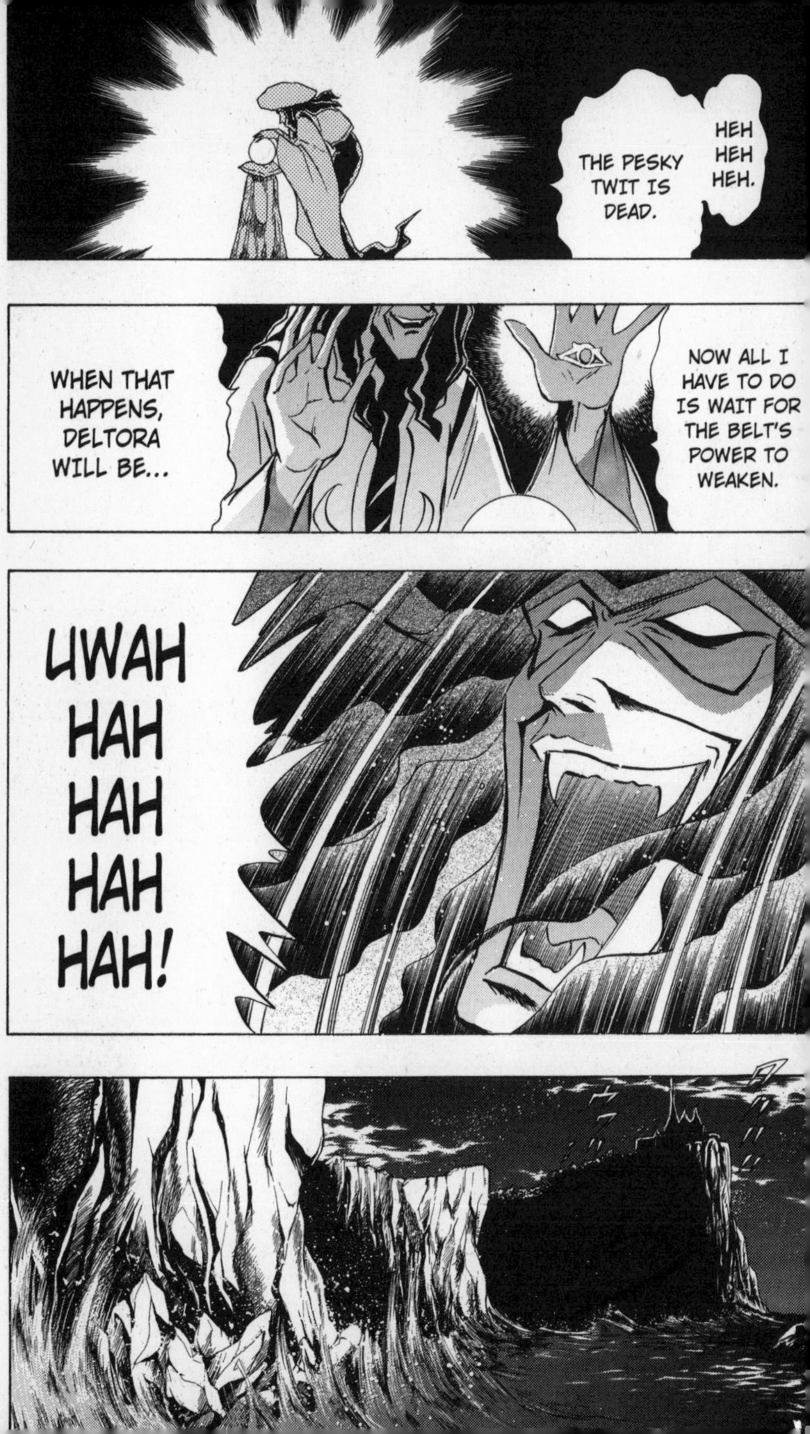
HEH HEH HEH.
THE PESKY TWIT IS DEAD.
NOW ALL I HAVE TO DO IS WAIT FOR THE BELT'S POWER TO WEAKEN.
WHEN THAT HAPPENS, DELTORA WILL BE...
UWAH HAH HAH HAH HAH!

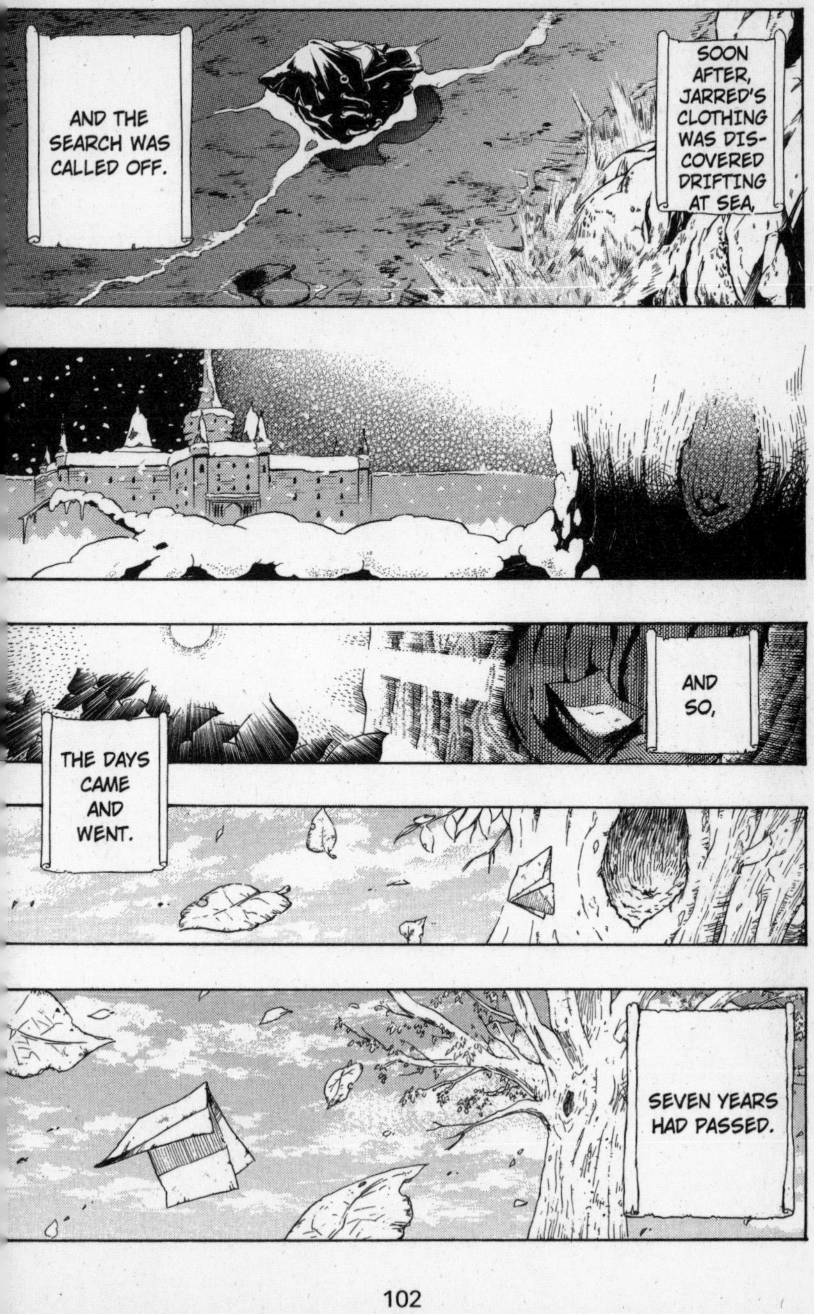
SOON AFTER, JARRED'S CLOTHING WAS DIS-COVERED DRIFTING AT SEA,
AND THE SEARCH WAS CALLED OFF.
AND SO,
THE DAYS CAME AND WENT.
SEVEN YEARS HAD PASSED.

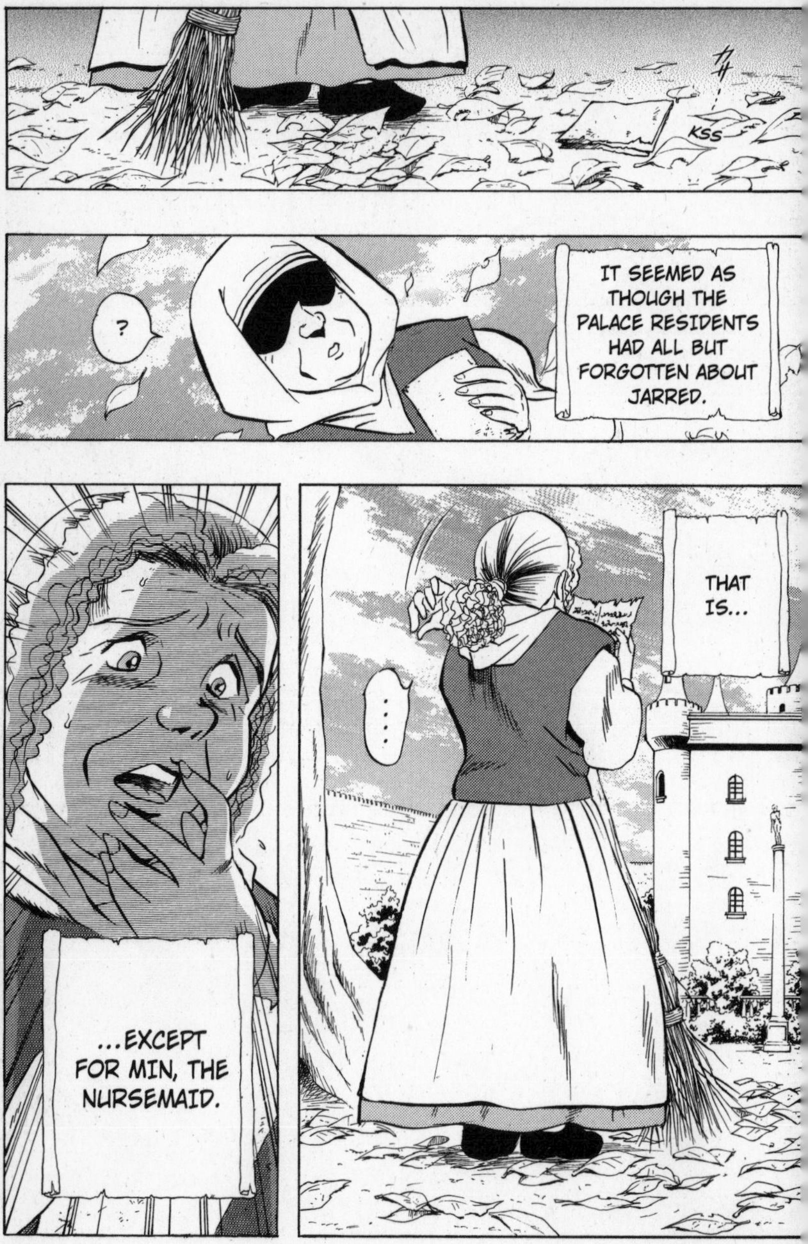
KSS
IT SEEMED AS THOUGH THE PALACE RESIDENTS HAD ALL BUT FORGOTTEN ABOUT JARRED.
?
THAT IS...
.....
...EXCEPT FOR MIN, THE NURSEMAID.

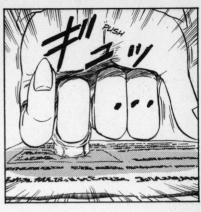

PUSH

PRAN-
DINE!

GYU...

HOW IS
THE CITY?

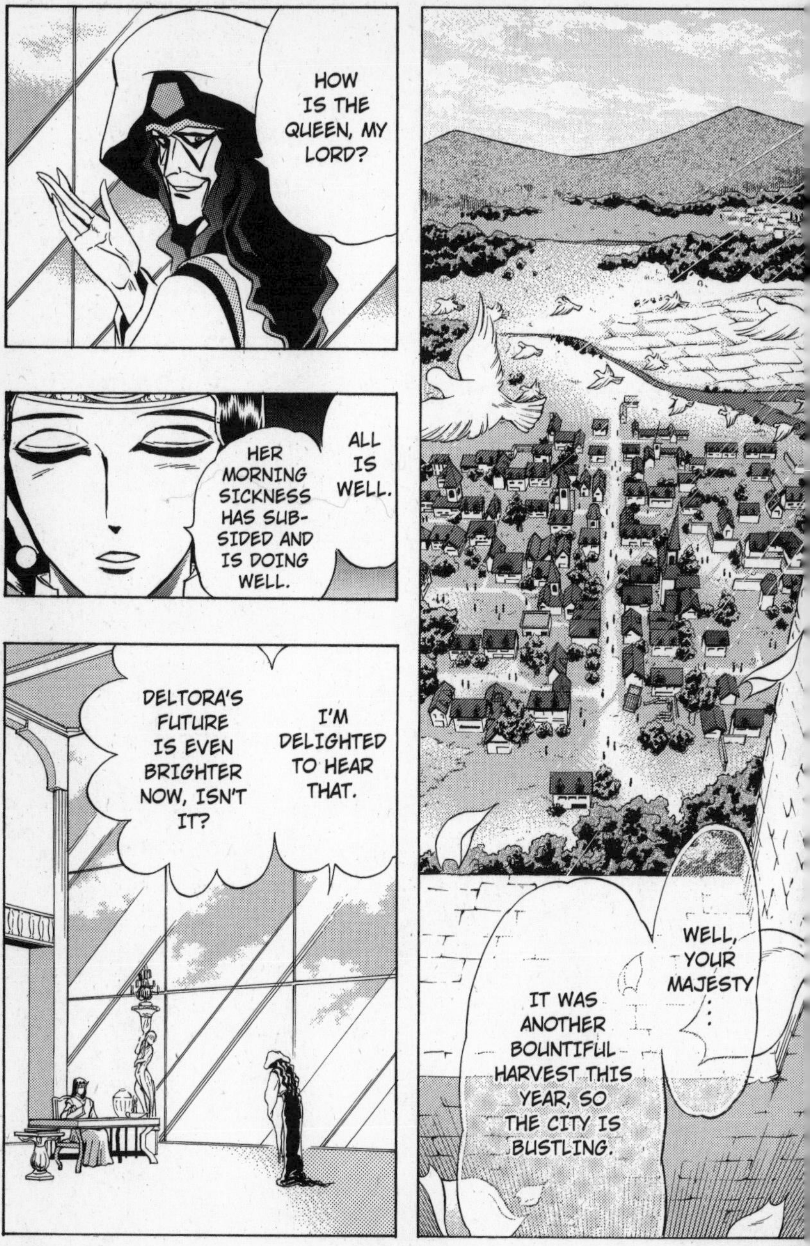
WELL, YOUR MAJESTY...
IT WAS ANOTHER BOUNTIFUL HARVEST THIS YEAR, SO THE CITY IS BUSTLING.
HOW IS THE QUEEN, MY LORD?
ALL IS WELL.
HER MORNING SICKNESS HAS SUB-SIDED AND IS DOING WELL.
I'M DELIGHTED TO HEAR THAT.
DELTORA'S FUTURE IS EVEN BRIGHTER NOW, ISN'T IT?

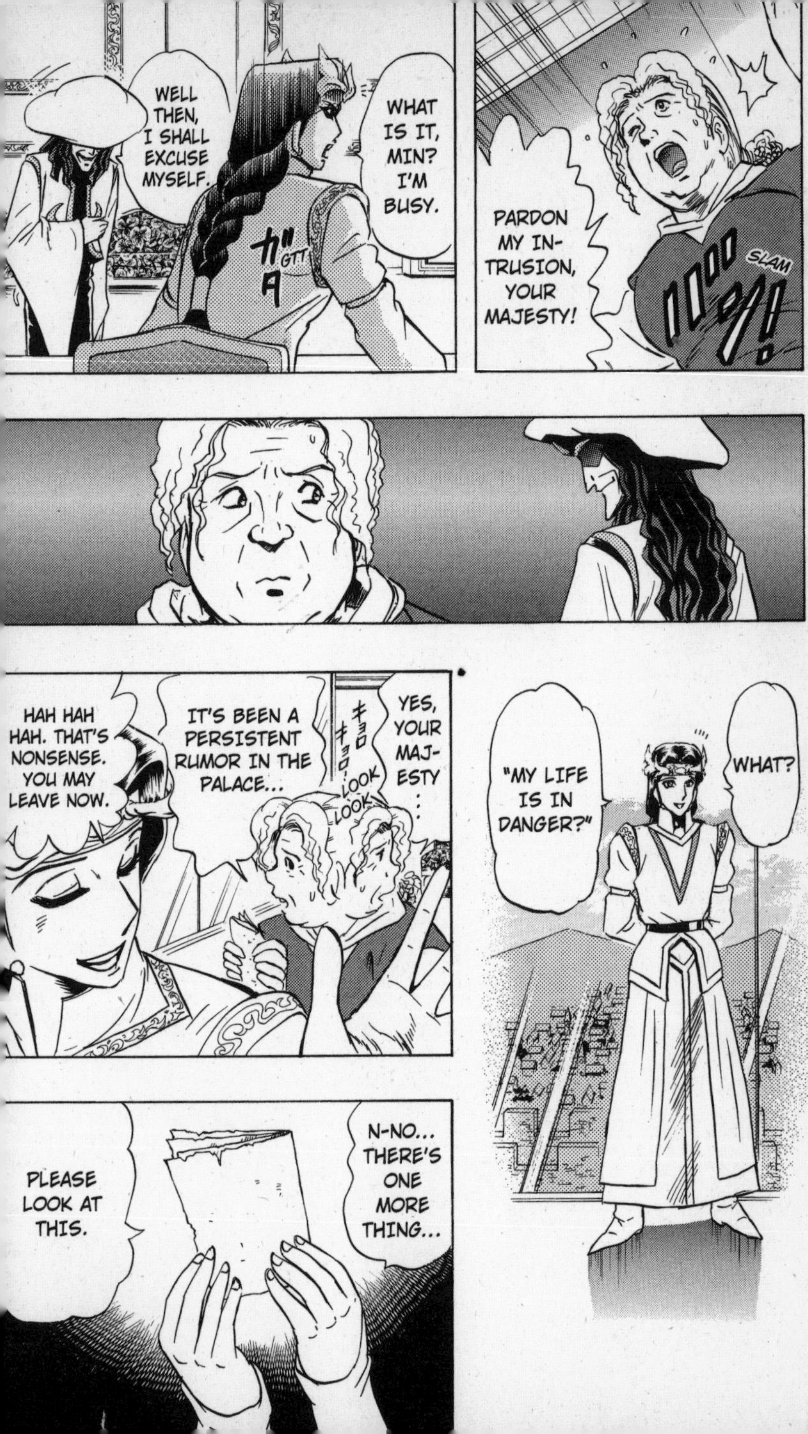
PARDON MY IN-TRUSION, YOUR MAJESTY!
SLAM
WHAT IS IT, MIN? I'M BUSY.
ガタ
GTT
WELL THEN, I SHALL EXCUSE MYSELF.
WHAT?
"MY LIFE IS IN DANGER?"
YES, YOUR MAJ-ESTY . . .
キョロキョロ
LOOK LOOK
IT'S BEEN A PERSISTENT RUMOR IN THE PALACE...
HAH HAH HAH. THAT'S NONSENSE. YOU MAY LEAVE NOW.
N-NO... THERE'S ONE MORE THING...
PLEASE LOOK AT THIS.

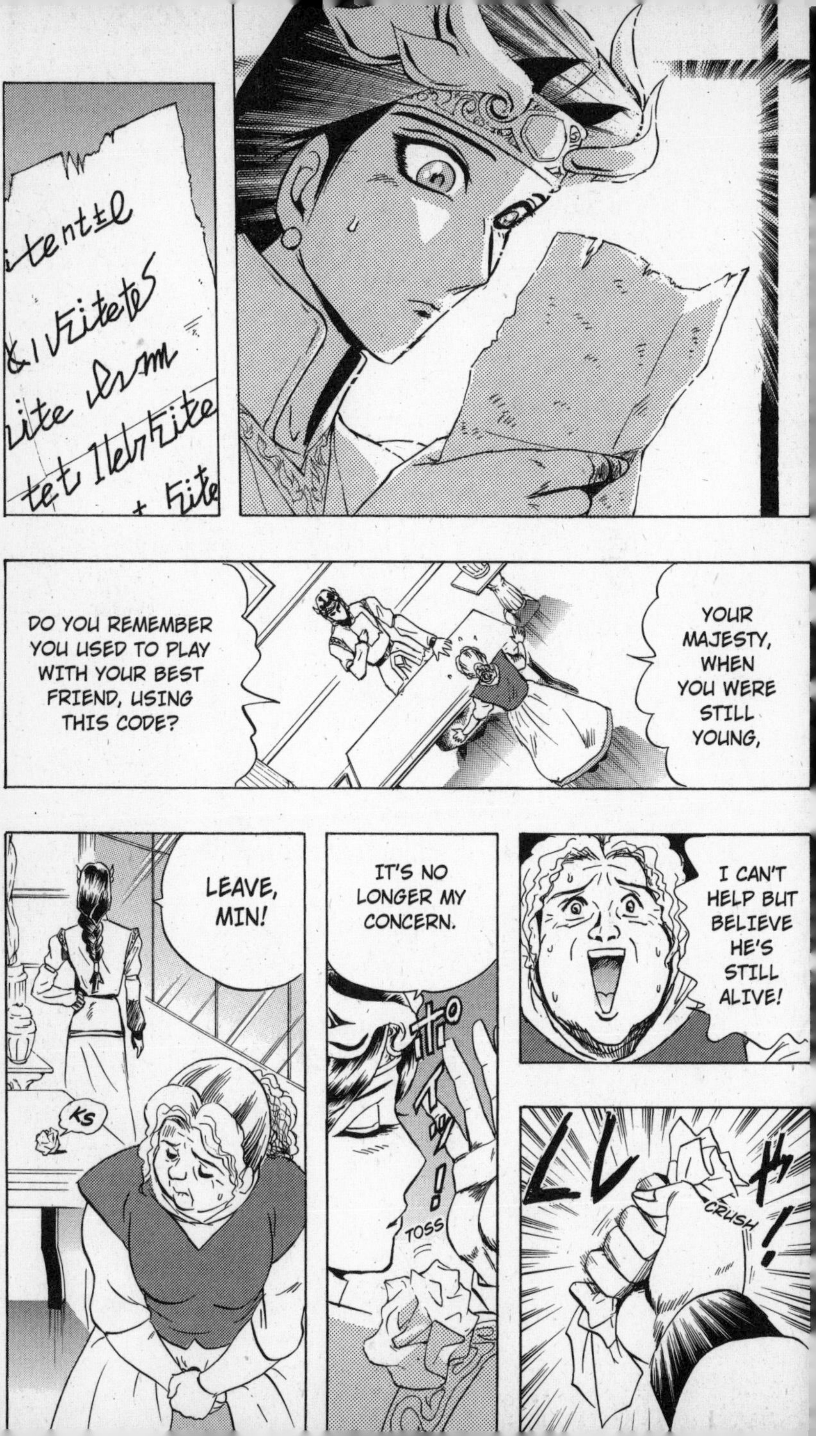
YOUR MAJESTY, WHEN YOU WERE STILL YOUNG,
DO YOU REMEMBER YOU USED TO PLAY WITH YOUR BEST FRIEND, USING THIS CODE?
I CAN'T HELP BUT BELIEVE HE'S STILL ALIVE!
CRUSH
IT'S NO LONGER MY CONCERN.
TOSS
LEAVE, MIN!
KS

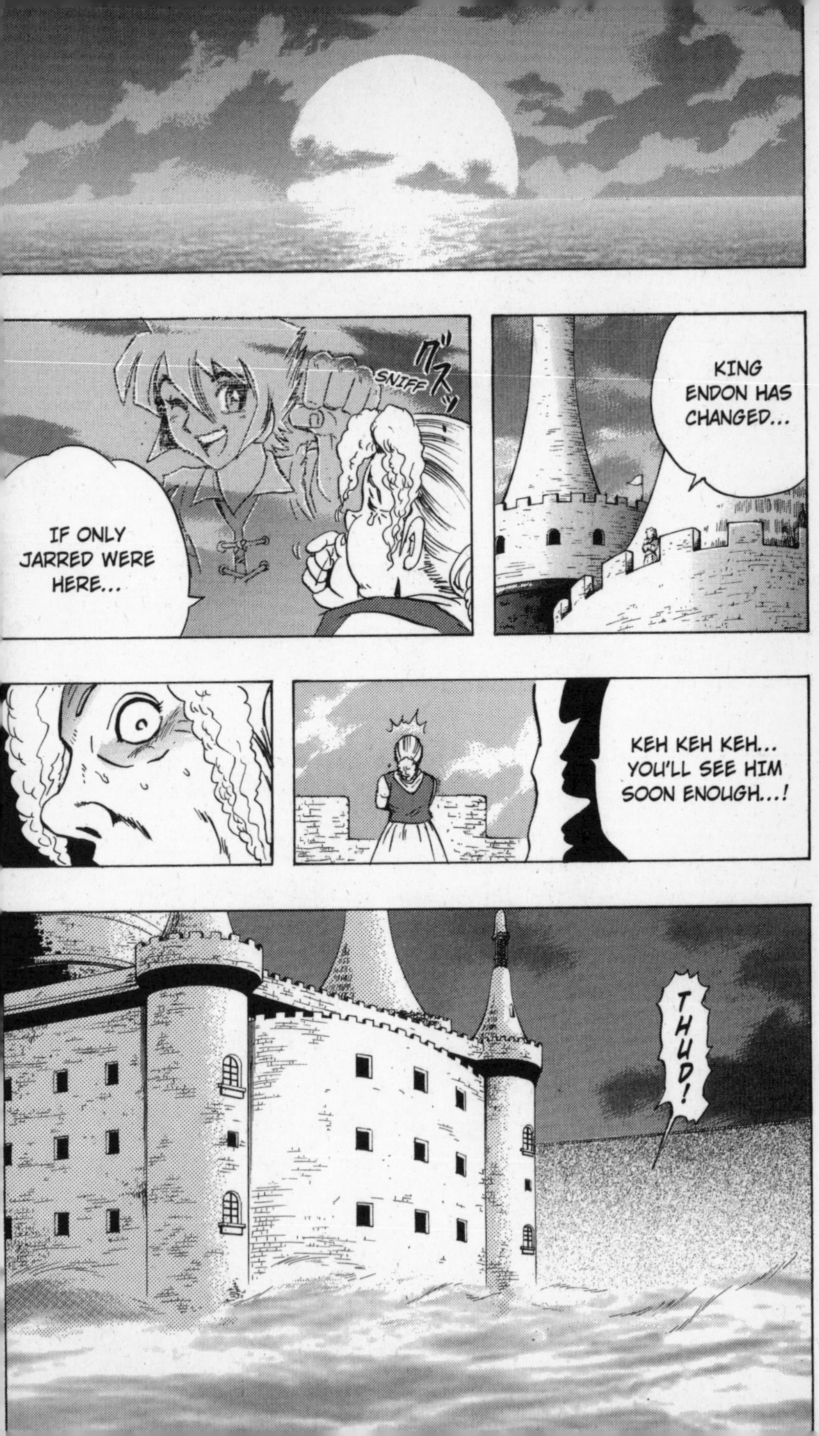
KING ENDON HAS CHANGED...
グスッ
SNIFF
IF ONLY JARRED WERE HERE...
KEH KEH KEH... YOU'LL SEE HIM SOON ENOUGH...!
THUD!

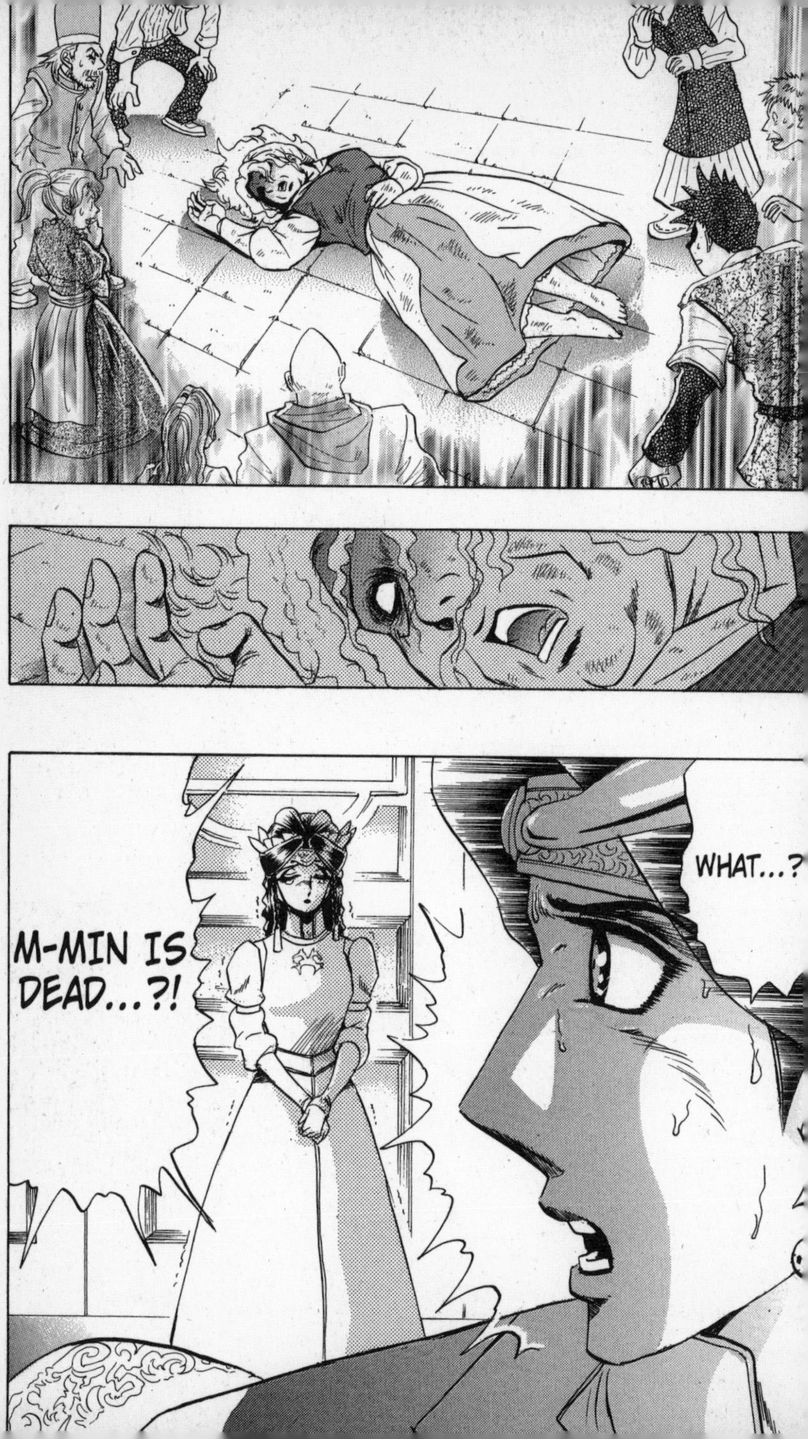
WHAT...?
M-MIN IS DEAD...?!

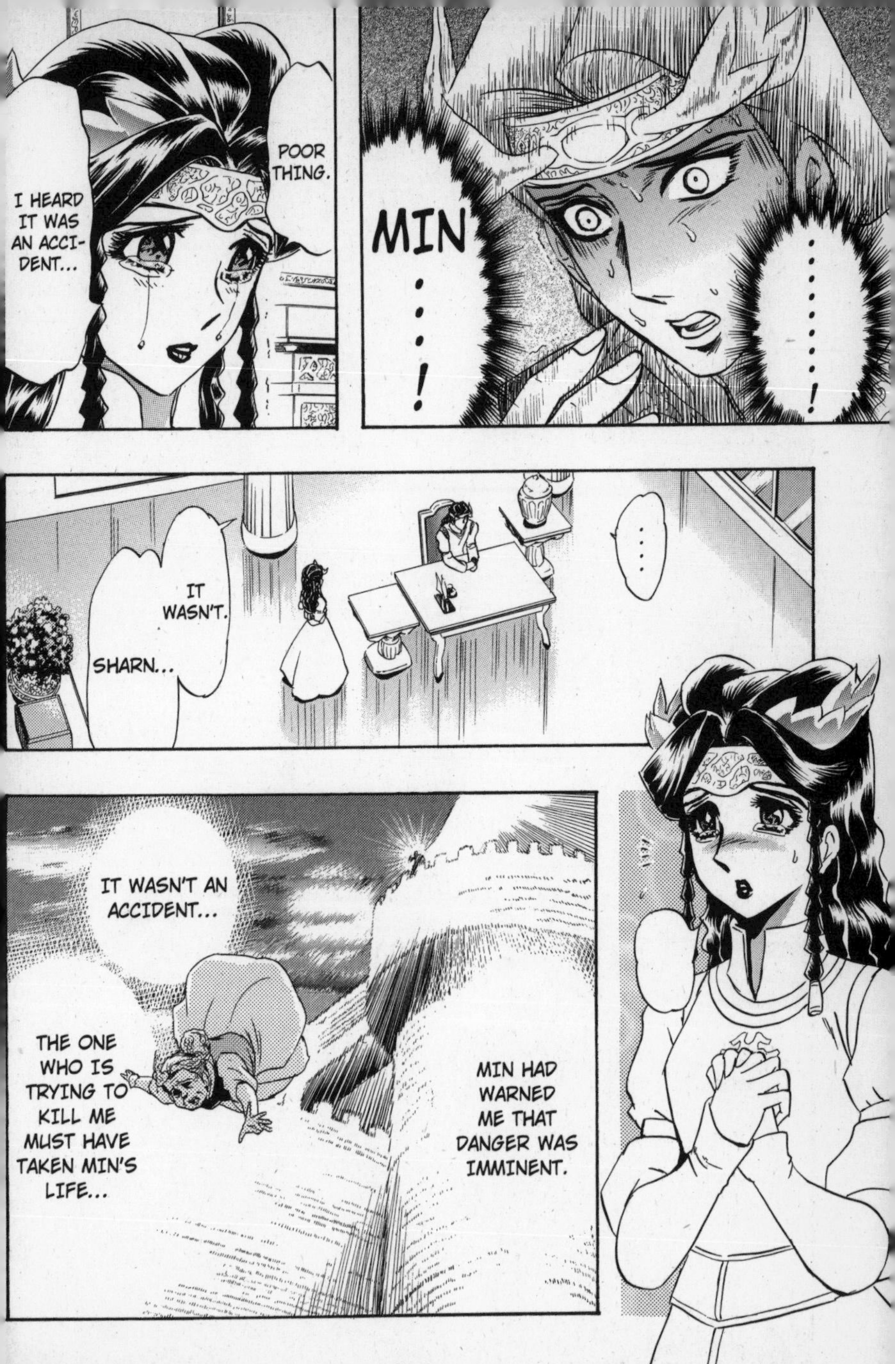
......!
MIN...!
POOR THING.
I HEARD IT WAS AN ACCI-DENT...
....
IT WASN'T.
SHARN...
IT WASN'T AN ACCIDENT...
MIN HAD WARNED ME THAT DANGER WAS IMMINENT.
THE ONE WHO IS TRYING TO KILL ME MUST HAVE TAKEN MIN'S LIFE...

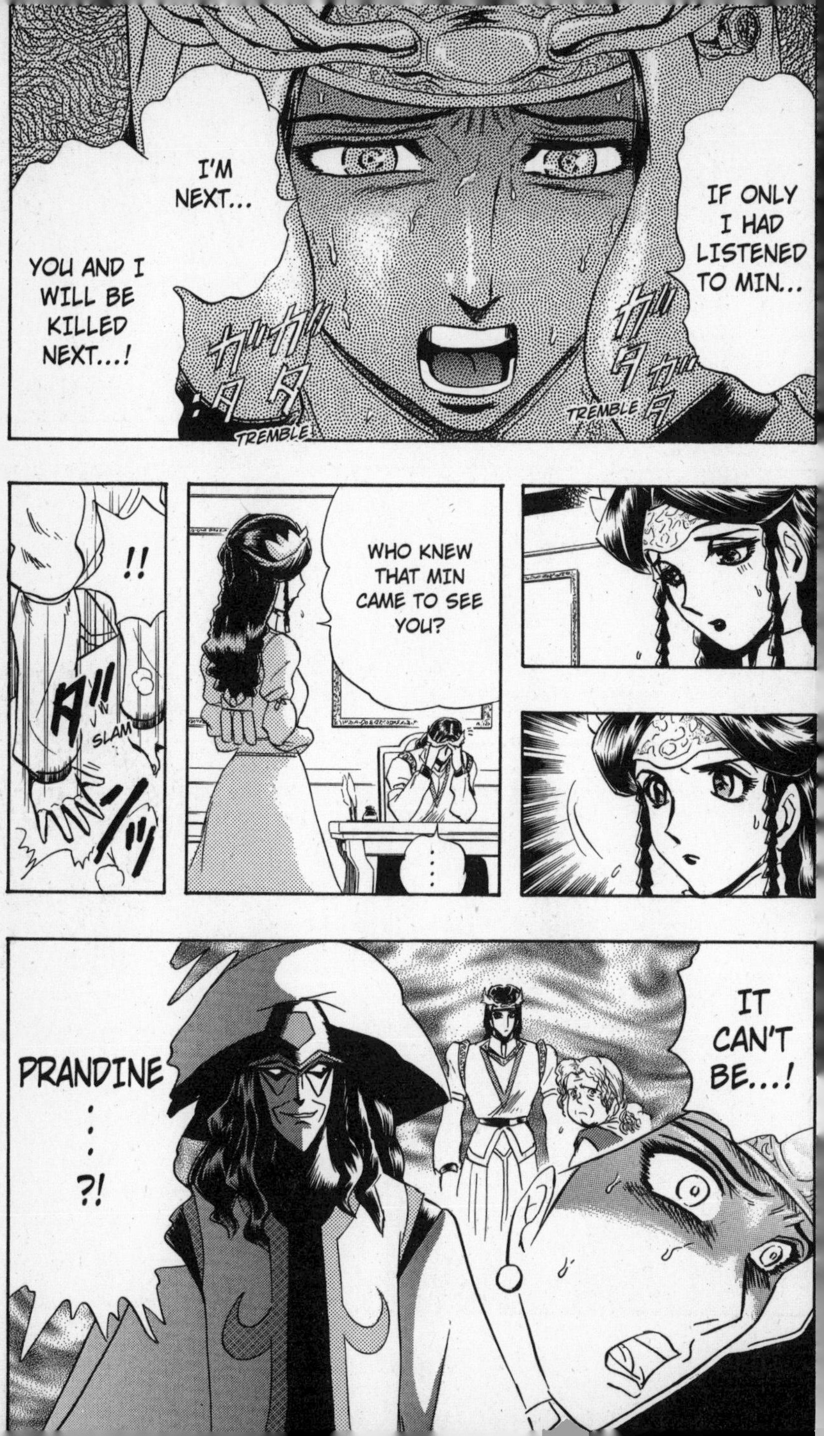
IF ONLY I HAD LISTENED TO MIN...
TREMBLE
I'M NEXT...
YOU AND I WILL BE KILLED NEXT...!
TREMBLE
WHO KNEW THAT MIN CAME TO SEE YOU?
....
!!
SLAM
IT CAN'T BE...!
PRANDINE...?!

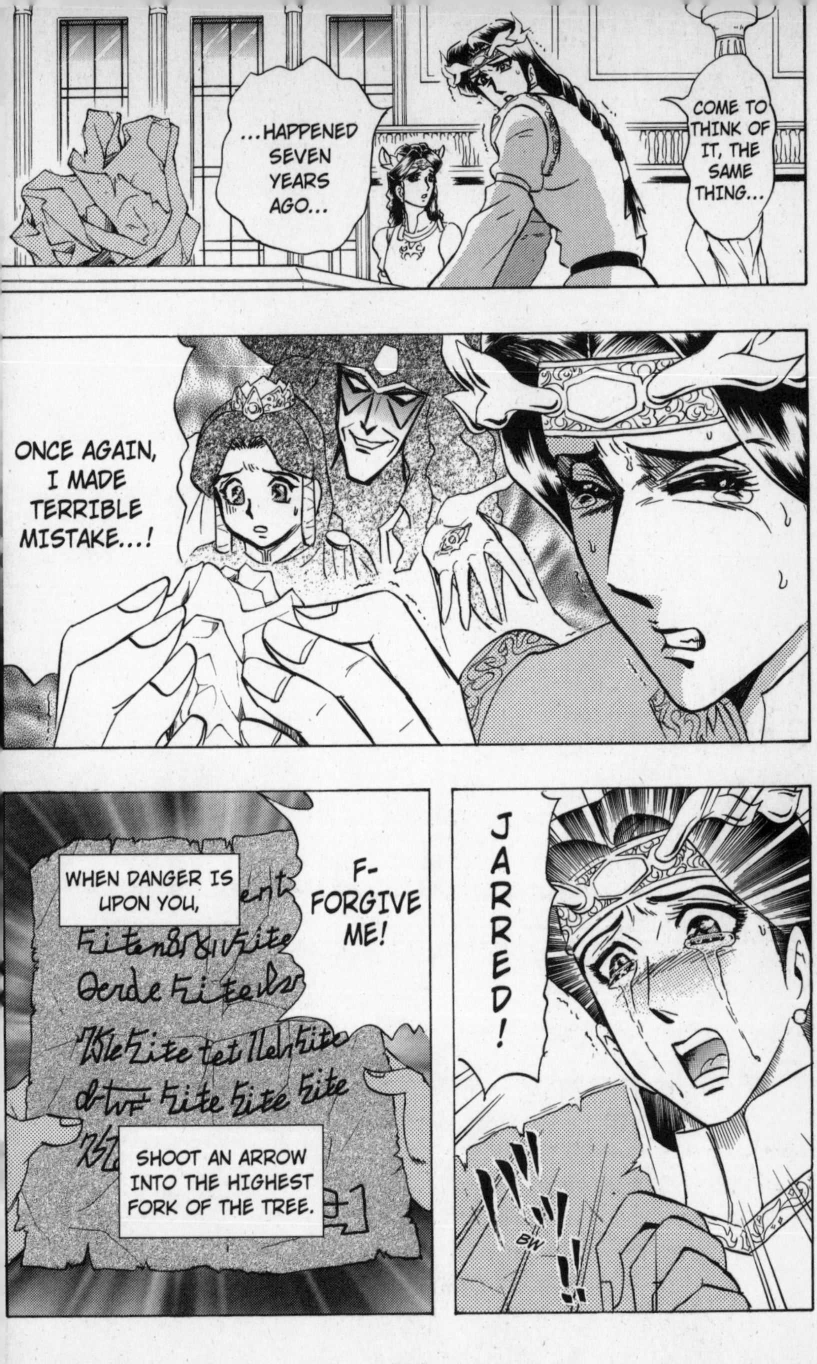
COME TO THINK OF IT, THE SAME THING...
...HAPPENED SEVEN YEARS AGO...
ONCE AGAIN, I MADE TERRIBLE MISTAKE...!
JARRED!
BW
F-FORGIVE ME!
WHEN DANGER IS UPON YOU,
SHOOT AN ARROW INTO THE HIGHEST FORK OF THE TREE.

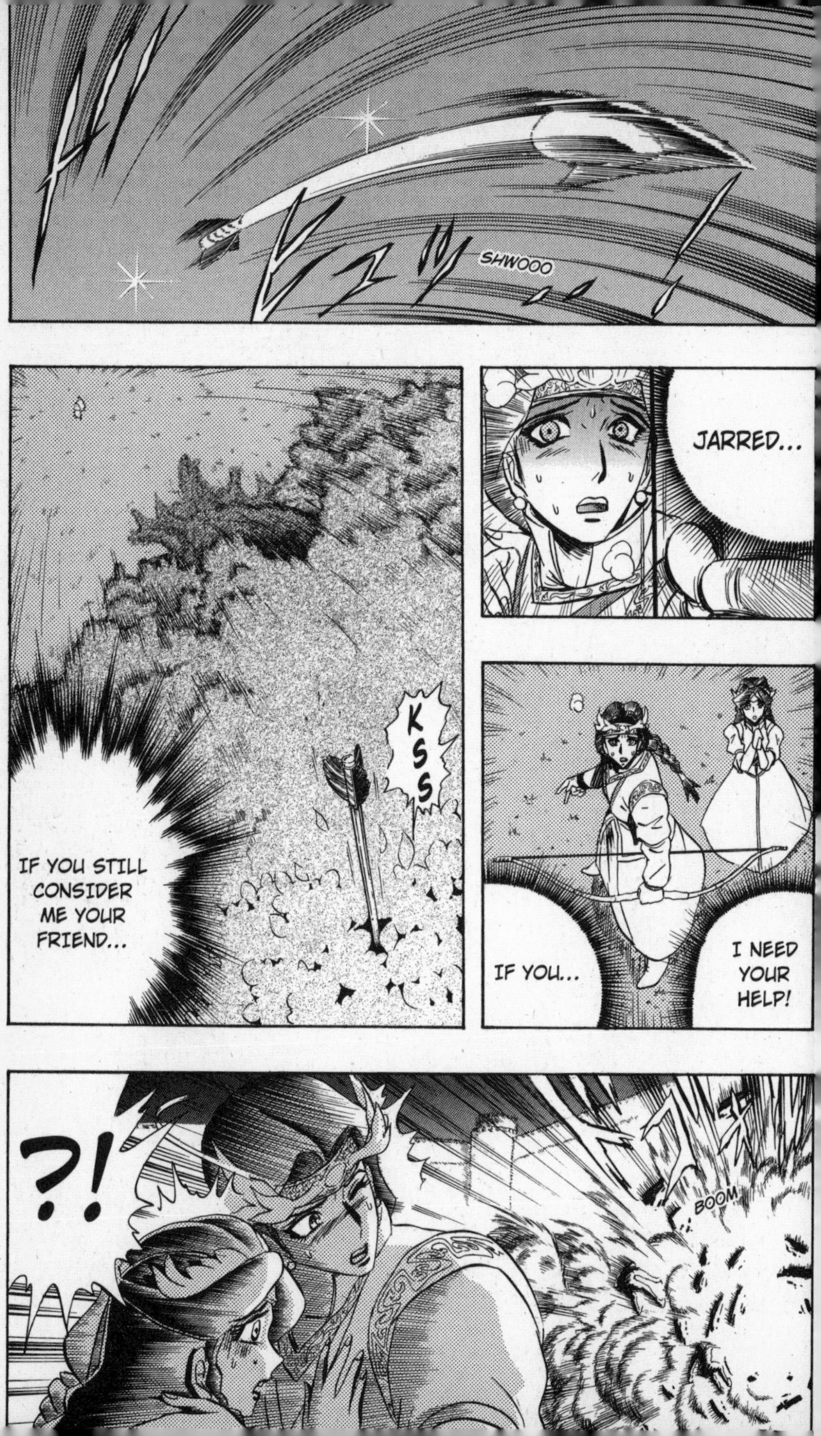
SHWOOO
JARRED...
I NEED YOUR HELP!
IF YOU...
KSS
IF YOU STILL CONSIDER ME YOUR FRIEND...
BOOM
?!

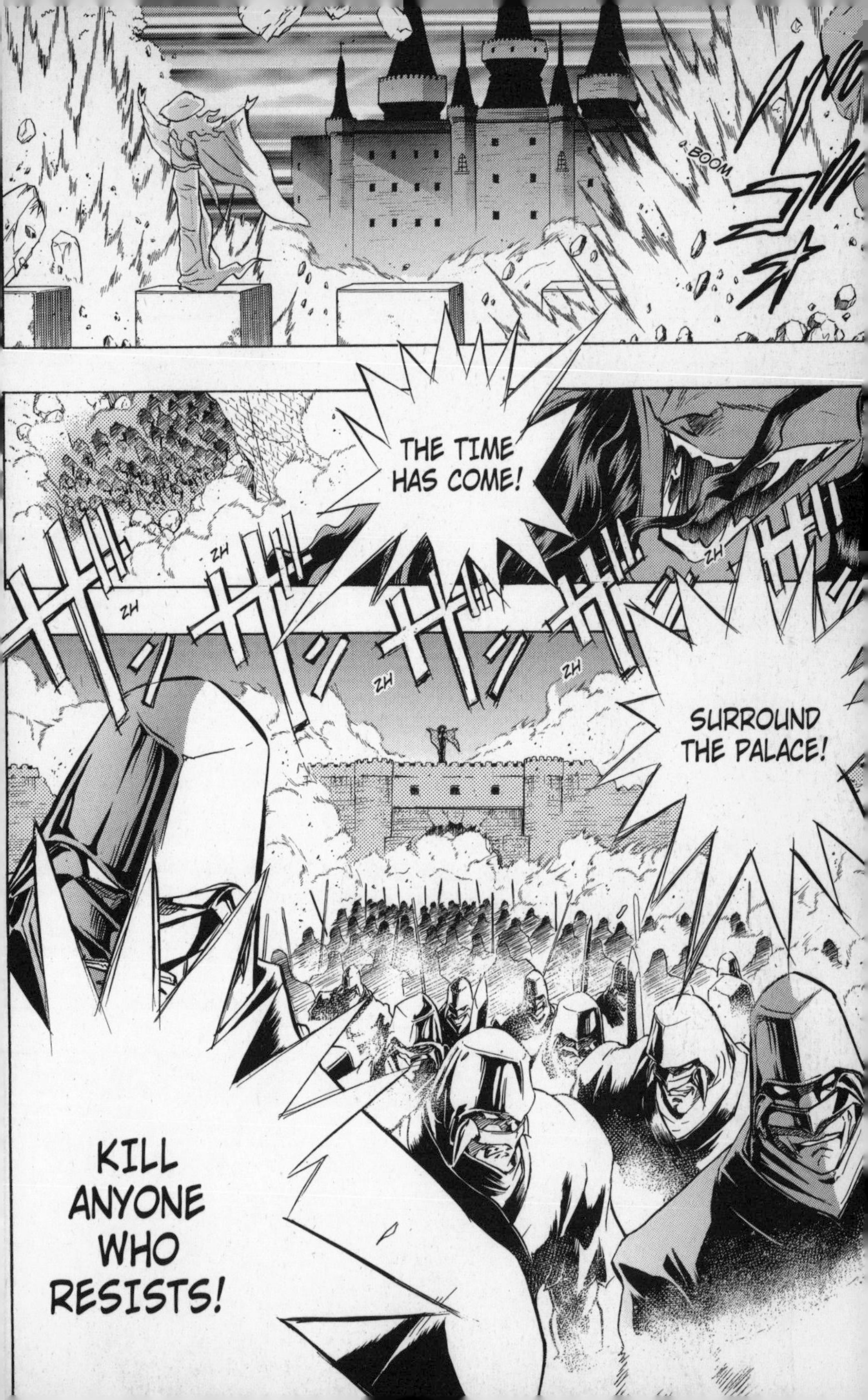
BOOM
THE TIME HAS COME!
ZH
ZH
ZH
ZH
ZH
SURROUND THE PALACE!
KILL ANYONE WHO RESISTS!

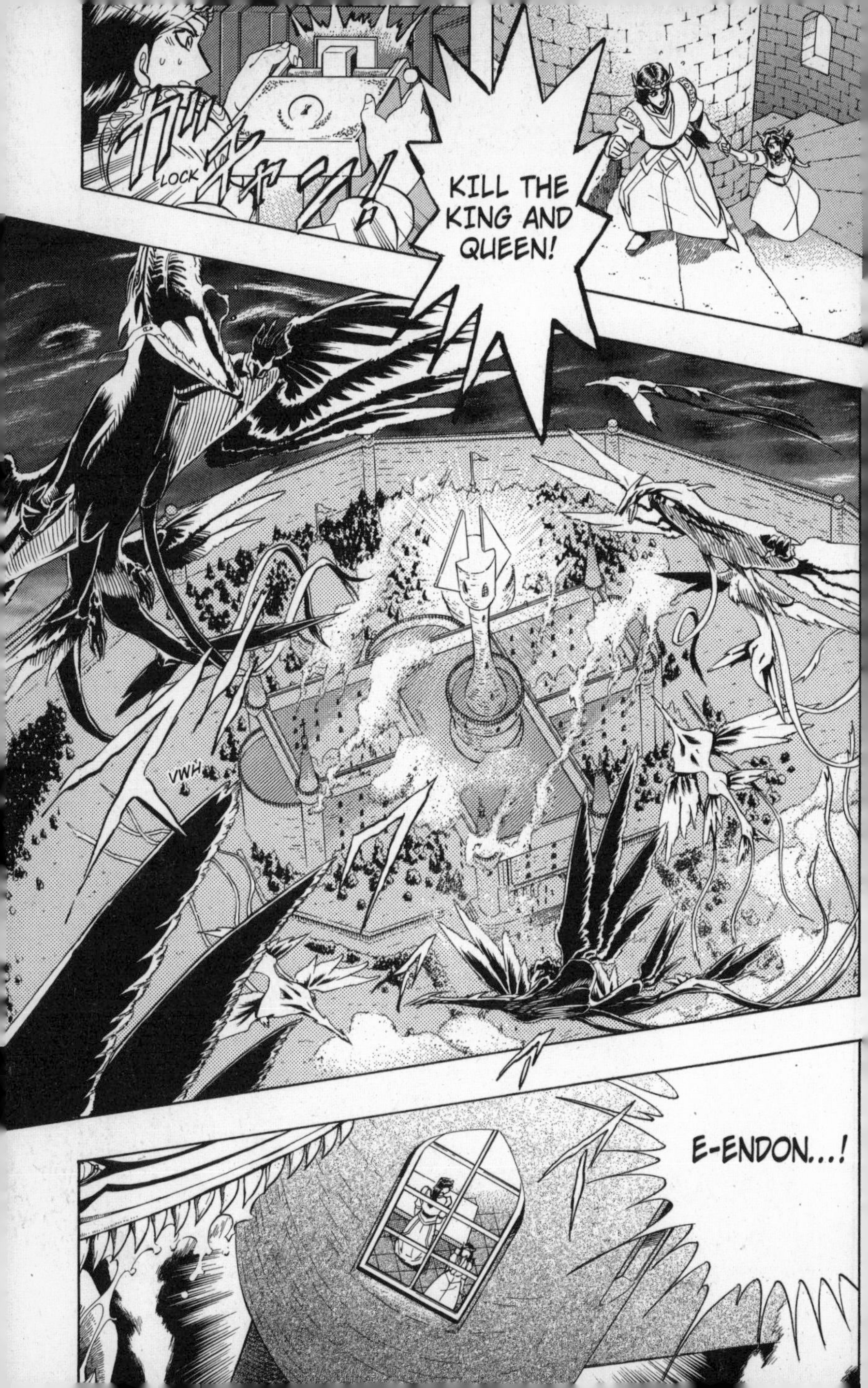
KILL THE KING AND QUEEN!
LOCK
VWH
E-ENDON...!

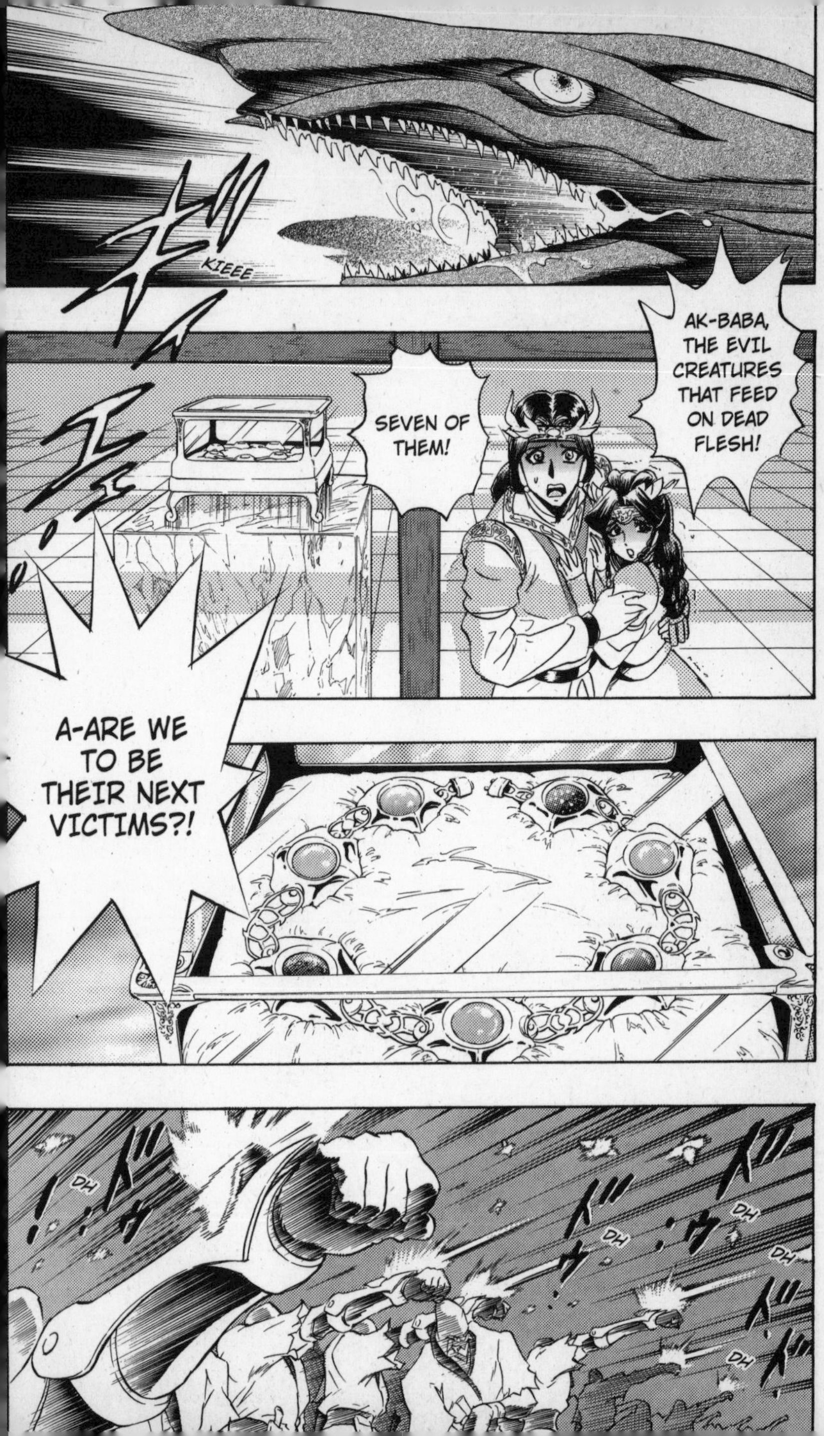
KIEEE
AK-BABA, THE EVIL CREATURES THAT FEED ON DEAD FLESH!
SEVEN OF THEM!
A-ARE WE TO BE THEIR NEXT VICTIMS?!
DH
DH
DH
DH
DH
DH

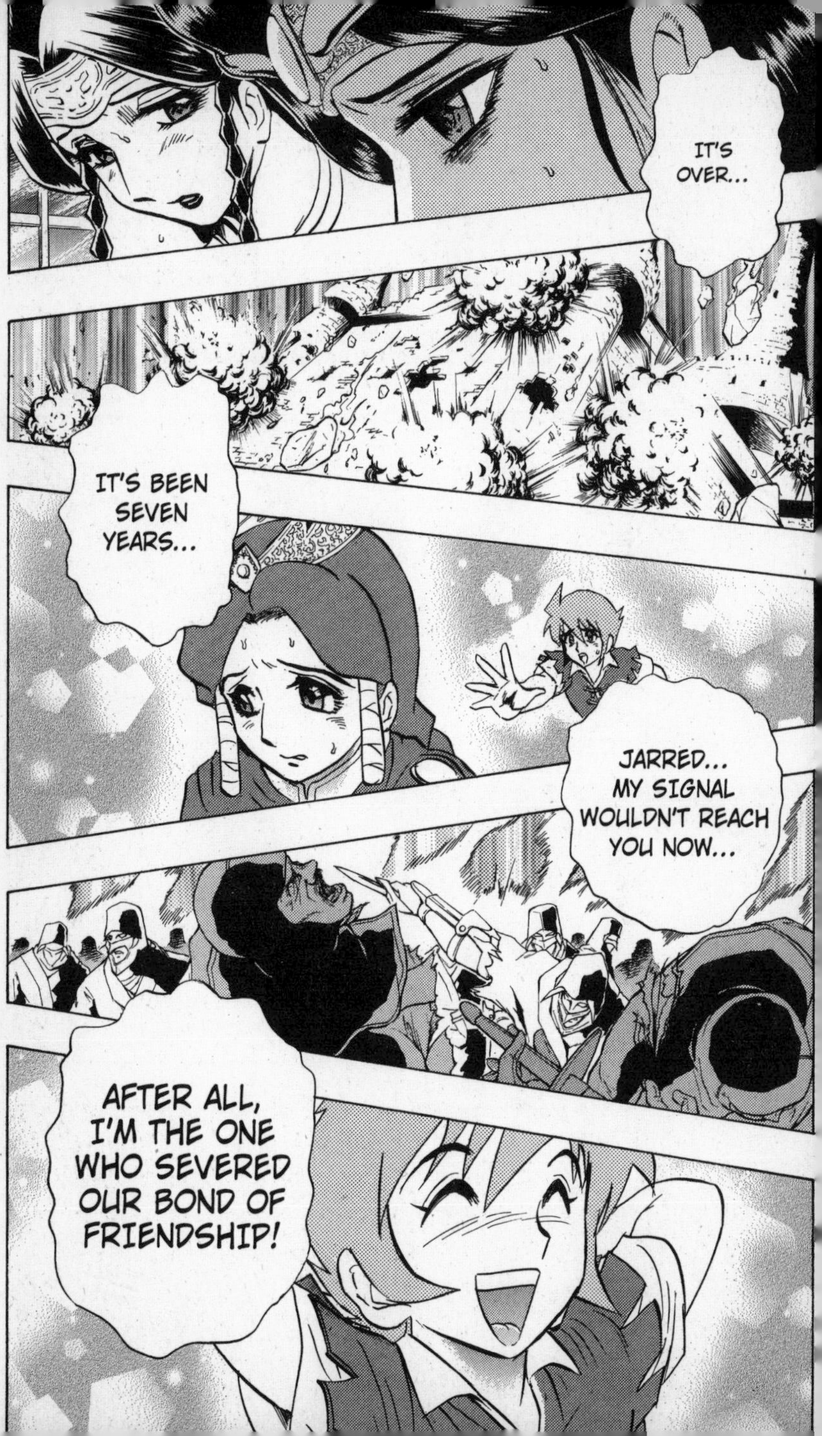
IT'S OVER...
IT'S BEEN SEVEN YEARS...
JARRED... MY SIGNAL WOULDN'T REACH YOU NOW...
AFTER ALL, I'M THE ONE WHO SEVERED OUR BOND OF FRIENDSHIP!

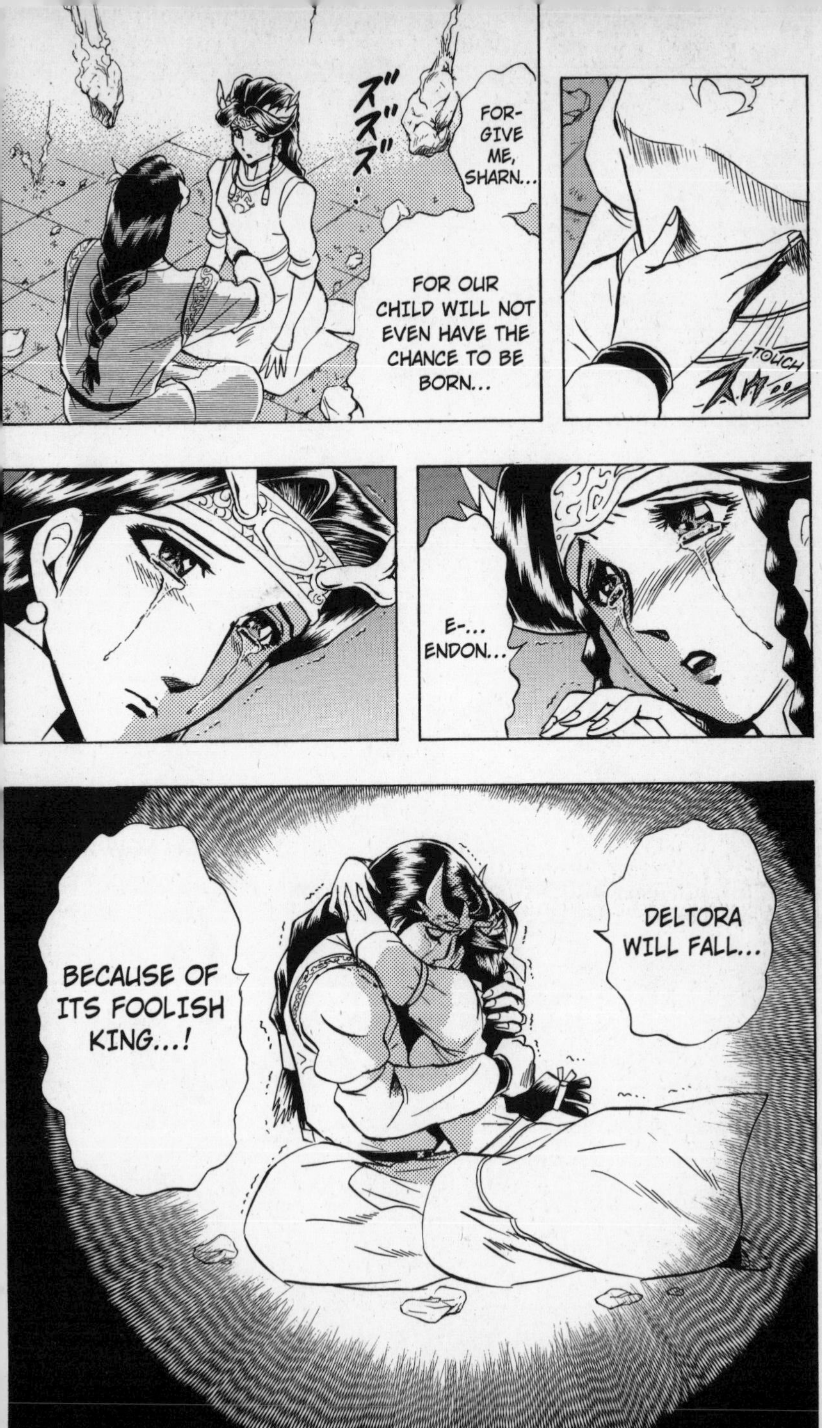
TOUCH
ズズズ…
FOR-GIVE ME, SHARN...
FOR OUR CHILD WILL NOT EVEN HAVE THE CHANCE TO BE BORN...
E-... ENDON...
DELTORA WILL FALL...
BECAUSE OF ITS FOOLISH KING...!

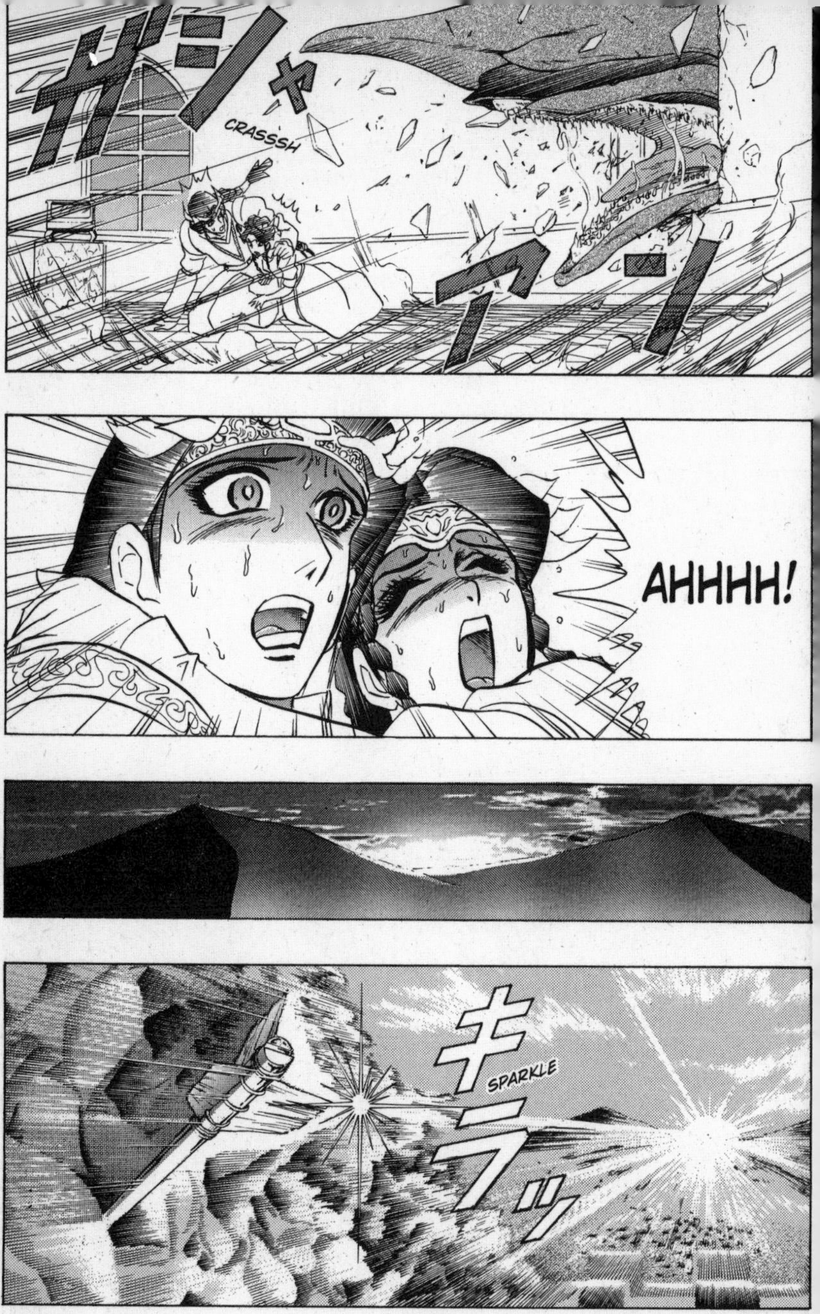
ガシャ
CRASSSH
アーン
AHHHH!
キラッ
SPARKLE

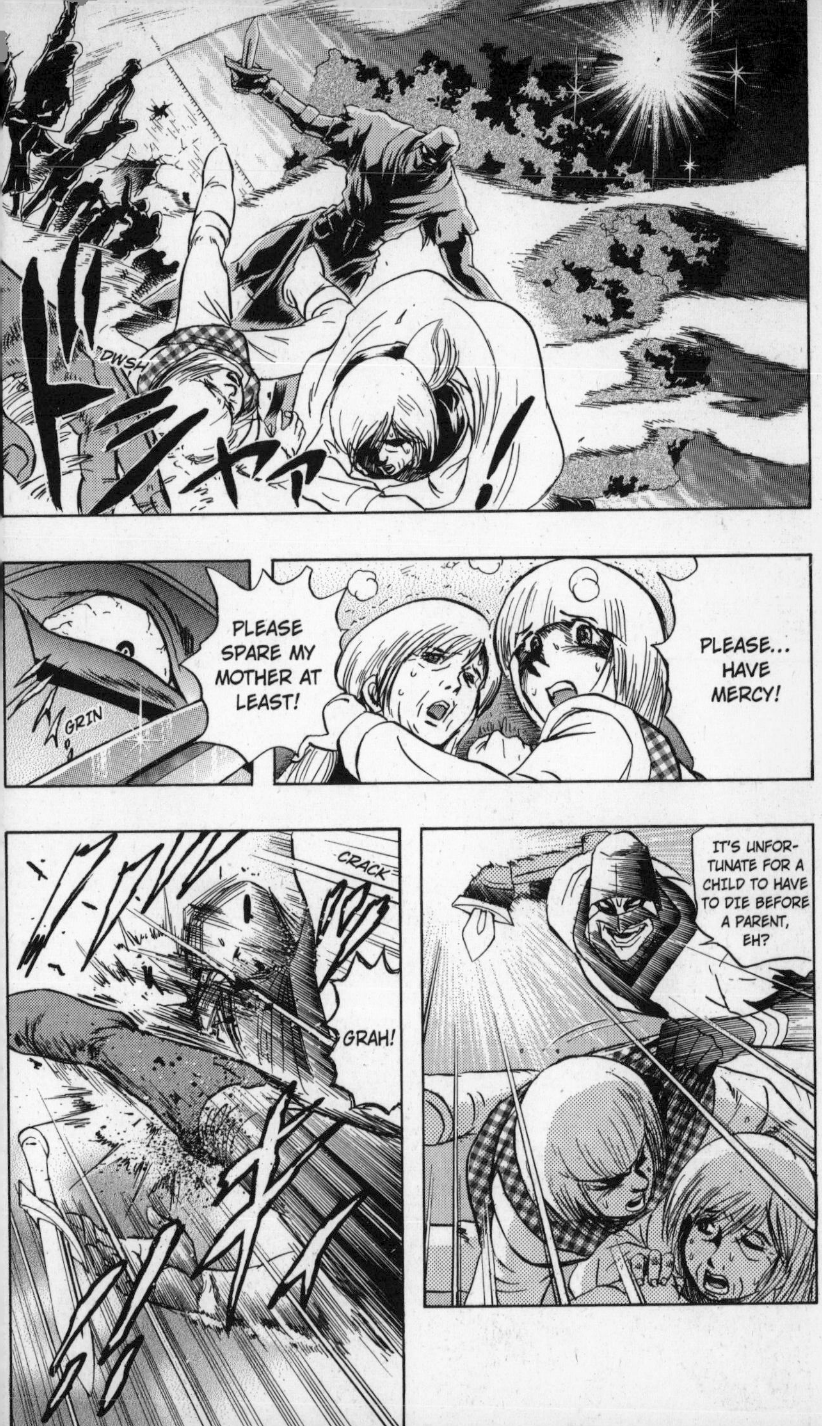
DWSH
PLEASE... HAVE MERCY!
PLEASE SPARE MY MOTHER AT LEAST!
GRIN
IT'S UNFOR-TUNATE FOR A CHILD TO HAVE TO DIE BEFORE A PARENT, EH?
CRACK
GRAH!

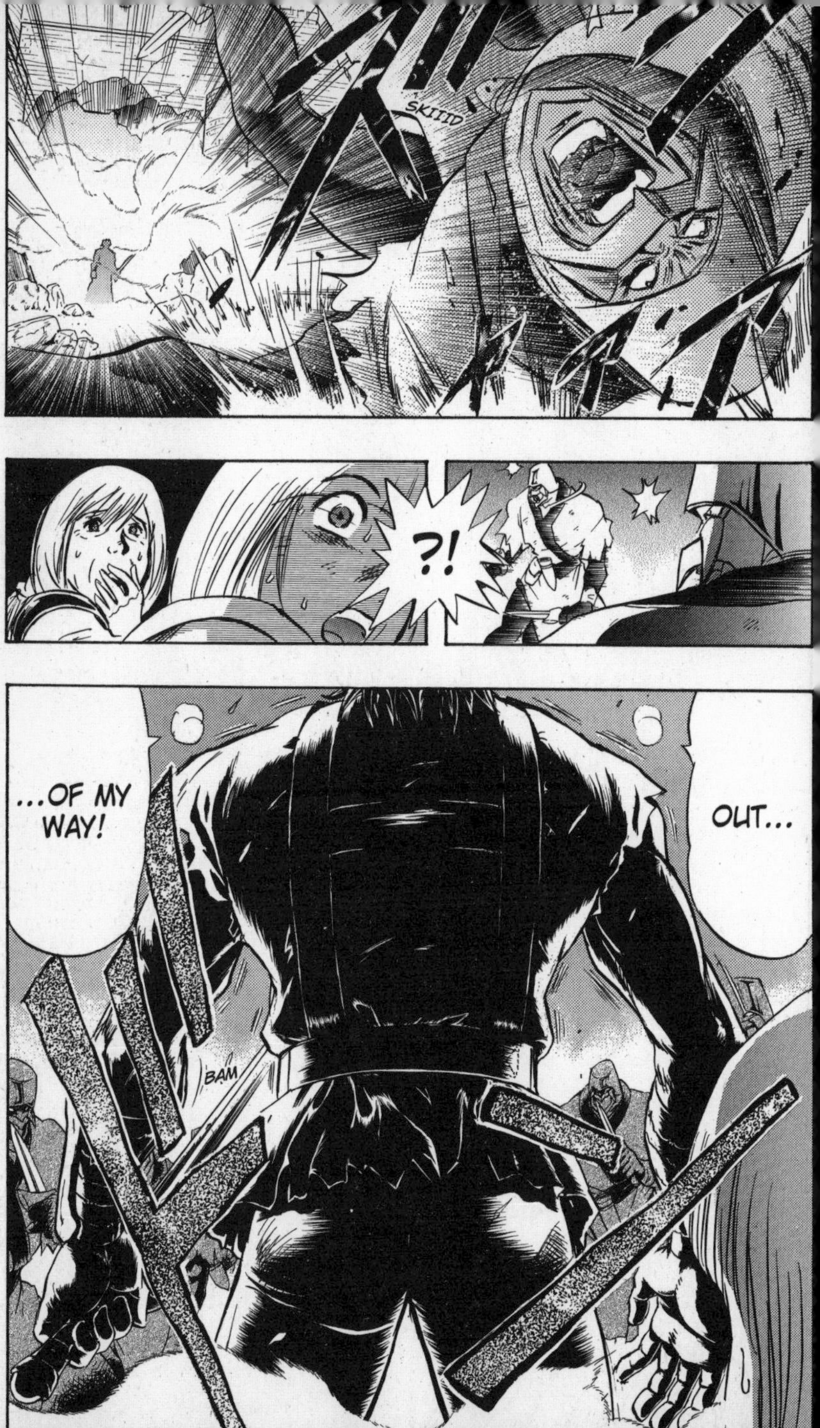
SKIIID
?!
OUT...
...OF MY WAY!
BAM

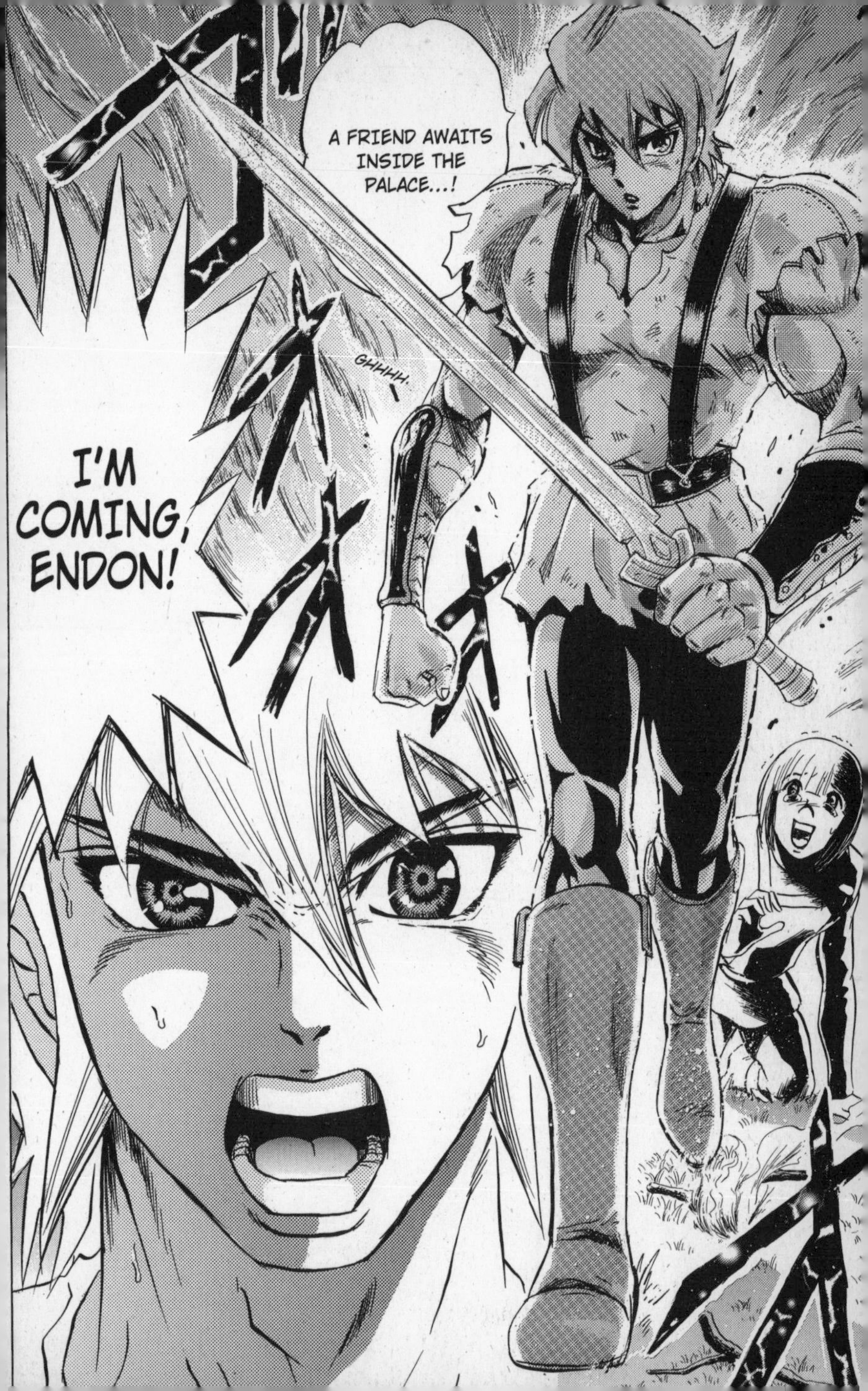
A FRIEND AWAITS INSIDE THE PALACE...!
GHHHH.
I'M COMING, ENDON!

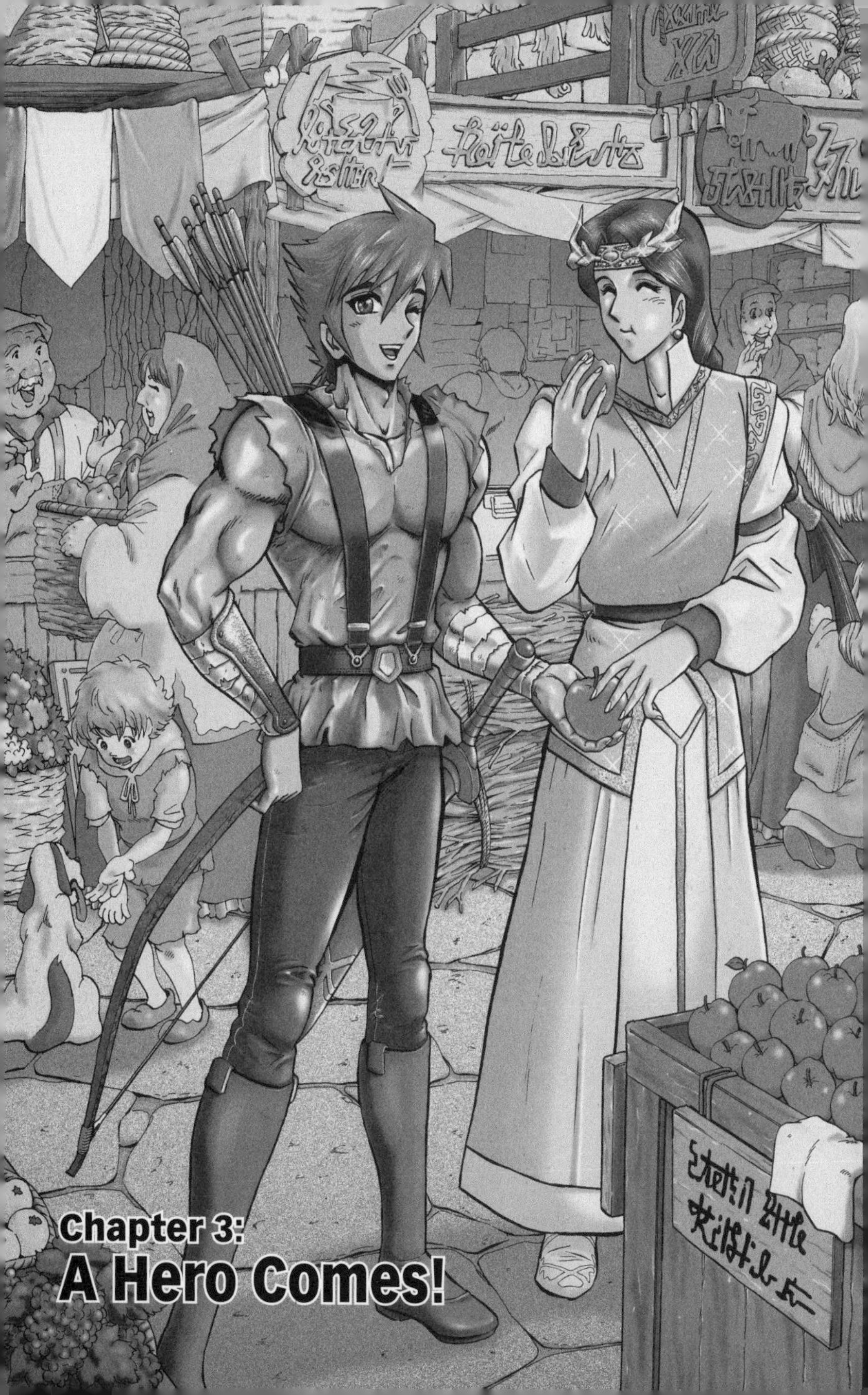
Chapter 3:
A Hero Comes!

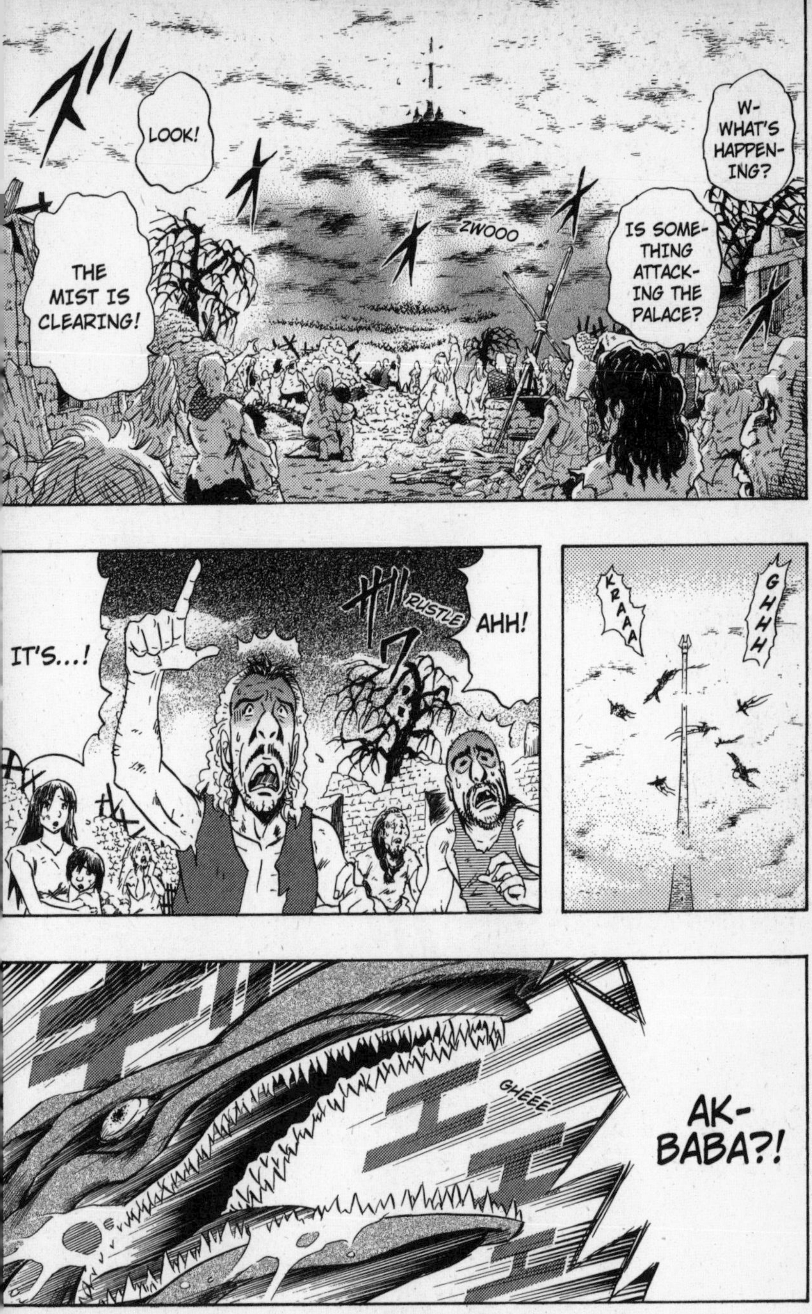
W-WHAT'S HAPPENING?
IS SOMETHING ATTACKING THE PALACE?
ZWOOO
LOOK!
THE MIST IS CLEARING!
GHHH
KRAAA
AHH!
RUSTLE
IT'S...!
GHEEE
AK-BABA?!

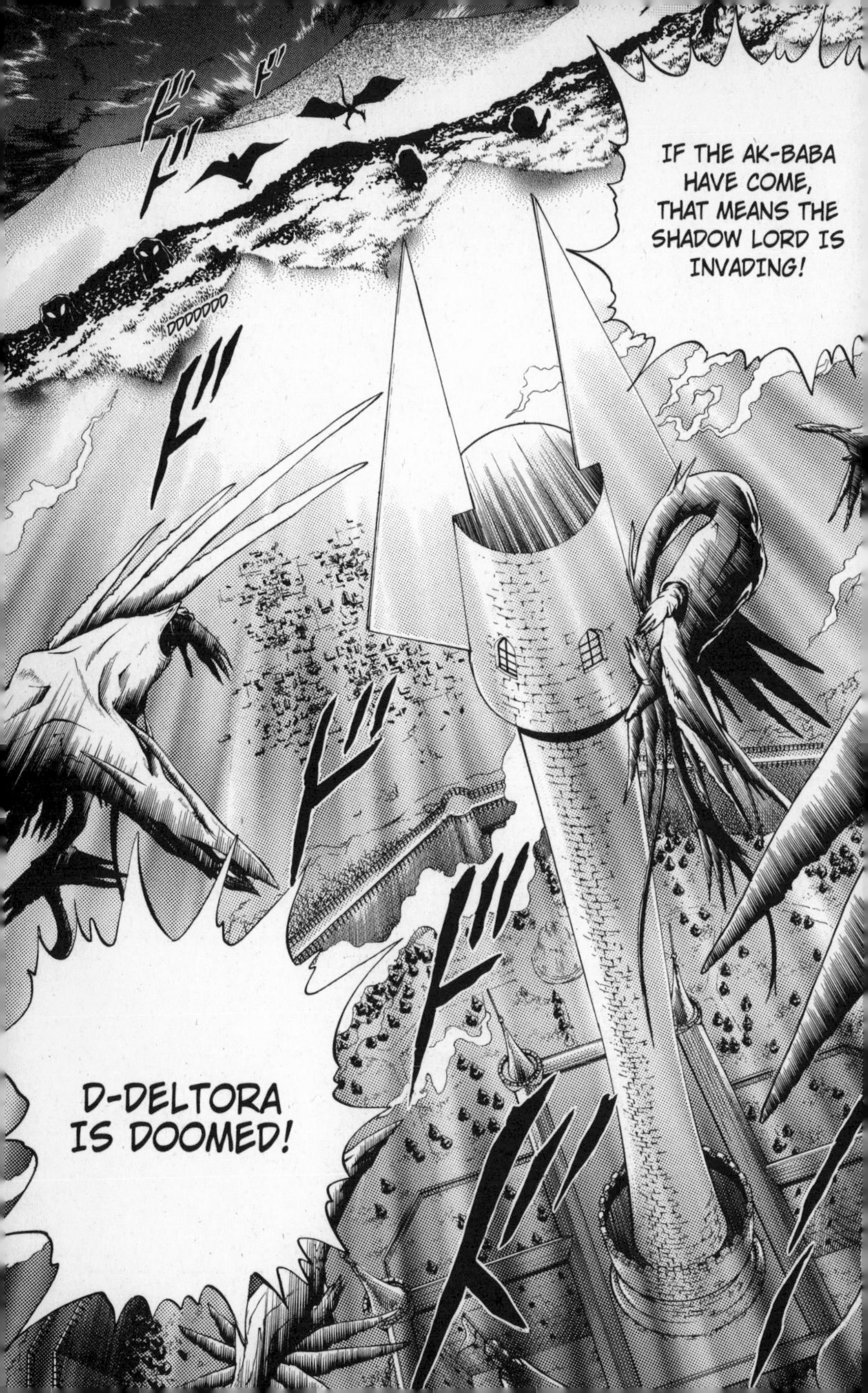
IF THE AK-BABA HAVE COME, THAT MEANS THE SHADOW LORD IS INVADING!
DDDDDDD
D-DELTORA IS DOOMED!

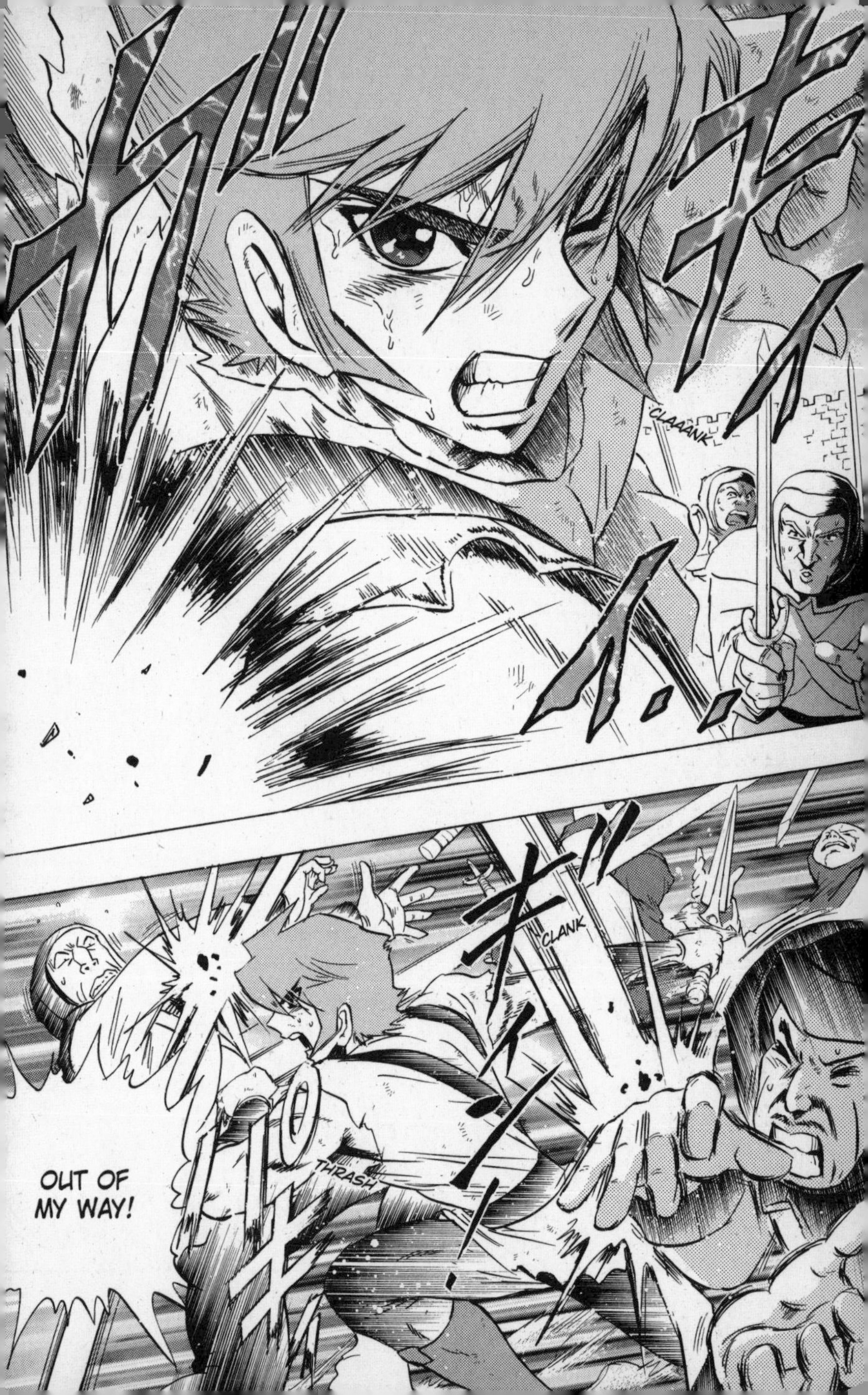
CLAAANK
CLANK
THRASH
OUT OF MY WAY!

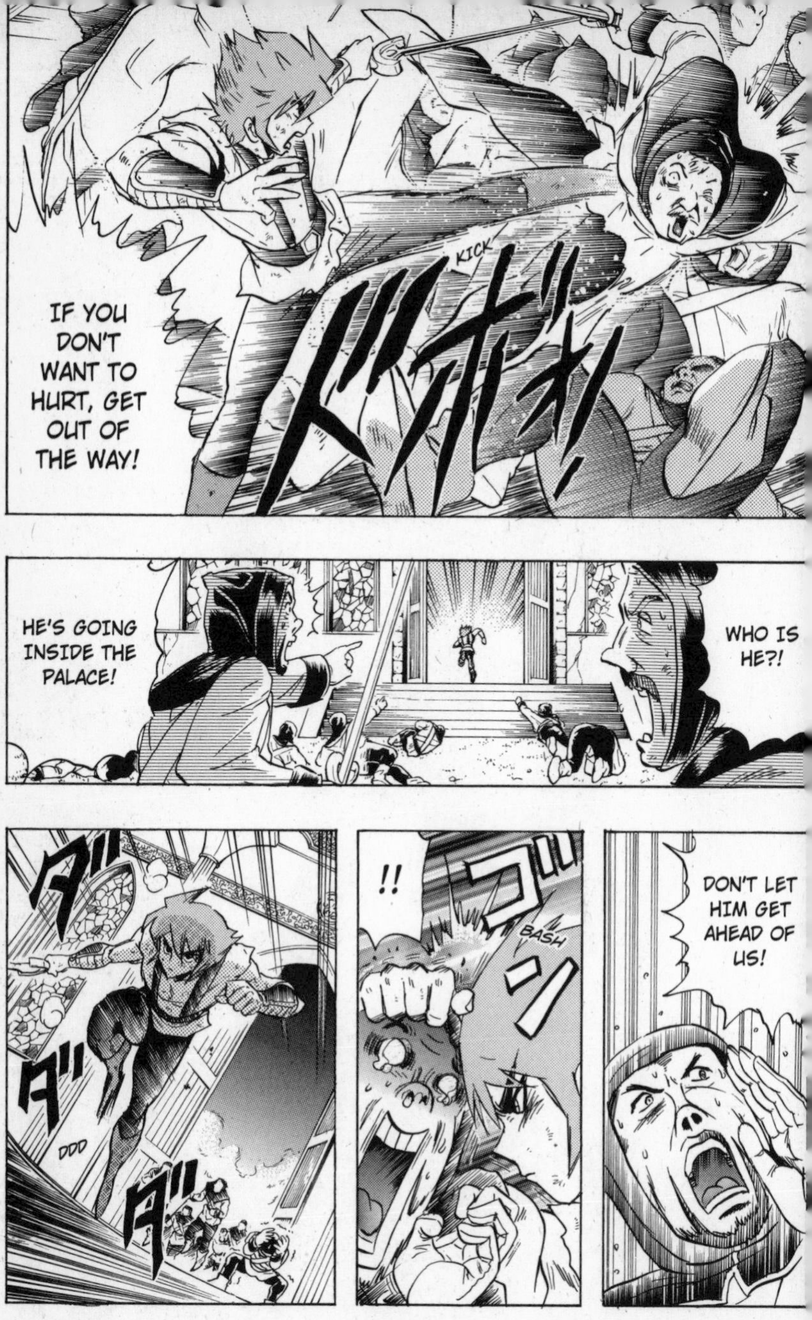
KICK
IF YOU DON'T WANT TO HURT, GET OUT OF THE WAY!
WHO IS HE?!
HE'S GOING INSIDE THE PALACE!
DON'T LET HIM GET AHEAD OF US!
!!
BASH
DDD

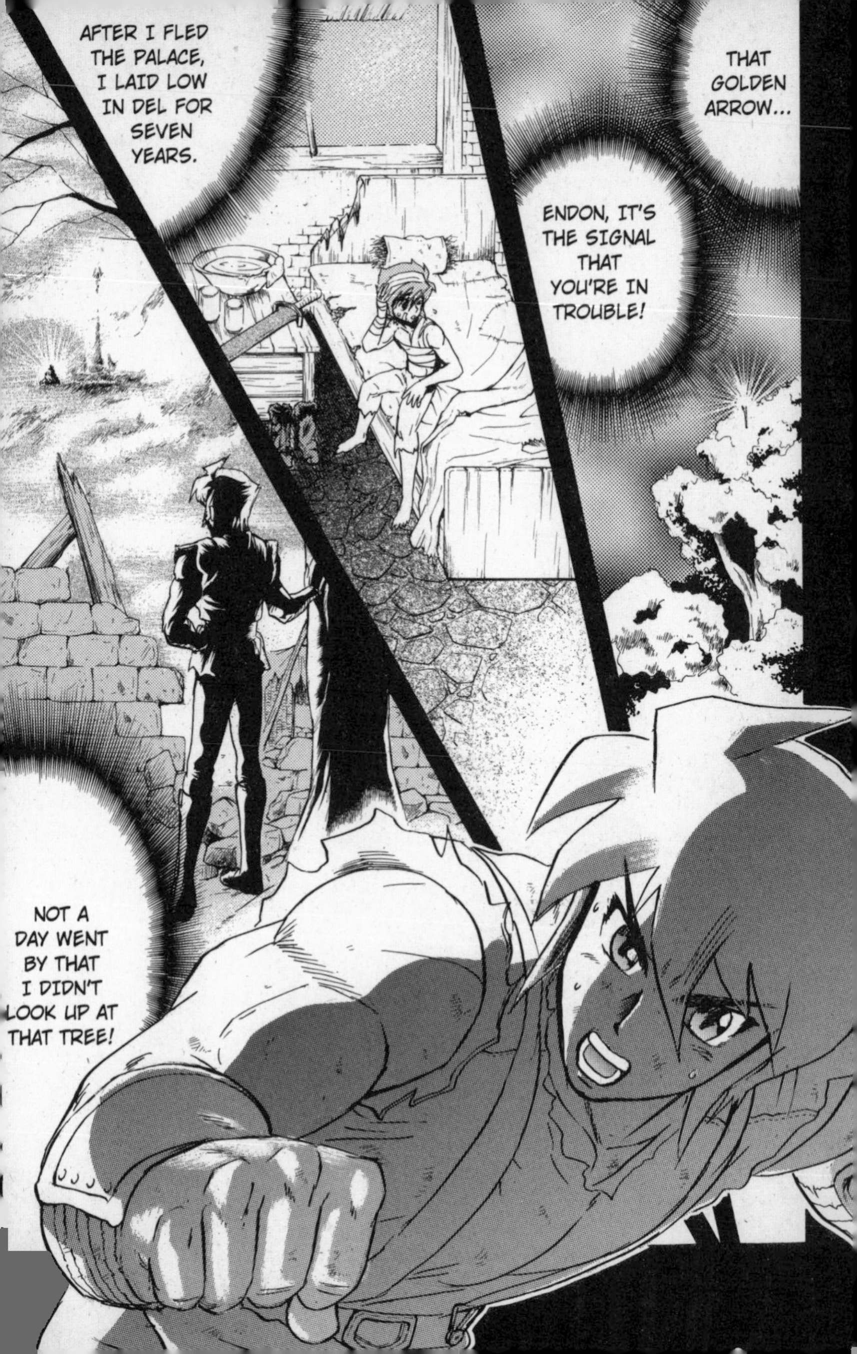

THAT GOLDEN ARROW...
ENDON, IT'S THE SIGNAL THAT YOU'RE IN TROUBLE!
AFTER I FLED THE PALACE, I LAID LOW IN DEL FOR SEVEN YEARS.
NOT A DAY WENT BY THAT I DIDN'T LOOK UP AT THAT TREE!

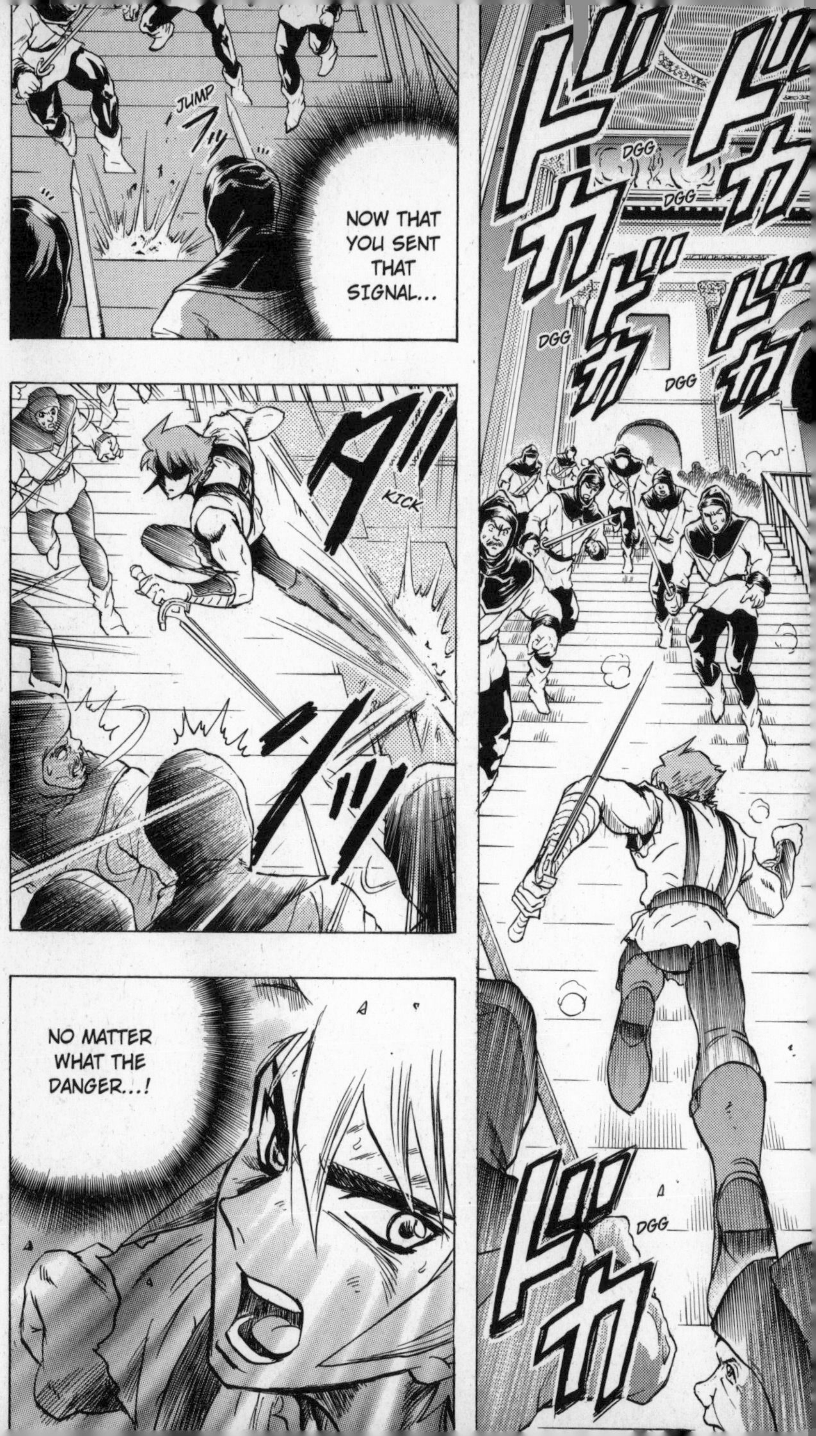
DGG
DGG
DGG
DGG
DGG
DGG
JUMP
NOW THAT YOU SENT THAT SIGNAL...
KICK
NO MATTER WHAT THE DANGER...!

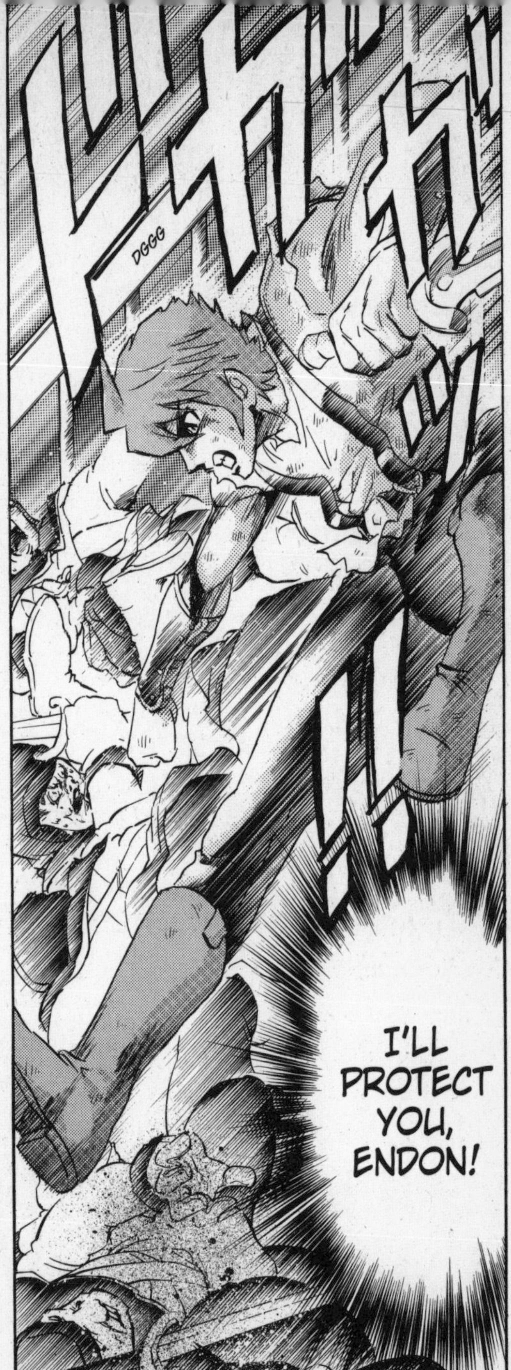
DGGG
!!
I'LL PROTECT YOU, ENDON!

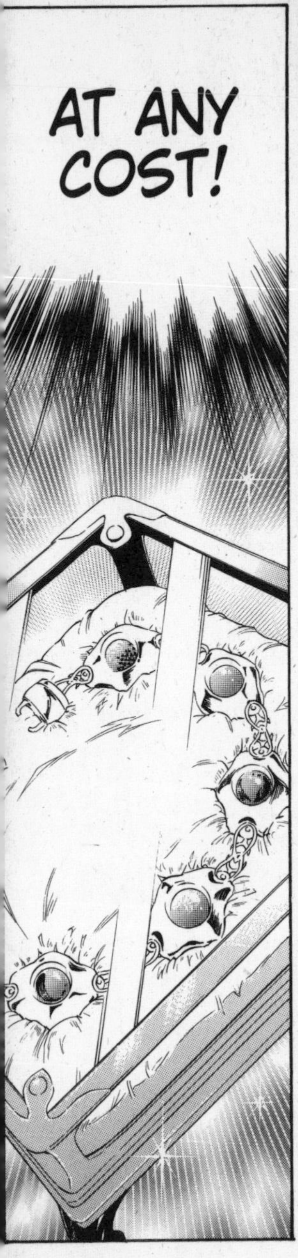
AT ANY COST!

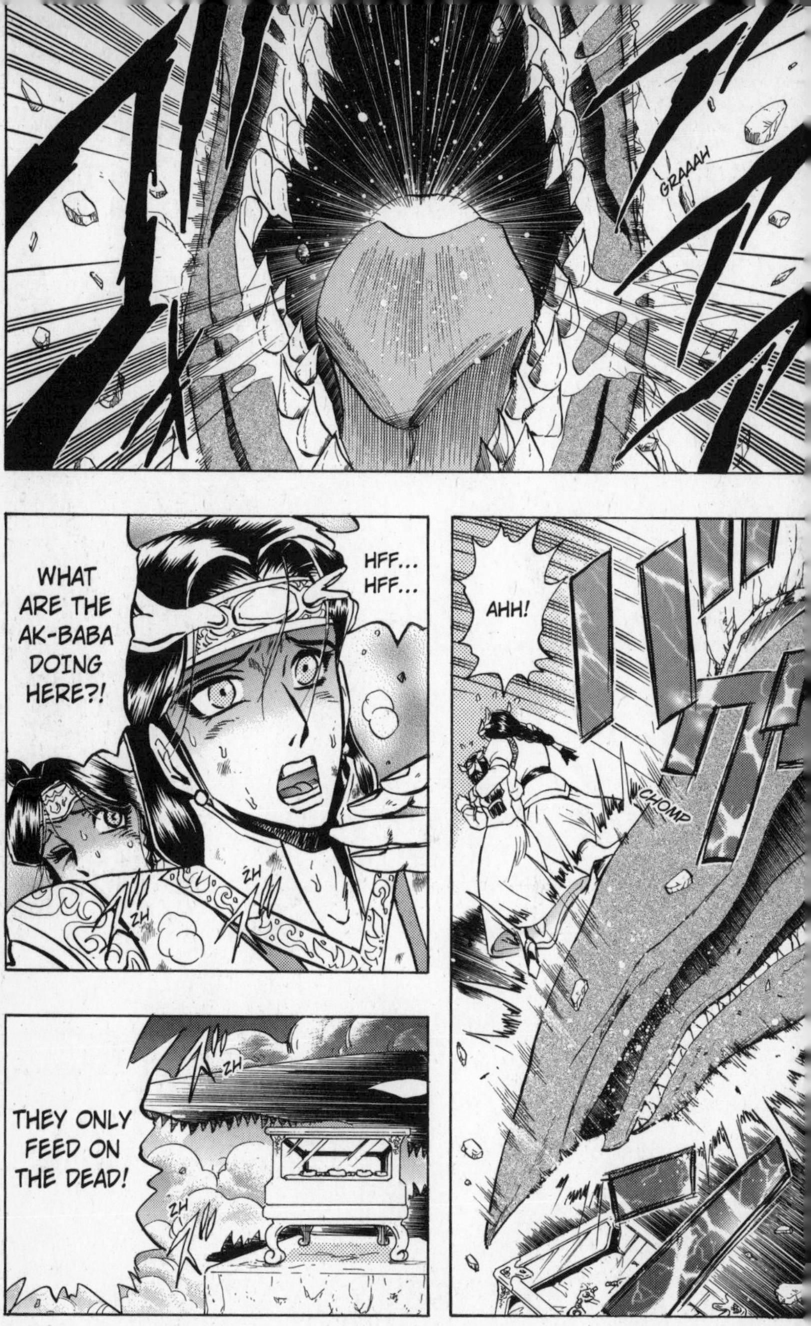
GRAAAH
AHH!
CHOMP
HFF... HFF...
WHAT ARE THE AK-BABA DOING HERE?!
ZH
ZH
ZH
THEY ONLY FEED ON THE DEAD!
ZH
ZH

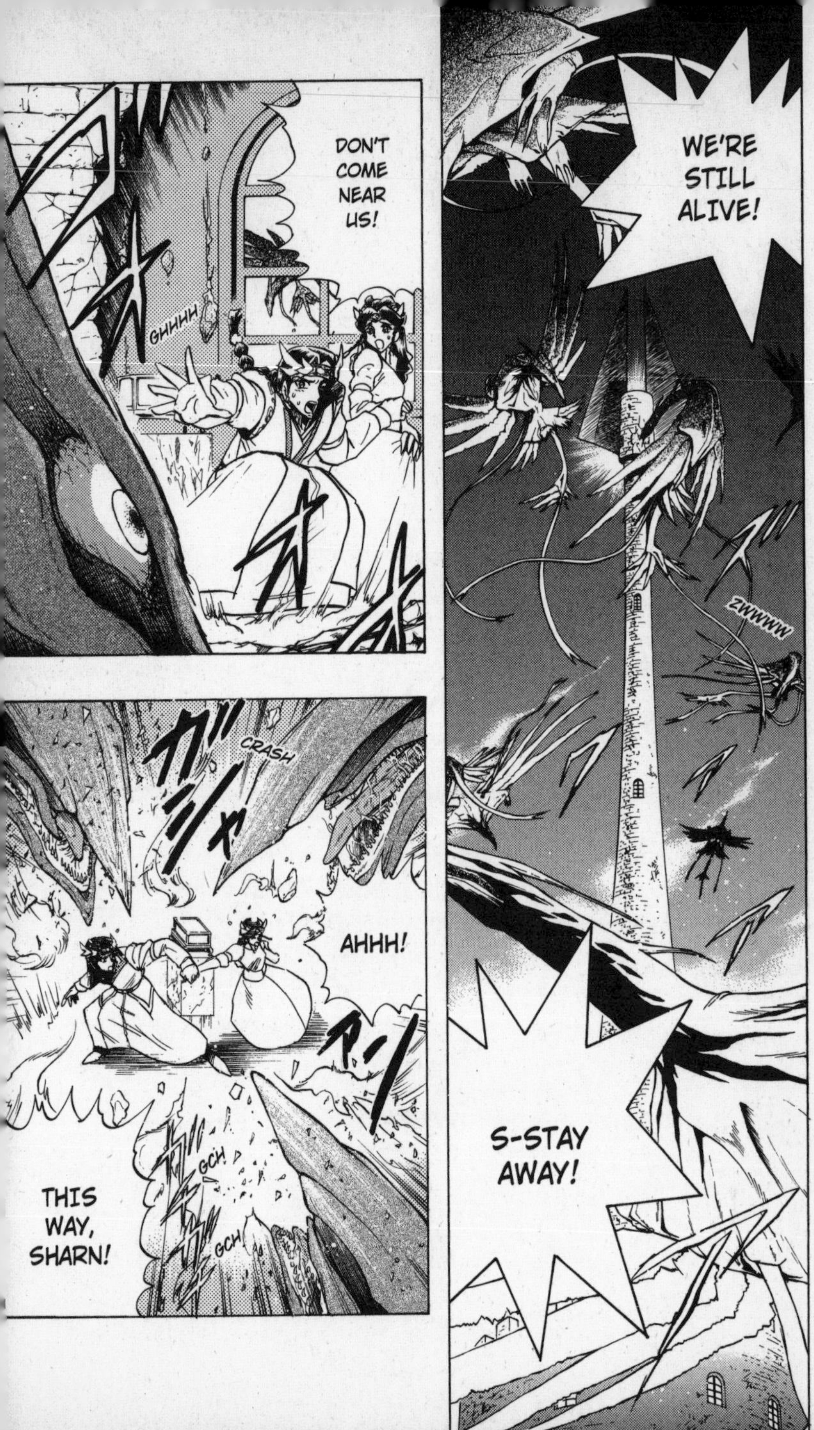
WE'RE STILL ALIVE!
ZWWWW
S-STAY AWAY!
DON'T COME NEAR US!
GHHHH
CRASH
AHHH!
GCH
GCH
THIS WAY, SHARN!

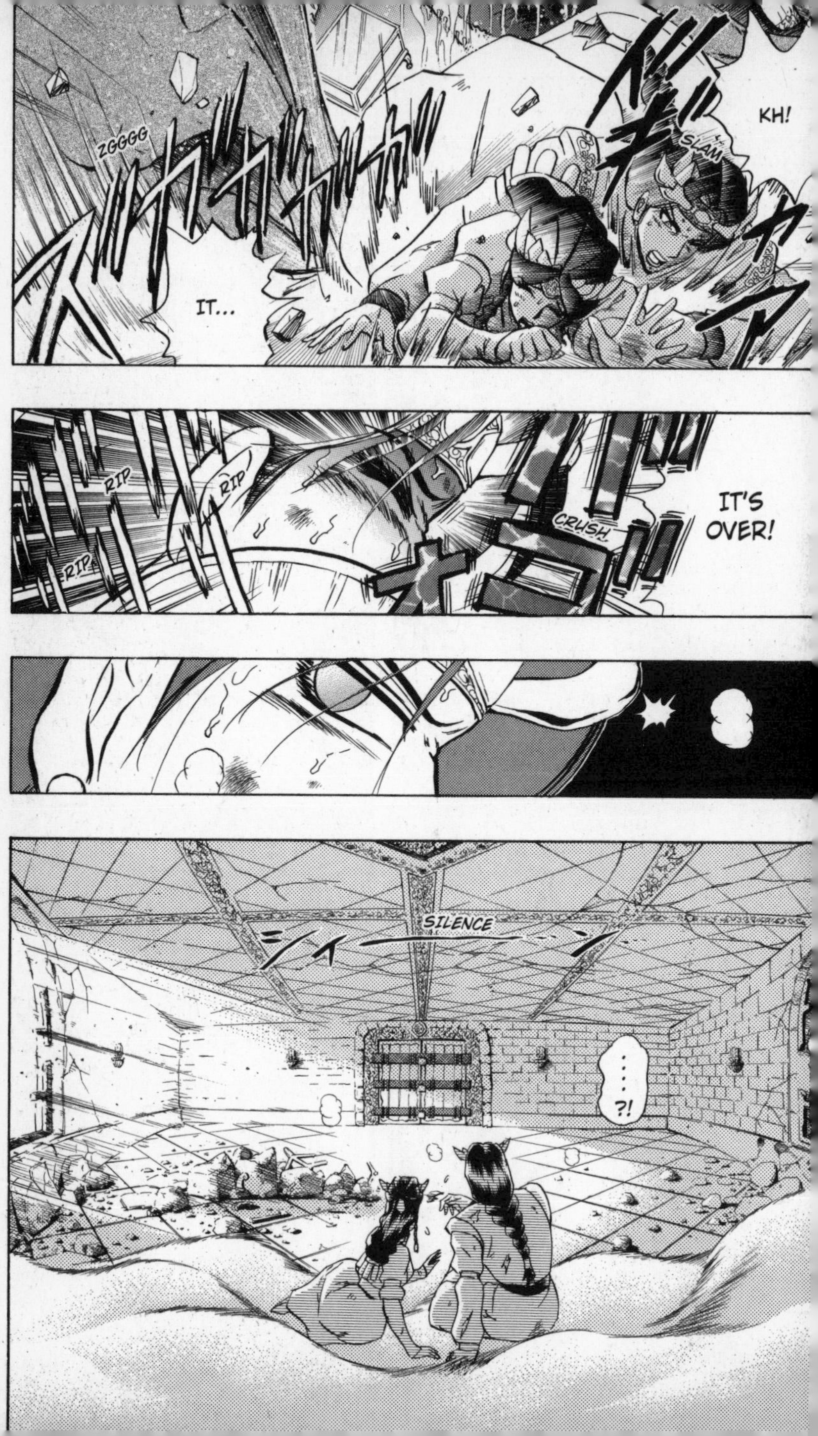
KH!
SLAM
ZGGGG
IT...
IT'S OVER!
CRUSH
RIP
RIP
RIP
SILENCE
.....?!

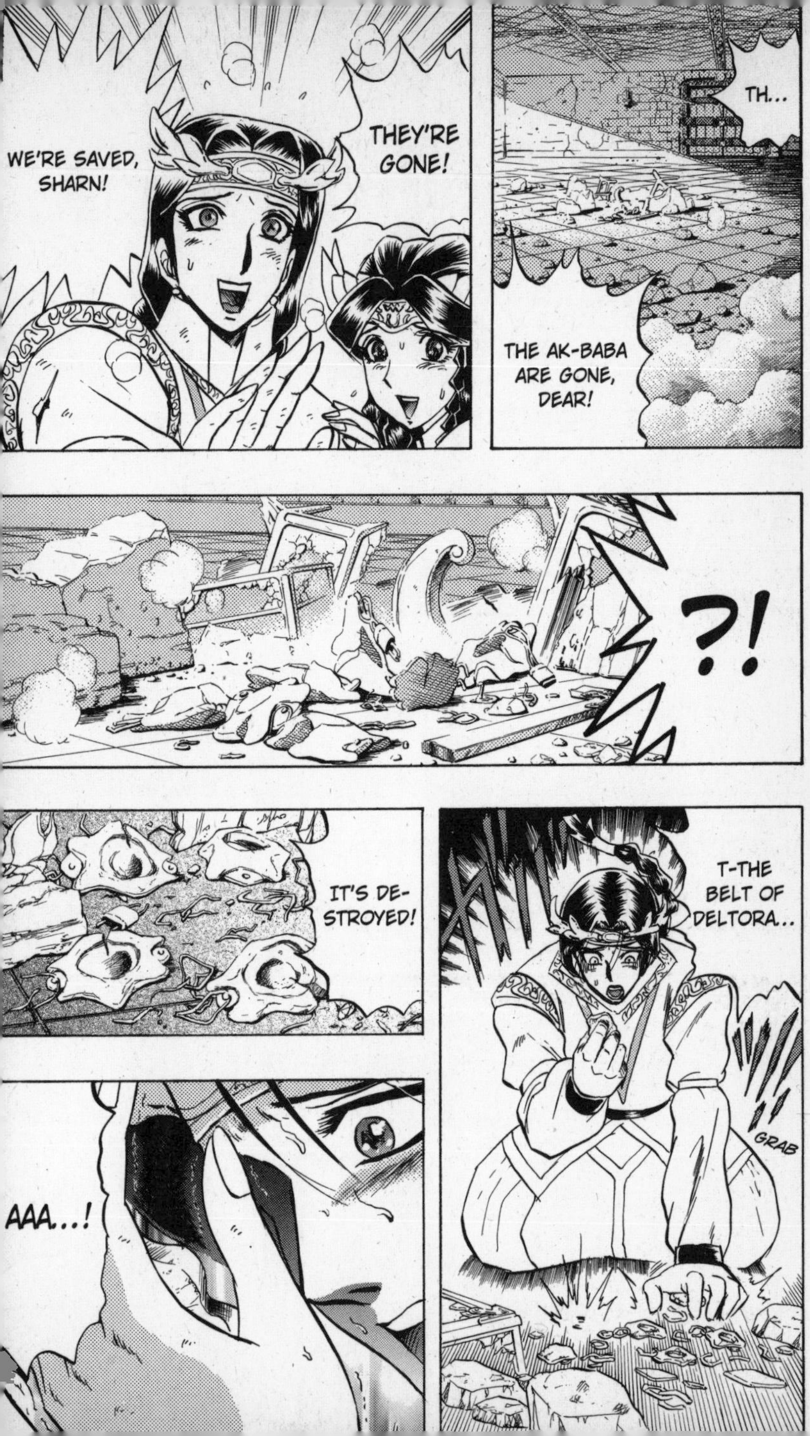
TH...
THE AK-BABA ARE GONE, DEAR!
THEY'RE GONE!
WE'RE SAVED, SHARN!
?!
T-THE BELT OF DELTORA...
GRAB
IT'S DE-STROYED!
AAA...!

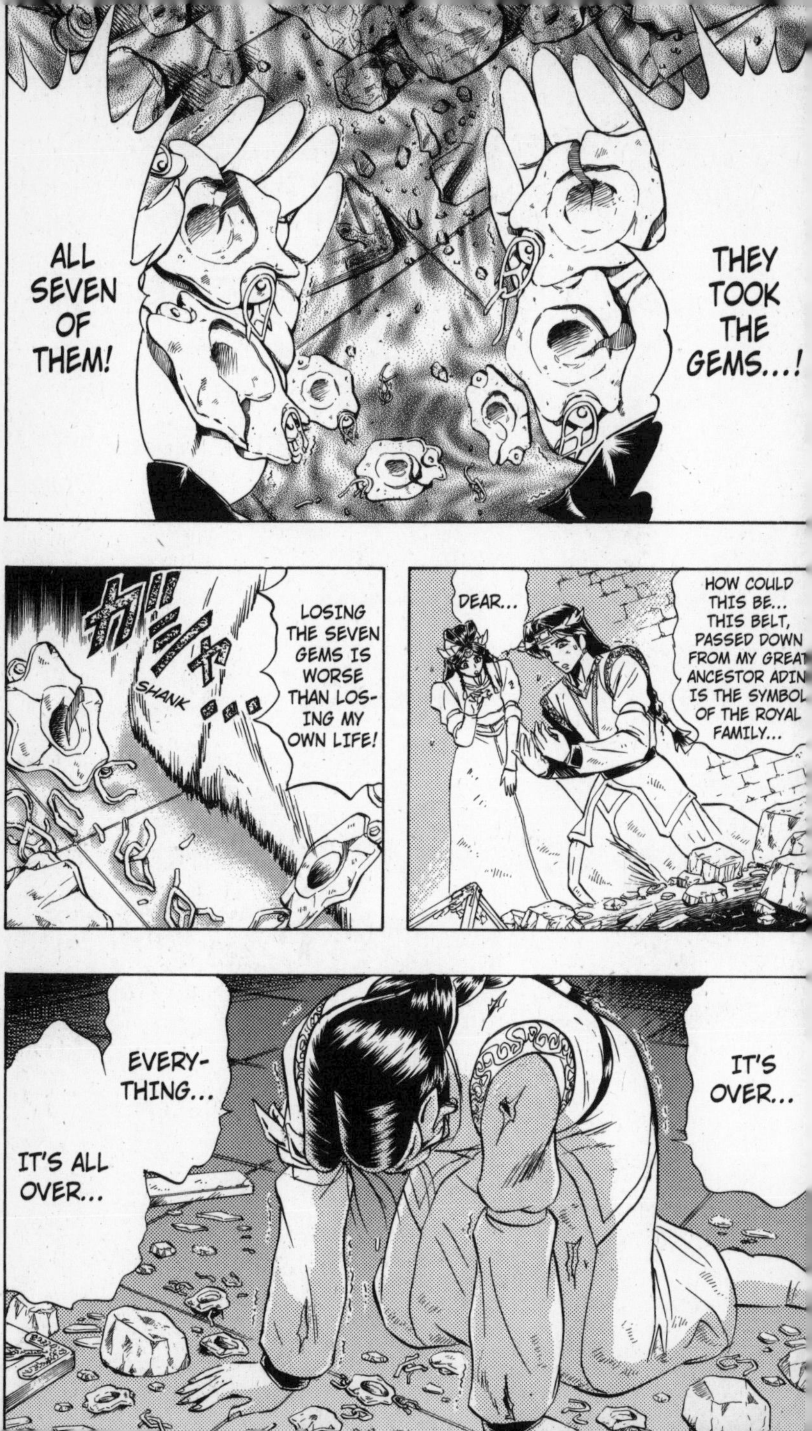
THEY TOOK THE GEMS...!
ALL SEVEN OF THEM!
HOW COULD THIS BE... THIS BELT, PASSED DOWN FROM MY GREAT ANCESTOR ADIN IS THE SYMBOL OF THE ROYAL FAMILY...
DEAR...
LOSING THE SEVEN GEMS IS WORSE THAN LOSING MY OWN LIFE!
SHANK
IT'S OVER...
EVERYTHING...
IT'S ALL OVER...

…?!

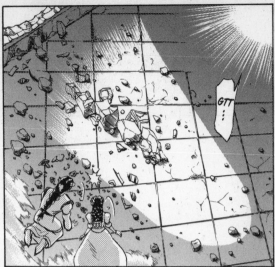

GTT…

GTT… GTT GTT

W-WHO'S THERE?!

ゴ''ト''ン
GTN

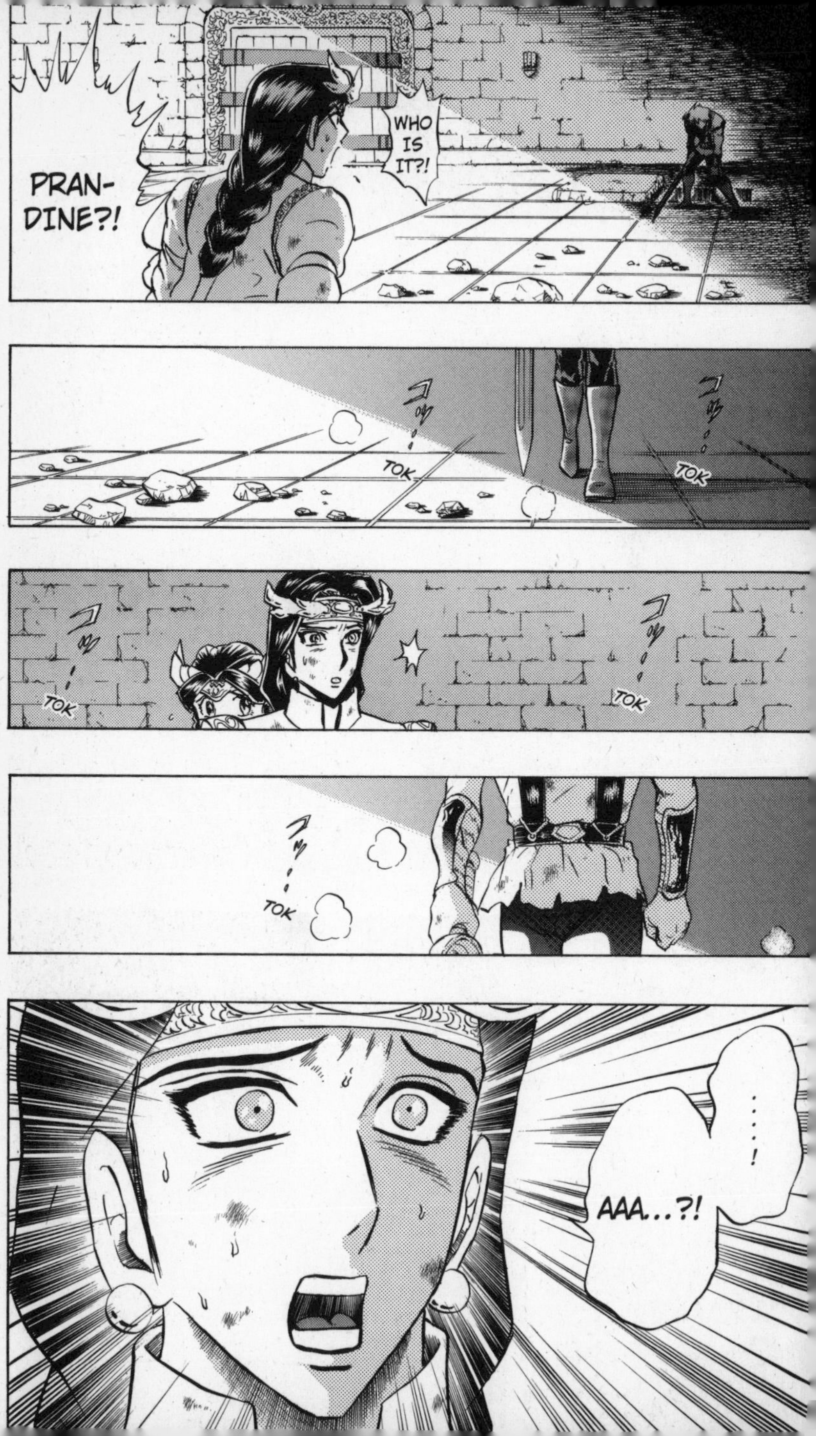
WHO IS IT?!
PRAN-DINE?!
TOK
TOK
TOK
TOK
TOK
....!
AAA...?!

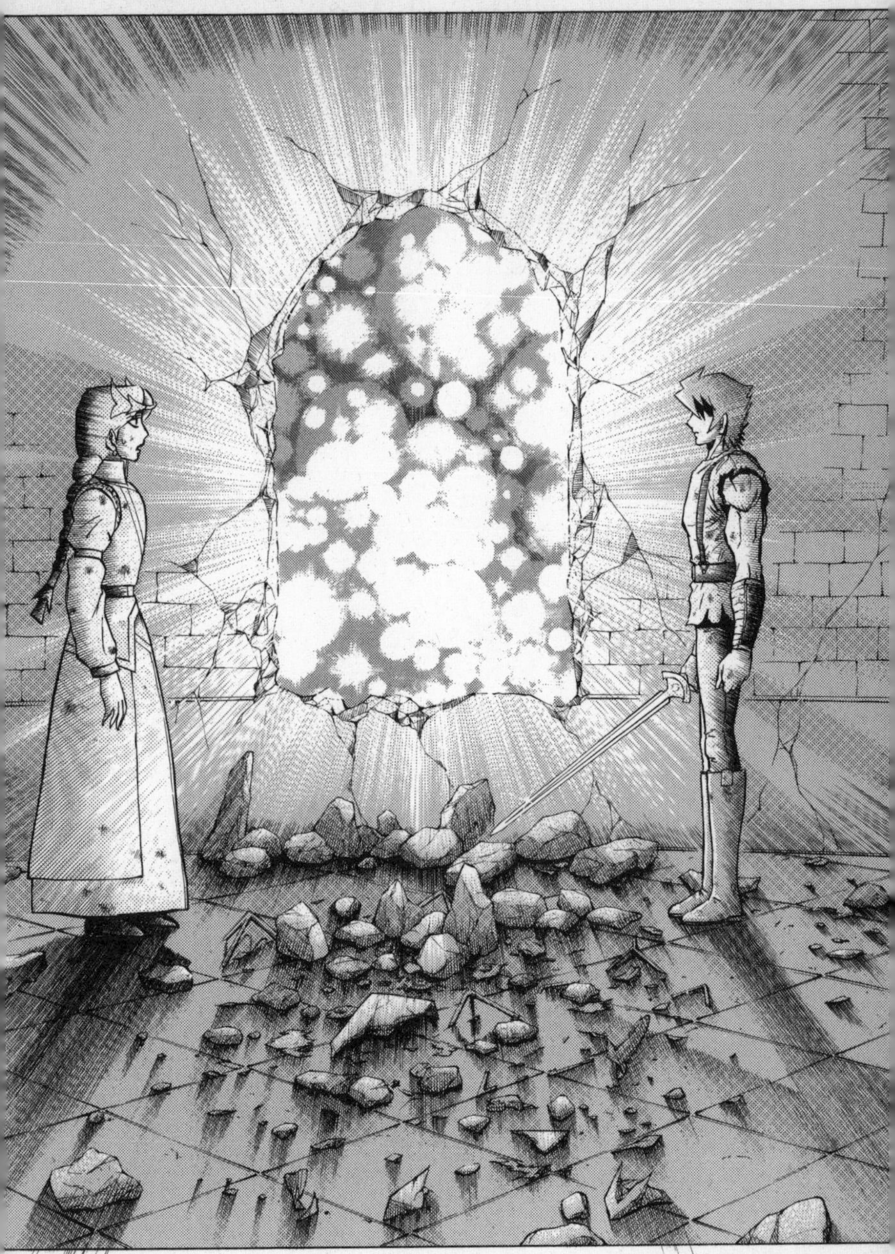

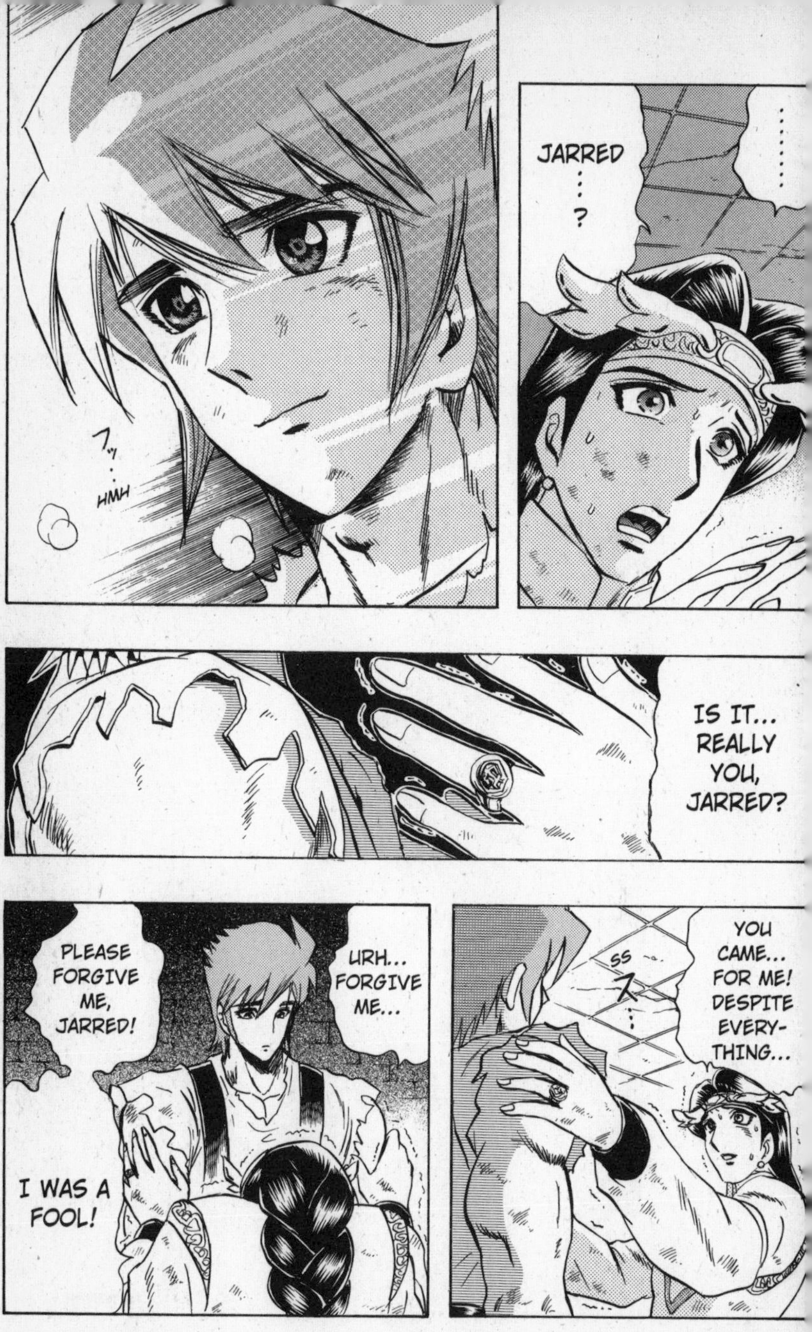
......
JARRED...?
HMH...
IS IT... REALLY YOU, JARRED?
YOU CAME... FOR ME! DESPITE EVERYTHING...
SS...
URH... FORGIVE ME...
PLEASE FORGIVE ME, JARRED!
I WAS A FOOL!

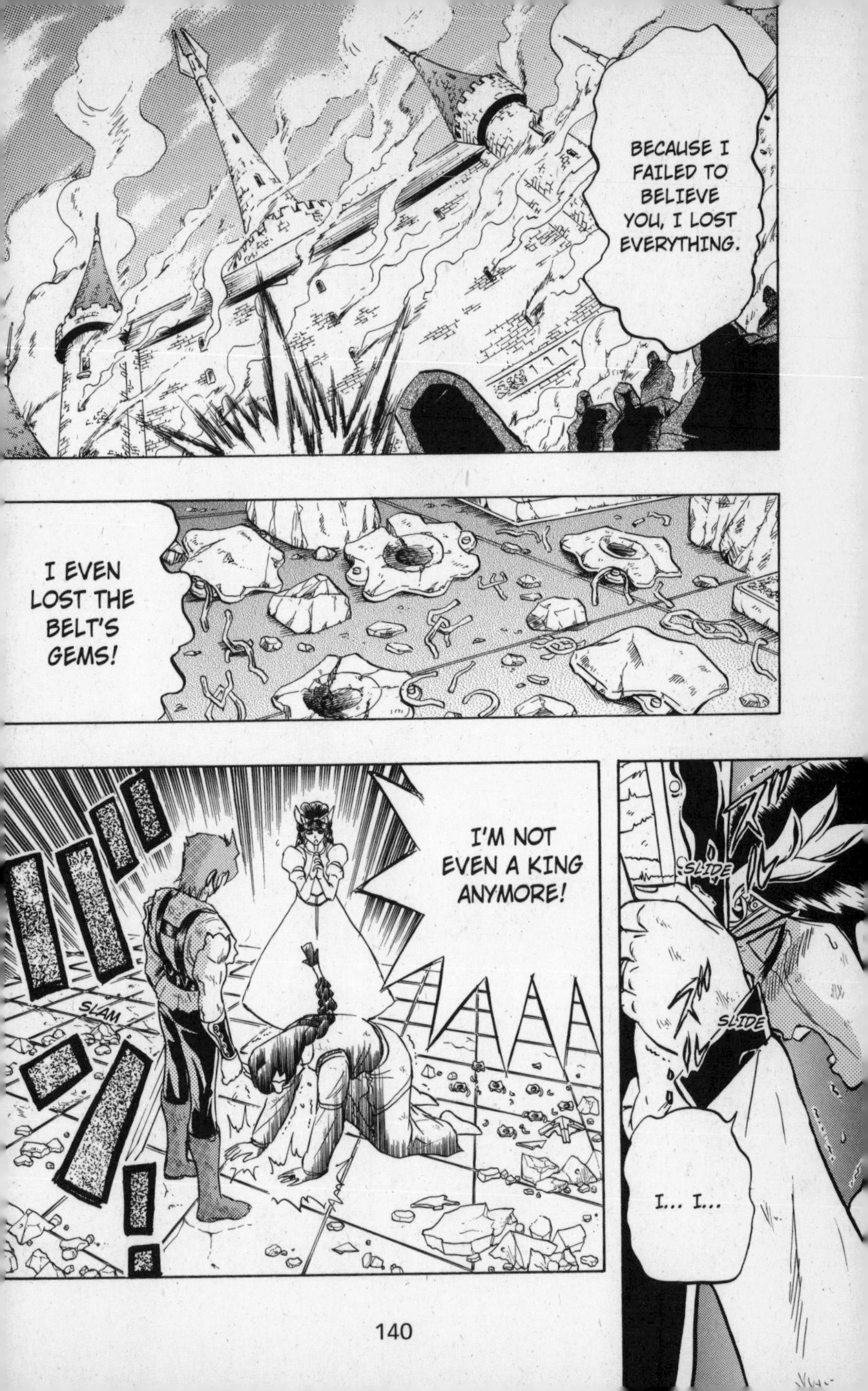
BECAUSE I FAILED TO BELIEVE YOU, I LOST EVERYTHING.
I EVEN LOST THE BELT'S GEMS!
SLIDE
SLIDE
I... I...
I'M NOT EVEN A KING ANYMORE!
SLAM

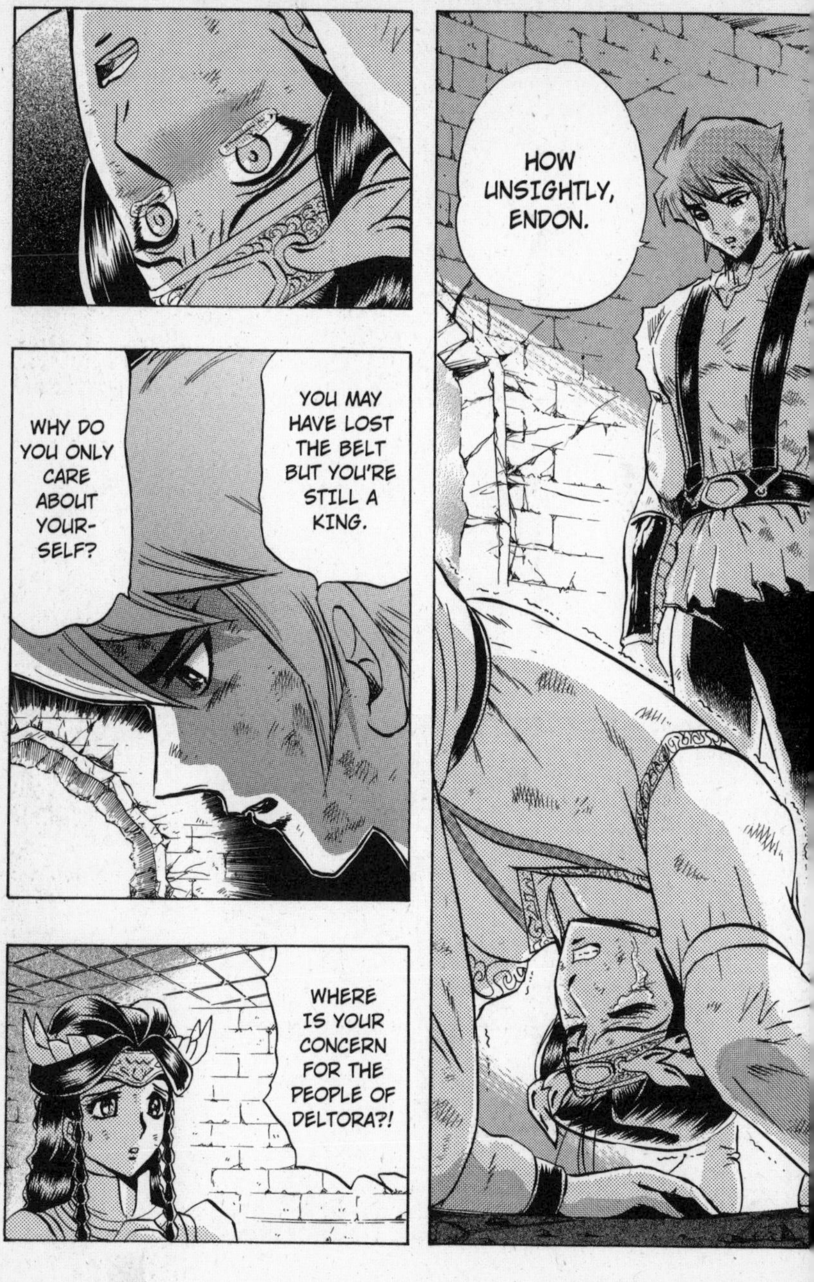
HOW UNSIGHTLY, ENDON.
YOU MAY HAVE LOST THE BELT BUT YOU'RE STILL A KING.
WHY DO YOU ONLY CARE ABOUT YOUR-SELF?
WHERE IS YOUR CONCERN FOR THE PEOPLE OF DELTORA?!

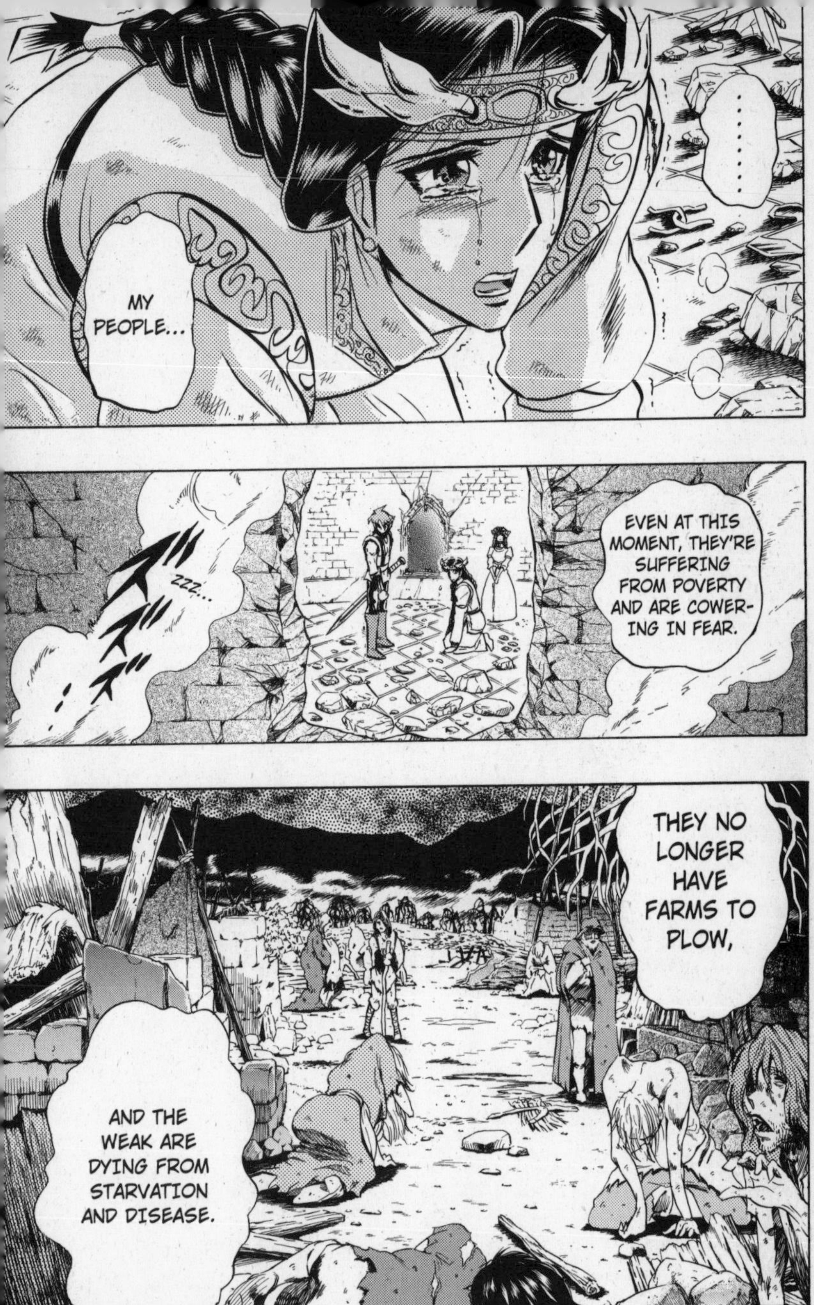
...
MY PEOPLE...
EVEN AT THIS MOMENT, THEY'RE SUFFERING FROM POVERTY AND ARE COWER-ING IN FEAR.
ZZZ...
THEY NO LONGER HAVE FARMS TO PLOW,
AND THE WEAK ARE DYING FROM STARVATION AND DISEASE.

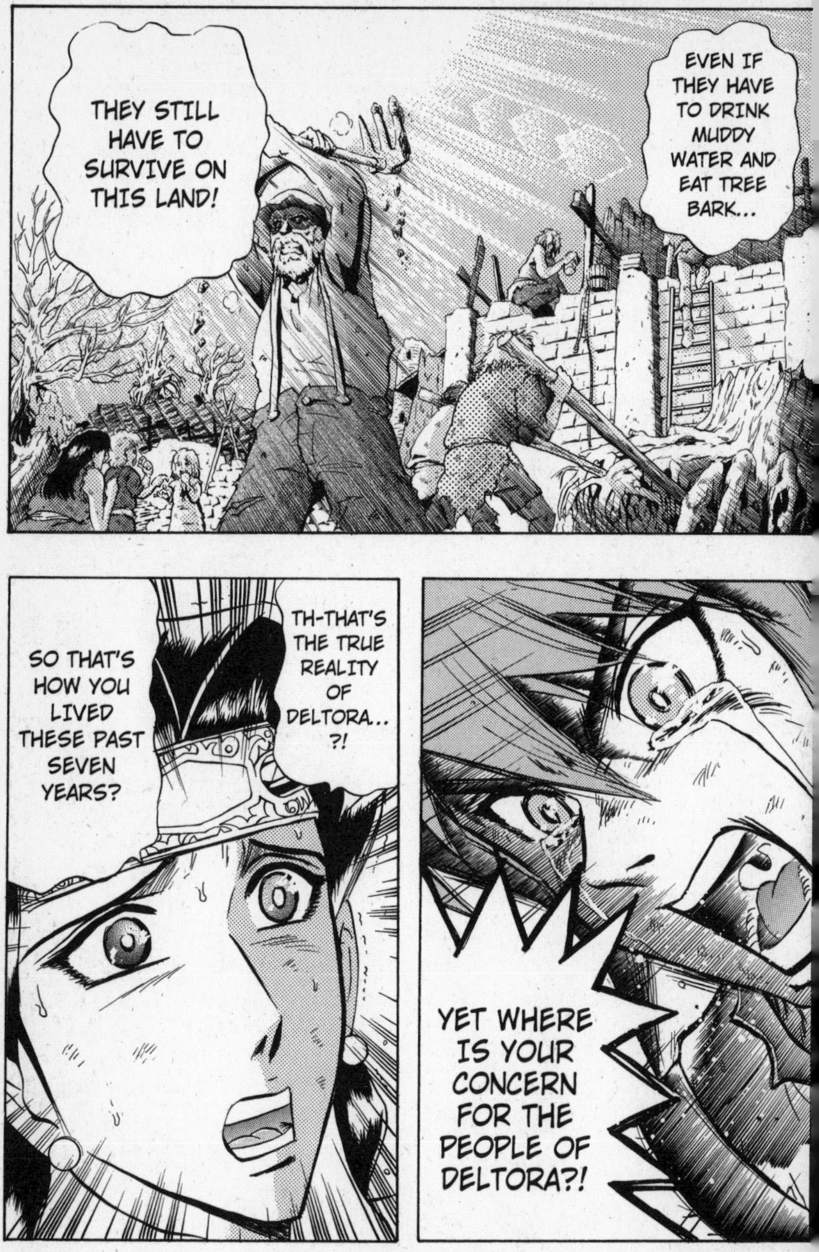
EVEN IF THEY HAVE TO DRINK MUDDY WATER AND EAT TREE BARK...
THEY STILL HAVE TO SURVIVE ON THIS LAND!
YET WHERE IS YOUR CONCERN FOR THE PEOPLE OF DELTORA?!
TH-THAT'S THE TRUE REALITY OF DELTORA...?!
SO THAT'S HOW YOU LIVED THESE PAST SEVEN YEARS?

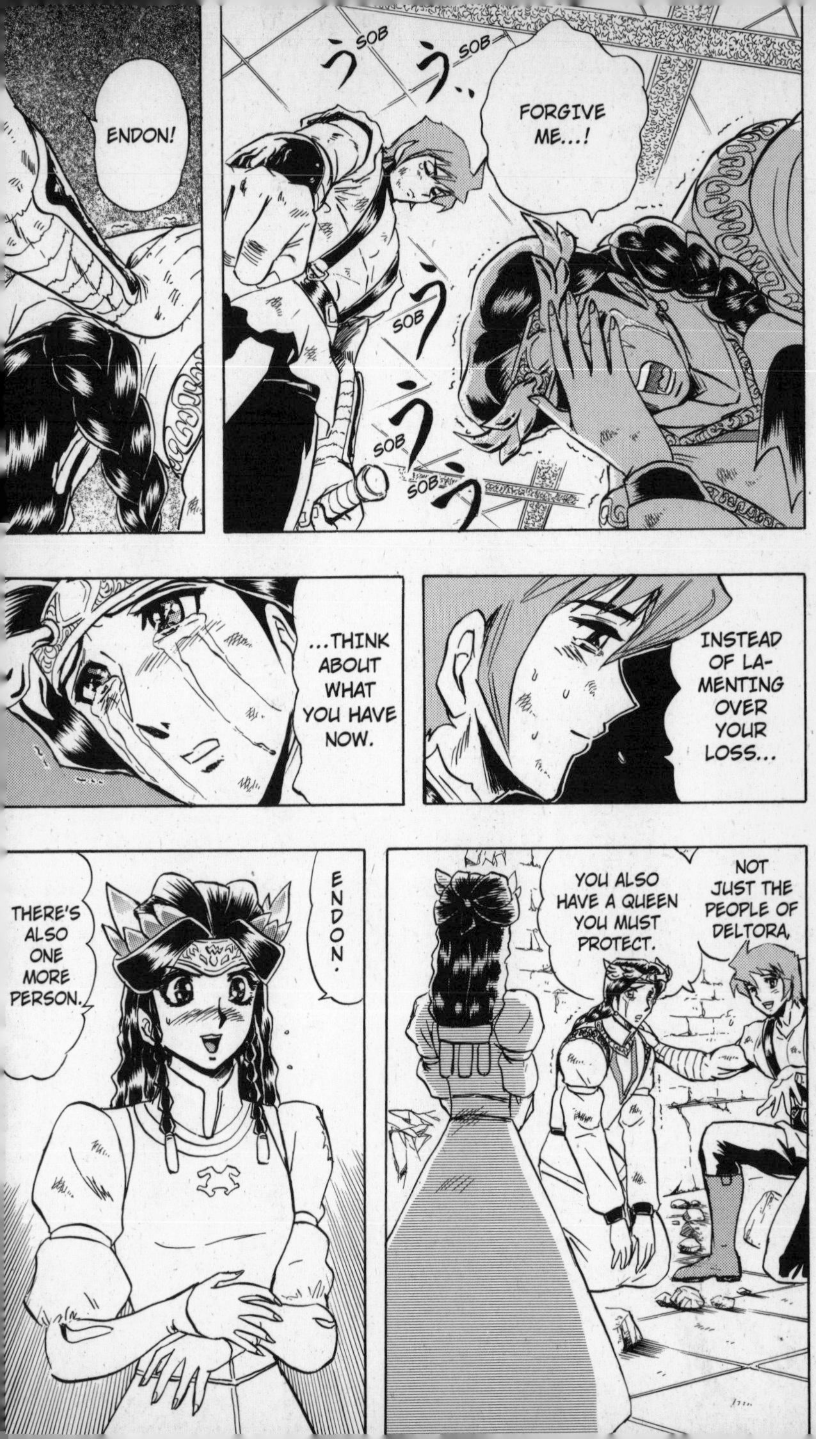
FORGIVE ME...!
う SOB
う SOB
う SOB
う SOB
う SOB
ENDON!
INSTEAD OF LA-MENTING OVER YOUR LOSS...
...THINK ABOUT WHAT YOU HAVE NOW.
NOT JUST THE PEOPLE OF DELTORA,
YOU ALSO HAVE A QUEEN YOU MUST PROTECT.
ENDON.
THERE'S ALSO ONE MORE PERSON.

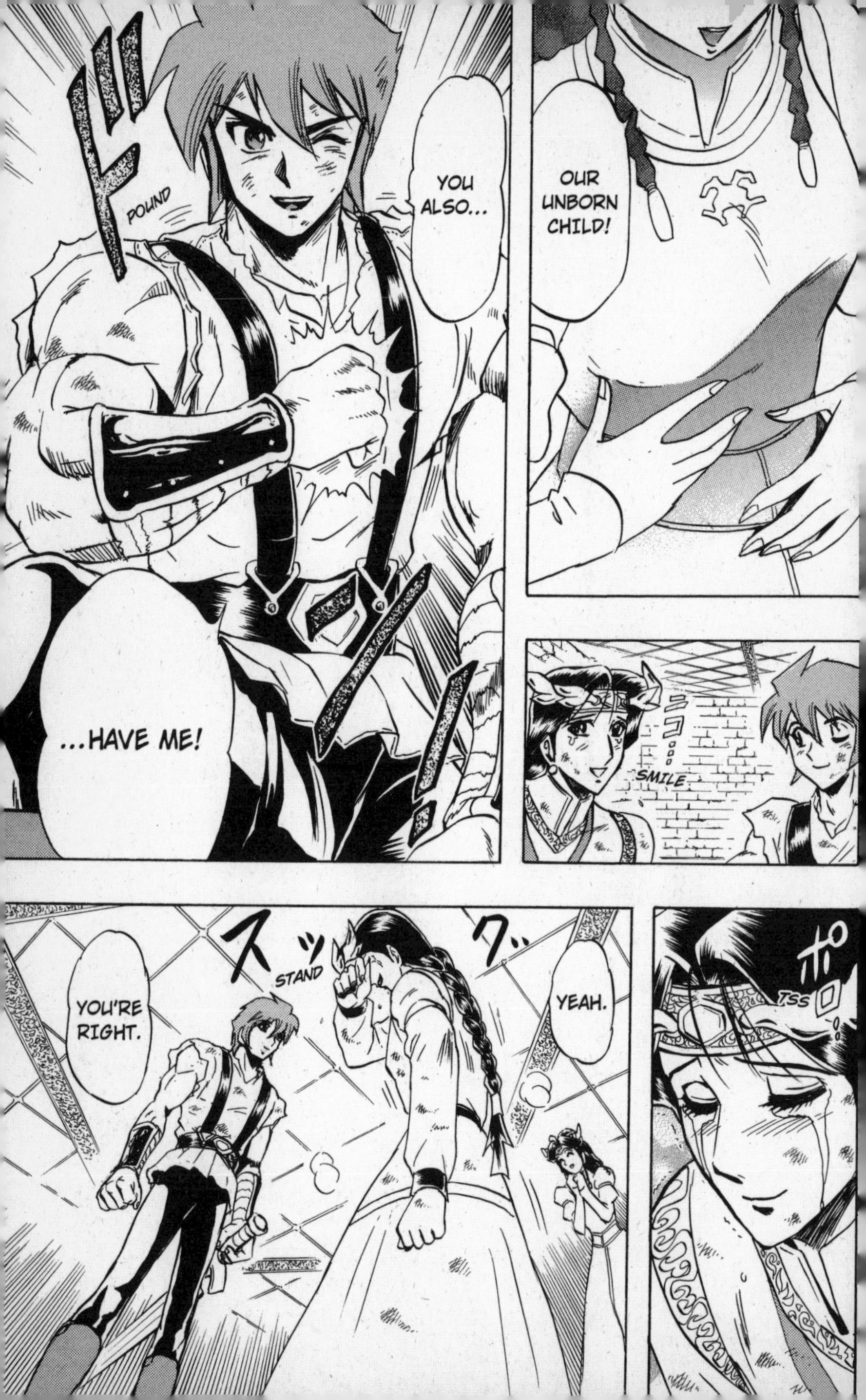

OUR UNBORN CHILD!
ニコ…
SMILE
YOU ALSO…
ド
POUND
…HAVE ME!
ポロ
TSS
YEAH.
スック
STAND
YOU'RE RIGHT.

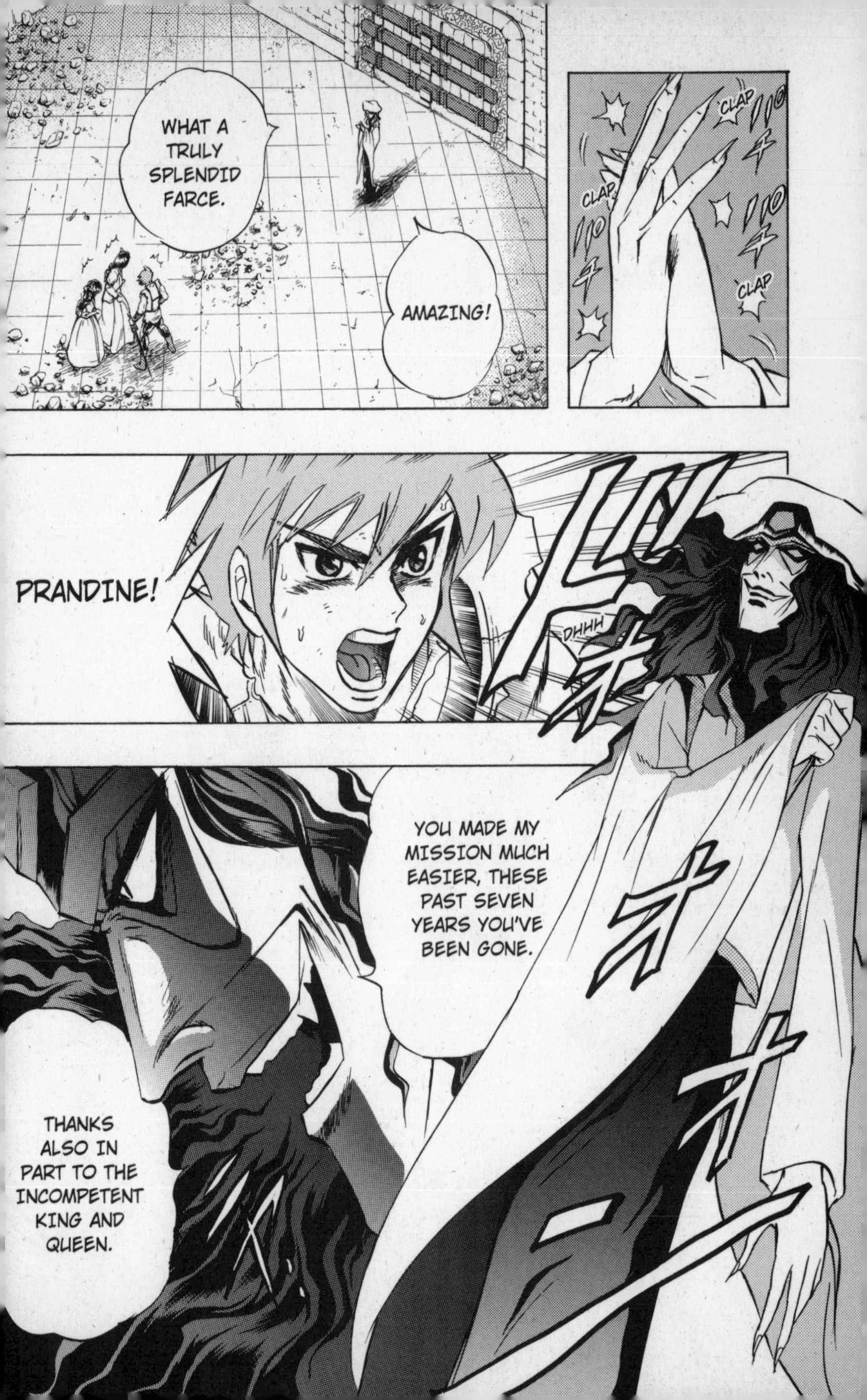
CLAP
CLAP
CLAP
WHAT A TRULY SPLENDID FARCE.
AMAZING!
PRANDINE!
DHHH
YOU MADE MY MISSION MUCH EASIER, THESE PAST SEVEN YEARS YOU'VE BEEN GONE.
THANKS ALSO IN PART TO THE INCOMPETENT KING AND QUEEN.

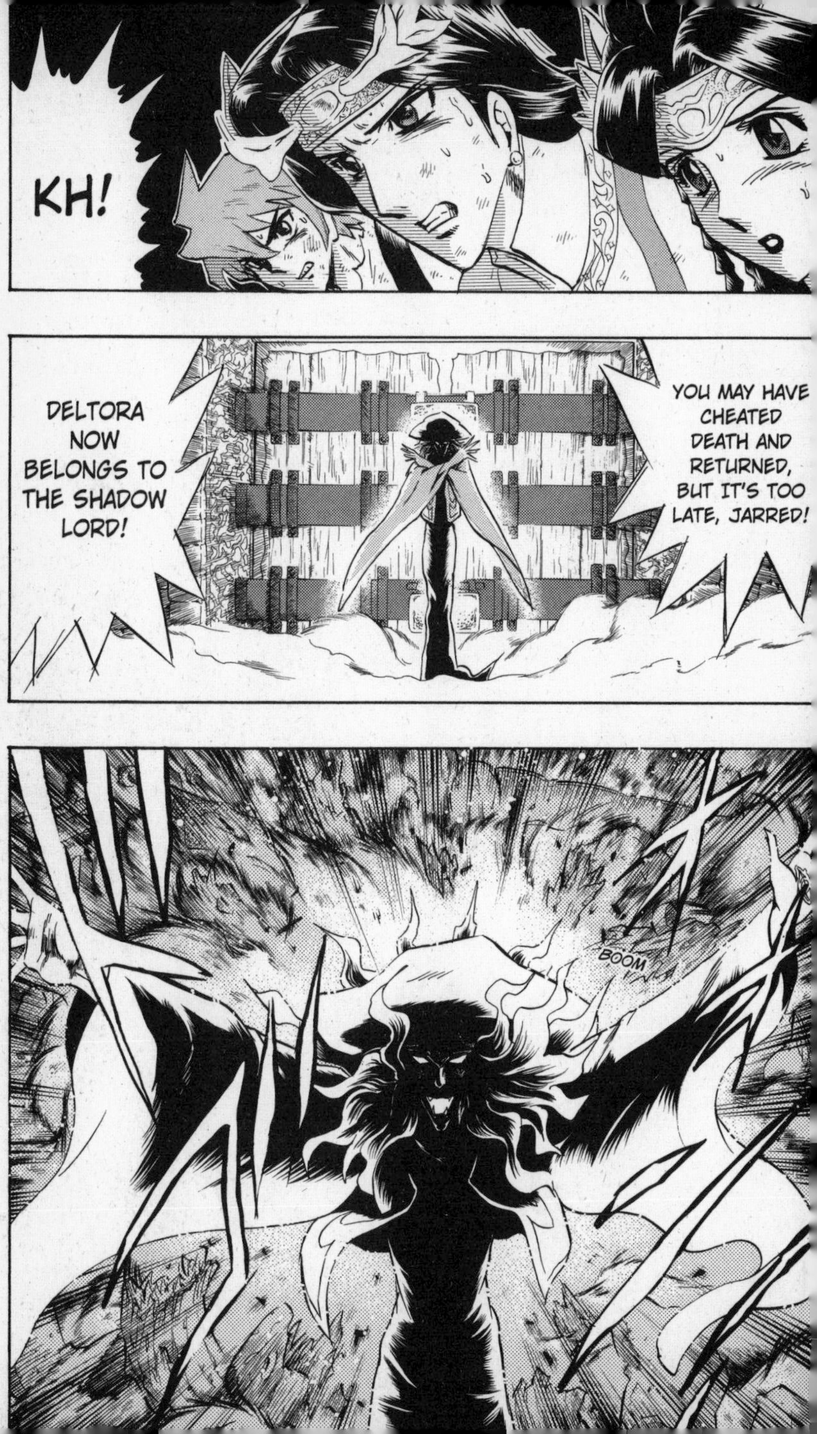
KH!
YOU MAY HAVE CHEATED DEATH AND RETURNED, BUT IT'S TOO LATE, JARRED!
DELTORA NOW BELONGS TO THE SHADOW LORD!
BOOM

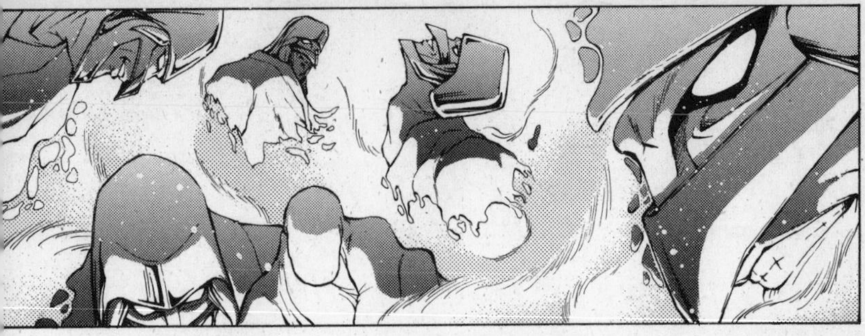
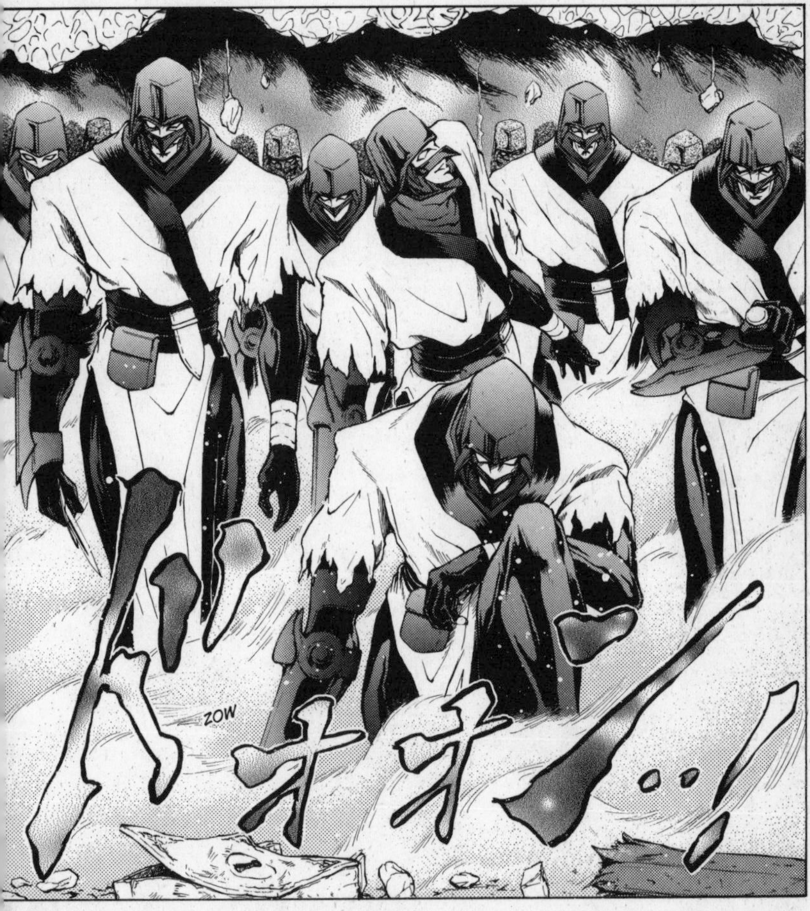
バオオ…!
ZOW

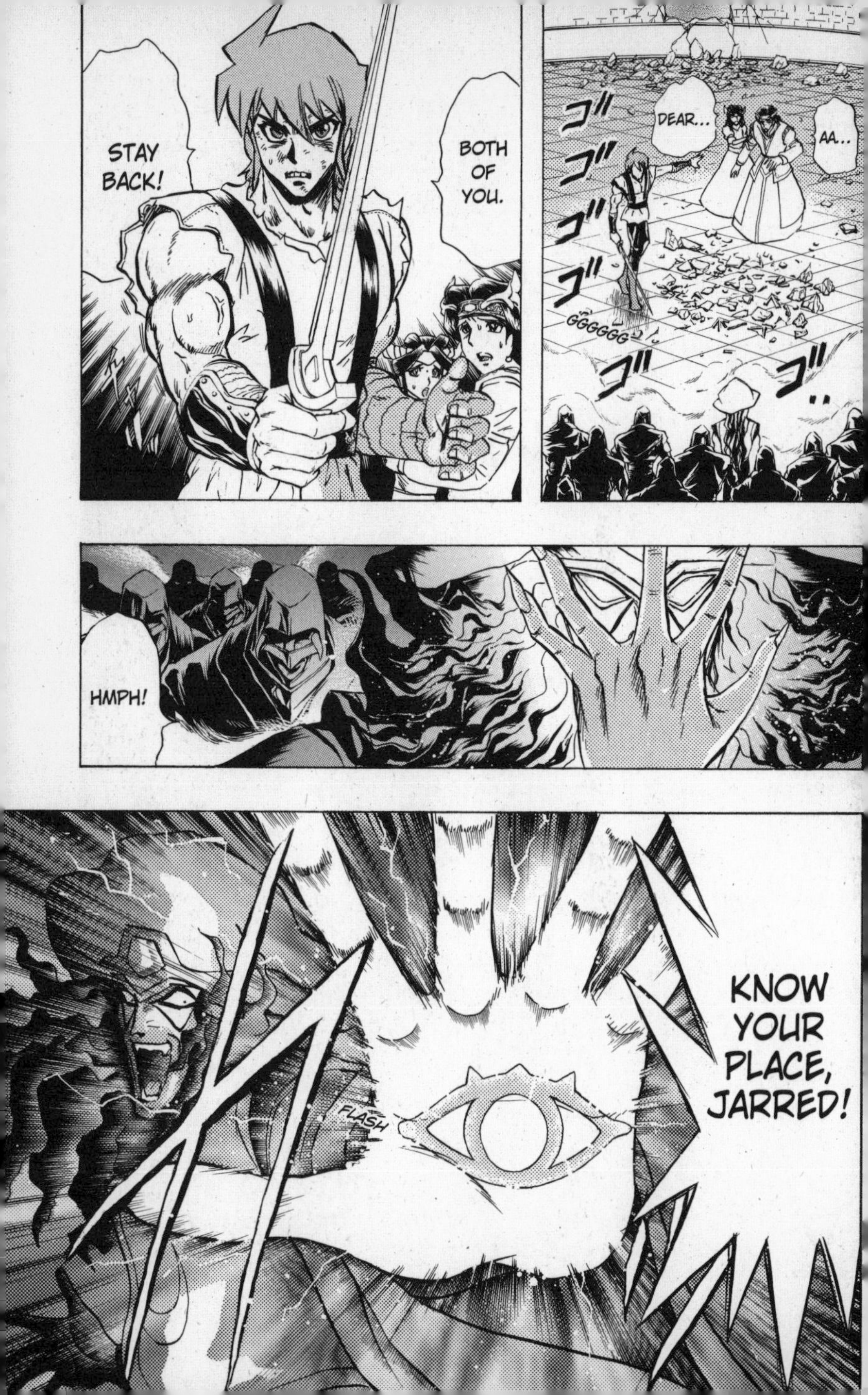
AA...
DEAR...
GGGGGG
BOTH OF YOU.
STAY BACK!
HMPH!
KNOW YOUR PLACE, JARRED!
FLASH

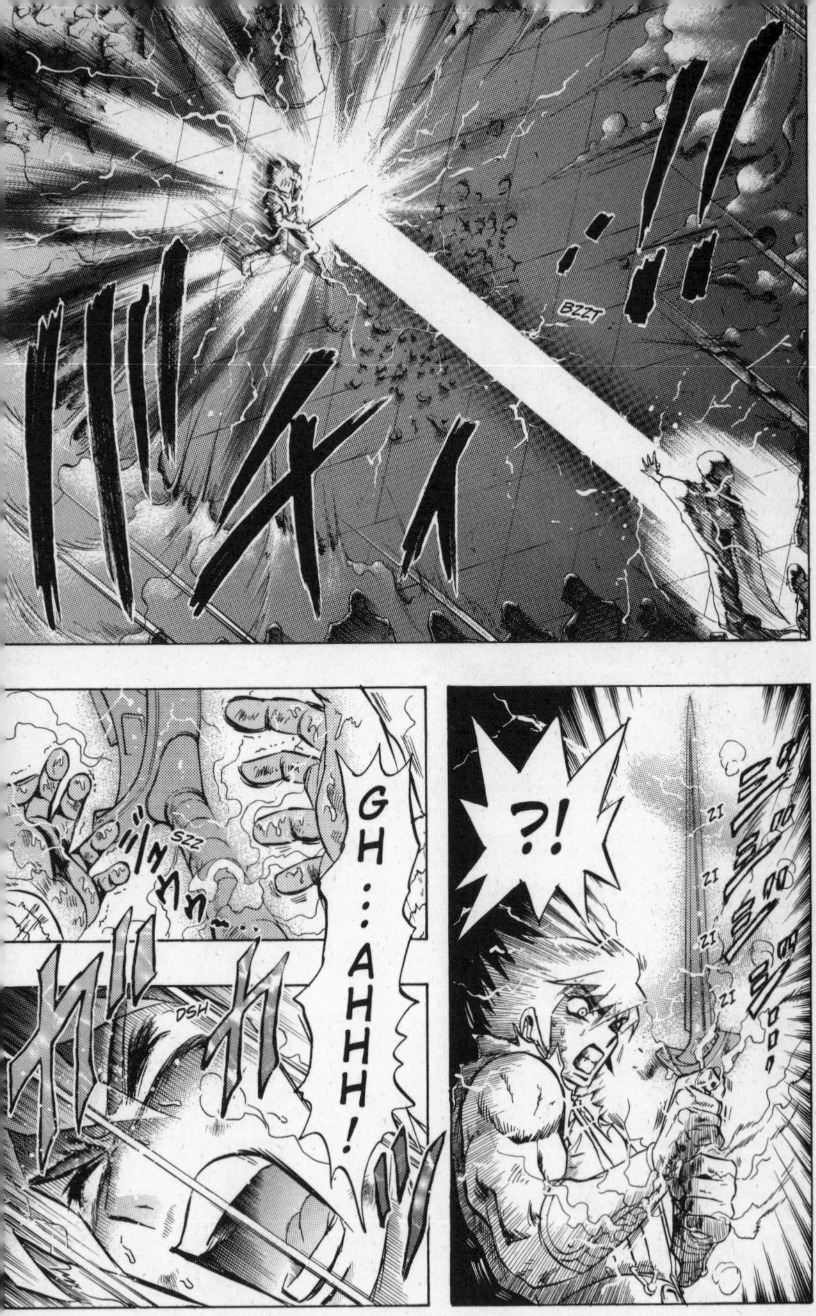
BZZT
SZZ
GH... AHHH!
DSH
?!
ZI
ZI
ZI
ZI

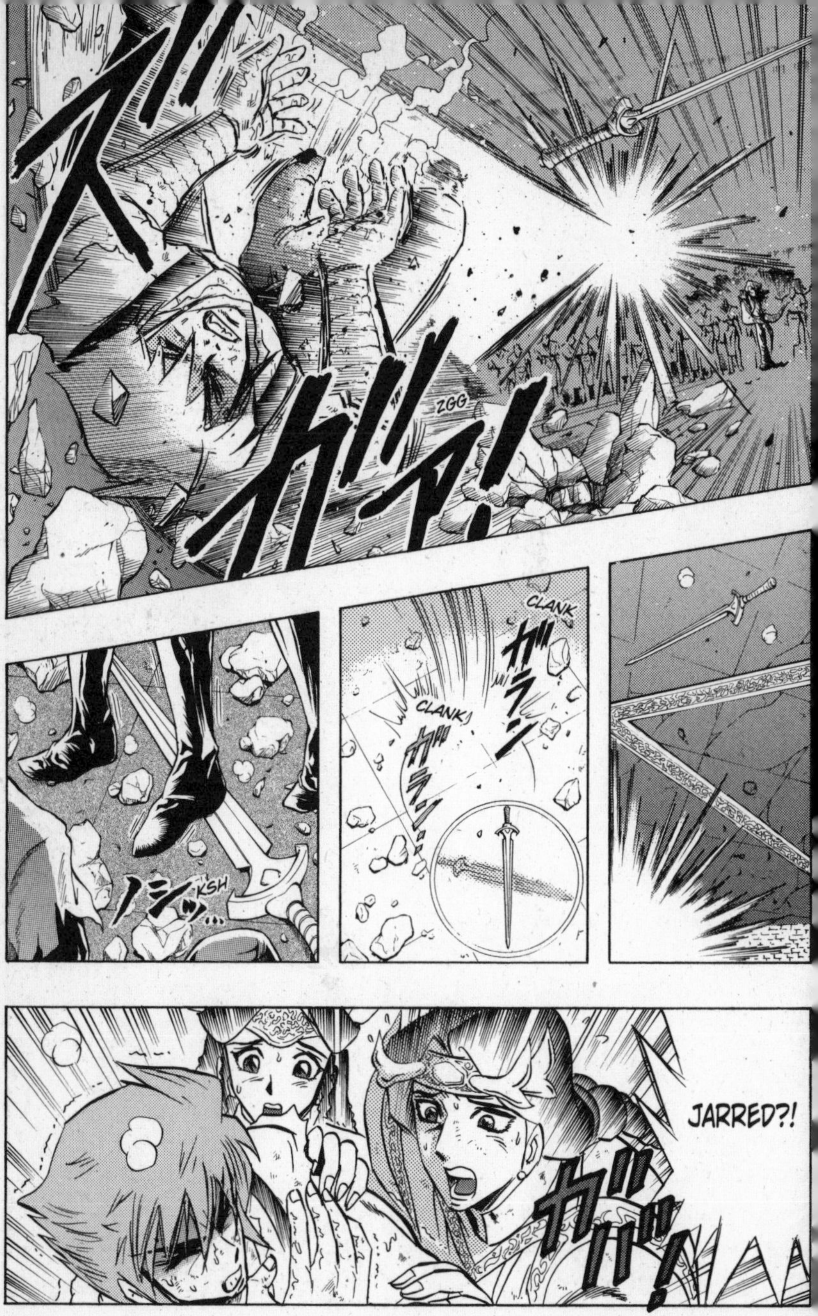
ZGG
CLANK
CLANK!
KSH
JARRED?!

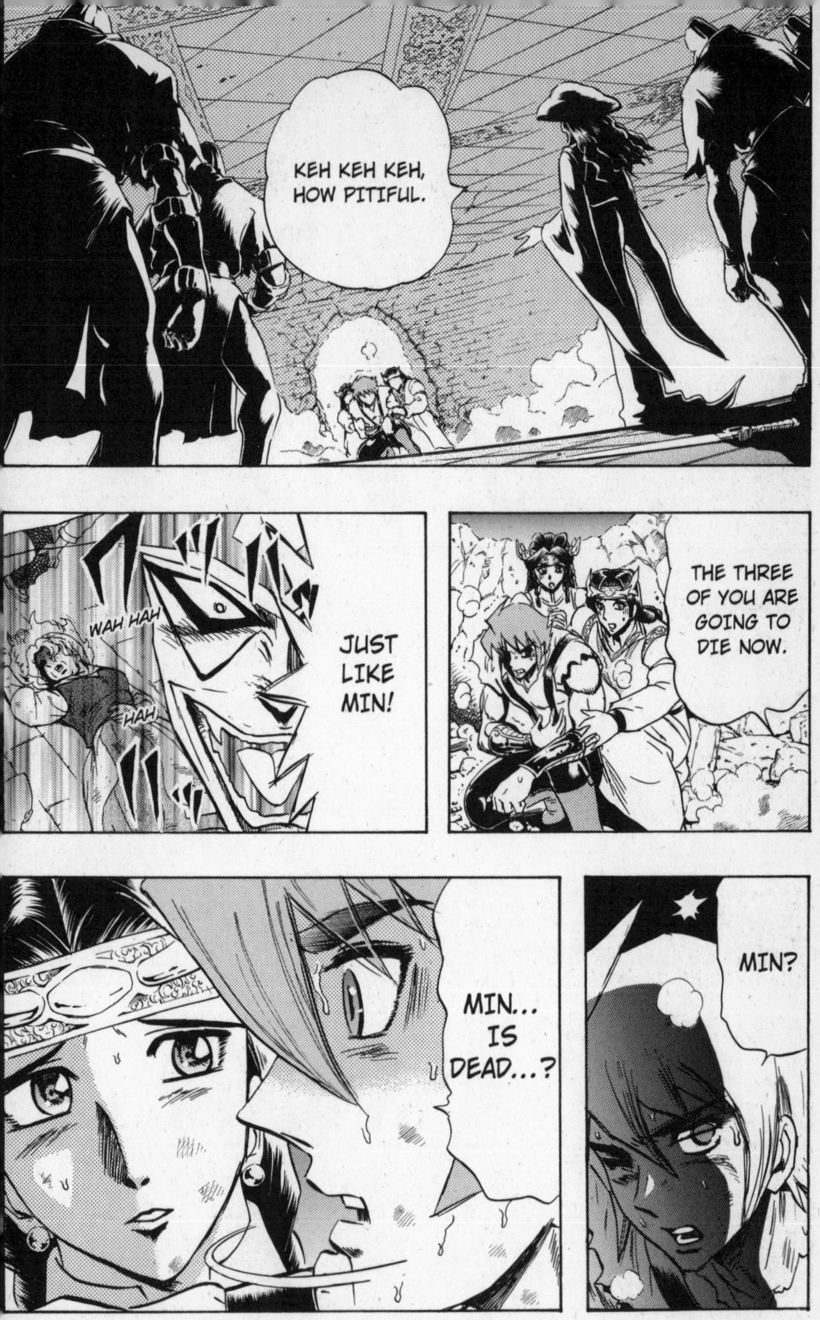
KEH KEH KEH, HOW PITIFUL.
THE THREE OF YOU ARE GOING TO DIE NOW.
JUST LIKE MIN!
WAH HAH
HAH
MIN?
MIN... IS DEAD...?

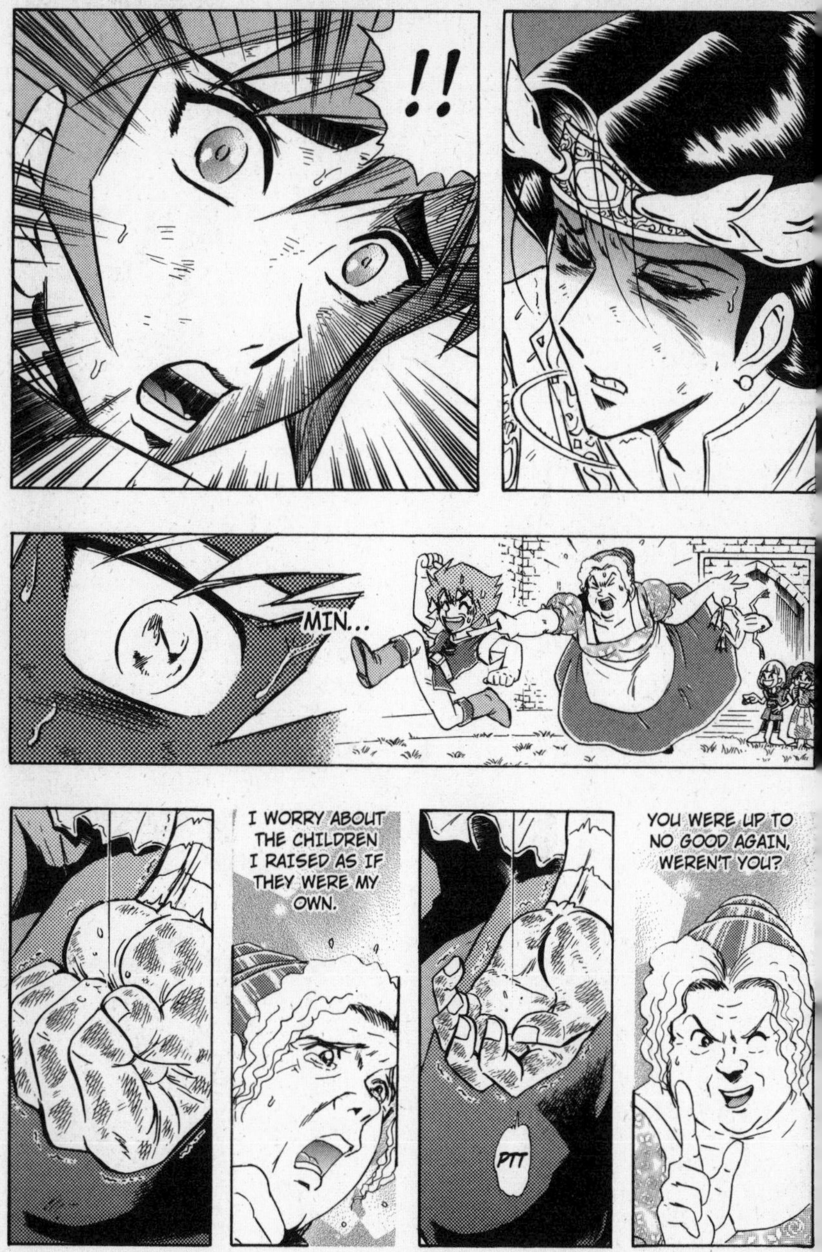
!!
MIN...
YOU WERE UP TO NO GOOD AGAIN, WEREN'T YOU?
PTT
I WORRY ABOUT THE CHILDREN I RAISED AS IF THEY WERE MY OWN.

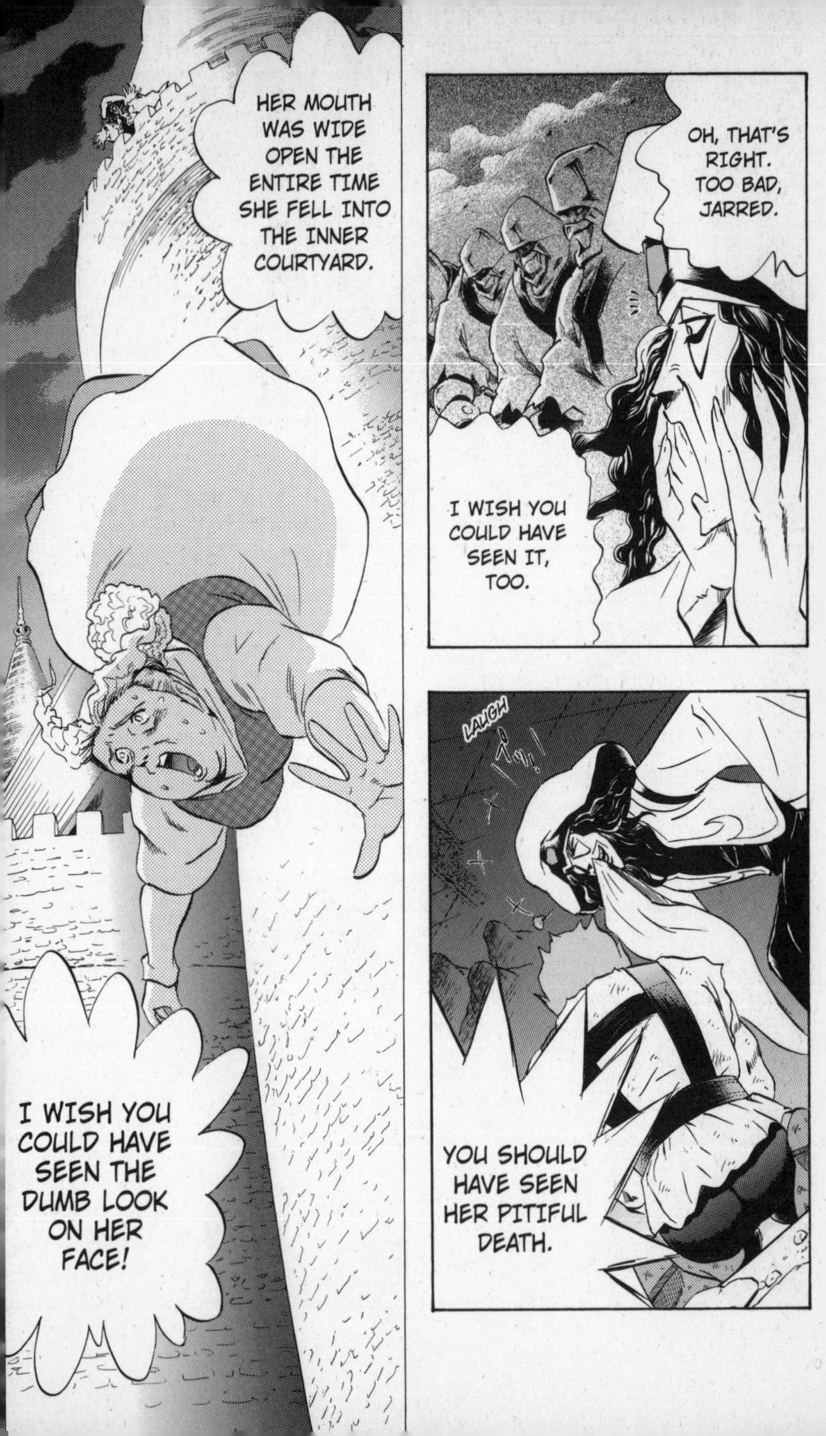
OH, THAT'S RIGHT. TOO BAD, JARRED.
I WISH YOU COULD HAVE SEEN IT, TOO.
LAUGH
YOU SHOULD HAVE SEEN HER PITIFUL DEATH.
HER MOUTH WAS WIDE OPEN THE ENTIRE TIME SHE FELL INTO THE INNER COURTYARD.
I WISH YOU COULD HAVE SEEN THE DUMB LOOK ON HER FACE!

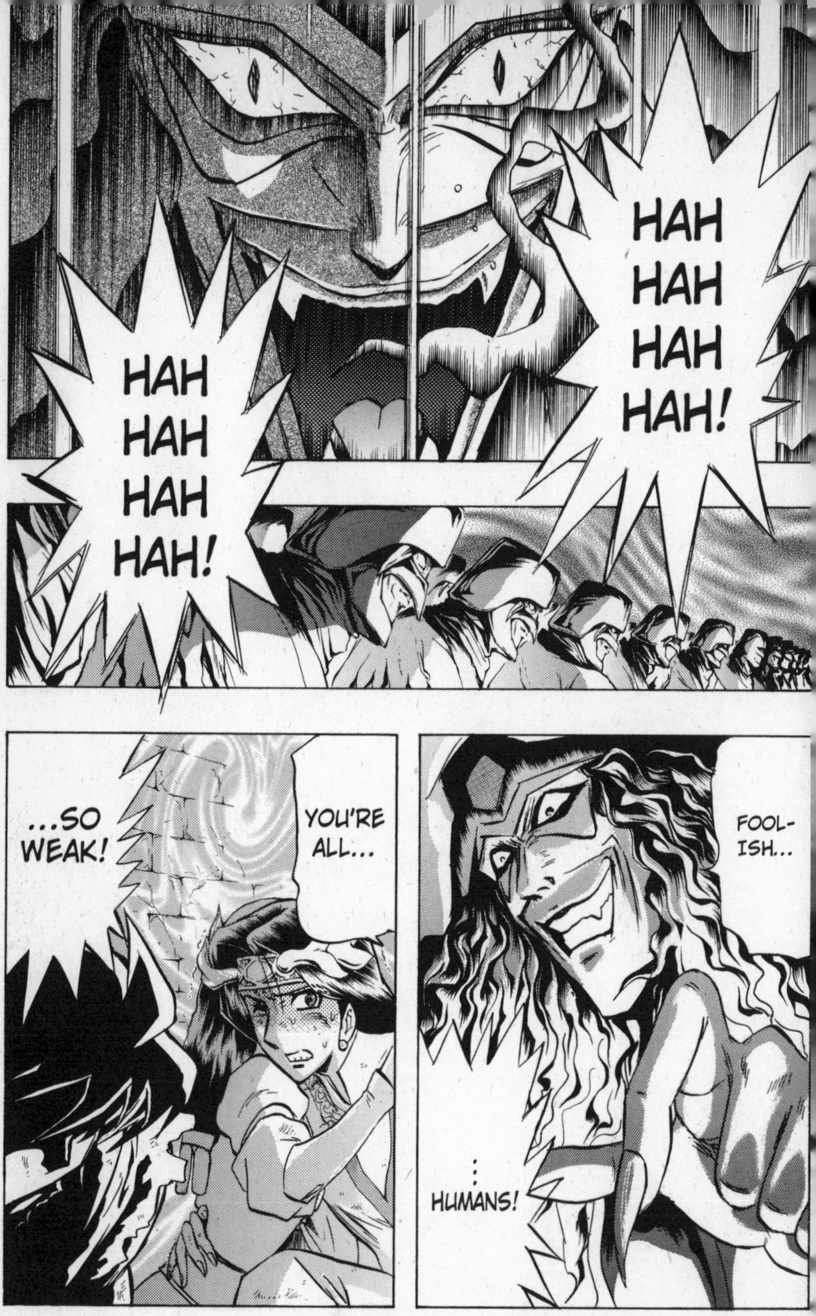
HAH HAH HAH HAH!
HAH HAH HAH HAH!
FOOL-ISH...
...HUMANS!
YOU'RE ALL...
...SO WEAK!

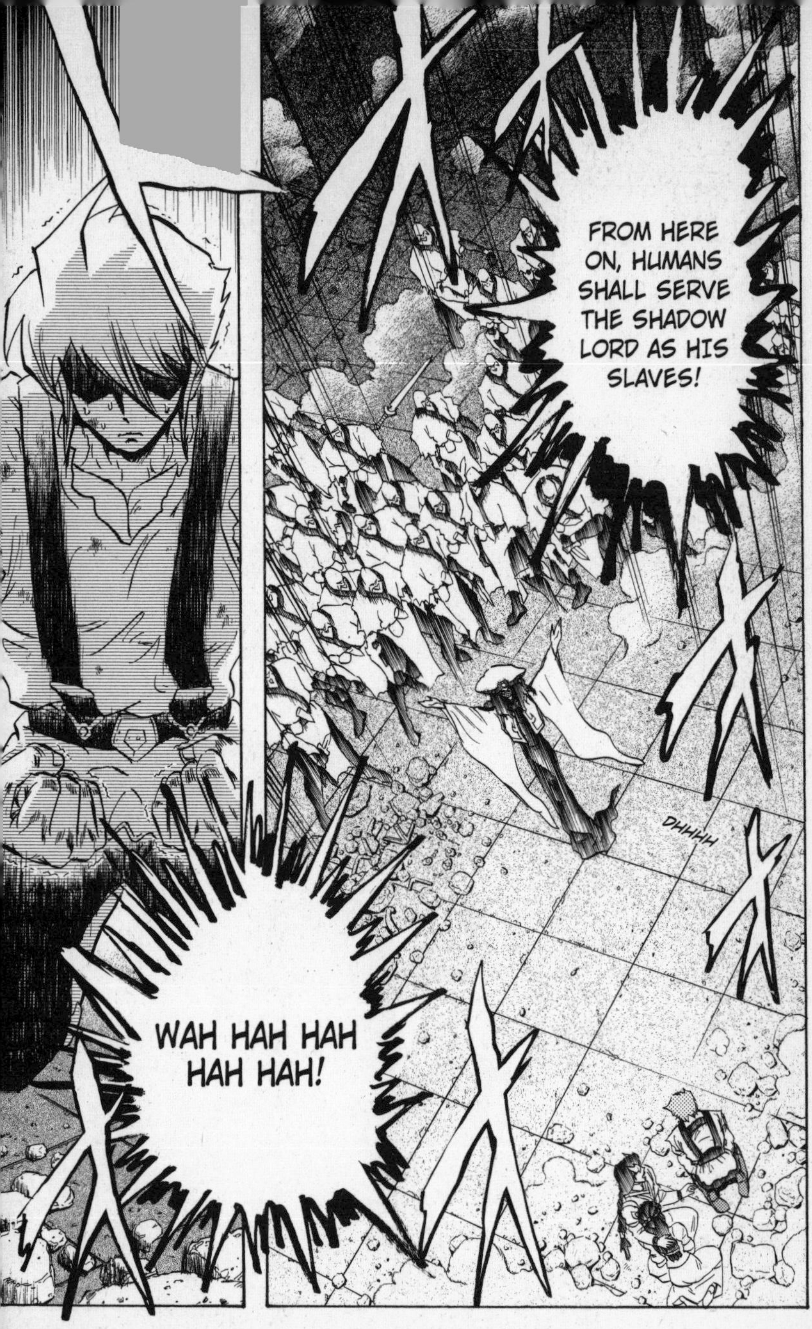
FROM HERE ON, HUMANS SHALL SERVE THE SHADOW LORD AS HIS SLAVES!
DHHHH
WAH HAH HAH HAH HAH!

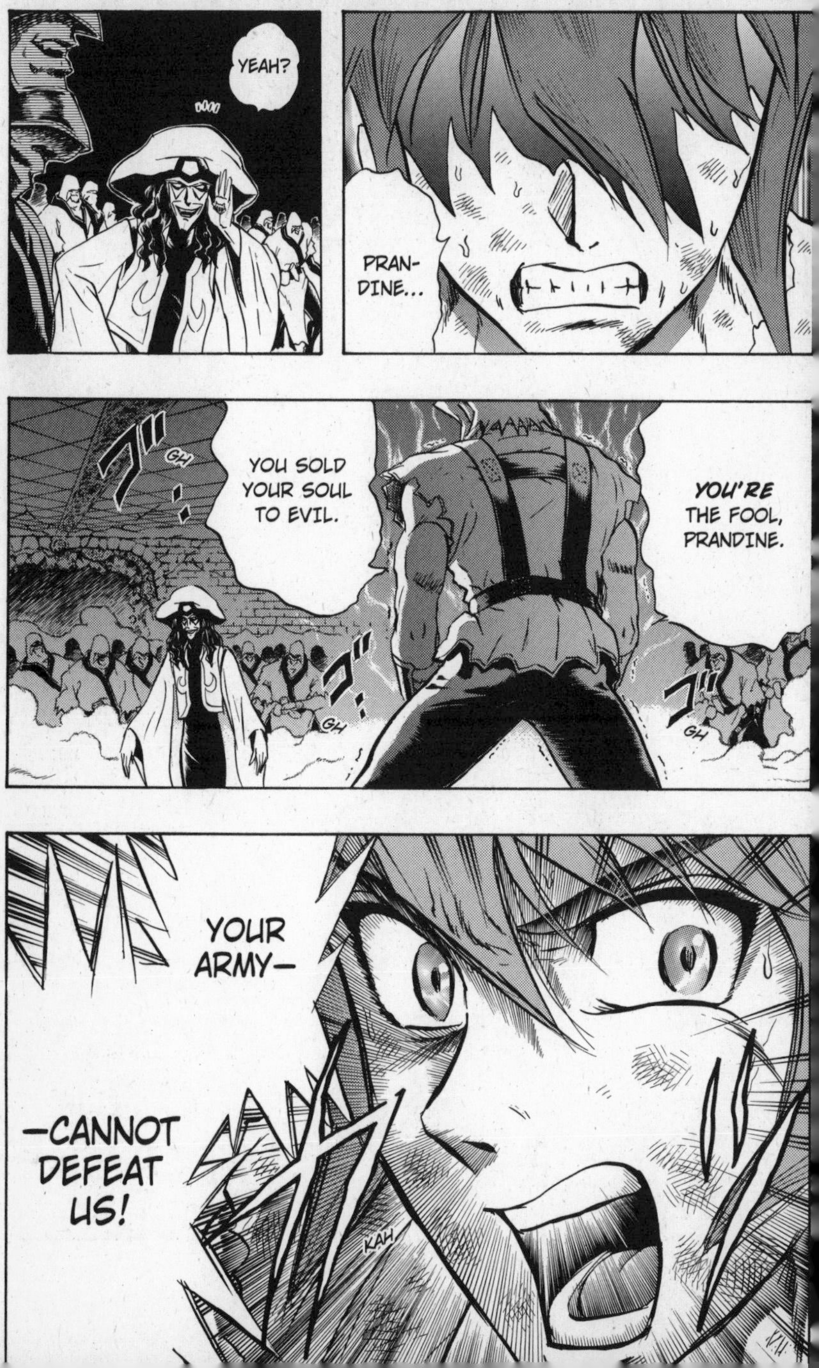
PRAN-
DINE...
YEAH?
YOU'RE THE FOOL, PRANDINE.
YOU SOLD YOUR SOUL TO EVIL.
GH
GH
GH
YOUR ARMY—
—CANNOT DEFEAT US!
KAH

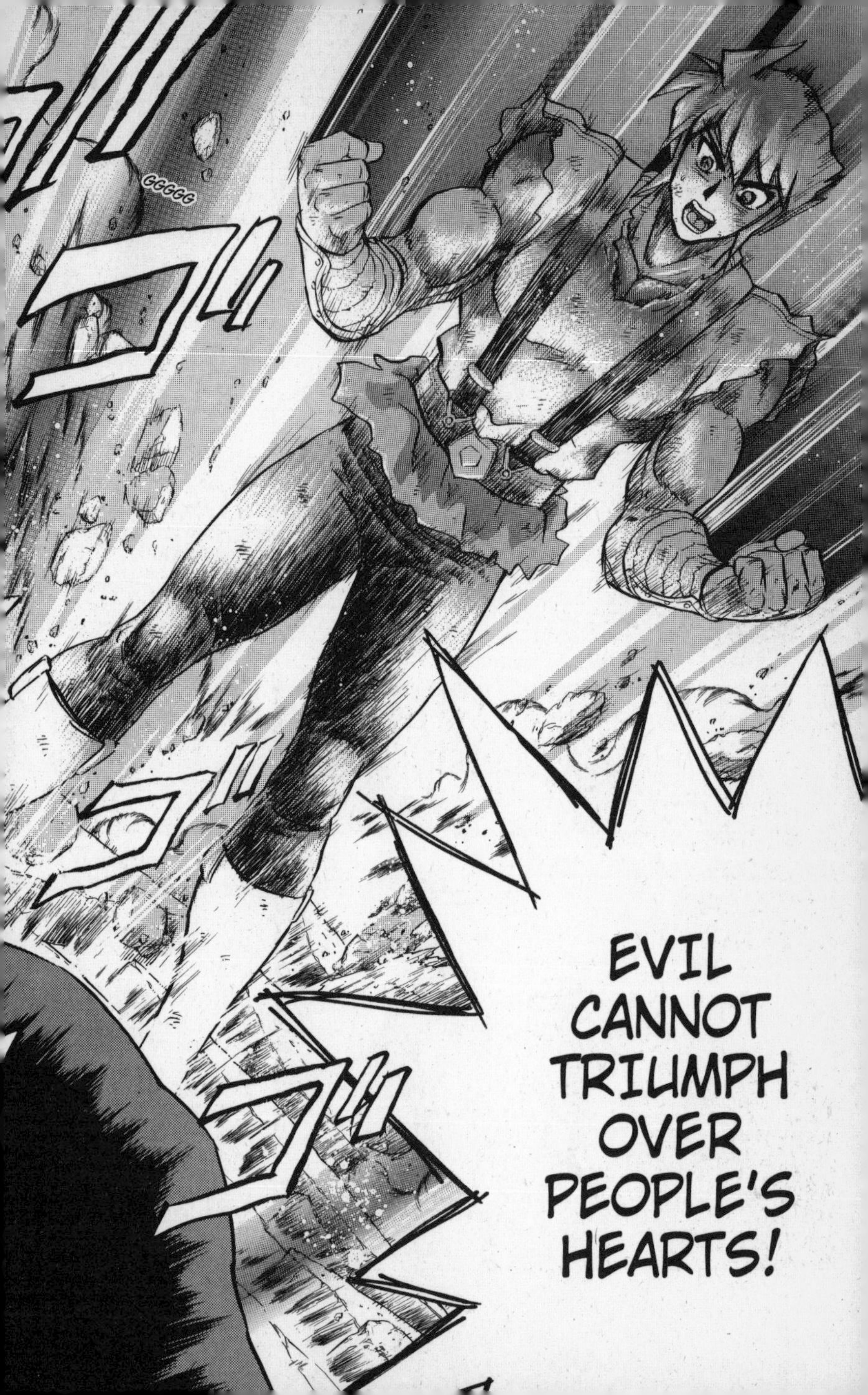
GGGGG
EVIL CANNOT TRIUMPH OVER PEOPLE'S HEARTS!

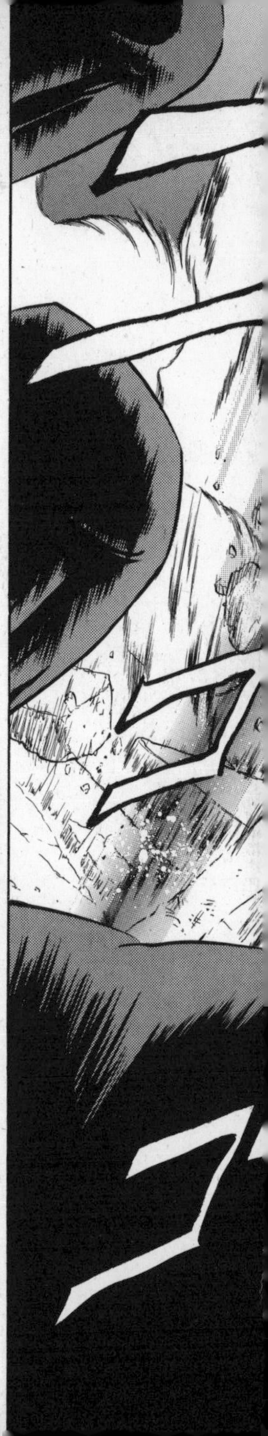

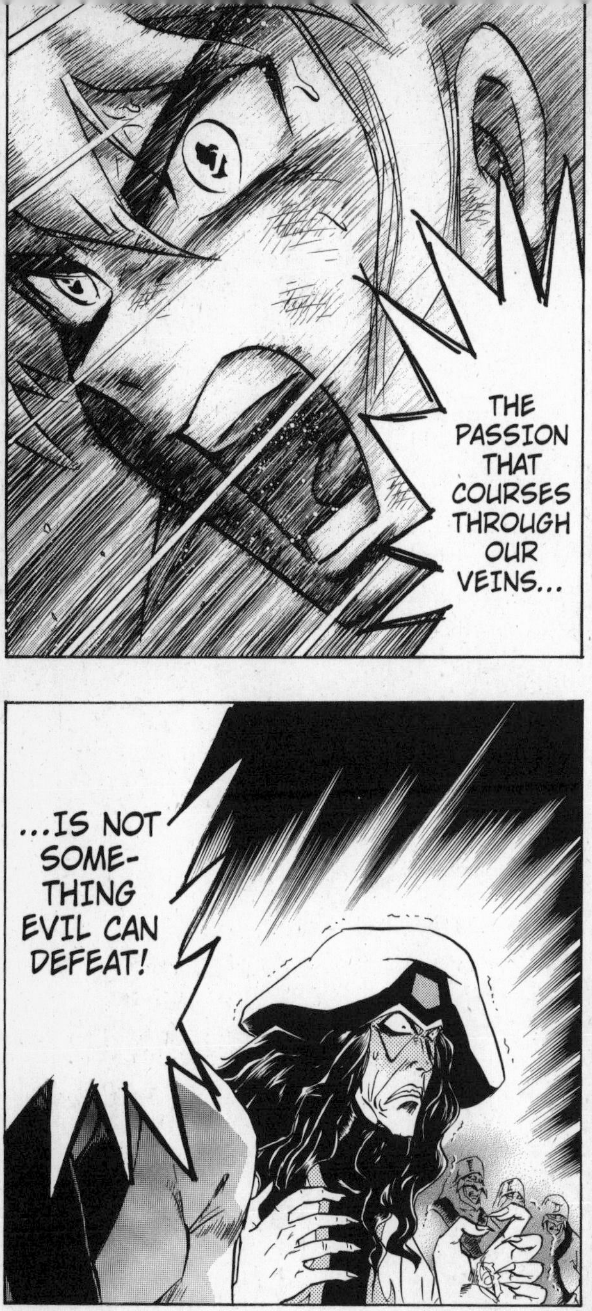
THE PASSION THAT COURSES THROUGH OUR VEINS...
...IS NOT SOME-THING EVIL CAN DEFEAT!

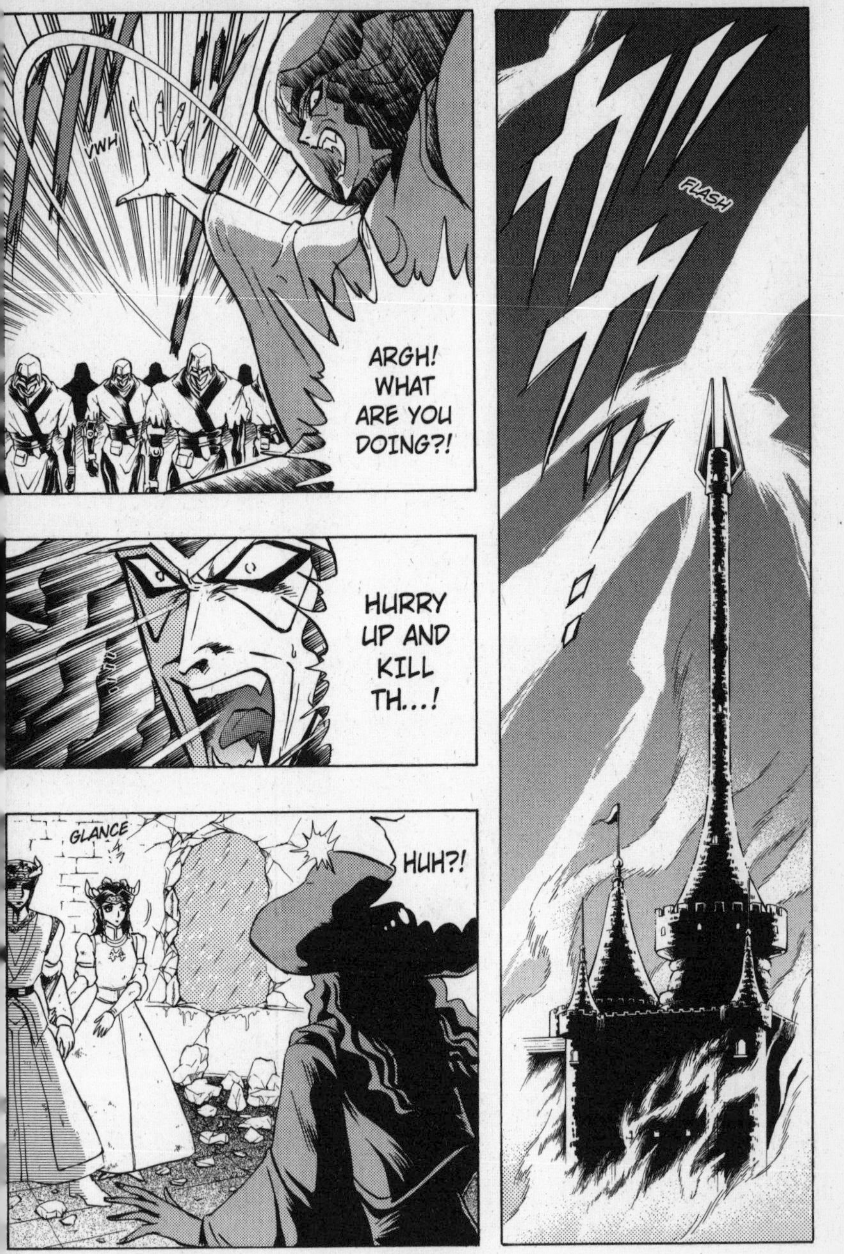
FLASH
ARGH! WHAT ARE YOU DOING?!
VWH
HURRY UP AND KILL TH...!
HUH?!
GLANCE

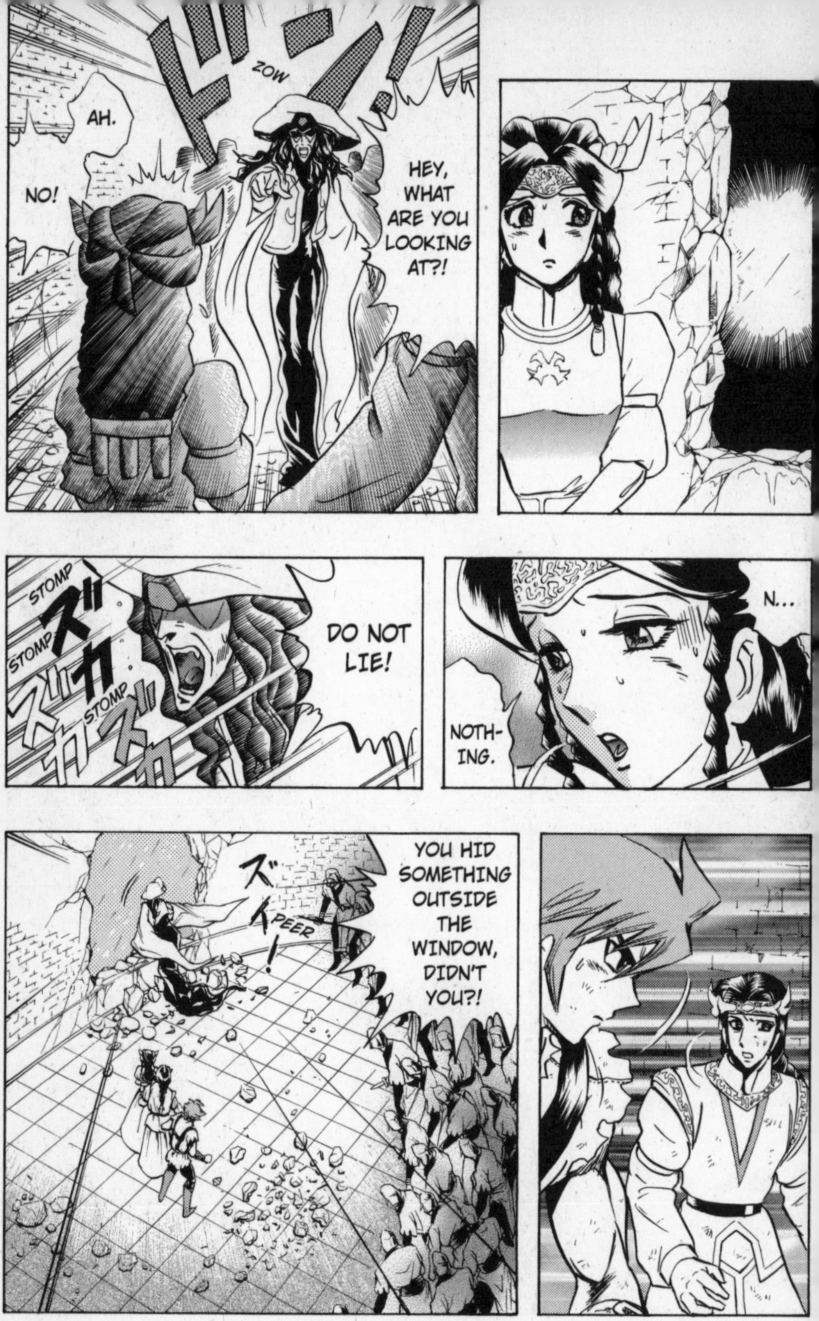
ZOW
HEY, WHAT ARE YOU LOOKING AT?!
AH.
NO!
N...
NOTH-ING.
DO NOT LIE!
STOMP
STOMP
STOMP
YOU HID SOMETHING OUTSIDE THE WINDOW, DIDN'T YOU?!
PEER

TSK. THERE'S NOTHING THERE.

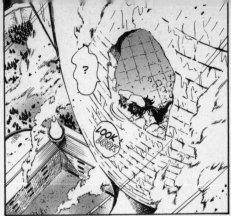

LOOK LOOK

DASH

?!

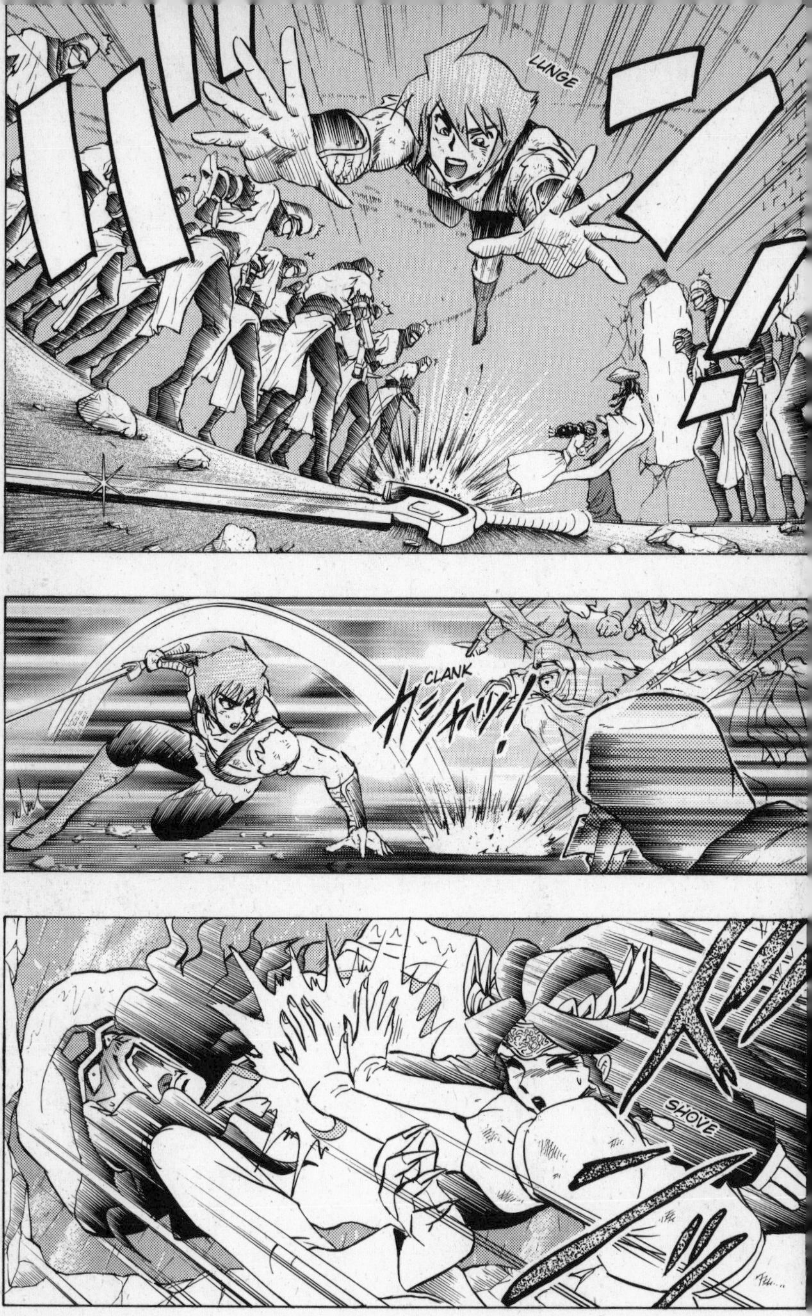
LUNGE
CLANK
SHOVE

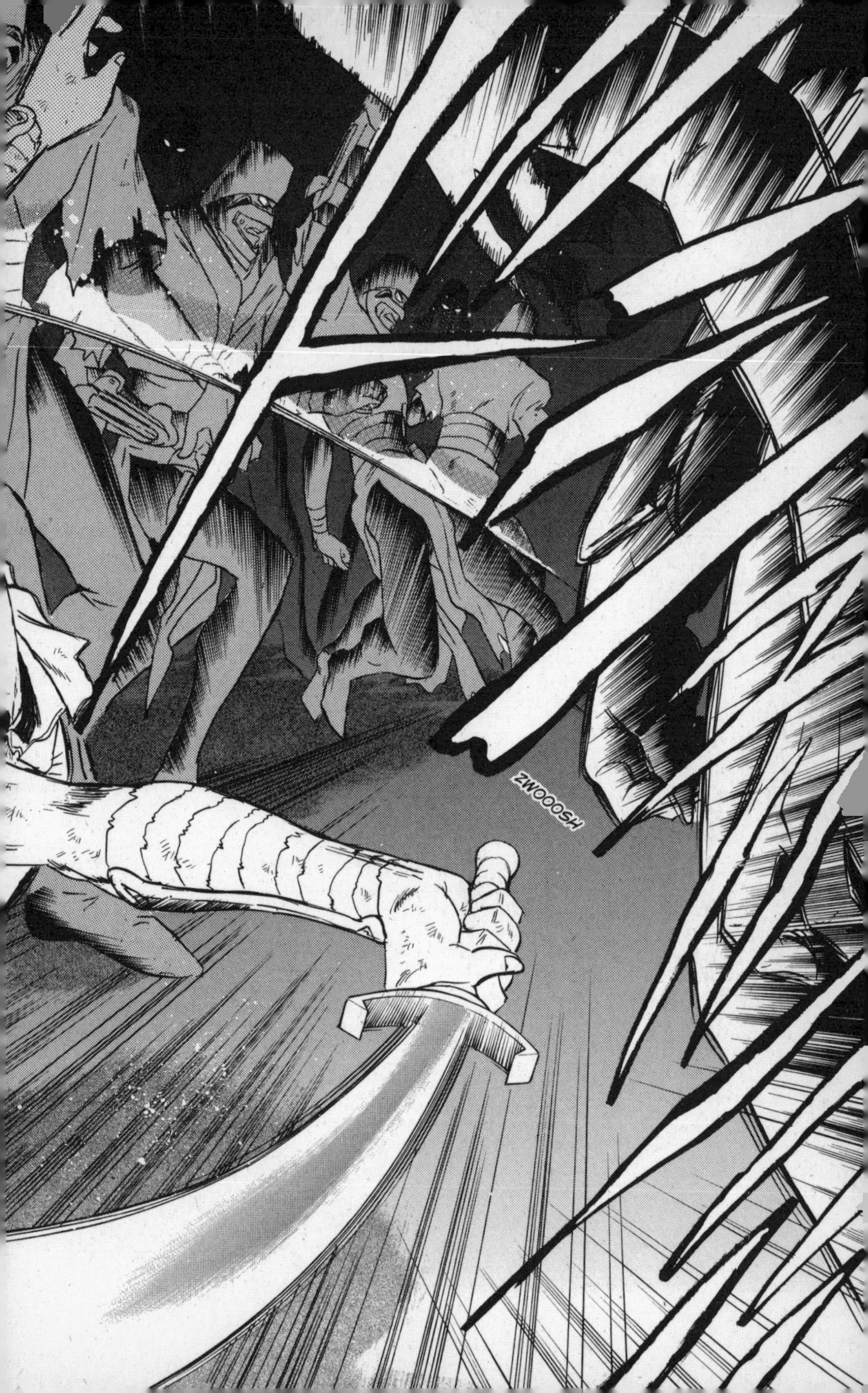
ZWOOOSH

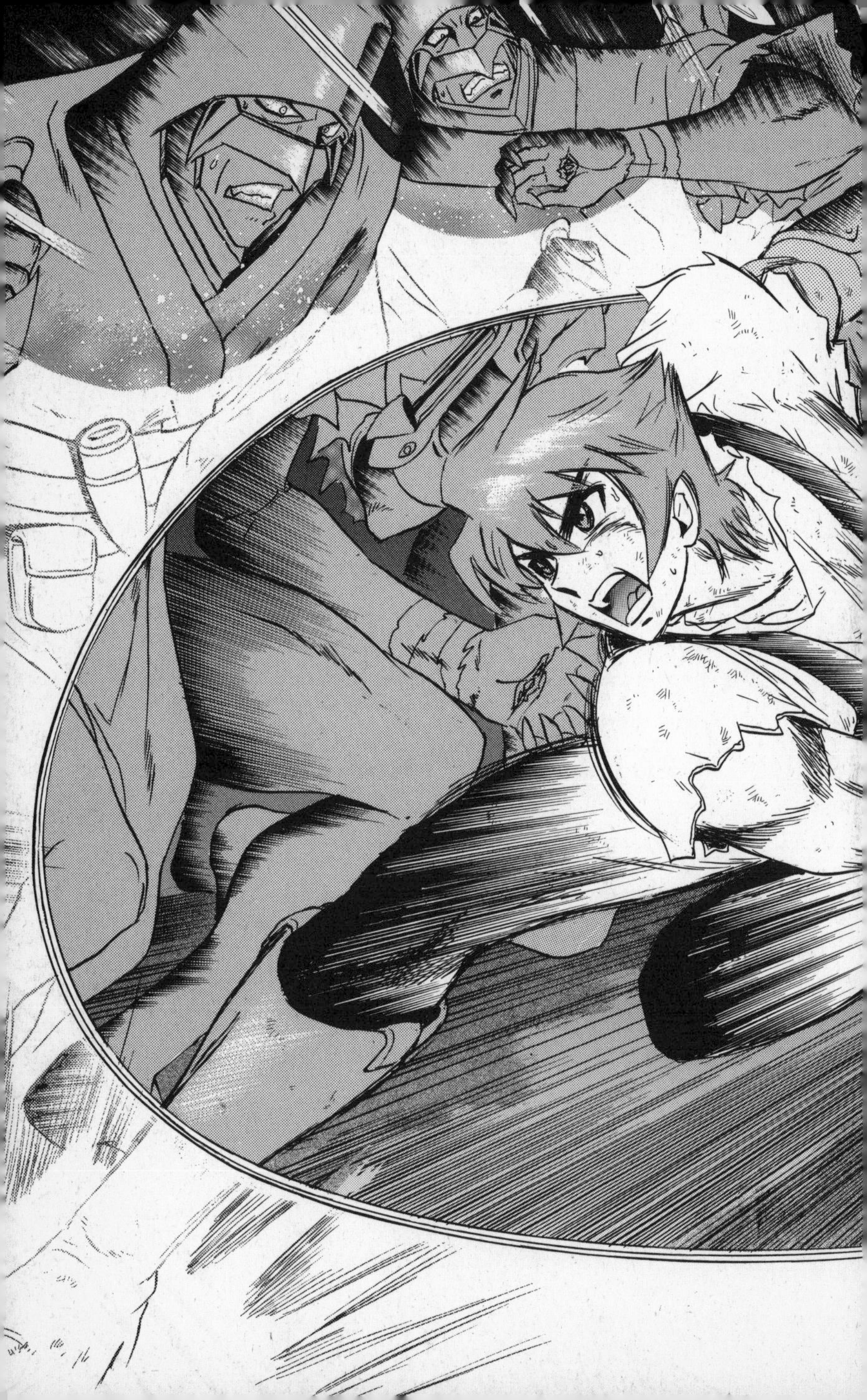

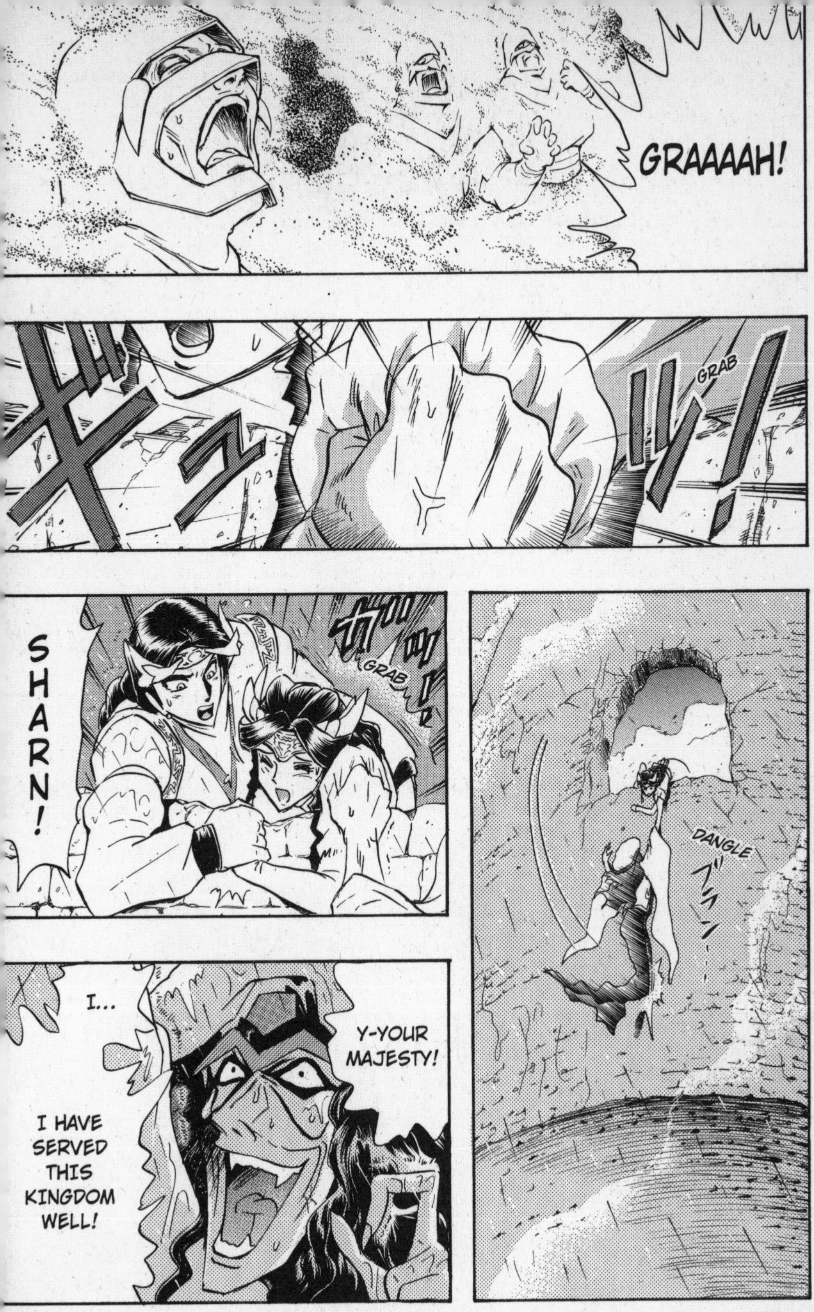
GRAAAAH!
GRAB
DANGLE
SHARN!
GRAB
Y-YOUR MAJESTY!
I...
I HAVE SERVED THIS KINGDOM WELL!

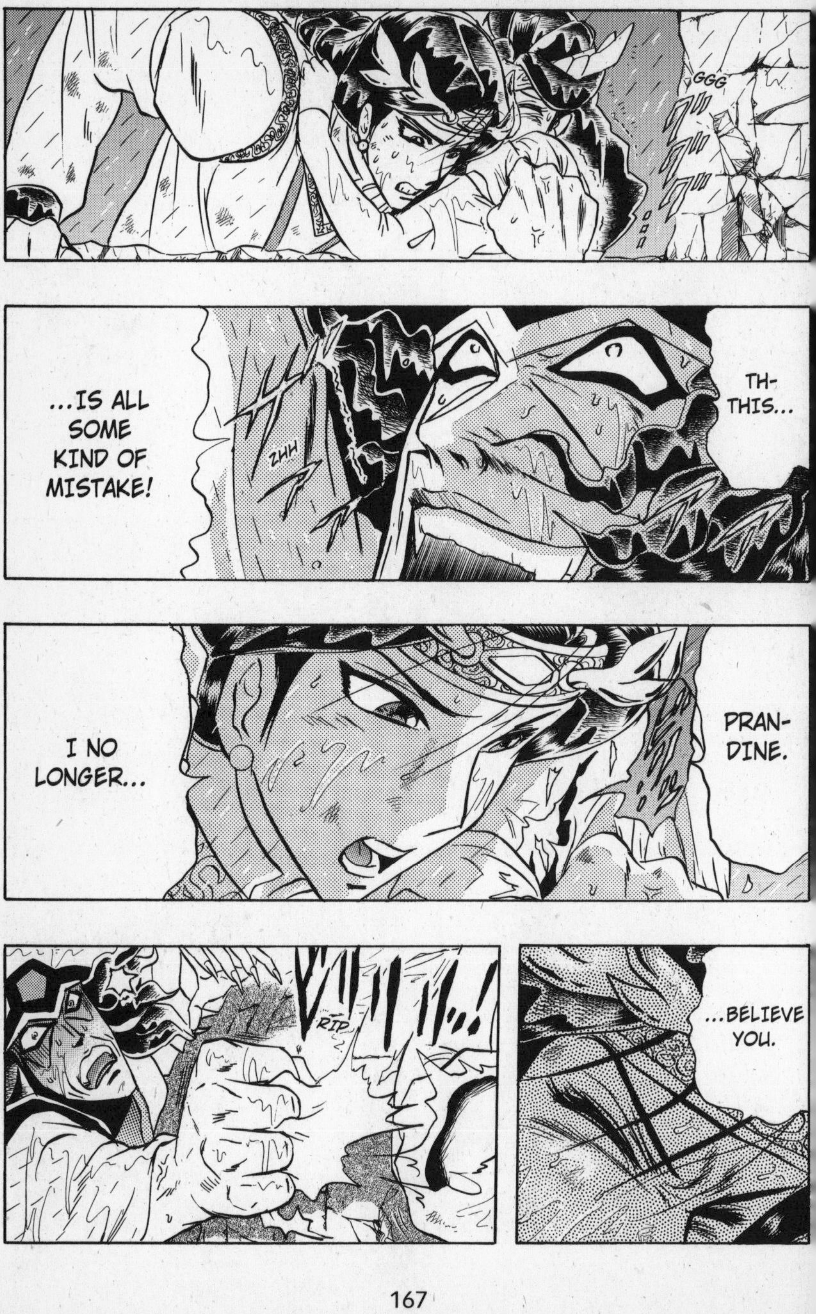
GGG
TH-
THIS...
ZHH
...IS ALL SOME KIND OF MISTAKE!
PRAN-
DINE.
I NO LONGER...
...BELIEVE YOU.
RIP

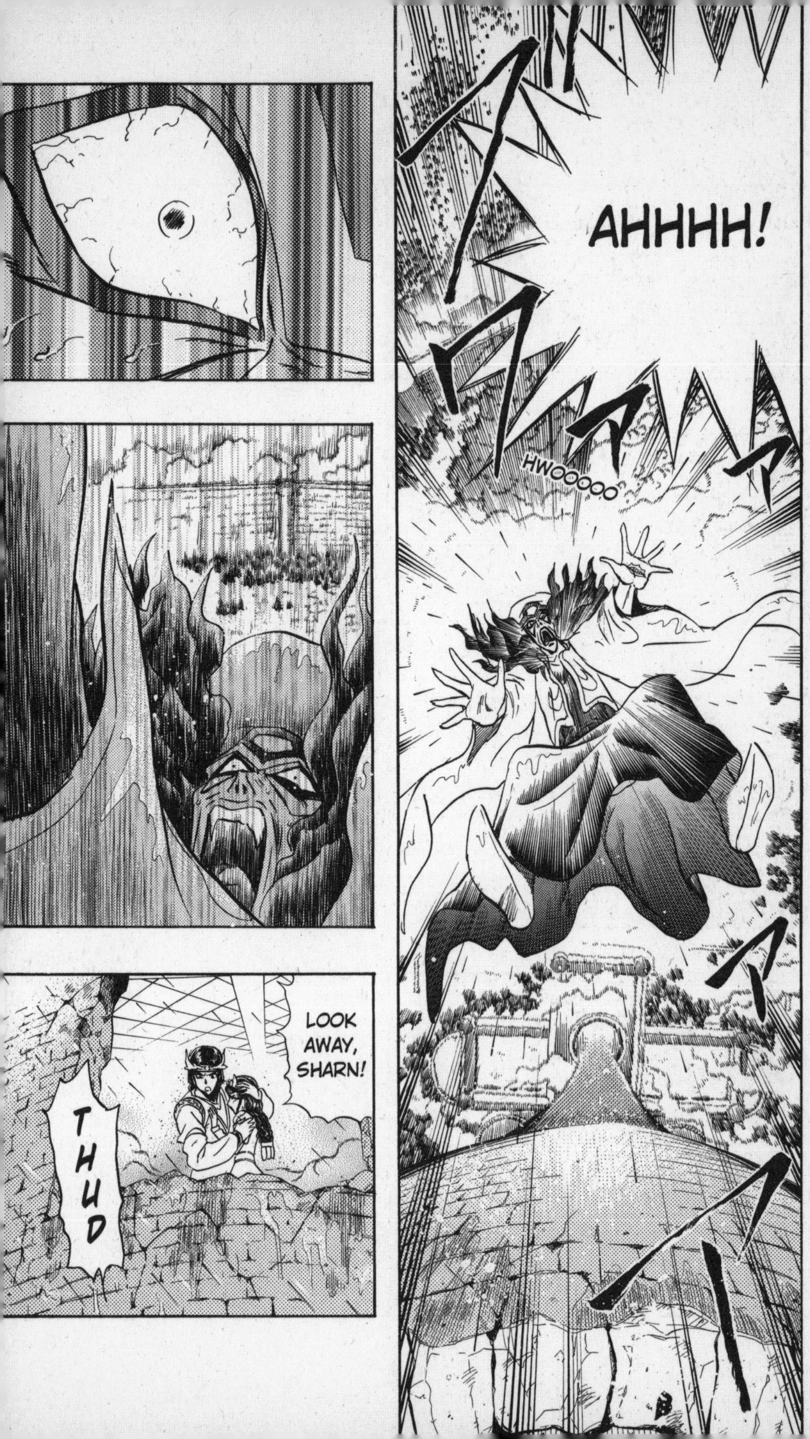
AHHHH!
HWOOOOO
LOOK AWAY, SHARN!
THUD

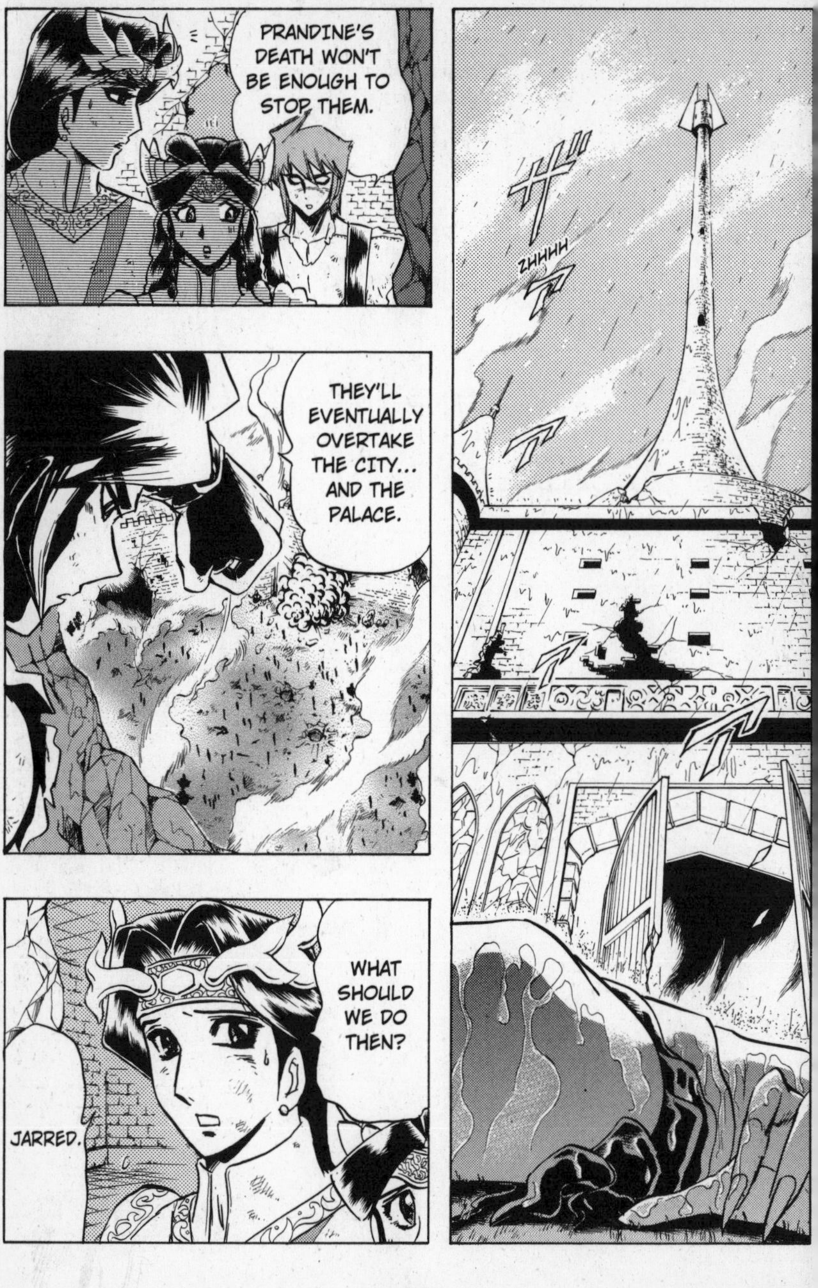
ZHHHH
PRANDINE'S DEATH WON'T BE ENOUGH TO STOP THEM.
THEY'LL EVENTUALLY OVERTAKE THE CITY... AND THE PALACE.
WHAT SHOULD WE DO THEN?
JARRED.

WAIT?

FIRST WE HIDEOUT IN THE CITY,

AND WAIT!

KII *Ky...!*

NOD

YEAH.

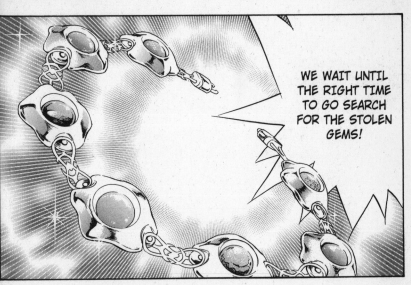

WE WAIT UNTIL THE RIGHT TIME TO GO SEARCH FOR THE STOLEN GEMS!

170

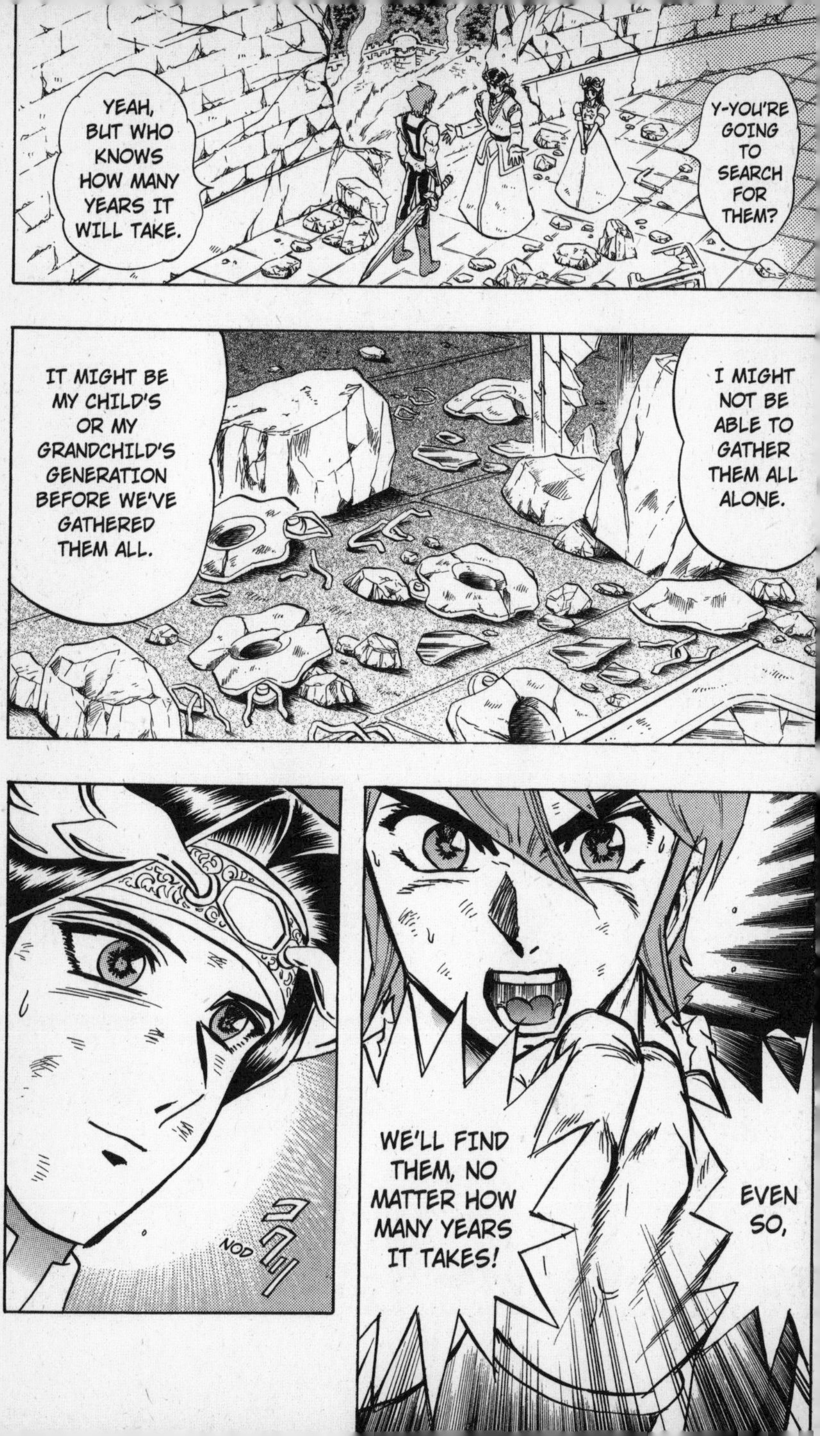
Y-YOU'RE GOING TO SEARCH FOR THEM?
YEAH, BUT WHO KNOWS HOW MANY YEARS IT WILL TAKE.
I MIGHT NOT BE ABLE TO GATHER THEM ALL ALONE.
IT MIGHT BE MY CHILD'S OR MY GRANDCHILD'S GENERATION BEFORE WE'VE GATHERED THEM ALL.
EVEN SO,
WE'LL FIND THEM, NO MATTER HOW MANY YEARS IT TAKES!
NOD

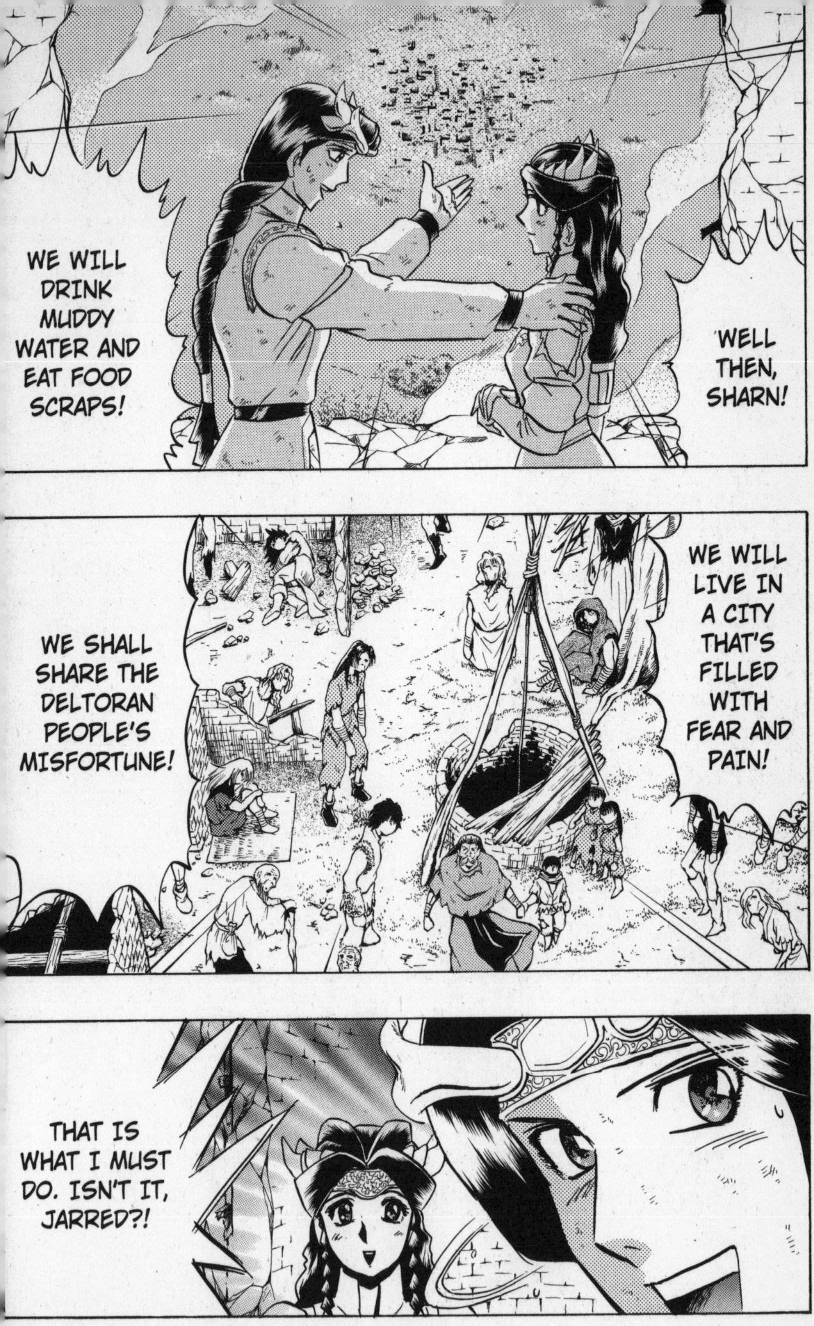
WELL THEN, SHARN!
WE WILL DRINK MUDDY WATER AND EAT FOOD SCRAPS!
WE WILL LIVE IN A CITY THAT'S FILLED WITH FEAR AND PAIN!
WE SHALL SHARE THE DELTORAN PEOPLE'S MISFORTUNE!
THAT IS WHAT I MUST DO. ISN'T IT, JARRED?!

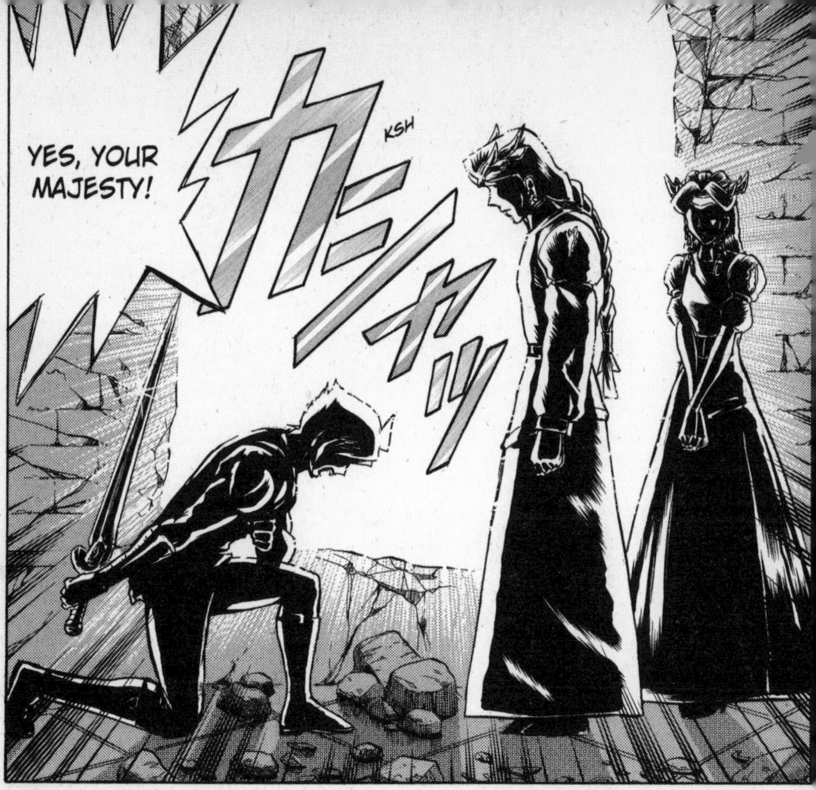
YES, YOUR MAJESTY!
カシャッ
KSH

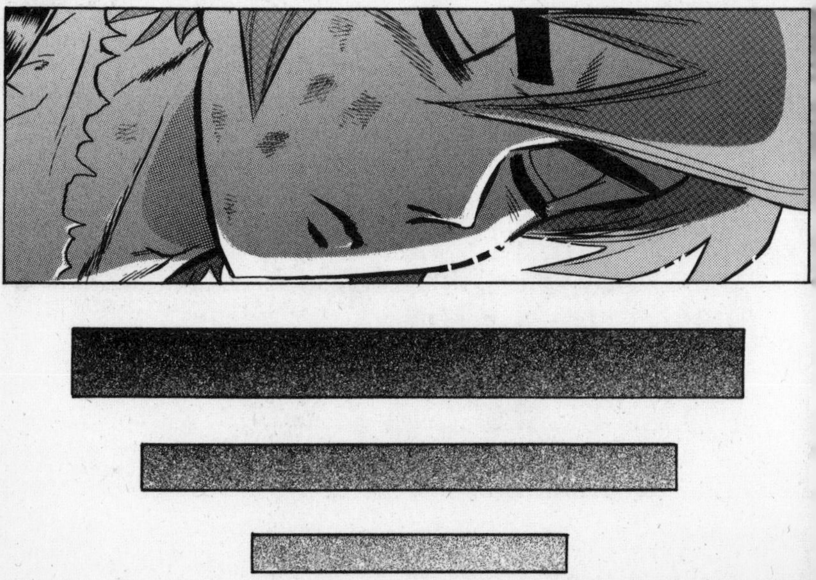

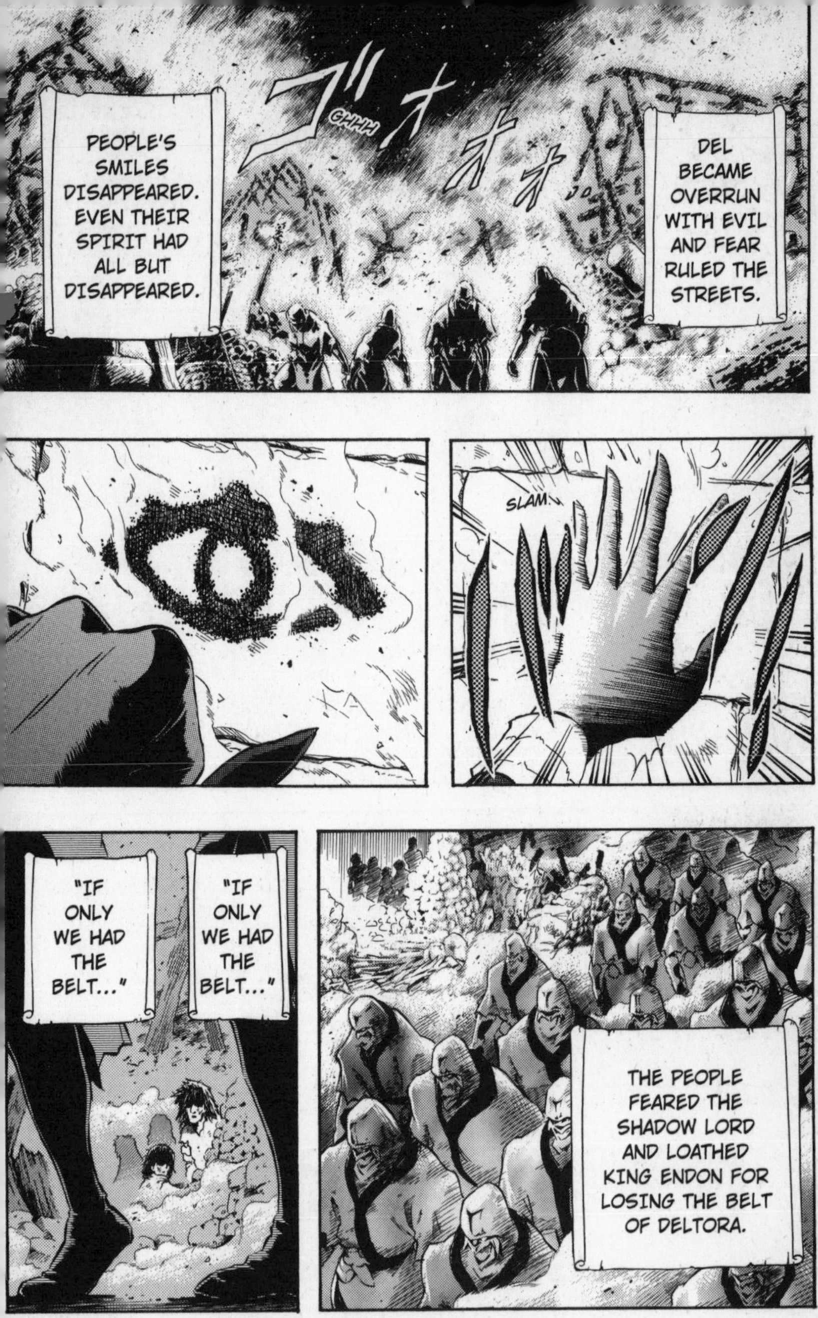
DEL BECAME OVERRUN WITH EVIL AND FEAR RULED THE STREETS.
GHHH
PEOPLE'S SMILES DISAPPEARED. EVEN THEIR SPIRIT HAD ALL BUT DISAPPEARED.
SLAM
THE PEOPLE FEARED THE SHADOW LORD AND LOATHED KING ENDON FOR LOSING THE BELT OF DELTORA.
"IF ONLY WE HAD THE BELT..."
"IF ONLY WE HAD THE BELT..."

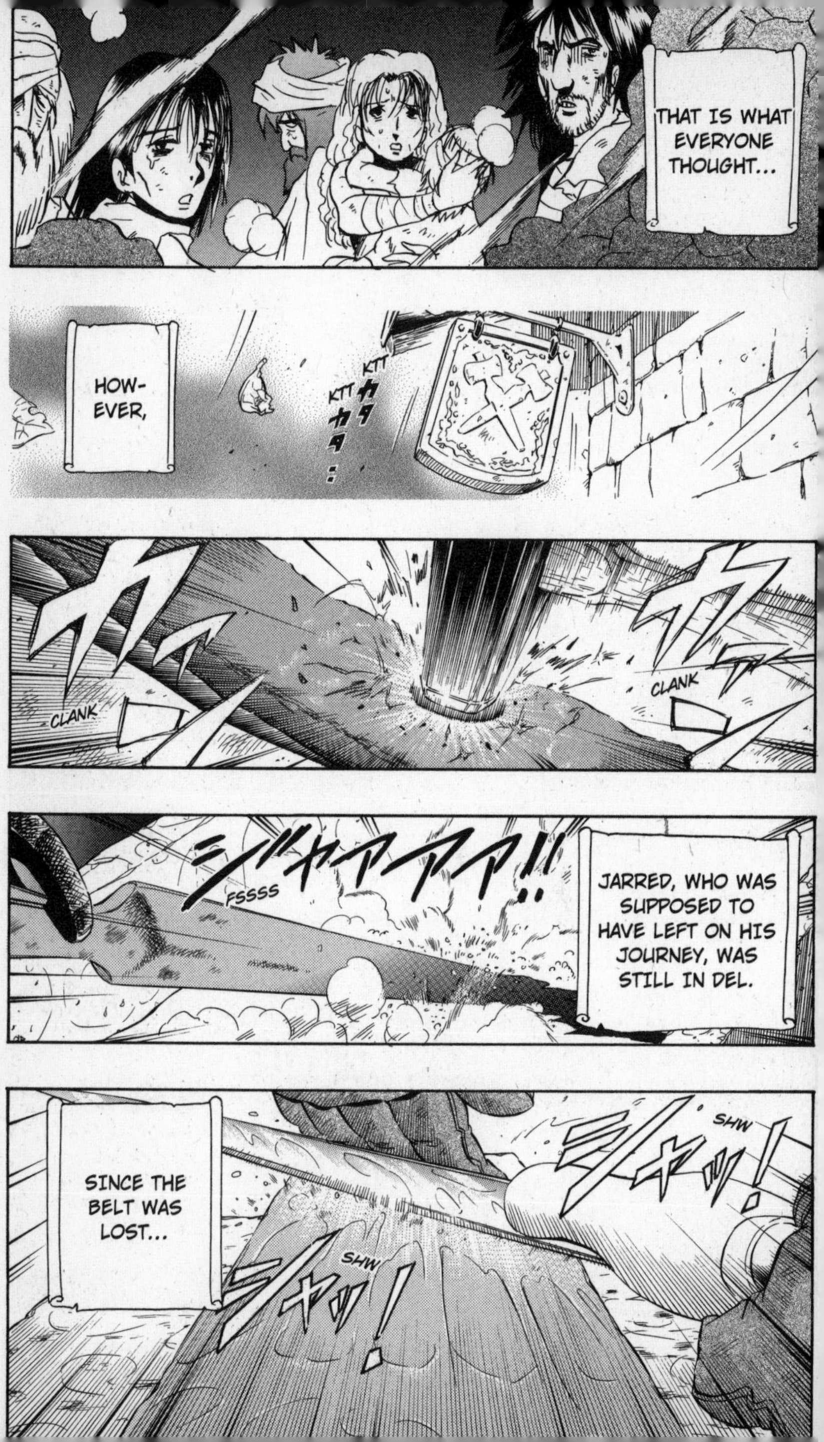
THAT IS WHAT EVERYONE THOUGHT...
HOW-EVER,
KTT
カタ
KTT
カタ
CLANK
CLANK
FSSSS
JARRED, WHO WAS SUPPOSED TO HAVE LEFT ON HIS JOURNEY, WAS STILL IN DEL.
SINCE THE BELT WAS LOST...
SHW
SHW

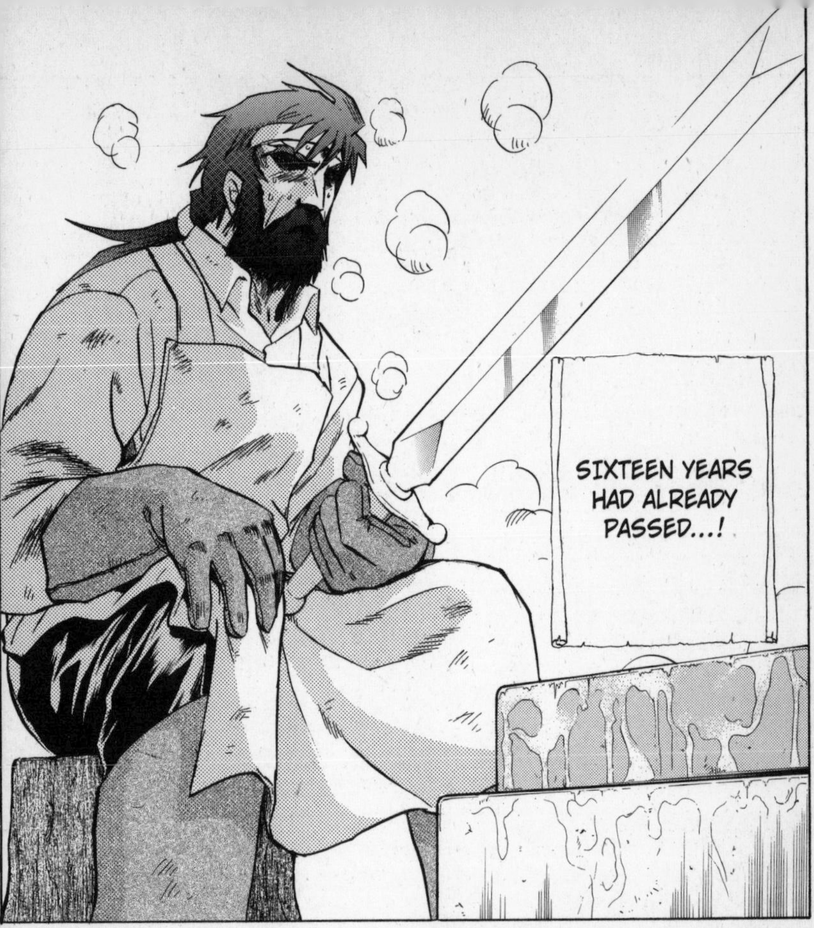
SIXTEEN YEARS HAD ALREADY PASSED...!
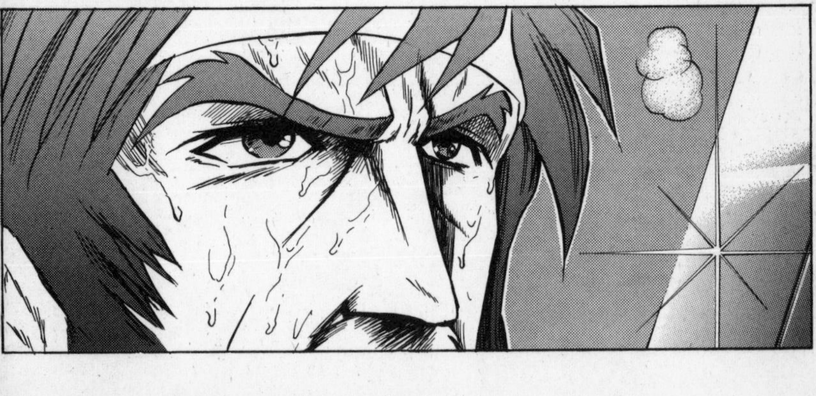

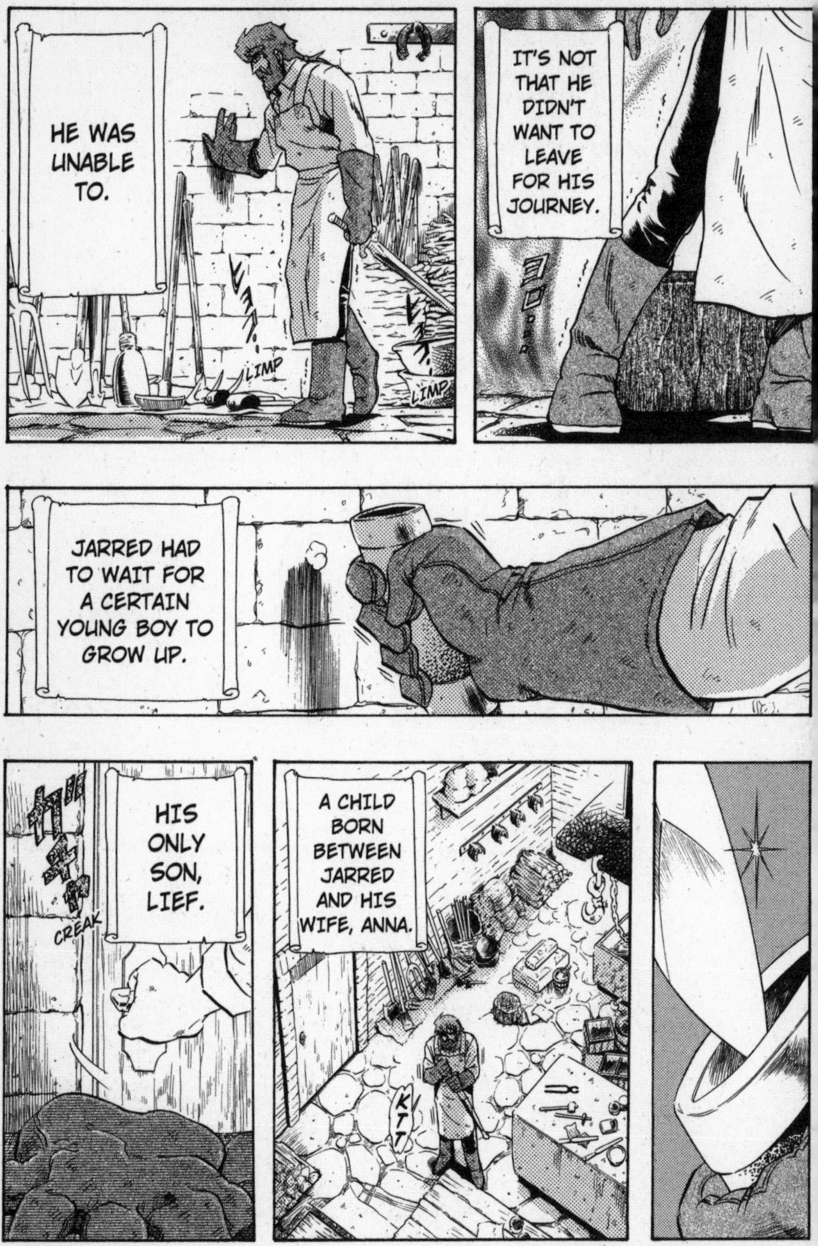
IT'S NOT THAT HE DIDN'T WANT TO LEAVE FOR HIS JOURNEY.
HE WAS UNABLE TO.
LIMP
LIMP
JARRED HAD TO WAIT FOR A CERTAIN YOUNG BOY TO GROW UP.
A CHILD BORN BETWEEN JARRED AND HIS WIFE, ANNA.
KTT
HIS ONLY SON, LIEF.
CREAK

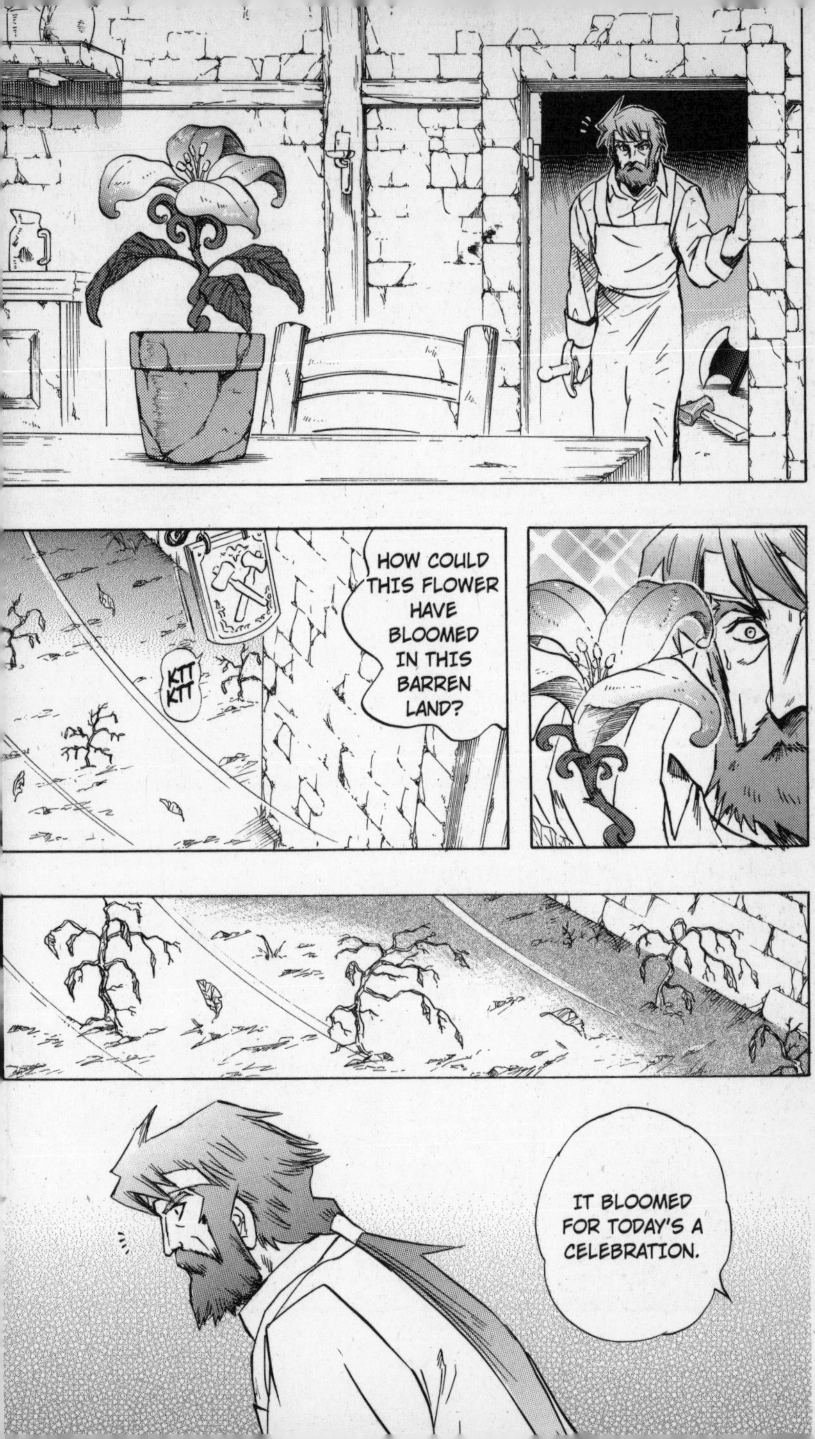
HOW COULD THIS FLOWER HAVE BLOOMED IN THIS BARREN LAND?
KTT KTT
IT BLOOMED FOR TODAY'S A CELEBRATION.

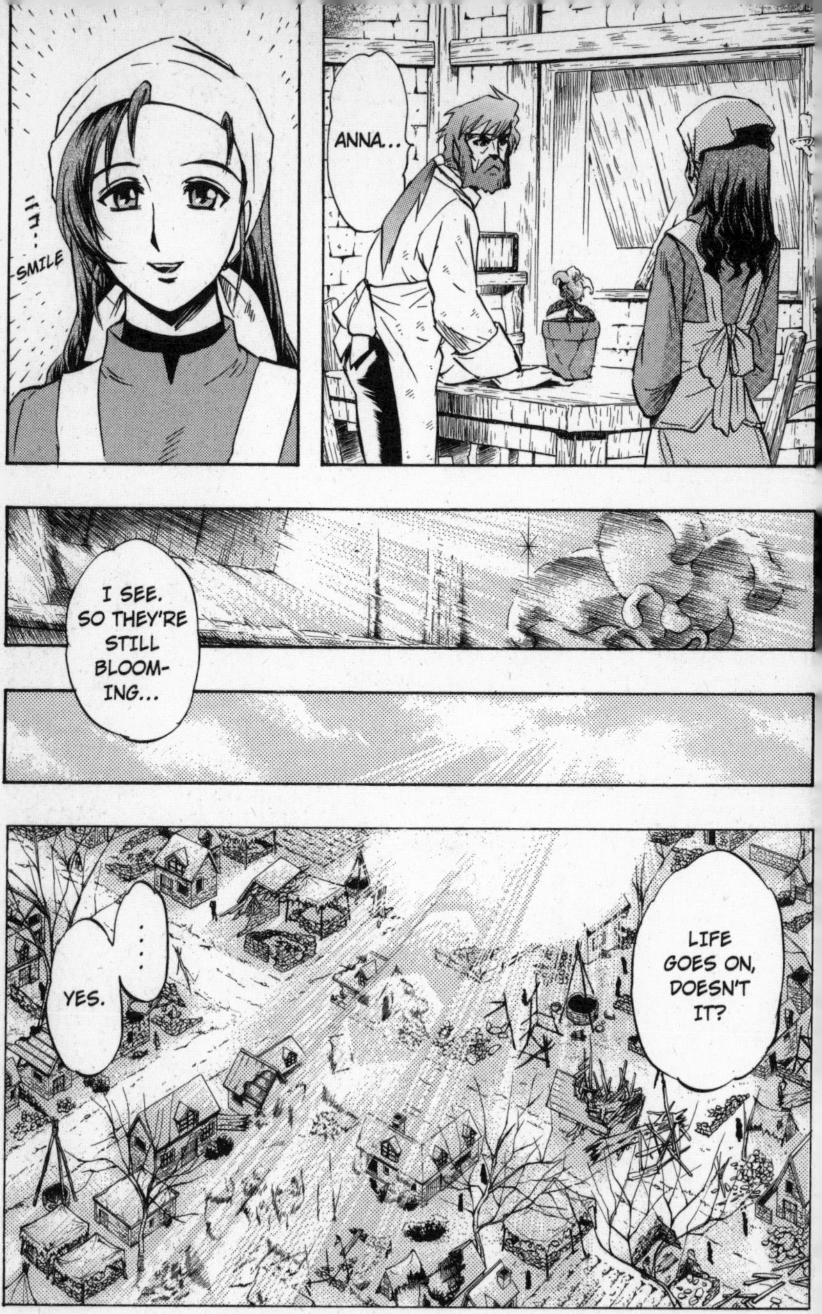
ANNA...
ニコ‥
SMILE
I SEE. SO THEY'RE STILL BLOOMING...
LIFE GOES ON, DOESN'T IT?
....
YES.

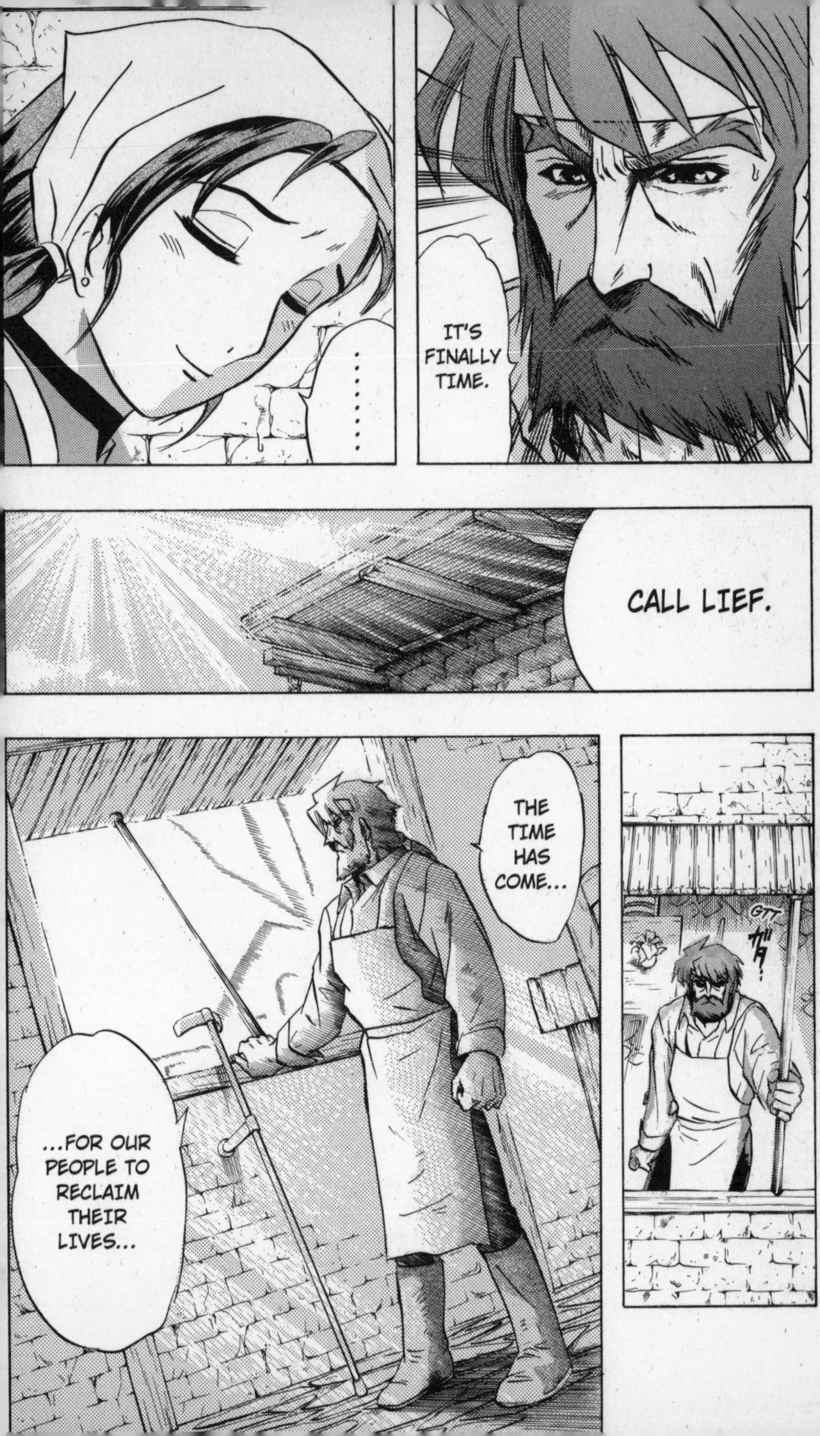
IT'S FINALLY TIME.
......
CALL LIEF.
GTT
THE TIME HAS COME...
...FOR OUR PEOPLE TO RECLAIM THEIR LIVES...

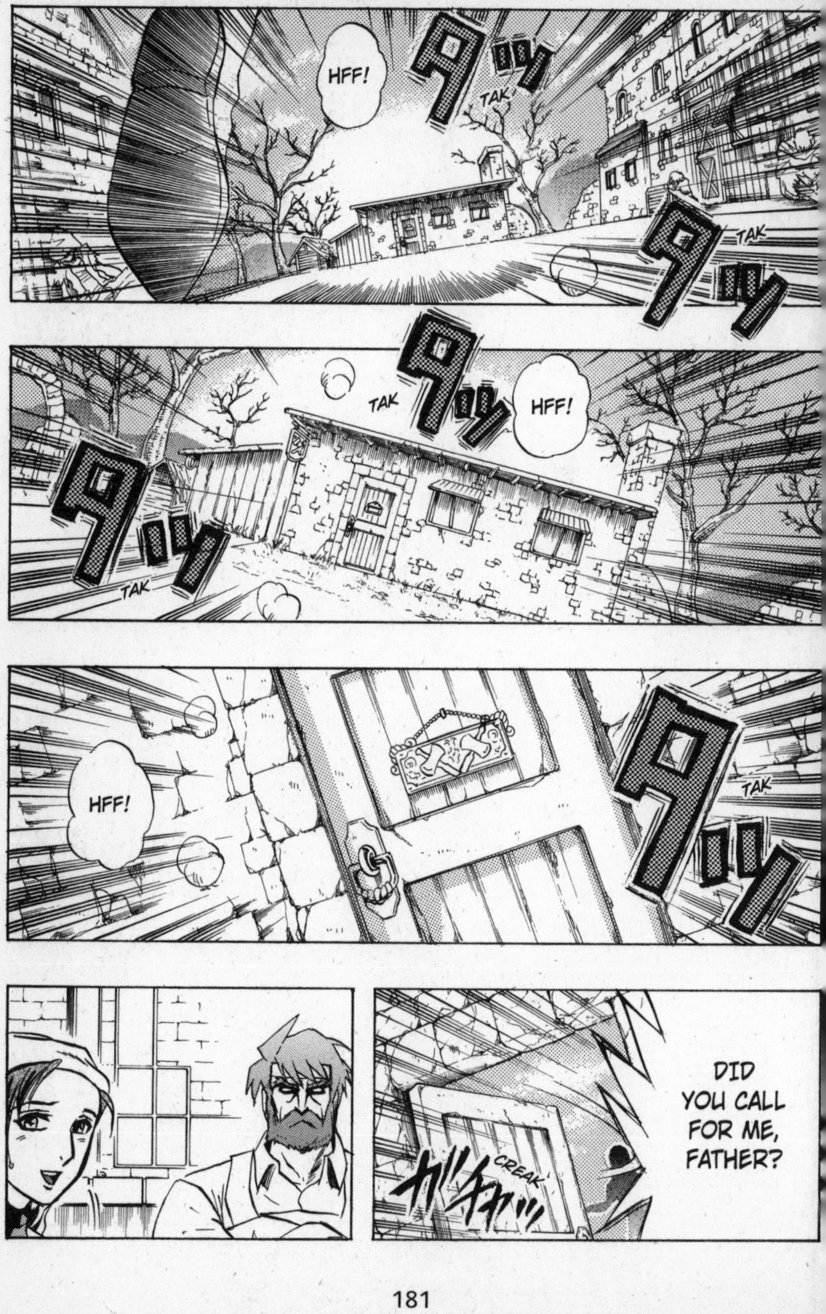
HFF!
TAK
TAK
HFF!
TAK
TAK
TAK
HFF!
DID YOU CALL FOR ME, FATHER?
CREAK

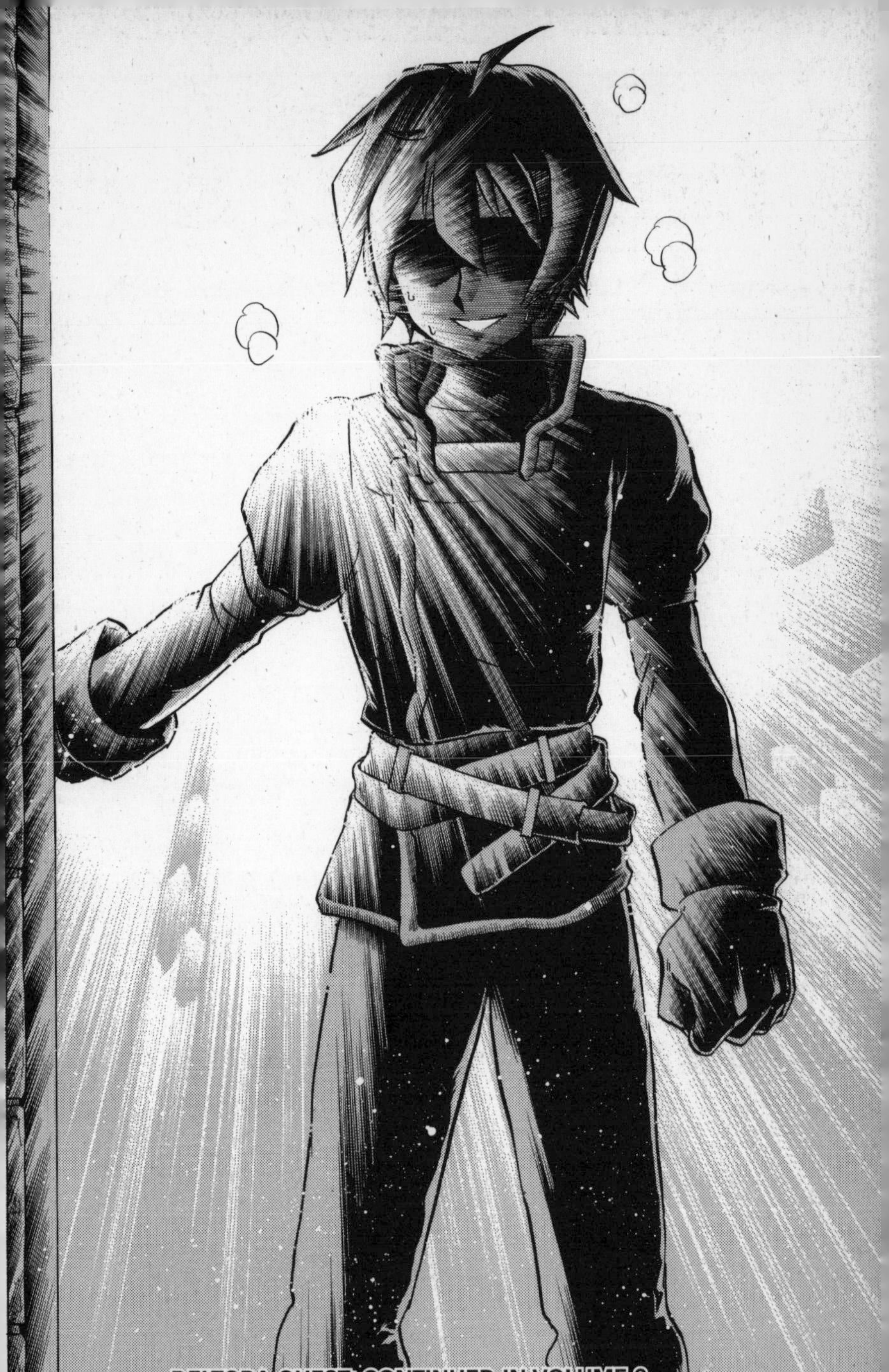

DELTORA QUEST: CONTINUED IN VOLUME 2

Bonus Section
Deltora Q & A

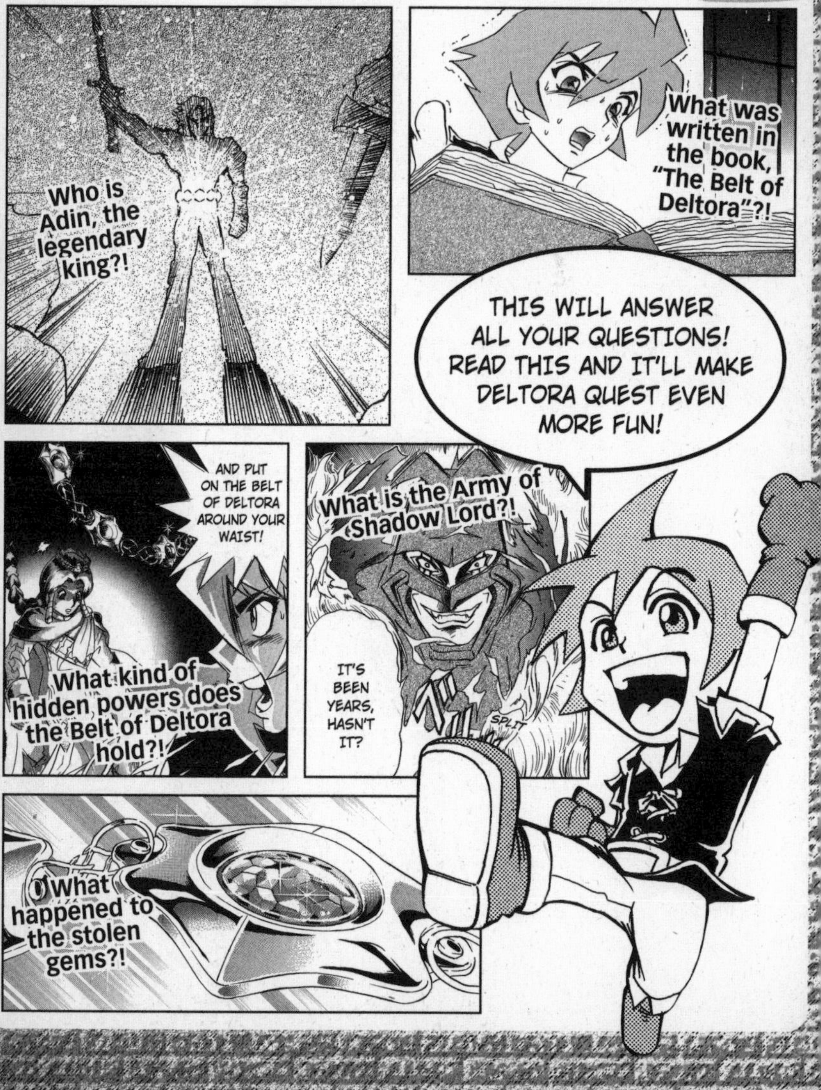
What was written in the book, "The Belt of Deltora"?!
Who is Adin, the legendary king?!
THIS WILL ANSWER ALL YOUR QUESTIONS! READ THIS AND IT'LL MAKE DELTORA QUEST EVEN MORE FUN!
What is the Army of Shadow Lord?!
IT'S BEEN YEARS, HASN'T IT?
SPLIT
AND PUT ON THE BELT OF DELTORA AROUND YOUR WAIST!
What kind of hidden powers does the Belt of Deltora hold?!
What happened to the stolen gems?!

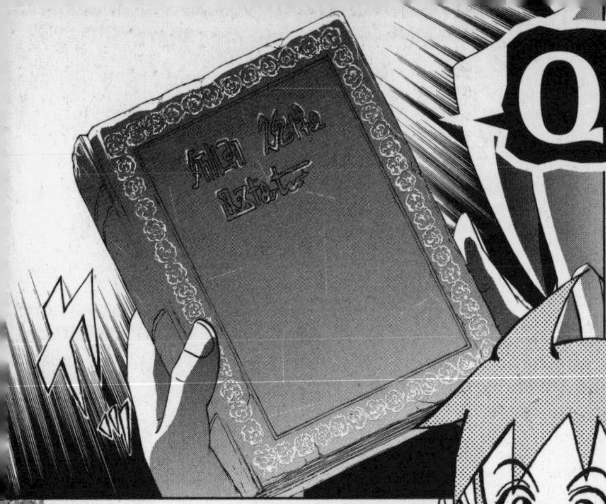

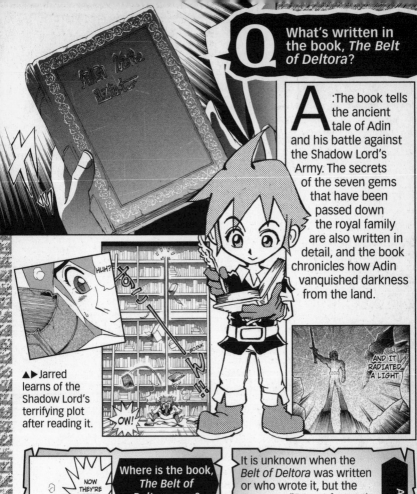

Q What's written in the book, *The Belt of Deltora*?

A: The book tells the ancient tale of Adin and his battle against the Shadow Lord's Army. The secrets of the seven gems that have been passed down the royal family are also written in detail, and the book chronicles how Adin vanquished darkness from the land.

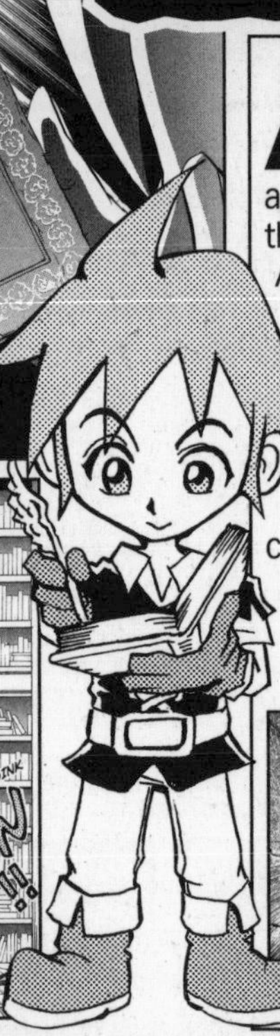

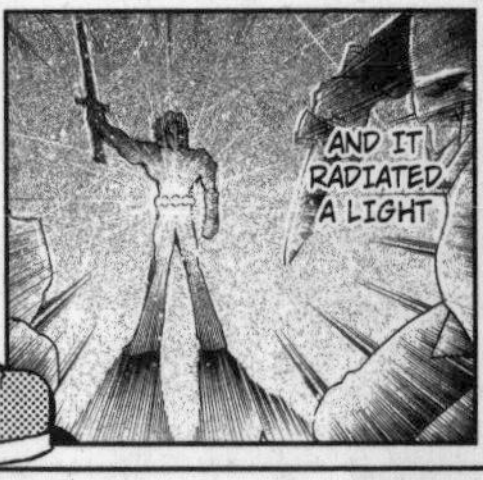
AND IT RADIATED A LIGHT

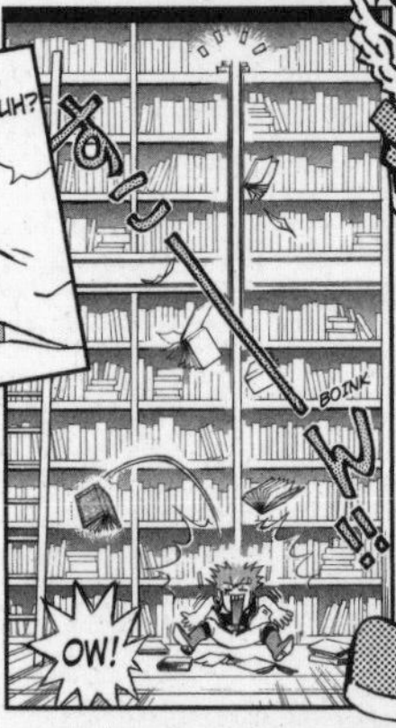
BOINK
OW!

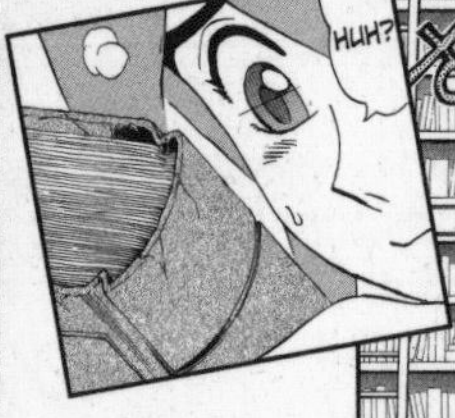
HUH?

▲▶Jarred learns of the Shadow Lord's terrifying plot after reading it.

A warning from previous kings and queens?!

It is unknown when the *Belt of Deltora* was written or who wrote it, but the message, "Do not forget the Shadow Lord's army!" must have been a warning from previous kings and queens.

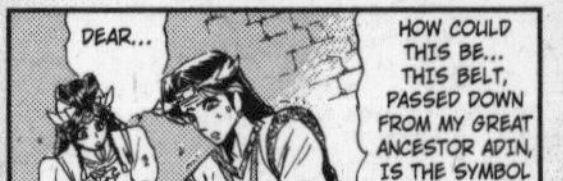
HOW COULD THIS BE... THIS BELT, PASSED DOWN FROM MY GREAT ANCESTOR ADIN, IS THE SYMBOL OF THE ROYAL FAMILY...
DEAR...

Where is the book, *The Belt of Deltora* now?

Jarred took the book with him when he fled the castle, so it wouldn't be lost again. The book is currently at Jarred's house...

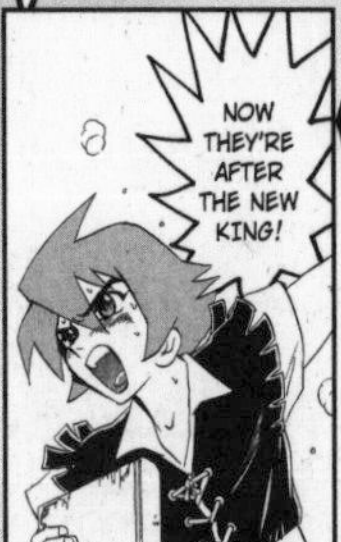
NOW THEY'RE AFTER THE NEW KING!

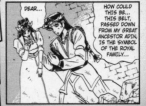

Q Who is Adin?

A: Adin was a blacksmith who rose up to protect the land of Deltora from the Shadow Lord's army. He is the great Hero who expelled the invading forces with the help of the seven tribes of Deltora. These tribes banded together under Adin and, after they defeated the Shadow Lord, Adin was made king and unified the country. He was a great king who pursued peace and was concerned with his people's well-being.

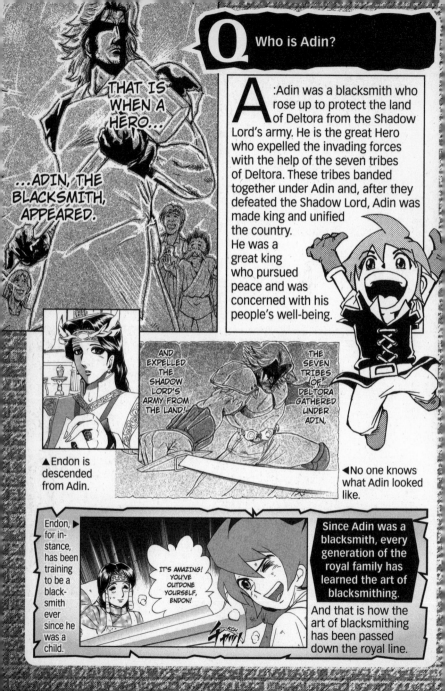

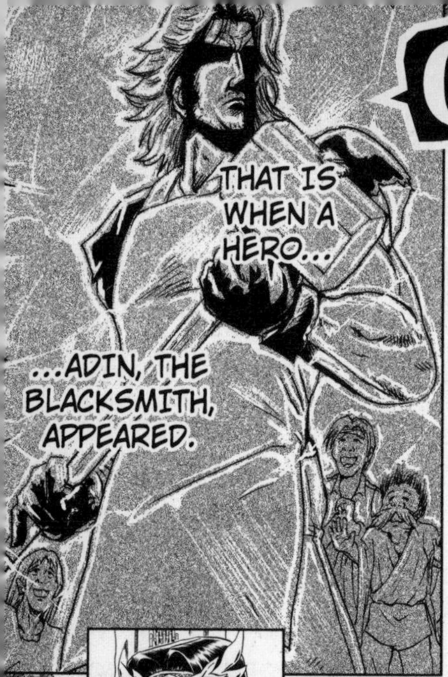
THAT IS WHEN A HERO...
...ADIN, THE BLACKSMITH, APPEARED.

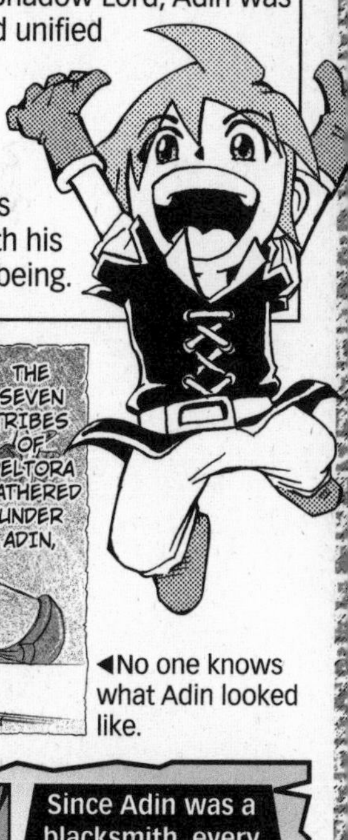

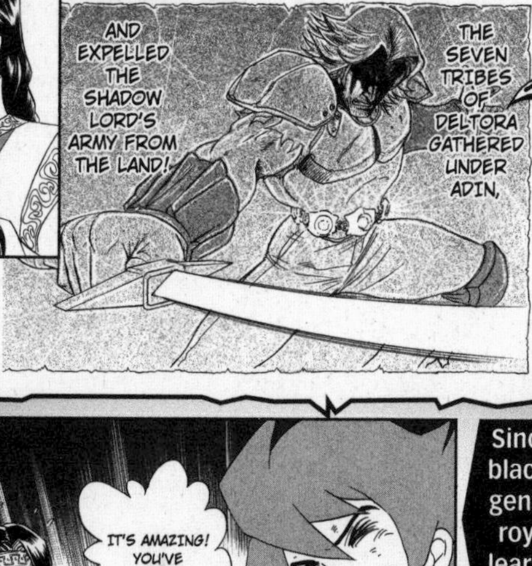
THE SEVEN TRIBES OF DELTORA GATHERED UNDER ADIN,
AND EXPELLED THE SHADOW LORD'S ARMY FROM THE LAND!

◀No one knows what Adin looked like.

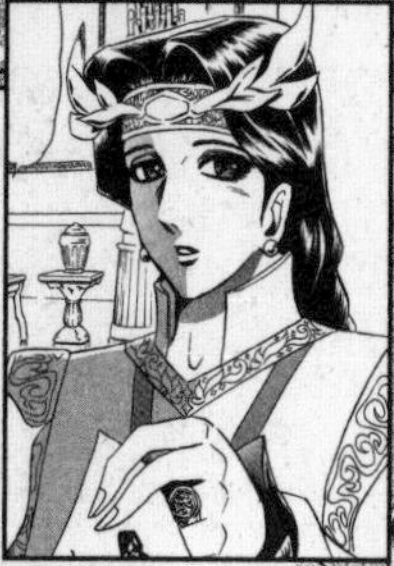

▲Endon is descended from Adin.

Since Adin was a blacksmith, every generation of the royal family has learned the art of blacksmithing.

And that is how the art of blacksmithing has been passed down the royal line.

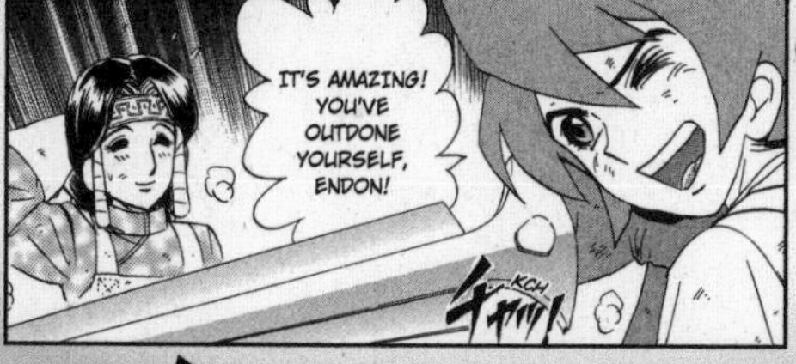
IT'S AMAZING! YOU'VE OUTDONE YOURSELF, ENDON!
KCH

Endon, ▶ for instance, has been training to be a blacksmith ever since he was a child.

Q What kind of secret powers does the Belt of Deltora have?

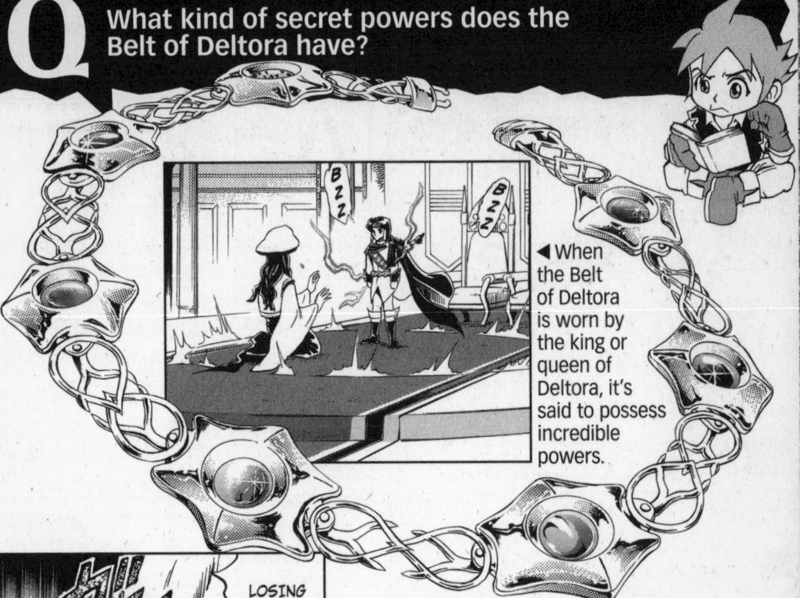
BZZ
BZZ

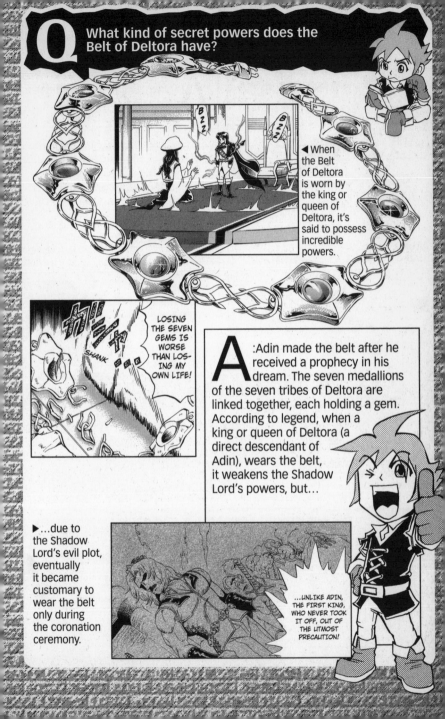

◀ When the Belt of Deltora is worn by the king or queen of Deltora, it's said to possess incredible powers.

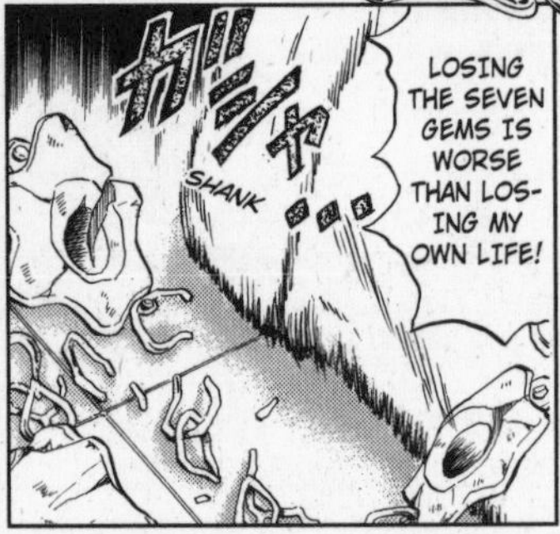
LOSING THE SEVEN GEMS IS WORSE THAN LOSING MY OWN LIFE!
SHANK

A:Adin made the belt after he received a prophecy in his dream. The seven medallions of the seven tribes of Deltora are linked together, each holding a gem. According to legend, when a king or queen of Deltora (a direct descendant of Adin), wears the belt, it weakens the Shadow Lord's powers, but...

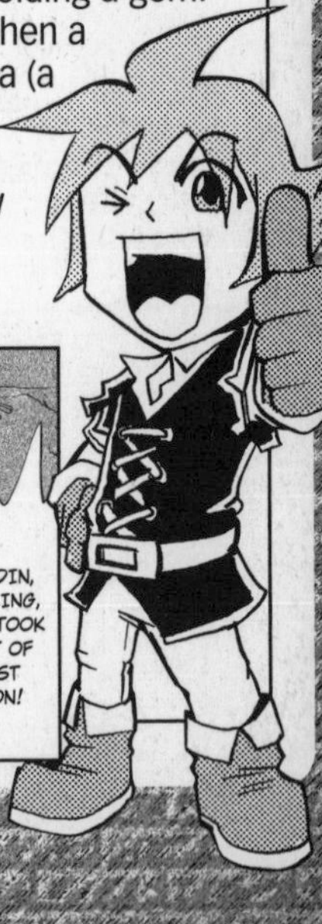

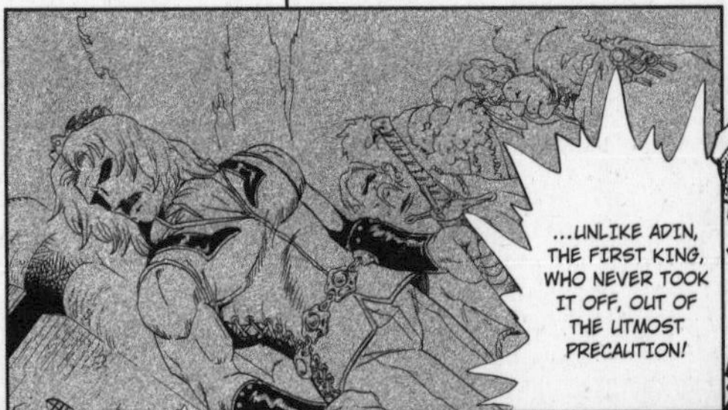
...UNLIKE ADIN, THE FIRST KING, WHO NEVER TOOK IT OFF, OUT OF THE UTMOST PRECAUTION!

▶ ...due to the Shadow Lord's evil plot, eventually it became customary to wear the belt only during the coronation ceremony.

Q Who is the man who defended the King from attack?

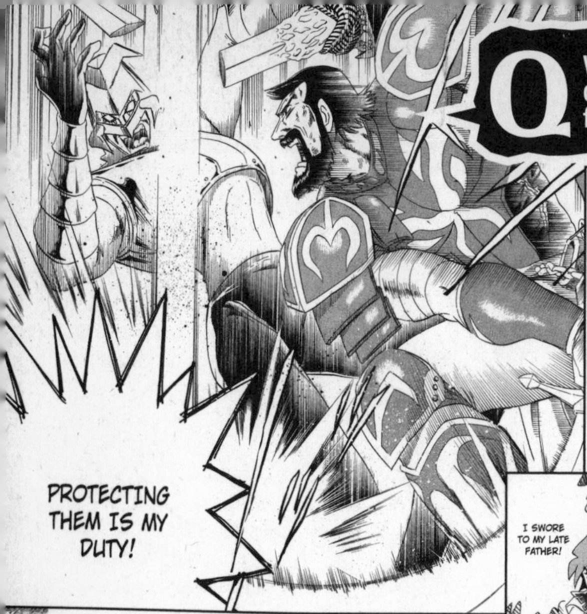

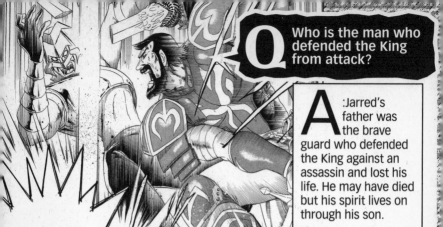

PROTECTING THEM IS MY DUTY!

A :Jarred's father was the brave guard who defended the King against an assassin and lost his life. He may have died but his spirit lives on through his son.

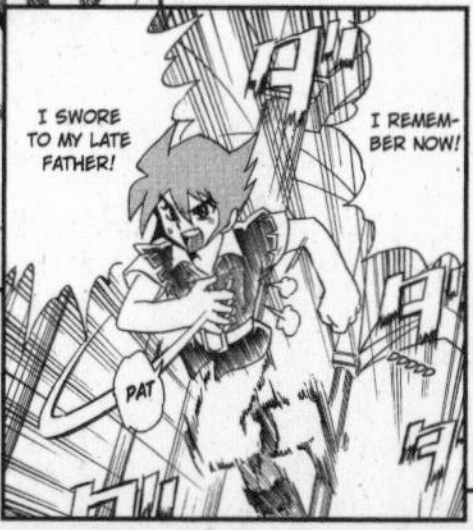

I REMEMBER NOW!
I SWORE TO MY LATE FATHER!
PAT

◀As he was dying, he taught his son the path he should take. Like Adin, he was a courageous man.

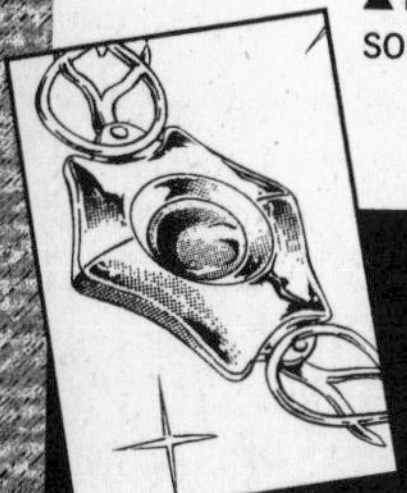

▲The Seven Gems are the source of the belt's powers.

Each gem has a special, mystical ability.

EMERALD – A green gem that symbolizes honor. It's said to detect the presence of evil.

LAPIS LAZULI – An azure blue stone with bits of shining silver that acts as a powerful talisman.

RUBY – A crimson gem. It has the power to tell the wearer when danger is near.

OPAL – Known as the gem of hope, it sparkles in all shades of the rainbow and is said to have the ability to predict the future.

TOPAZ – A golden stone that is said to connect to the spirit world.

AMETHYST – A stone that symbolizes innocence and power. It's said to have the ability to calm one's soul.

DIAMOND – The gem symbolizes strength and innocence. It's said to lend its strength to those who are righteous.

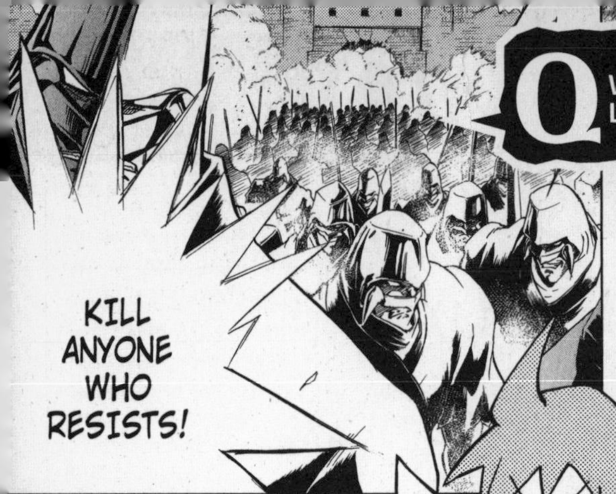
KILL ANYONE WHO RESISTS!

Q What is the Shadow Lord's army?

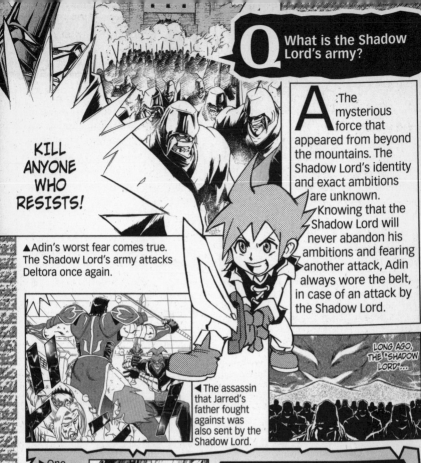

A:The mysterious force that appeared from beyond the mountains. The Shadow Lord's identity and exact ambitions are unknown.

Knowing that the Shadow Lord will never abandon his ambitions and fearing another attack, Adin always wore the belt, in case of an attack by the Shadow Lord.

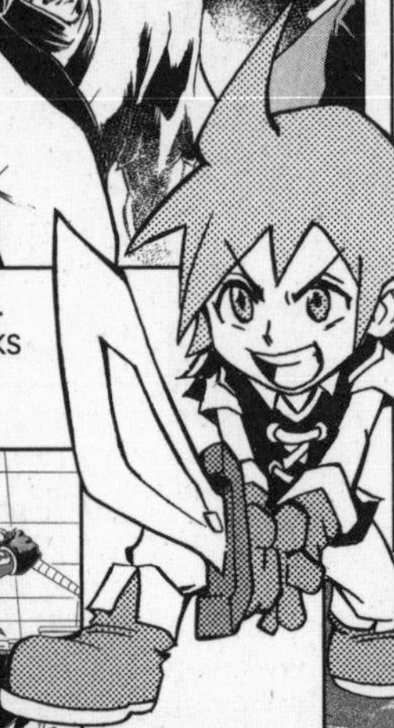

▲Adin's worst fear comes true. The Shadow Lord's army attacks Deltora once again.

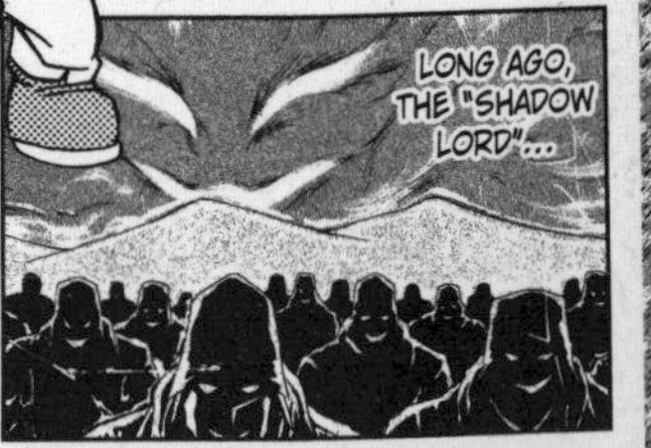
LONG AGO, THE "SHADOW LORD"...

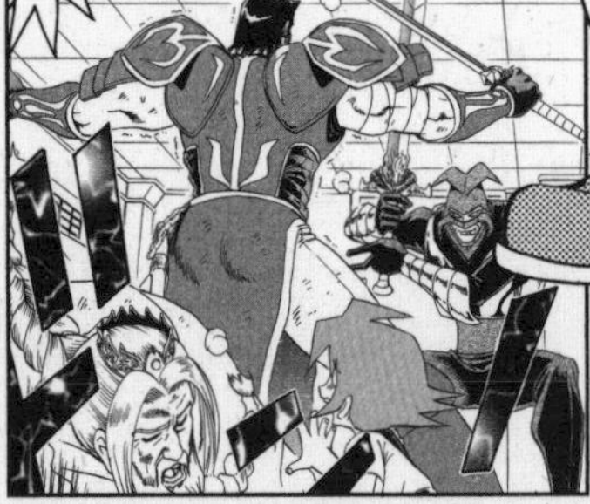

◀The assassin that Jarred's father fought against was also sent by the Shadow Lord.

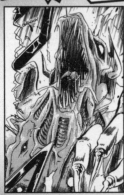

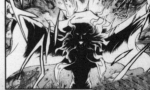

Deltora is always at risk for another attack by the Shadow Lord.

The Shadow Lord's assassins lurk in the dark corners of Deltora. Don't let your guard down for a single moment in this land.

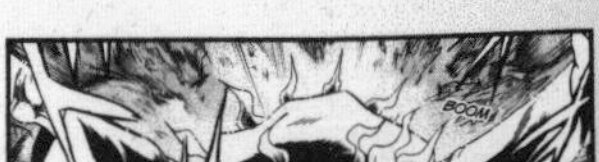
BOOM

▶They could be closer than you expect, like Prandine!

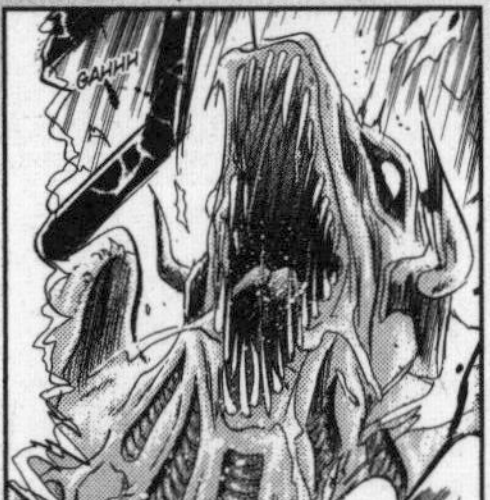
GAHHH

▶One assassin was disguised as a townsman. The Shadow Lord is always looking for an opportunity to strike!

ALL SEVEN OF THEM!

THEY ONLY FEED ON THE DEAD!

▲The Ak-baba destroyed the belt and scattered the seven gems.

Q Where did the stolen gems go?

A: Once the Ak-baba stole the gems, they were strewn about the land. According to rumors, it's said they were taken to seven different— and extremely dangerous—areas, but nobody knows for sure. Will the seven gems come together and peace be restored once again?

DREAD MOUNTAIN

THE SHIFTING SANDS

LAKE OF TEARS

CITY OF THE RATS

DEMON CAVE

MAZE OF THE BEAST

FORESTS OF SILENCE

PREVIEW OF *DELTORA QUEST 2*

We're pleased to present you a preview from *Deltora Quest 2*. Please check our website (www.kodanshacomics.com) to see when this volume will be available in English. For now you'll have to make do with Japanese!

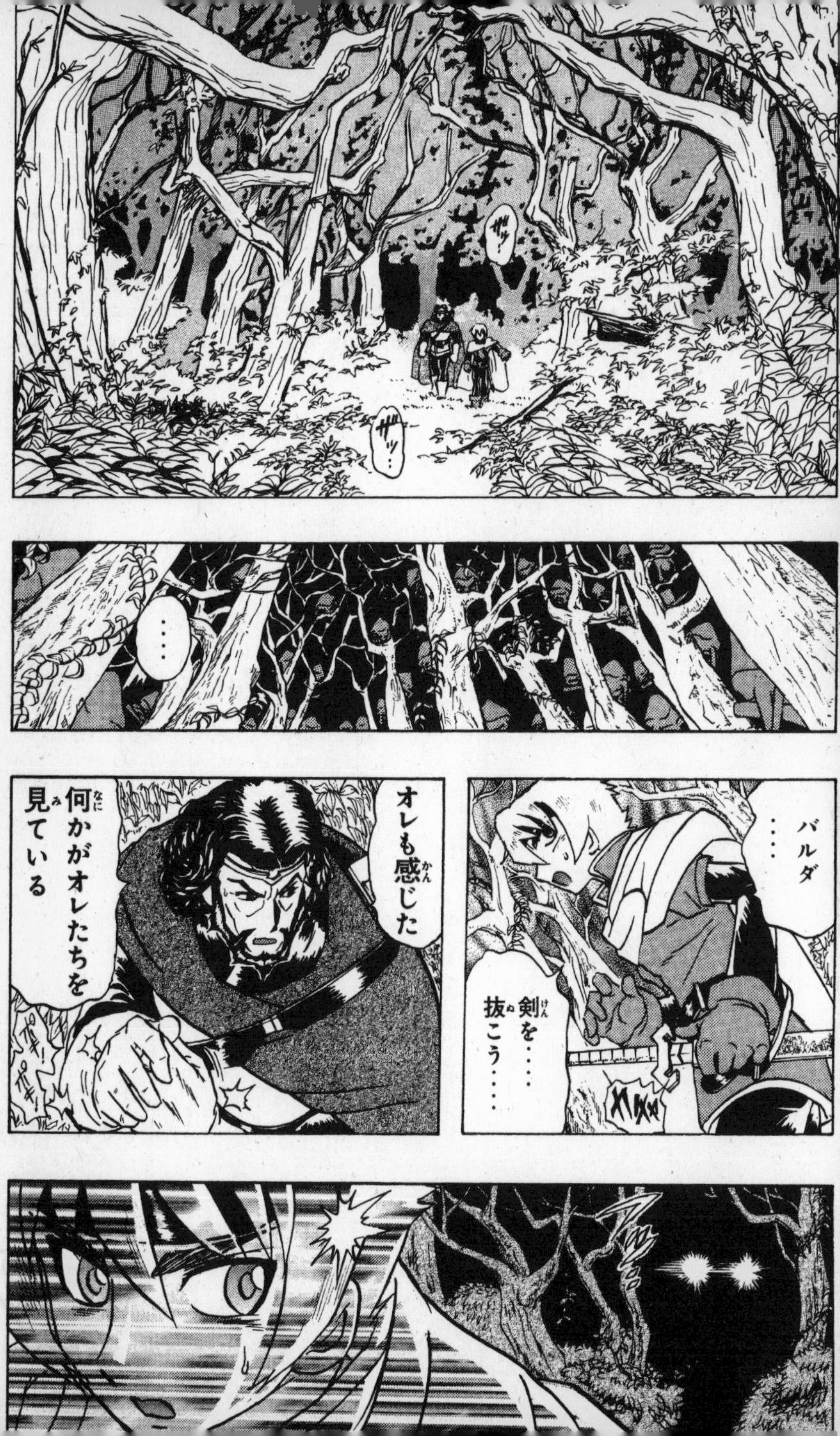
ザッ!
ザッ…
……
バルダ……
剣を……抜こう……
オレも感じた
何かがオレたちを見ている
ポキ!ポキ!

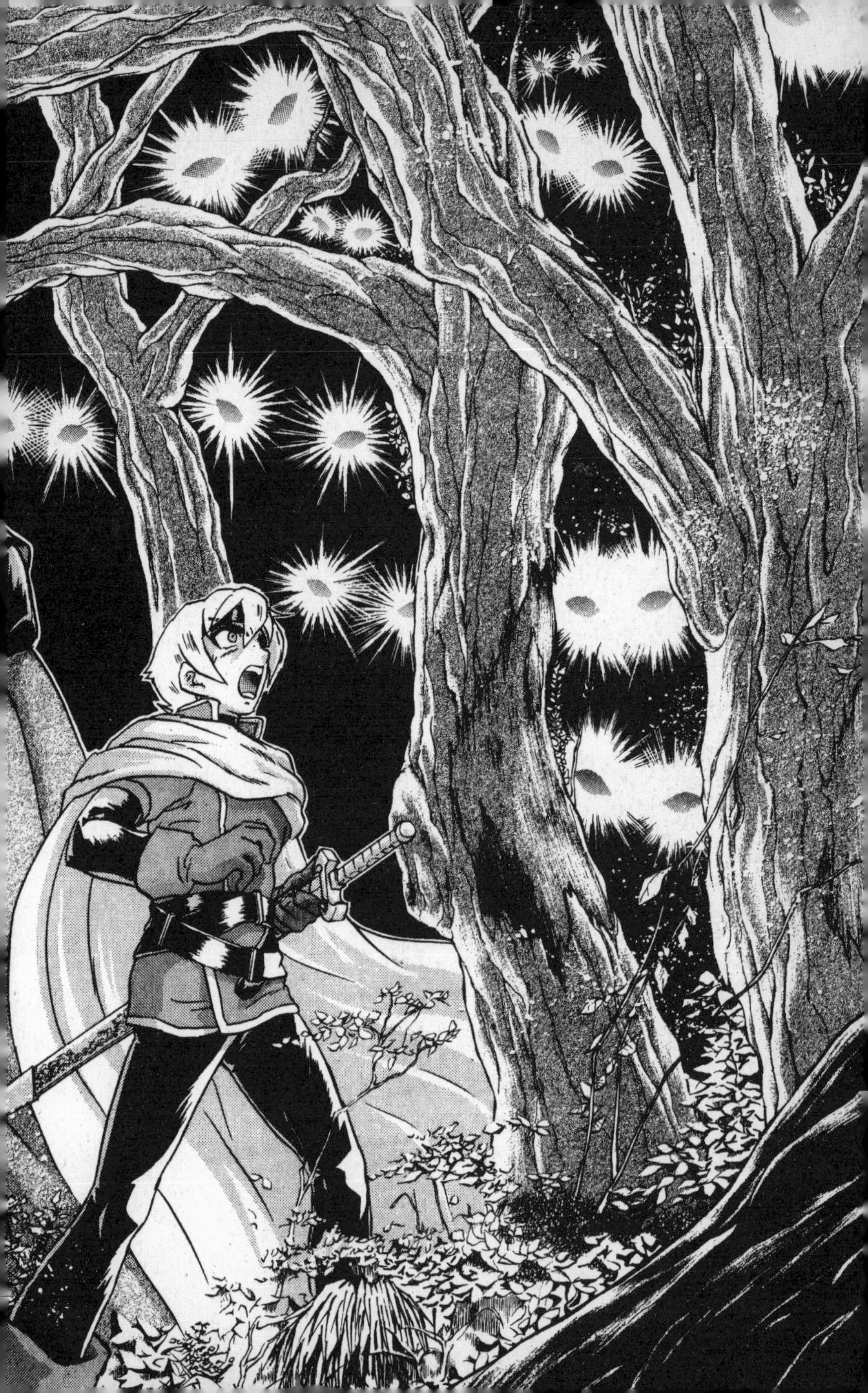

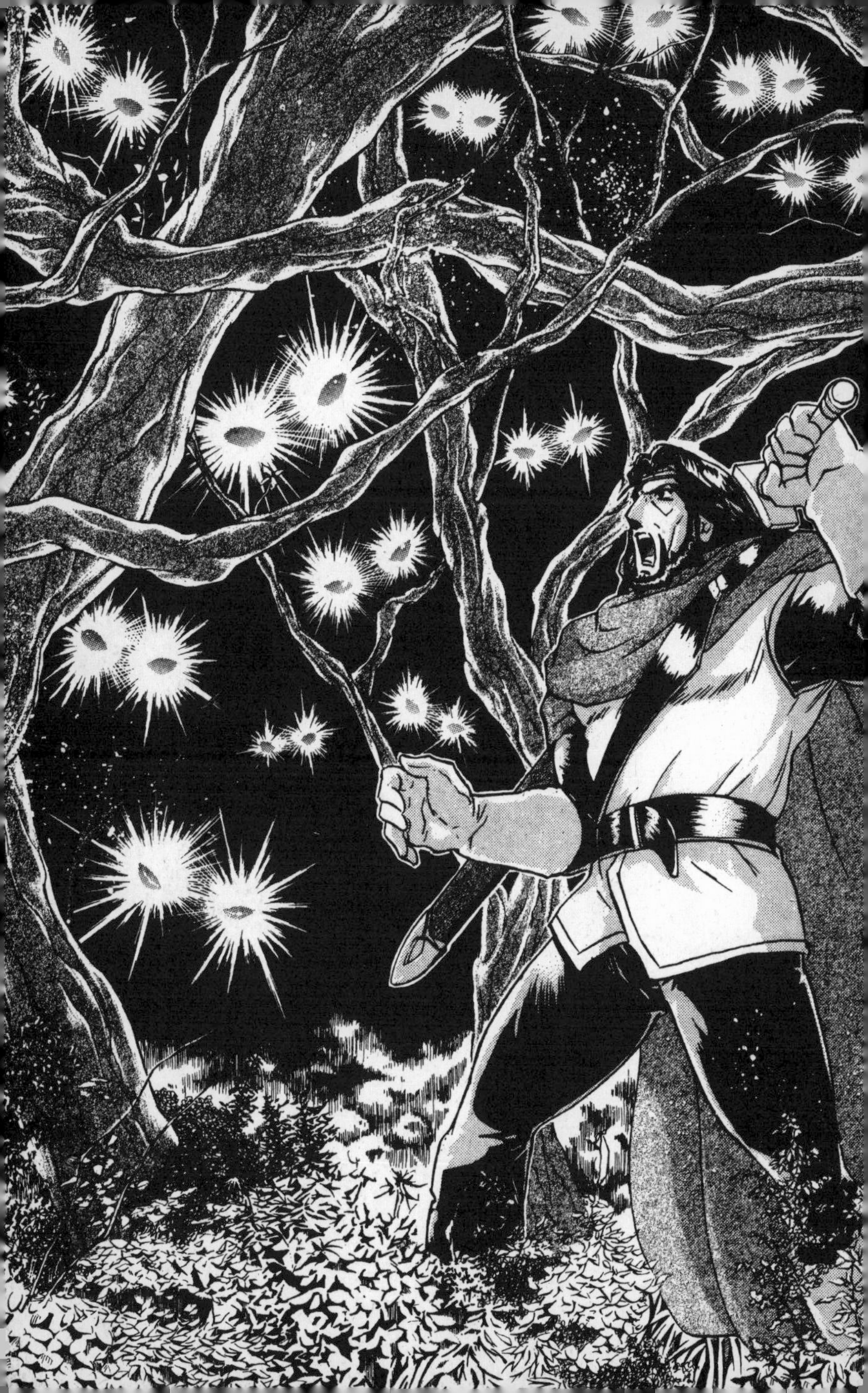

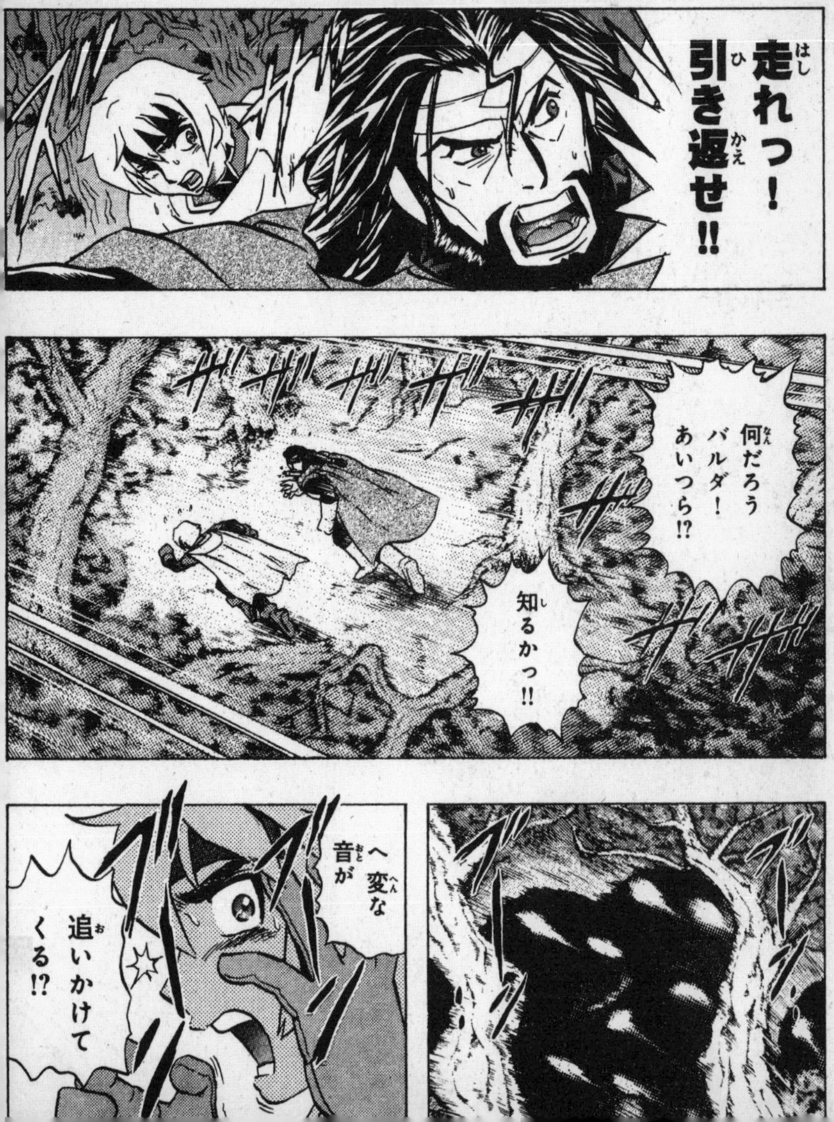
走れっ！引き返せ!!
何だろう バルダ！あいつら!?
知るかっ!!
へ 変な音が 追いかけてくる!?

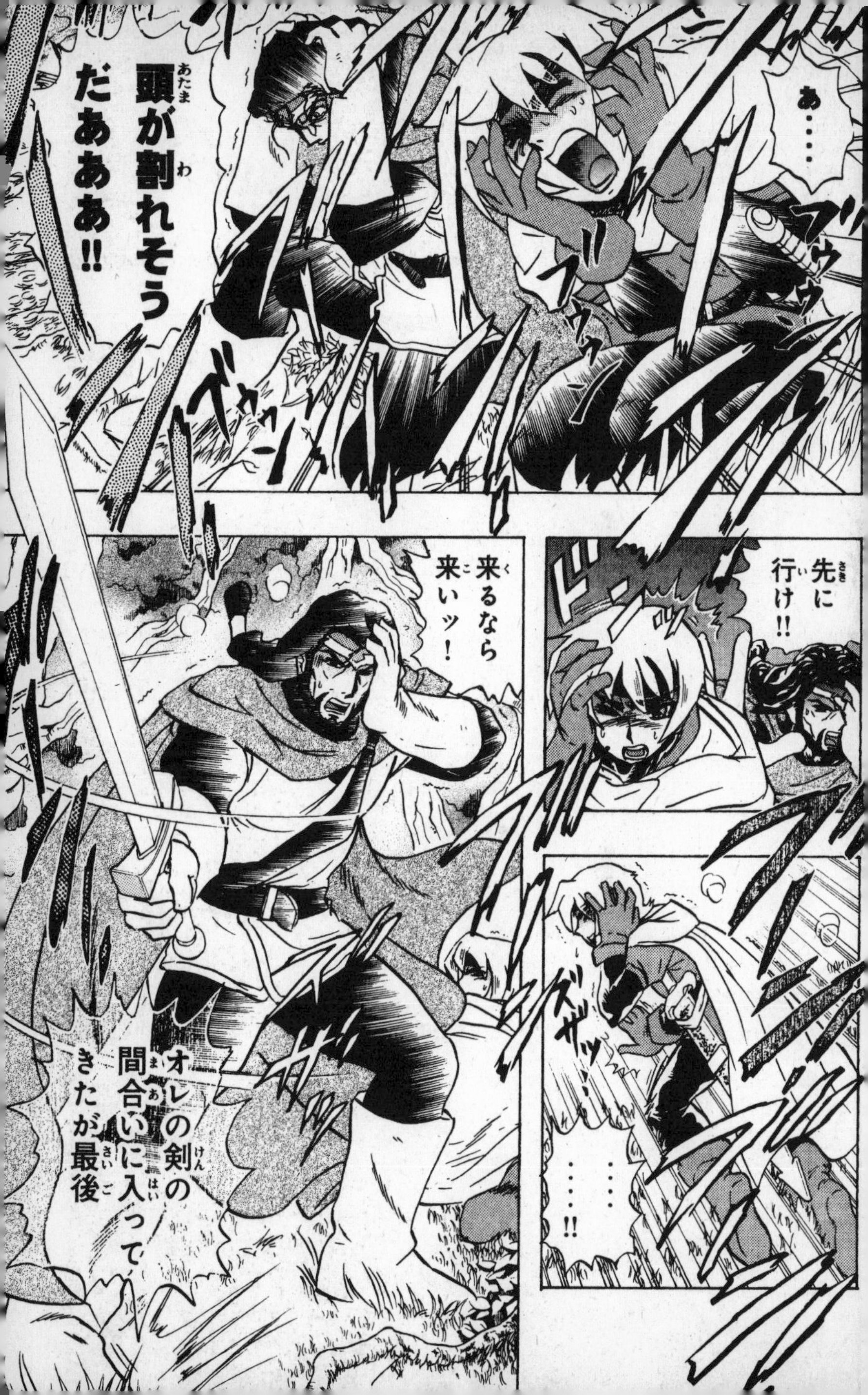

あ……
頭が割れそうだあああ!!
先に行け!!
来るなら来いッ!
……!!
オレの剣の間合いに入ってきたが最後

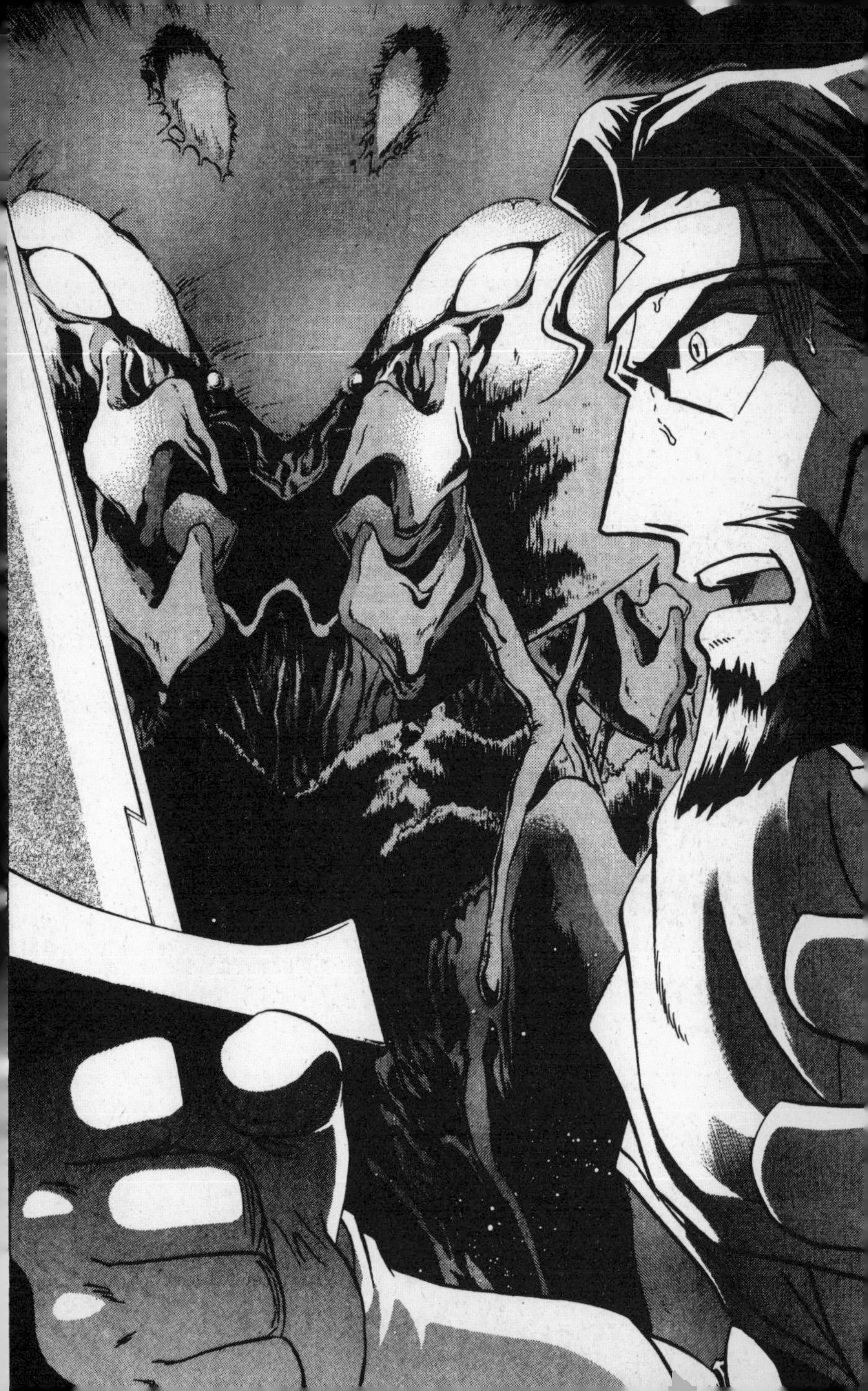

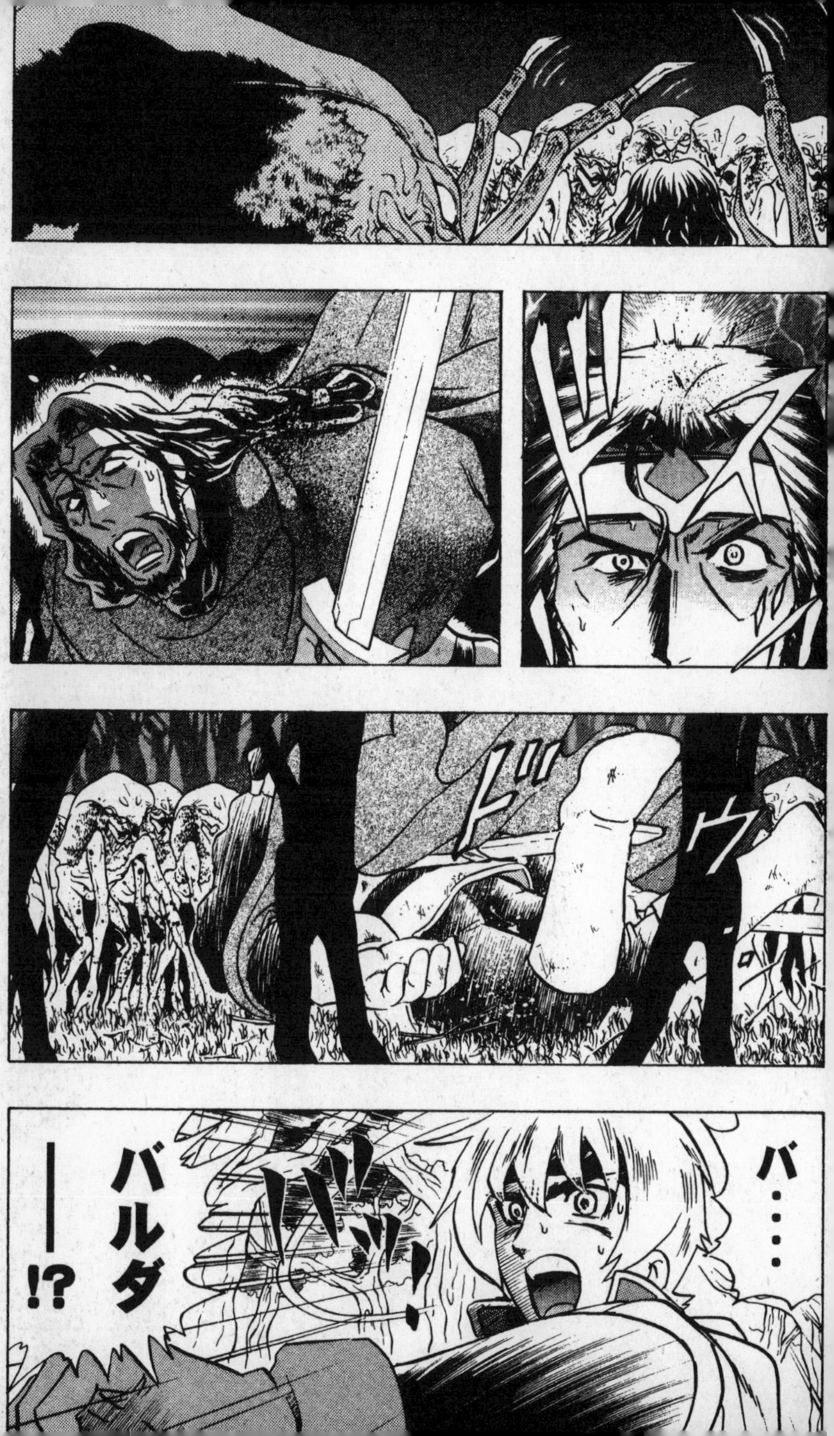
バ……
バルダ——!?

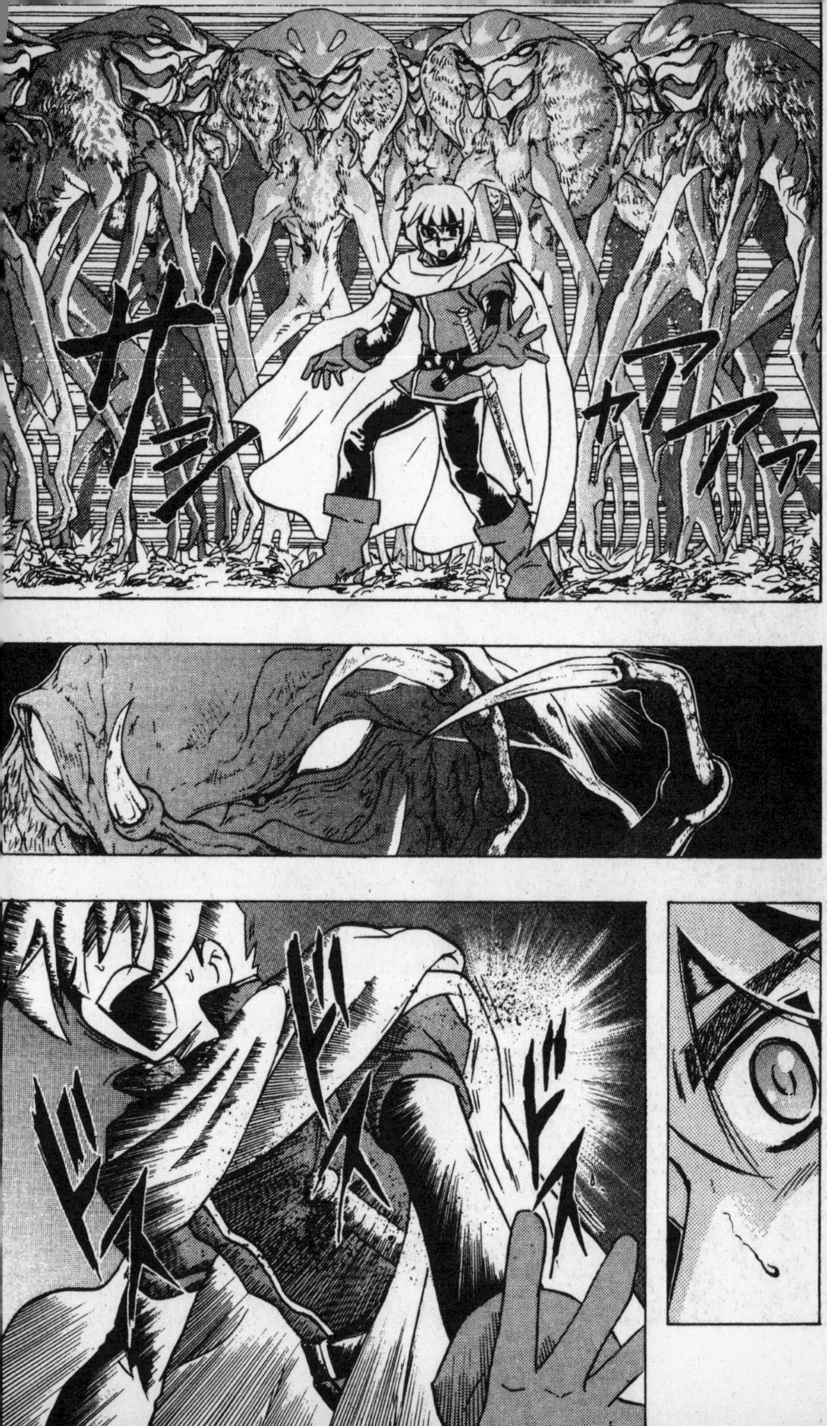

ザシ
ドド
ドド
ドド

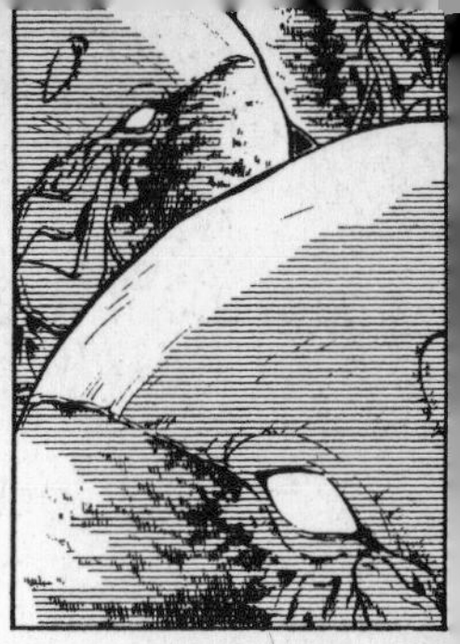

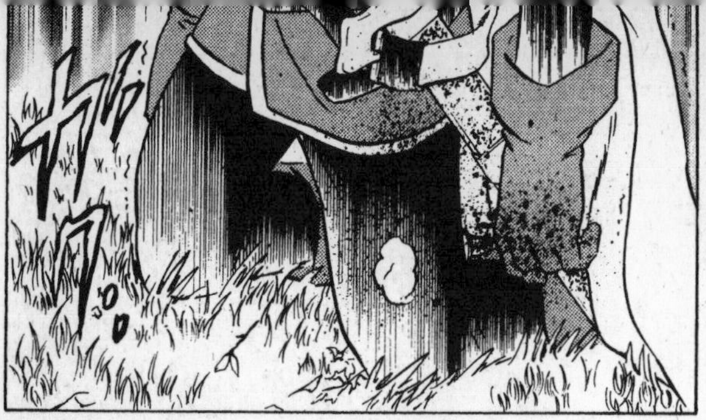

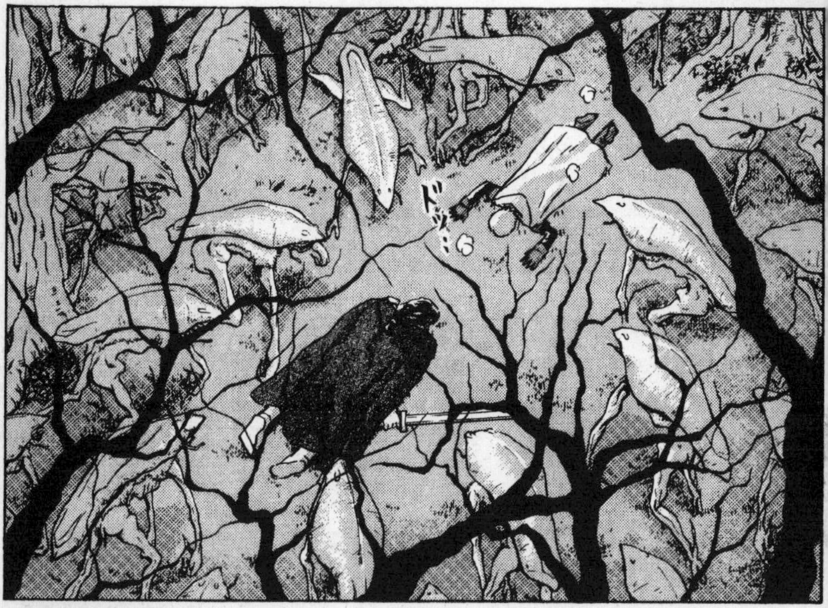
ドッ…

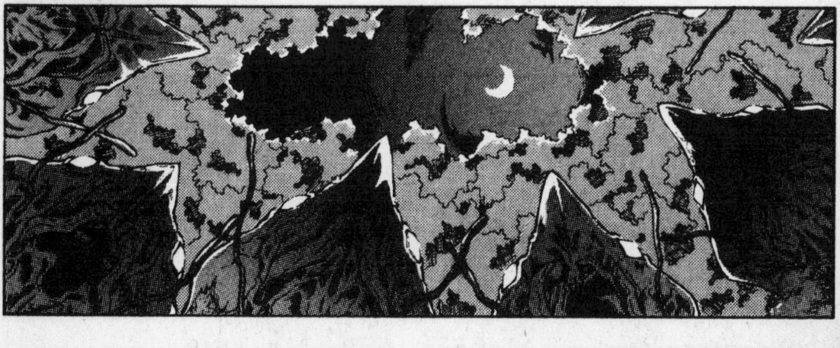

BY KEN AKAMATSU

Negi Springfield is a ten-year-old wizard teaching English at an all-girls Japanese school. He dreams of becoming a master wizard like his legendary father, the Thousand Master. At first his biggest concern was concealing his magic powers, because if he's ever caught using them publicly, he thinks he'll be turned into an ermine! But in a world that gets stranger every day, it turns out that the strangest people of all are Negi's students! From a librarian with a magic book to a centuries-old vampire, from a robot to a ninja, Negi will risk his own life to protect the girls in his care!

Ages: 16+

Special extras in each volume! Read them all!

KC
KODANSHA COMICS

VISIT WWW.KODANSHACOMICS.COM TO:
• View release date calendars for upcoming volumes
• Find out the latest about new Kodansha Comics series

Negima © 2004 Ken Akamatsu / KODANSHA LTD. All rights reserved.

FROM HIRO MASHIMA,
CREATOR OF **RAVE MASTER**

Lucy has always dreamed of joining the Fairy Tail, a club for the most powerful sorcerers in the land. But once she becomes a member, the fun really starts!

Special extras in each volume! Read them all!

RATING T AGES 13+

VISIT WWW.KODANSHACOMICS.COM TO:
- View release date calendars for upcoming volumes
- Find out the latest about new Kodansha Comics series

Fairy Tail © 2006 Hiro Mashima / KODANSHA LTD. All rights reserved.

TOMARE!

[STOP!]

You are going the wrong way!

Manga is a completely different type of reading experience.

To start at the *beginning*, go to the *end*!

That's right! Authentic manga is read the traditional Japanese way—from right to left, exactly the opposite of how American books are read. It's easy to follow: Just go to the other end of the book, and read each page—and each panel—from the right side to the left side, starting at the top right. Now you're experiencing manga as it was meant to be.